AMERICAN JOURNAL
OF NUMISMATICS
28

Second Series, continuing
The American Numismatic Society Museum Notes

THE AMERICAN NUMISMATIC SOCIETY
NEW YORK
2016

ISSN: 1053-8356
ISBN 978-0-89722-348-5

Printed in China

Contents

American Journal of Numismatics

Ute Wartenberg
David Yoon
Editors

Oliver D. Hoover
Managing Editor

Editorial Committee

John W. Adams
Boston, Massachusetts

Jere L. Bacharach
University of Washington

Gilles Bransbourg
American Numismatic Society

Andrew Burnett
British Museum

Evridiki Georganteli
Harvard University

Kenneth W. Harl
Tulane University

Paul T. Keyser
IBM T. J. Watson Research Center

John M. Kleeberg
New York, New York

John H. Kroll
Oxford, England

Eric P. Newman
St. Louis, Missouri

Ira Rezak
Stony Brook, New York

Stephen K. Scher
New York, New York

Stuart D. Sears
Westport, Massachusetts

Peter van Alfen
American Numismatic Society

Bernhard Weisser
*Münzkabinett
Staatliche Museen zu Berlin*

AJN Second Series 28 (2016) pp. 1–63

Seleukos I's Victory Coinage of Susa Revisited:
A Die Study and Commentary

PLATES 1–21   LAURE MAREST-CAFFEY*

This contribution presents the results of a die study of the victory coinage minted at Susa under the authority of Seleukos I Nikator and proposes a commentary on the historical significance of the series and its iconography. The appearance of new coins on the market since the publication of the last die study allows a revision of previous findings. The estimated number of original dies has been reduced to fewer than 30 for tetradrachms. The sequence of control marks has also been slightly altered thanks to new die links and discoveries concerning imitations. It is argued that the coinage, probably minted after the Battle of Ipsos in 301, was conceived with a Persian audience in mind and testifies to the Seleukid policies of conciliation towards local populations.

A large silver coin featuring a helmeted male head hovers like a sun over a watercolor reconstruction of city walls on the cover of a recent monograph on the early history of the Seleukid Empire.[1] The tetradrachm, minted at Susa under the authority of Seleukos I Nikator, was probably selected to represent the same ruler and founder of the largest Hellenistic kingdom issued from the conquest of Alexander the Great. The choice of illustration exemplifies the importance of the coinage known as the trophy or victory type for numismatists and

*University of California, Berkeley (lmarestcaffey@berkeley.edu).
1 Grainger 2014.

(art) historians alike. The series offers much needed evidence concerning early Seleukid minting practices, portraiture, iconography, and policies.

Numerous coins have appeared on the market since the publication of the last die study nearly two decades ago along with a detailed study of the numismatic production at Susa under Seleukos I.[2] The present article first proposes to lay the foundation for further work on the mint with an updated die study of the victory coinage and its imitations. Second, it provides a commentary on the historical significance of the type. Moving away from the traditional *interpretatio graeca*, it argues that the coinage was conceived and circulated as an "eastern" coinage, materializing Seleukid policies of fusion with local populations, particularly the Persian elite. The obverse iconography mined the polysemy of power imagery to further the ideological and political agenda of the new ruler. This paper proposes to push the date of the types' inception after the Battle of Ipsos in 301 and questions the occurrence of an early secession of Persis from the empire as an impetus for minting.[3] Numismatic evidence suggests a more peaceful and cooperative relationship between the Seleukid Empire and local elite in Persis than previously thought.

History of Scholarship

The history of recent scholarship on the victory coinage goes back to the late nineteenth century with the work of Percy Gardner and Ernest Babelon, who identified the portrait as that of Seleukos I.[4] Babelon first noticed the distinctive spots of a panther on the helmet, which have since been of great significance for identifying the portrait. Fifty years later, Edward Newell systematically studied the series in his two foundational volumes on Seleukid mints.[5] He accepted Gardner and Babelon's identification but stressed the Dionysiac undertones of the iconography. Newell divided the type between two different mints, Susa and Persepolis, on account of control marks and provenience. The identification tide turned in favor of Alexander the Great with an article by Robert Hadley.[6] In a 1980 article, Arthur Houghton demonstrated through close associations of monograms, symbols, style, and fabric that the type originated from Susa alone.[7] Brian Kritt published in 1997 a detailed study of the production and role of the Susian mint under Seleukos I, in which he reorganized and redated the overall

2 *ESMS.*
3 All Seleukid dates are BC.
4 Gardner 1878: xviii, 4; Babelon 1890: xv–xvi. The interest in Seleukid coinages can be traced to the sixteenth century, but methodological changes in the early nineteenth century created a gap in the scholarship (Callataÿ Forthcoming).
5 *ESM:* 107–125, 154–161; *WSM:* 25–26.
6 Hadley 1974.
7 Houghton 1980.

and internal sequences of issues, including the trophy type.[8] His work served as a basis for the entry on Susa in the current standard reference on Seleukid coinage.[9]

In the intervening years since those publications new data have become available—mainly in the form of new coins appearing on the market—with a promising potential since the statistical coverage has until now been low (Table 2). Furthermore, the current dating of the beginning of the trophy coinage, c. 305/4, has been questioned on iconographic and numismatic grounds,[10] while the theory concerning a putative secession of Persis in c. 295 has come under attack in historical and archaeological scholarship.[11] The last two decades have also enriched and nuanced our understanding of Seleukid administration and strategies, particularly concerning policies vis-à-vis conquered territories and peoples in the eastern part of the empire.[12]

Table 1. Overview of the victory coinage in standard references.

Reference	Mint, group	Proposed date	Classification (denomination)
ESM	Susa - Series II, Group A	300-298	300 (drachm)
	Susa - Series II, Group B	300-298	301 (tetradrachm) 302 (drachm)
	Persepolis, Group A	300 and later	413 (tetradrachm) 414 (drachm) 415 (hemidrachm) 416 (obol)
	Persepolis, Group B	300 and later	417 (tetradrachm) 418 (drachm) 419 (hemidrachm) 420 (tetradrachm) 421 (tetradrachm)
	Persepolis, Group C	300 and later	422 (tetradrachm) 423 (obol) 424 (tetradrachm) 425 (drachm) 426 (tetradrachm) 427 (drachm)
WSM	Persepolis, Group B	300 and later	421A (tetradrachm)

8 *ESMS*.

9 *SC*. For a summary of dates and classifications, see Table 1 and Concordance.

10 Iossif 2004.

11 Wiesehöfer 1994: 91–96; Callieri 2007: 115–146.

12 Among others, see Sherwin-White and Kuhrt 1993; Wiesehöfer 1994; Aperghis 2004; Capdetrey 2007; Klose and Müseler 2008; Wiesehöfer 2011; Wiesehöfer 2013; Kosmin 2014.

Reference	Mint, group	Proposed date	Classification (denomination)
ESMS	Susa, Group 2	305-298/7	I (tetradrachm) J (tetradrachm) JA (tetradrachm) *ESM* 426 (tetradrachm) *ESM* 427 (drachm) *ESM* 424 (tetradrachm) *ESM* 425 (drachm) K (hemidrachm) L (tetradrachm) *ESM* 421A M (drachm) *ESM* 421 (tetradrachm) *ESM* 422 (tetradrachm) *ESM* 423 (obol) N (tetradrachm) *ESM* 413 (tetradrachm) *ESM* 414 (drachm) *ESM* 415 (hemidrachm) *ESM* 416 (obol) *ESM* 417 (tetradrachm) *ESM* 418 (drachm) *ESM* 419 (hemidrachm) O (tetradrachm) *ESM* 420 (tetradrachm) P (drachm) *ESM* 300 (drachm)
	Susa, Group 3a	298/7-295/4	Q (tetradrachm) *ESM* 302 (drachm) *ESM* 301 (tetradrachm) R (drachm)
SC	Susa	c. 305/4-295	173 (tetradrachm) 174 (drachm) 175 (hemidrachm) 176 (obol)
	Probably from Persis	after 305/4	195 (tetradrachm)
	Other non-Susian issues	after 305/4	196 (tetradrachm) 197 (drachm)
	Imitations	after 305/4	198 (drachm) 199 (drachm)
	Imitations in the name of Antiochos from Drangiana	294-281 or later	226 (drachm) 227 (hemidrachm) 228 (obol)

Table 2. Estimated original number of dies and coverage for tetradrachms.

	Sample	Observed dies	Singletons	Estimated original dies (Carter)	Coverage (Esty)
ESMS	105*	67	49**	148.82 ± 17.46	0.53
Marest-Caffey	191	26	5***	27.25 ± 0.75	0.97

* Excluding five specimens with unidentified obverse dies.
** Three flagged as potentially imitative by Kritt.
*** Three, different from Kritt's, are potentially imitative.

DIE STUDY

A fresh start was needed to test previous findings, particularly the sequence of dies and estimates of the original output, in light of an enlarged sample. The emerging die linkage—now much improved—dictated the progression of the work.[13] The tightly-knit cluster composed of a small portion of Group 1.4 and the entirety of Groups 1.5 through 1.8—representing nearly a third of the corpus—served as a nexus to reconstruct the whole sequence.[14] Shared control marks allowed for rebuilding the sequence backwards from 1.4 to 1.1. What remained formed two distinct clusters sharing die links and control marks—1.9–1.10 and 1.11–1.12. The latter presents the Helios head symbol that appears on late Alexandrine types from Susa and was thus placed last.[15] The engravers' varying skills, poor quality of some images, and modern tooling of some recently-discovered coins sometimes made the identification of individual dies difficult, but imaging software was used to remedy these issues. No tetradrachm remains unclassified, although two were sorted without any image available, using the results of previous die studies.

The sequence presented in this study largely confirms previous findings with the exception of the inversion of the varieties *SC* 173.9 and 173.11, and the exclusion from the official production of *SC* 173.6–173.8 as imitative, and *SC* 173.13 as anomalous (see Concordance). The fractional coinage—drachms, hemidrachms, and obols—was organized mainly according to the sequence provided by the tetradrachms. However the presence of control mark combinations unseen among the tetradrachms indicates that the production of different denominations was not always concomitant. The order within each Group of the fractional coinage was often arranged stylistically since few die links were found and should thus be regarded as provisional. A new variety of drachms has appeared, Group 2.3, and

13 Most of the comments about die linkage concern tetradrachms, unless noted otherwise, since the sample of fractional coinage mainly presents "loose" dies.

14 New numbers have been assigned to the Groups, since those used in *SC*, which were based on *ESMS*, no longer reflect the chronological sequence as shown below (see Concordance).

15 *ESMS*: 38, Group 3b.

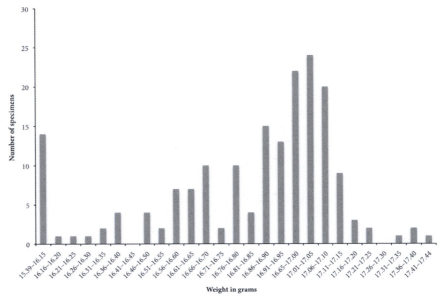

Figure 1. Tetradrachm weight frequency.

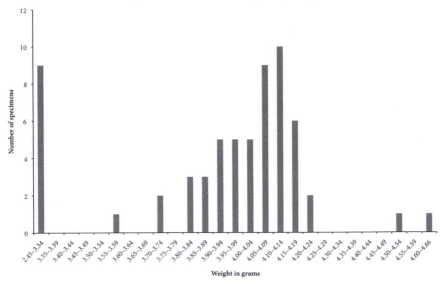

Figure 2. Drachm weight frequency.

its place in the sequence is secure thanks to an obverse die link. *SC* 174.3 is here considered imitative, and *SC* 174.6 and 174.7 have been inverted. Two varieties of obols using the same control marks seen on tetradrachms have also been added.

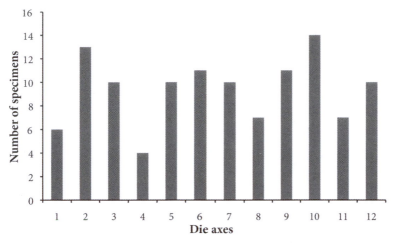

Figure 3. Tetradrachm die axis frequency.

The most drastic departure from previous results concerns the statistical coverage and estimated production. The coverage has been radically improved with an expanded sample and a reduced number of observed dies (Table 2). The fact that past estimates were too high is supported by the low number of new obverse dies that have appeared since the publication of *ESMS*, while the size of the sample has nearly doubled.[16] Consequentially, the estimated output of the coinage has greatly been reduced, from a surprisingly large production of about one hundred and fifty dies to fewer than thirty. This has significant repercussions on our understanding of the series' function as discussed below.

Metrology and Die Axes

The frequency of tetradrachm and drachm weights show clusters just below the standard early Hellenistic Attic weight of respectively about 17.25 g and 4.25 g (Figs. 1 and 2).[17] Wear, especially since some coins clearly had a long circulation life, and the paucity of archaeologically-excavated and hoard specimens explain the long tailing edge of the graphs. Indeed, coins that have appeared only recently on the market, some of which probably come from a new hoard to still be reconstructed (Table 3,"Persia" Hoard), present a higher average weight and narrower deviation. Very few of the specimens are overweight, keeping in line with the standard *al pezzo* production method of silver and gold coinage at the time.

16 Only four new obverse dies have surfaced: A2, 12, 13, and 26. If previous estimates were correct, more should have appeared statistically (*ESMS*: 67–68).

17 For discussions of early Hellenistic standards, see Mørkholm 1982; Le Rider and Callataÿ 2006: 28–31.

No fixed rule seems to guide the die axes (Fig. 3). Punctual clusters probably indicate a worker's preference or contemporaneity of production rather than a specific practice of the mint.

Die Groups

Since the present identification of individual dies often deviates from that of previous studies, my reasoning is presented below.

1.1-1.3 or the "Horizontal Ear Group"[18]

The three Groups share the Boeotian shield symbol or several letters and monograms such as BE and 𝔼 with early Alexandrine issues from Susa.[19] They also form a homogenous stylistic cluster distinguished by the small, horizontal bull's ear of the helmet that lacks the more naturalistic helix and prominent striations indicating scaphae seen on later dies. The coins in this cluster also share a common obverse die, A3, whose progressive wear clearly indicates that Group 1.1 precedes 1.2. It results that 1.3 must follow, which is confirmed independently by the die link between coin nos. 14 and 15.[20]

For the internal organization of Group 1.1, P5 must be the last reverse die of A1 because of the wear pattern observed on nos. 9 and 10. The order of earlier reverse dies is more difficult to determine due to the poor state of preservation of some coins and the obvious modern tooling of others. However, the appearance of two horizontal lines near the eye seen on some obverses and the widening of Nike's wings on the reverse dies can be used to reconstruct the sequence. Unfortunately nos. 4-6, probably coins from the recent "Persia" Hoard, were tooled after their discovery to bring out key features, such as the panther spots, and enhance their commercial appeal.[21]

Interestingly, none of the extant fractional coinage bears these sets of control marks and symbol, thus highlighting, along with the rapid succession of combinations, the experimental beginning of the series.

1.4 and 1.5

A die link provides evidence for the succession of Group 1.4 to 1.3. This Group encompasses a large portion of the total issue—nearly a quarter. The monograms 𝔸 and 𝕄 are reused from the "Horizontal Ear" Group. The numerous obverse dies share a consistent style featuring a well-proportioned profile with a classicizing

---

18 *ESMS*: 53.

19 ESMS: 35, Group 1.

20 Unlike Kritt, I find that no.13 (=*ESMS* Tr.6) shares an obverse die with nos. 11 and 12 (= *ESMS* Tr.4-5). I believe that the discrepancy in the configuration of the skin around the neck is due to wear. The characteristic pattern of panther spots at the back of the helmet seen on these three coins supports their association.

21 Unfortunately this practice seems to plague the recent market. Such "touched-up" coins are indicated in the Catalogue.

nose and little modeling, panther spots carefully arranged in rows, and bull's ear tilting slightly upward.[22]

The internal sequence of this Group is less certain although die links and stylistic affinities form several clusters. Obverses A5 to A8 present several links and obvious stylistic similarities with the obverse A4.[23] Several "loose dies" are positioned next in the sequence, although the order could be slightly altered and some specimens even demoted to the rank of imitations of good quality.[24] An unusual feature characterizes the end of obverse A7 and beginning of A8: the appearance of simultaneous reverse dies P19 and P20. Group 1.4 ends with the die-linked obverses A14 and A15 since coin no. 65 ushers in a new combination of control marks.

The next Group, featuring the reused monogram ℞, is stylistically consistent with the previous.[25] The serial arrangement of its obverse dies is provided by several links. Obverse A17 introduces a new iconographical feature: a spotted *nebris* as opposed to the pleated version of the earlier design.[26] A17 must be the last obverse of 1.5 since it carries over to the next Group.

An interesting new control mark combination, Ⓐ ΔΙ (Group 2.3), now appears among the drachms. A die link clearly places it immediately before Ɛ ΔΙ (Group 2.4). Although it could mean that such a set of control marks also existed among the tetradrachms, the continued use of obverse die A17 between the end of 1.5 and the beginning of 1.6 makes this hypothesis unlikely. Mint officials were simply not always producing different denominations simultaneously.[27]

---

22 It is probably within this Group that my identification of individual dies departs the most from Kritt's. The style is indeed so consistent that identification can be arduous. Superimposition of images through computer imaging software was most helpful.

23 A5 through 7 are very similar dies, but the patterns of spots on the helmet and cheek piece are different. The phenomenon, seen elsewhere in the sequence, cannot be explained by a simple recutting of the die. I hope to discuss this phenomenon elsewhere.

24 My criteria for identifying imitative specimens are discussed below. Here, the singletons 57 and 58 have slightly deviant styles and share some features with imitations. However their weight, fabric, general appearance, and quality compare well with the official issue. They remain provisionally in the official issue.

25 Following Newell, Kritt expressed the possibility that the monogram ⚹ might be a variant of ℞ (*ESM*: 156; *ESMS*: 54).

26 Kritt saw another occurrence of stylistic change in the transformation of the monogram from ⚹ to ⚹ (*ESMS*: 53). However better preserved specimens of the reverses of his Tr.34-37 show that it remains constant as ⚹. Nevertheless, the assertion that the pleated skin precedes the spotted version on the obverses is confirmed. Groups 1.11-12 return to the pleated design at the end of the sequence.

27 Group 2.6 presents another such case.

1.6-8 or the "Thin Head Group"[28]

The combination of control marks Ɛ ΔI presents the first discontinuity in the sequence.[29] Up to this point a new set always reused at least one monogram, letter or symbol from a previous one. ΔI is attested in Alexandrine issues, which Kritt places earlier in the overall production at Susa.[30] Obverse A17 is replaced with an obverse of a different style, characterized by a thin, long face with a strong brow and small chin. This obverse is used through the next two sets of control marks, ℤ ΔI (Group 1.7) and ⚹ MI (Group 1.8). The degradation of A18, particularly a long crack running vertically along the cheek piece, provides a solid basis for organizing reverses.

1.9-10

This cluster is not linked to the previous through any die or control mark, although AX has been seen earlier in 1.3. Two major styles are distinguishable. The first shares many characteristics with that of Groups 1.3-1.4, although the skin tied around the neck is spotted rather than pleated. The second, which appears around the switch from Group 1.9 to 1.10 with obverse A22, is one of the finest of the entire issue, sometimes nicknamed that of the "Pasargadae Master."[31] It is characterized by a detailed modeling of the face and neck with a special attention to the bone structure, a well-proportioned helmet with a narrow neck guard, and a spotted skin worn high on the neck.

The appearance of a crack at the back of the helmet, below the horn, provides evidence for the internal sequence of A19. The relative order of reverses P52, 53 and 57 seems secure, while that of P54-56, where the crack on the obverse is at an advanced stage, is more ambiguous. Singleton 128 may be imitative and its position relative to A19 is uncertain.[32] The internal sequence of A21 is provided by a defect appearing above the helmet and on the neck. A22 must be the last obverse die of Group 1.9 since its reverse die P71 introduces a new group and style. A defect between the neck guard and cheek piece of A23 gives the internal order of its reverses.

My decision to exclude SC 173.13 from the official issue needs to be discussed at this point since the variety is clearly related to this group. The new monogram ⋈ appears on other types from Susa.[33] Kritt posited that this variety—then only

---

28 ESMS: 55.

29 The second—and last—break happens at the very end of the sequence with Groups 1.11-1.12.

30 ESMS: 34–47.

31 Kritt nicknamed the engraver "Pasargadae Master" on account of several examples of such fine craftsmanship found in the Pasargadae Hoards (ESMS: 56).

32 Stylistic oddities such as the shape of the helmet may indicate an imitative production. The poor quality of the only available image precludes any definitive judgment.

33 ESMS: 35.

known from a single coin (*ESMS* Tr. 91 = 9.A2)—"should probably be regarded as parallel" to 1.9 and 1.10 since it is stylistically attributable to the "Pasargadae Master" and its obverse very close to but distinct from A22. However this variety cannot simply be inserted in between since A22 links Groups 1.9 and 1.10. Nor can it be placed before or after on account of style. The only logical conclusion was indeed to place it in an awkward parallel position.

Three new coins presenting the same reverse as 9.A2 help make sense of the situation (Fig. 4). The first of these (9.A1) links the new variety to two groups that are not sequential: it is related to Group 1.4 on account of the die and to 1.9–10 because of the style of 9.A2–4's obverse die. Furthermore, the reverse of 9.A4 presents the incongruous letter H instead of the monogram ꝳ, although it is otherwise identical to the reverses of 9.A1-3. The die could have been recut, but we would still be left with the problematic obverse A5 on 9.A1, which contradicts the whole sequence. A closer look at these coins reveals several incongruities that further isolate Group 9A. The inscription on the reverses often lacks the *puntelli* so distinctive of ancient Greek numismatic inscriptions and presents a strangely rectilinear lettering.[34] The surfaces seem rather odd, even seen on photographs. These specimens also favor die axes between 11 and 1, while the whole sample is more varied. Finally the elegant volute of the brow guard, the uniquely rounded spots on the helmet, and the idiosyncratic pleats of Nike's drapery are unparalleled in the rest of series. The coins related to *SC* 173.13 must be set aside pending further evidence.

<h3 style="text-align:center">1.11 and 1.12</h3>

These two varieties are clearly related. They share two control marks, AP and ꝲ, but the latter include the Helios head symbol added in between. Both the letters and monogram are new but the Helios head symbol places this cluster at the end of the issue since it is also found on late Alexandrine types from Susa.[35] A die link among drachms supports this sequence. The distinctive style of this cluster presents, on the obverse, a nearly neckless head with brutish features, and a long bull's ear curving up; and, on the reverse, an idiosyncratic hatching of the wings, reversed configuration of Nike's arms, and undecorated shield on the trophy.

1.11 and 1.12 share the obverse die A25, which clearly indicates the relative order through its wear, particularly with the appearance of a defect in the dotted border at right. The internal order of P81-84 is difficult to ascertain. Obverse A26 must be last.

---

34 This is most obvious in 9.A3-4.
35 *ESMS*: 38, Group 3b.

Figure 4. Anomalous group 9.A1 (top left), 9.A3 (bottom left), 35 (top right), and 148 (bottom right).

Silver-Plated and Imitative Coins

Twenty-nine tetradrachms were found to be imitative (Group 5 in the Catalogue).[36] The survival rate of these coins is extremely low with 21 obverse dies.[37] They are not arranged sequentially but rather according to stylistic affinities and/or perceived degrees of "deviation." Not only is this group mainly composed of "loose" dies but it is not possible to use the official control marks as a basis for organization as well.[38] Such a number may seem improbably high. Nevertheless three arguments support the reasoning for distinguishing some specimens from the official issue, even though they do not offer a sweeping explanation for such a phenomenon.

    First, it is certain that the victory coinage represented a popular type for "barbarous imitations." Houghton listed no less than ten drachms, six hemidrachms, and eleven obols, all of them struck with a different obverse die.[39] They feature a variety of barbarous inscriptions, unprecedented control marks, and designs sometimes simplified to the point of abstraction. To these must be added specimens struck in the name of Antiochos, including a tetradrachm presenting an unusual style (5.T1).

---

36 Most of the following comments concern tetradrachms, unless noted otherwise. The fractional coinage varies widely in weight and quality. The list of imitative fractional coinage in the Catalogue should be considered tentative, especially since available images were often of extremely poor quality.

37 Seven tetradrachms from *ESMS* (Tr.8, 9, 11, 43-45, 104) were demoted. Five of these are singletons and two shares dies with silver-plated specimens. Three singletons, Tr.43-45, had already raised doubt in Kritt's mind (*ESMS*: 55).

38 This is well illustrated by the example of Group 5.B. Wear on the obverse die—the appearance of a defect between the cheek piece and neck guard—indicates that B1 precedes B2 and yet this contradicts the official issue.

39 Houghton 1980: 11–13.

Second, over half of the imitative tetradrachms are either plated or related through a die link to a *monnaie fourrée*. While it has been suggested that some official issues could be silver-plated, the extant evidence does not support such a conclusion for the victory coinage.[40] No die links have been found between an official die and a plated specimen. Although such debasement is attested at a later period, Seleukos I would have had little reason to perpetuate such a fraud, especially since his coffers were still brimming with the fabulous quantities of Persian bullion inherited from Alexander's conquest.

Third, of the remaining imitative coins that are not plated or in the name of Antiochos—12 specimens—only Group 5.C and 5.A1 are not singletons. Since the coverage of the present die study is extremely high, it seems logical to suspect any singleton that also presents a number of incongruities. The identification of imitations may seem subjective, but long hours spent scrutinizing the entire sample train the eye to spot oddities. Nevertheless, a set of specific criteria was used to this end: blundering of the inscription, unparalleled control marks, unusual styles, misunderstanding of the original iconography, and anachronism in the design. None of these characteristics alone represents a particular stigma, but the combination does especially when the coin also happens to be a singleton.

The imitations form a very heterogeneous group on several levels. The fabric and style of the coins, faithfulness to the original inscriptions, and the engraver's skill vary considerably from one specimen to the next. On one side of the spectrum, some coins display excellent craftsmanship, suggesting that the engravers were likely trained in the Greek tradition. The obverse of Group 5.F compares rather well with coins from the official Group 1.4. The odd style of the reverse, uneven fabric, and disconnection from the official sequence betray its imitative nature. The same could be said of 5.C2-3 with the addition of the anachronistic spotted skin. On the other end of the spectrum, crude imitations feature incomplete, blundered or nonsensical inscriptions, compositions simplified and stylized nearly to the point of abstraction, and widely varying weights and metal composition.

Lack of evidence unfortunately does not to allow us to locate imitative mints with certainty. The only hoard featuring an imitation (5.L1) was reconstructed and has no provenience record (Table 3, "Frataraka" Hoard). The content suggests that it likely originated from Persis, possibly from the area of Persepolis.[41] Among the four trophy-type coins present in the hoard, the imitation appears the freshest, suggesting that the imitative mint did not produce any such coins before the end of the official issue. Yet any further argument concerning an absolute chronology based on wear would be highly speculative since the Frataraka coinage is not securely dated. Several coins of good quality but deviant style featuring two Aramaic letters as control marks (5.I1, J1; 6.A1; 8.A1) could be associated with a

---

40 Houghton 1980: 10–11; Hoover 2008b: 243–245.
41 Wiesehöfer 1994: 64; Wiesehöfer 2007.

Figure 5. Reuse of obverse die A18: 112 (left) and 5.A1 (right).

mint in Persis.[42] It is also possible that the imitative Persid mint had ties with the official mint at Susa. This hypothesis is supported by the use of an official—albeit much worn—obverse die to strike an imitative tetradrachm (Fig. 5).[43]

A distinct group of imitations in the name of Antiochos were discovered further east, probably in the Helmand Valley at the western edge of the Baluchistan desert.[44] The producing mint, sometimes located in the ancient province of Drangiana, mainly struck fractions—drachms, hemidrachms, and obols—in a characteristic, simplified style.[45]

Anomalous coins

Several irregularities such as blundered inscriptions, unparalleled control marks and symbols, misunderstood composition, and awkward style mark some specimens listed in the Catalogue as anomalous (Group 9). The tetradrachms 9.A1-4 have already been discussed. 9.B1 presents striking incongruities such as the inversed inscription and the high relief of the lower edge of the *nebris*, creating an anachronistic bust format. The fabric, particularly the thin, bulging line around the reverse, is also troubling. 9.C1 features on the obverse an oddly feminine profile, of a more modern sensibility, and on the reverse a blundered inscription, misunderstood iconography, and altogether awkward style.

COMMENTARY

Intended Audience(s)

The matter of intended audience(s) of the trophy type needs to be addressed at the outset, since it constitutes a premise for many interpretations and permeates the present commentary. It has often been assumed that the coinage targeted a Greek audience because it was struck on the early Hellenistic Attic standard. The Achaemenids used a different, bimetallic monetary system with the gold *daric*

---

42 *ESMS*: 28–30.

43 The atypical reverse with its deviant monogram and vertical inscription could be at first construed as the product of an unskilled engraver. The case is not so simply resolved. If placed at the end of A18's life cycle, it contradicts the sequence of official control marks.

44 Houghton 1980: 11–13; *SC*: 88–89.

45 An unpublished tetradrachm in the name of Antiochos (5.T1), brought to my attention by Arthur Houghton, might be related to this group.

weighing about 8.35-8.40 g and silver *siglos* about 5.50-5.60 g. However, weight standards do not necessarily align with the ethnic background of the consumers, particularly in the eastern satrapies of the Seleukid Empire. During the Achaemenid period, the coinage of Persian weight did not circulate east of the Euphrates, where metal was still predominantly weighed rather than counted.[46] Conversely, hoard evidence shows that foreign coinages, especially from Athens and Aegina, were commonly used throughout the western part of the Persian Empire.[47] By the time of Alexander the Great's conquest, Susiana, Persis, and other eastern satrapies were very poorly monetized and their populations could not have been attached to any particular currency.

Furthermore, the monetary output in the early days of the Macedonian conquest incorporated a variety of standards and cultural references.[48] Mazaios, a satrap under the Achaemenids and reinstated in Babylonia by Alexander, was granted the right to mint between 331 and 328 a silver coinage of Attic weight, featuring a Persian iconography and Aramaic legend. Local populations readily adopted this syncretic type as demonstrated by the popularity of imitations. Alexander, too, minted coinages of Persian weight and mixed iconography. Babylonian tetradrachms derived from an Athenian type continued to be issued during the same period. Thus, the major novelty for local populations in the eastern satrapies was not the introduction of Greek types and weights, but rather the use of minted precious metal *tout court*.

The hoard evidence shows that the majority of Susian production as a whole was consumed in the eastern satrapies, mainly Persis and Characene and more rarely in Media and Babylonia (Table 3, below). No coin of the trophy type has been found west of those satrapies.[49] Soldiers, the primary receivers of such silver coinages, needed to be paid and Susa remained, with Ekbatana, the easternmost mint of the Seleukid Empire until new mints were founded in Baktria after 290. The geographical concentration of findspots does not, in itself, resolve the issue of intended audience(s), since Greek and local veterans coexisted in many areas of the Seleukid Empire. However, it should be noted that the Iranian Plateau was rather lightly settled by Greek colonies.[50] Interestingly, the most important settlement of the area, the refoundation of Susa as Seleukeia on the Eulaios by military— probably Macedonian—settlers, yielded no coin of the trophy type despite several archaeological campaigns.[51]

---

46 Joannès 1994.

47 Le Rider 1999: 1044–1055; Duyrat 2005: 383–386.

48 Among others, see Le Rider 1999: 1078–1085; Le Rider 2003: 267–329; Duyrat 2005: 386–390, 400–405; Briant 2006: 312–314.

49 *ESMS*: 81.

50 Cohen 2013: 27–32.

51 Le Rider 1965; Cohen 2013: 194–199.

Two distinct pieces of evidence clearly support that local populations used the victory coinage, despite its Attic weight. First, several tetradrachms present Aramaic graffiti on their obverses.[52] Although not all of these have been translated, it seems that the inscriptions spell Persian names and possibly the term for "governor."[53] Second, imitations featuring Aramaic letters as control marks (5.I1-J1; 6.A1; 8.A1) indicate that the trophy type was circulated widely enough in Persis to be copied. This evidence, combined with the geographical focus of the monetary output of Susa, a former Achaemenid capital, severely undermines the assumption that the victory coinage singled out a Greek audience.

Rather than favoring the standard *interpretatio graeca* of the type's iconography, we should understand the polysemous nature of the coinage as a sign of an acute awareness to different "communities of response," including the Persian elite in the eastern satrapies.[54] Seleukos I promoted a policy of conciliation as exemplified in other aspects of his rule such as his reliance on local administration and Persian affiliation.[55]

Obverse

One of the main points of contention in the study of the obverse has long centered on the identity of the helmeted male head. The singularity of the representation suggests a portrait, but its idiosyncrasies stymie most attempts at such empirical identification as is practicable with later Seleukid types. Babelon and Newell both identified the obverse as a portrait of Seleukos I.[56] Babelon, however, stressed similarities of the obverse with that of Alexandrine types such as the youthful and idealized features, covered head, and feline skin tied around the neck. Newell added that the idiosyncratic panther spots of the *nebris* highlighted the connection between Alexander and Seleukos, both of whom had "conquered" India like Dionysos.

Decades later, Hadley doubted this identification because of the lack of perceived individuality, quite unlike later numismatic portraits of Seleukid rulers.[57] Further, he noted that the portrait bears little resemblance with posthumous coins representing Seleukos struck by his son Antiochos I Soter and the Pergamene ruler Philetairos.[58] Hadley also added that since Seleukos was not officially deified until after his death in 281, the overt assimilation with Dionysos would have been inappropriate. Of the two remaining possible identifications, either Dionysos or

---

52 See coins 48, 50, 51, 142, 170, 176, 177 in the Catalogue and Ad10 in the Addendum.

53 *ESMS*: 125.

54 Others have shown the importance of taurine imagery in local contexts (Hoover 2011; Iossif 2012).

55 Seleukos wed a Sogdian noblewoman, Apama, and never repudiated her unlike most of Alexander's generals (Arr. *An.* 7.4.6). His son and heir, Antiochos, was thus of mixed ethnic background.

56 Babelon 1890: xv–xvi; Newell 1938: 156–158.

57 Hadley 1974.

58 *SC* 309, 322, 323.

Alexander assimilated to Dionysos, Hadley argued in favor of the latter on the grounds that the former would have been a "most atypical representation" of the god while Alexander had been compared to Dionysos during his lifetime. He concluded that it would have been appropriate for Seleukos to adopt Alexander as the "tutelary divinity of his realm" and to commemorate him on his coinage.

In the latest attempt to comprehensively tackle the issue of identification, Oliver Hoover convincingly objects to Hadley's argument concerning deification, stressing that there are several parallels for placing portraits with divine attributes on obverses before the establishment of any official cult—e.g. coins of Ptolemy and Demetrios Poliorketes.[59] Furthermore, ruler cult in the Hellenistic period was a complex and multifaceted phenomenon, and a distinction should be made between civic and dynastic cults.[60] Although Seleukos was not officially deified before his death and the Seleukid dynastic cult was probably not established before the reign of Antiochos III, civic cults were already attested during Seleukos's lifetime.[61] Like other Diadochs, he received *isotheoi timai*, honors equal to those of the gods, with statues, sacrifices, processions, sanctuaries, festivals, and games.

The particularism of the head on the obverse and absence of iconographic comparanda, especially the helmet, eliminate the god Dionysos from the list of possible identifications, although the panther skin and bull's horns have been associated with the god.[62] The basic principle of physiognomic identification— the empirical comparison of the physical features of the head seen on the victory coinage with securely identified portraits—is straightforward enough. Unfortunately its practical application reaches a methodological impasse in this case. The helmet conceals much of the face, particularly the hairline, which is usually diagnostic in the case of Alexander, even under a headdress. The portrait also lacks the strong particularism seen on posthumous coins presenting the— sometimes horned—head of Seleukos or the ageless heroism of the bronze bust from the Villa of the Papyri (Fig. 6, below).[63] Nor does it present the image of the wonder boy Alexander with his flowing mane of hair as seen on posthumous numismatic types or earlier sculptural representations such as the Dresden type and the Azara herm.[64]

---

59 Hoover 2002: 52–54.

60 Among others, see Debord 2003; Virgilio 2003a; Van Nuffelen 2004; Chaniotis 2007.

61 The earliest sources concerning Seleukid civic cult are two decrees from Ilion to be dated from the lifetime of Seleukos, probably soon after the battle of Koroupedion in February 281 when the ruler took control of Asia Minor (*OGIS* 212; Robert 1937: 172–184; Virgilio 2003b: 229–231). For discussions of possible dates for the establishment of the official dynastic cult—mainly 206/5 and 200—see Ma 1999: 272–276; Debord 2003: 293–294.

62 For the iconography of Dionysos, see Veneri and Gasparri 1986; and for the association with Alexander, see Stewart 1993: 78–86, 231–243; Houghton and Stewart 1999; Iossif 2004: 263–265.

63 For Seleukos's portraits, see Fleischer 1991: 73–74, 159, no. 21.

64 For Alexander's portraits, see Smith 1988: 73–74, 100–101; Fleischer 1991: 5–19; Stewart 1993: 42-52.

Figure 6. Portrait of Seleukos I Nikator from the Villa of the Papyri at Herculaneum.
Naples, Archaeological National Museum, 5590. Author's photo.

We are left with the idiosyncrasies of the portrait, particularly the prominent
helmet and skin tied around the neck. Most interpretations privilege a Greek
understanding of the iconography and overlook the potency of the attributes in
a Persian context. Such a reading associates the bull's horns both with Dionysos
and Poseidon, and the panther skin exclusively with the former. The association
of panther imagery with military conquest through the spotted helmet recalls
Dionysos as conqueror of India, a feat that both Alexander and Seleukos had
reproduced to some extent. However, we must contend with the likelihood that
the main audience of the coinage was Persian, not Greek.

The victory coinage could be understood by a Persian audience because of
its polysemous use of power imagery. The horns on the helmet would have been
read as a very potent symbol of power by the Persian elite since such attributes
were associated with divine and royal authority since the third millennium BC.[65]
Furthermore, the configuration of the horns themselves supports the local origin
of the intended audience. The horn in the background points forward while that
in the foreground extends back in a Near Eastern "composite" perspective. In the
Greek tradition, both appendices would have been represented from the same
angle of view, pointing forth.[66] There is no doubt that this arrangement was not

65 Selz 2008; Winter 2008.
66 This topic is addressed in more detail in Marest-Caffey Forthcoming.

Figure 7. Detail of a rider wearing a Persian garb on the Alexander Sarcophagus.
Istanbul, Archaeological Museum, 370. Author's photo.

left to chance. The horns on coins issued by Antiochos I featuring the posthumous portrait of his father present a Greek configuration in the western part of the empire (*SC* 323) and a Near Eastern design in the east (*SC* 469, 471, 472).

The panther skin, which is often identified as Dionysiac in a Greek context, could have a very different significance for a Persian audience, conjuring a mental image of local authority. The so-called Alexander Sarcophagus provides evidence for the representation of the spotted skin in a local context.[67] On one of the pediments, a rider in traditional Persian dress including trousers and headdress called *kyrbasia*, perhaps the Sidonian king Abdalonymos, wears an ochre *chlamys* with brown spots, clearly imitating a panther skin, and sits on a saddlecloth possibly similarly decorated (Fig. 7).[68] The comparison between the helmeted head on the trophy type and horseman on the Alexander Sarcophagus is justified

---

67 The sarcophagus was found in the royal nekropolis of Sidon in 1877 and has usually been connected with Abdalonymos, a local dynast appointed by Alexander. Heckel prefers to identify the satrap Mazaios as the *Grabherr*. Although the details of the iconography and identity of most participants are uncertain, it is agreed that it should be dated to the last quarter of the fourth century BC (Stewart 1993: 294–306, figs 101–106; Heckel 2006).

68 The saddlecloth was clearly painted since a shadow of the fringed edge is still visible. Remnants of paint below the rider's thigh suggest that the cloth was spotted although more work on the polychromy would be needed to determine the exact nature of the decoration.

Figure 8. Horseman-type tetradrachm minted at Ekbatana, c. 295 (x 1.5).
Private Collection.

by the appearance of a figure linking both representations on a coinage minted by Seleukos I at Ekbatana in c. 295 (Fig. 8; *SC* 203, 209, 213). The rider wears both the horned helmet and spotted *chlamys*, and sits on spotted saddlecloth.[69] By the time the sarcophagus was carved—probably within a decade of the beginning of the trophy series—the panther-spotted skin was associated with a local ruler in Persian dress.

Although identification has long been of particular interest for scholars, no one has suggested that the ambiguity of the portrait may be purposefully catering to different communities of response. A Macedonian audience could have identified the image as Alexander the Great, although Seleukos himself had been associated with taurine imagery.[70] Horned portraits of the Diadoch are attested both in literary sources and material evidence, most notably on posthumous coins and official seals from Seleukeia on the Tigris and Uruk.[71] A Persian audience probably would have been more comfortable reading it as Seleukos because of the checkered relations between Alexander and the local elite. On the contrary, Seleukos had found support in Persis against Antigonos. The Seleukids never exhibited a strong Alexandrine ideology as opposed to most early Hellenistic rulers contrary to Hadley's argument.[72] Seleukos proved very conservative in his deployment of Alexander's portrait and used it on a single, short-lived issue of gold and bronze types minted at Babylon, Susa, and Ekbatana in c. 300–298.[73]

69 When the Ekbatana horseman type was first published, it was identified as Alexander the Great (Houghton and Stewart 1999: 28–29). As convincingly argued by Hoover (2002: 58-59), and Miller and Walters (2004), the rider need not be Alexander nor the horned horse Boukephalas. Fresher specimens of the type have appeared since the publication of the first article and confirm that panther spots adorn the saddlecloth (Fig. 8).

70 Hoover 2011; Iossif 2012.

71 A clay sealing from Uruk representing a ruler standing in a heroic pose could offer an illustration of the horned statues of Seleukos mentioned by Appian. See Lindström 2003: 48, fig. 63.

72 Hadley 1974: 13.

73 *SC* 101, 183, 188-190, 219, 222-223. For discussions of the numismatic use of

Interestingly, the findspots—when documented—point to a wider dispersion of these coins than in the case of the trophy type.[74] Their iconography—clearly indebted to earlier Alexandrine and Ptolemaic types—reuses a decades-old and by then familiar representation of the Macedonian conqueror with an elephant headdress and shows no great innovation. Furthermore, many feature Alexander's iconic forelock peeking from under the headdress or the telltale *mitra* headband associated with Dionysos, none of which are ever found on the victory coinage.[75]

Indeed, the iconography of the trophy type could apply to Seleukos himself. Once ruler of the eastern portion of the empire, Alexander's successor harnessed the powerful symbolism of the bull on his coinage, effective both among the Greek and Persian population, first with the "butting bull" on bronze series and later with the numerous iterations of horned horseheads and elephants on different issues.[76] Appian relates an anecdote featuring Seleukos and a bull to explain the horned statues of the king.[77] During a sacrifice performed by Alexander, the Macedonian general, who was of large and powerful build, mastered an escaping bull.[78] Regardless of the veracity of the story, the persona of Seleukos already became associated with taurine lore and imagery during his lifetime since Appian's likely source, Hieronymos of Kardia, was a contemporary of the events.[79] The horned helmet seen on the trophy type later became a symbol of the Seleukid kings and other rulers in eastern satrapies.[80]

A new approach to the obverse shows that the idiosyncrasies of the portrait, especially the horned, spotted helmet and the panther skin, could be understood as polysemous iconographic elements exploited by the Seleukids to further their political and ideological agenda in the eastern satrapies of the empire. The trophy coinage should thus be seen as one of the iconographic and numismatic experiments characterizing the years following the consolidation of the eastern border of the Seleukid Empire and reorganization of the eastern provinces. The period culminated with the nomination of Antiochos, Seleukos' son and heir by

Alexander's image, see Hoover 2002: 54–56; *SC*: 6–7; Dahmen 2007: 14–15, 117–118.

74 According to *SC*, specimens were found in Persia, Urumia, in the excavations at Failaka, Seleukeia, and Susa, possibly in the Oxus Hoard, in the excavations at Istakhr, as well as in Tehran and Punjab.

75 For Alexander's anastole, see Smith 1988: 58–64; Stewart 1993: 52–56, 105–122; Dahmen 2007: 6–17; Hölscher 2009: 26–32.

76 Iossif 2012.

77 The only extant visual evidence is a colossal marble head with bases for missing horns, which was identified as a posthumous portrait of Seleukos (Antakya, Hatay Archaeology Museum, 14319). See Houghton 1986; Smith 1988: 100–101; Stewart 1993: 337–338.

78 App. *Syr.* 9.57.

79 For later sources, see *Historia Alexandri Magni* 2.28; Libanius, *Orationes* 11.92-93 (Erickson 2013: 120–125).

80 For instance, a bronze coinage from Aï Khanoum dating from the reign of Antiochos I features a horned Macedonian helmet alone on the reverse (*SC* 448-451).

his Persian wife, as coruler and regent over these eastern territories in 294. During this time, new iconographic types and Persian-weight issues were minted in the easternmost workshops at Babylon, Susa, and Ekbatana, integrating elements of Greek and Persian visual vocabulary.[81]

Reverse

The following commentary argues that the pointed iconography of the reverse would be better understood if the beginning of the victory coinage were down-dated from c. 305/4 to after the battle of Ipsos in 301. It will not be possible to redate the series based on numismatic grounds until a new study of the *entire* Susian production under Seleukos I is conducted in light of new discoveries. The dating hinges on several historical landmarks. Seleukos returned to Babylon c. 312/1, progressively regained control over the satrapy during a bitter struggle with Antigonos spanning several years, and finally extended his authority to Susiana, Media, and Persis. The victory coinage must postdate 305/4 (when the Macedonian general took the title of king according to literary sources). Two other dates are of crucial importance: c. 304/3 (when Seleukos ended the Indian campaign with a diplomatic agreement with the Mauryan king Chandragupta) and 301 (when Seleukos was instrumental in defeating Antigonos at the battle of Ipsos).

The hoard evidence is unfortunately of little help to narrow an absolute chronology since few of the hoards were archaeologically excavated and many have been reconstructed (Table 3). Two of the hoards excavated at Pasargadae by the British Institute of Persian Studies in 1962 and 1963 contained trophy-type tetradrachms and drachms from Susa along with Alexandrine types in the name of Philip and Alexander of various geographical origins. Hoard II was found sealed below a thick layer of debris associated with the end of Period II of the Tall-e Takht, an elevated structure dating back to the Achaemenid period and transformed into a citadel by Darius I.[82] As the freshest coins in the hoard, the "trophies" provided a chronological benchmark for the dating of the destruction layer. Accepting Newell's dating of the trophies and factoring in the wear of the coins, the excavator dated the end of Period II to c. 280, the year of Seleukos' death, a "period of nationalist unrest."[83] Since the destruction layer is not dated independently from the hoard, the end of Period II has been redated several times, including to c. 295 by Kritt.[84] The argument becomes circular: the coins date the destruction layer, which in turn supports the dating of the coins. Furthermore, recent archaeological work at the Tall-e Takht and preliminary reports suggest a more complex stratigraphy with signs of destruction carbon-dated to the Achaemenid period.[85]

---

81 See the following types: *SC* 88-91, 102-104, 163, 173-182, 184-187, 203, 209, 213, 220-221.
82 Stronach 1978: 146–159.
83 Stronach 1978: 155–156.
84 *ESMS*: 70–72.
85 Askari Chaverdi and Callieri 2010.

Table 3. Coin hoards containing trophy-type coins.

Hoard	Reference	Content	Including trophy type
Near East, 1981	*CH* VII, 66	8+ AR incl. Alexander III, Demetrios Poliorketes, Seleukos I	1 tetradrachm (Group 1.8)
Babylonia, c. 1900?	*IGCH* 1761	108+ AR incl. Alexander III, Philip III, Mazaces, Tyre, Seleukos I	1 hemidrachm (Group unknown)
Mesopotamia, before 1920	*IGCH* 1764	94+ AR incl. Alexander III, Philip III, Demetrios Poliorketes, Lysimachos, Eumenes I, Seleukos I, Antiochos I, Antiochos II, Seleukos II, Antiochos Hierax	1 hemidrachm (Group unknown)
Pasargadae I, Persis, 1962	Jenkins 1965: 42-44; Stronach 1978: 185-198; *IGCH* 1795	14+ AR incl. Alexander III, Philip III, Seleukos I	3 tetradrachms (Group 1.5 = no. 82; Group 1.10 x 2 = nos. 157, 171); 3 drachms (group 2.5 x 2 = nos. 211, 232; Group unknown)
Pasargadae II, Persis, 1963	Jenkins 1965: 44-49; Stronach 1978: 185-198; *IGCH* 1794	34 AR incl. Alexander III, Philip III, Seleukos I	8 tetradrachms (Group 1.6 x 2 = nos. 84, 88; Group 1.9 x 2= nos. 129, 134; Group 1.10 x 3 = nos. 153, 165, 168; Group 1.11 = no. 178)
Qazvin, Media, 1964	*IGCH* 1796; *CH* I, 38	ca. 150 AR incl. Alexander III, Seleukos I, Antiochos I (coregency)	1 tetradrachm (Group 1.1 = no. 2); 1 drachm (Group 2.4 = no. 203)
Persepolis, Persis, 1934-1935	*IGCH* 1797	10 AR incl. Seleukos I, Vahbarz, Baydād, Vādfradād	1 tetradrachm (Group 1.9 = no. 141)
"Frataraka," probably from Persis, 1986	*ESMS:* 132-137; *CH* IX, 481	AR incl. Seleukos I, Ardaxšīr Vahbarz, unknown Persid ruler	4 tetradrachms (Group 1.4 x 2 = nos. 24, 33; Group 1.10 = no. 170; imitation = 5.L1); 3 drachms (Group 2.5 = nos. 224, 229, 239)
"Persia," probably from Persis, c. 2007	Commerce	c. 900 AR incl. Alexander III, Philip III, Seleukos I	c. 100

Seeking to close the gap between Antigonid and Seleukid series minted at Susa and offer a scenario of continuous production, Kritt dated the beginning of the Alexandrine issues from 311 and the subsequent victory coinage, which bears the name of Seleukos and his royal title, from 305/4.[86] While Kritt's relative chronology convincingly places the early Alexandrine types of Susa before the trophy type based on symbols and monograms, his absolute chronology is debatable.[87] First, the adoption of the royal title in 305/4 only provides a *terminus post quem*, not an absolute date for the beginning of the victory coinage. Second, as shown by Panagiotis Iossif, Seleukos, like most of Alexander's successors, did not start inscribing the royal title on his coinage immediately upon its adoption but much later in most mints.[88] Lastly, recent numismatic work concerning the nature and importance of the so-called "Uncertain Mint 6A" in Babylonia, which produced some of the earliest coinage bearing the name and title of Seleukos, suggests that the incorporation of the royal title on coins should be down-dated to the period following the return of Seleukos to Babylonia, shortly before Ipsos, and related to the Macedonian tradition of acclamation as king by the troops.[89]

The battle of Ipsos in 301 appears a more probable historical benchmark for the dating of the Susian coins on iconographic and numismatic grounds. Iossif has used the detailed iconography of the reverse to argue convincingly that the trophy coinage commemorates Seleukos' momentous victory.[90] The 12-rayed Macedonian star prominently displayed on the trophy's shield unequivocally identifies the vanquished army as dominantly Macedonian. Between 311 and 301, Seleukos did not win any battle of consequence against such an army since most of his military operations were located in the East. Nike crowning, assembling, or holding a trophy constituted a widely recognizable motif across space—Pyrrhos in Epiros and Agathokles in Sicily displayed it on their coinages[91]—and time— the Seleukids, and usurpers, reused it several times.[92] Yet none of these iterations present the prominent and charged Macedonian starburst. The iconography also undermines the interpretation that the trophy may be referencing Seleukos' Indian campaign as it is sometimes argued to support the 305/4 dating. To be sure, Seleukos' *anabasis* was ultimately successful, consolidating the eastern border of his empire and earning him a sizable—and later extremely useful—herd of war

---

86 The assumption that the mint was producing continuously and that the transfer of allegiance from Antigonos to Seleukos happened in 311 is problematic (see note 95 below). For the intermittent nature of minting operations, see Callataÿ 2012: 41–42.

87 *ESMS*: 48, 65. In a more recent contribution, Kritt (2016: 65) maintains the dating of the victory coinage to 305–295.

88 Iossif 2004: 253-254.

89 Taylor 2015. Agency, and most particularly military achievements, constituted the central aspect of the definition of Macedonian kingship (Virgilio 2003b).

90 Iossif 2004: 255–260.

91 *BMC* 1, 379.

92 *SC* 388-390, 455-469 (Antiochos I); 776-780 (Seleukos II); 949 (Molon).

elephants. However, this success was diplomatic rather than military. The terms of the treaty stipulated that Seleukos hand over to Chandragupta the easternmost satrapies and receive in exchange five hundred Indian elephants, while a marriage alliance sealed the treaty.[93] It also seems that the Indian campaign ended in 304/3 rather than at the earlier date.[94]

Kritt dated the end of the victory coinage to c. 295 and associated this event with a revolt in Persis.[95] A heated debate concerning the status of the satrapy within the Seleukid Empire has emerged, usually pitting numismatists against historians and archaeologists. Persis was the center of power in the Achaemenid period, but it did not enjoy the same preeminence under the Seleukids. While all scholars acknowledge that the area enjoyed *some* form of independence at *some* point between Seleukid control at the end of the fourth century and Arsacid rule in the second half of the second century, few agree about the beginning, duration, and nature of this independence. The main controversy centers on the chronology and significance of Persid coins, usually known as "Frataraka" because of the title of the local rulers inscribed in Aramaic. Some numismatists have associated the end of the trophy coinage, dated as early as 295, with the beginning of independence in Persis. Indeed, several Seleukid coins were overstruck by Frataraka rulers and others coexisted with Persid coinages in hoards such as the "Frataraka" and Persepolis Hoards (Table 3).[96] However, the evidence does not warrant such a hasty conclusion, especially since the Frataraka coinage cannot be independently dated and probably served a commemorative purpose. Historians and archaeologists object that literary, epigraphic, and archaeological evidence points rather to a certain continuity of the Seleukid presence in Persis until the second century. The proponents of this understanding tend to support a low chronology, which dates the beginning Frataraka dynasty to the late third or early second century at the earliest.

Let us first review the evidence marshaled by Kritt:

> I [Kritt] will argue that the Persepolis and Frataraka hoards imply an early date for the independence of the Persid dynasty. The absence in these hoards

93 Kosmin 2014: 32–37.

94 Kosmin 2014: 276 n. 8.

95 Using magisterial terms, Kritt estimated that the victory coinage was produced for about ten years. The calculations were based on principles of continuous production at Susa between 311 and 280 and regular "magisterial terms" evidenced in the successive control marks (*ESMS*: 63-64). However, there is no evidence to support such a hypothesis, especially in the early days of the empire. Seleukos struggled for control over Babylon until 308. It is thus unclear whether he could have stuck coins at Susa as early as 311. The notion of "yearly terms" is also problematic. For a summary of the various interpretations of control marks in the Hellenistic period, see Callataÿ 2012.

96 Discussions of the Frataraka coinages are found in *ESMS*: 132-137; Hoover 2008a: 213–215; Klose and Müseler 2008; Curtis 2010.

of Seleucid coins later than the trophy series could imply a date as early as 295 B.C. There is evidence of hostility to the Greeks among the natives of Persis, going back to the time of Alexander, as well as indications of Seleucid intentions of holding Persis. There is also both literary and archeological support for Seleucid garrisons in Persis, and in particular at Persepolis. As discussed below, the evidence from Pasargadae strongly suggests the possibility of a violent revolt in Persis c. 295 B.C.

Thus the role of Susa may have involved military operations in southern Persia intended to hold Seleucus' eastern flank from possible Persid insurrection, while his main force was off to the west to fight Antigonus. (…)

If Persis was lost in 295, it seems no coincidence that the trophy coinage ceased virtually immediately. Then the purpose of this type, celebrating Seleucus' conquest of the east, could be seen as signifying Seleucid intentions to control Persis, and projecting the image of Seleucid power into that region.[97]

The hoard evidence and overstrikes indeed support an early date, despite low survival rates (Table 4).[98] The fact that no coin issued by a successor of Antiochos II was overstruck by a Frataraka ruler renders the low chronology extremely unlikely, even taking into consideration the poor monetization of Persis under the Achaemenids and the continued preference for exchange in kind.[99] It would otherwise have meant hoarding Seleukid coins for over a century before overstriking them! The first Frataraka dynast, Ardaxšir, should be considered a contemporary of the later years of Seleukos' reign or of the beginning of Antiochos I's rule at the very latest since the "Frataraka" Hoard contained specimens of the trophy type along with coins of the first two Persid rulers. Ardaxšir also overstruck coins minted by Seleukos I and Demetrios Poliorketes. The Frataraka rulers probably came in relatively rapid succession since the latest Seleukid coin overstruck by Vadfradad I is dated c. 261.

The second part of Kritt's argument has however been convincingly challenged by historians and archaeologists. First, the few extant accounts regarding tensions between Greeks and Persid populations, and Seleukid involvement are contradictory, not datable with any certainty, and point to sporadic events.[100] Second, recent archaeological work supports a rather continuous Greek presence in Persis until the second century BC.[101] Finally, as already discussed above, the

97 *ESMS*: 82–83.

98 Using overstruck Seleukid coins, Hoover (2008a: 213-215) reorganized the order of Frataraka rulers, originally presented by Newell (1938: 160) and Alram (1986: 162–186).

99 Joannès 2005; Duyrat 2005.

100 Engels 2013: 33–36. For a list of sources, see Klose and Müseler 2008: 8–9.

101 Callieri 2007; Askari Chaverdi and Callieri 2013; Cohen 2013: 32, 181–200; Wiesehöfer 2013.

argument concerning the Pasargadae Hoards is circular and the related destruction layer may date from the Achaemenid period.

Table 4. Chronologies and overstrikes by Frataraka rulers.

Ruler	High chronology	Low chronology	Type and date of undertype
Ardaxšir	early 3rd century	late 3rd or early 2nd century	-1 trophy-type tetradrachm, after 301* -1 tetradrachm of Demetrios Poliorketes, c. 295*
Vahbarz	1st half of 3rd century	1st half of 2nd century	
Baydad	1st half of 3rd century	1st half of 2nd century	-1 Alexandrine tetradrachm of Seleukos I from Ekbatana, after c. 295 (Hoover 2008a: no. 31)
Vadfradad I	mid 3rd century	mid 2nd century	-1 trophy-type tetradrachm, after 301 (Hoover 2008a: no. 32) -1 horsehead-type tetradrachm of Antiochos I, after 281 (Hoover 2008a: no. 33) -1 drachm of Antiochos II, c. 261 (Klose and Müseler 2008: no. 2/23)*

* From personal communication with Scott VanHorn, who identified the undertypes.

Using several links between the Susian and Frataraka coinages, this paper argues in favor of a high chronology incorporating the current—more sympathetic and complex—understanding of Seleukid policies.[102] Rather than signifying an early Persid independence—and thus latent weakness and intrinsic inadequacy of the Seleukid Empire—the emergence of a local Persian "dynasty" might be the sign of a successful Seleukid policy of fusion and adaptation to local customs. It is now widely accepted that the title *frataraka* featured on the Persid coins is rather modest and relates to a sub-satrapal function attested in Achaemenid Egypt. It even simply refers to a "foreman" in Baktrian documents dating from the mid- to late fourth century.[103] Other numismatic evidence points to a scenario of limited Persid autonomy under Seleukid control. Indeed, the obvious Seleukid influence on the obverse portraits and manufacture of the Frataraka coinage, the production of trophy-type coins with Aramaic letters as control marks, and the popularity of the trophy type for local imitations would make little sense in the case of an open Persid revolt. The local rulers may have been granted some form of autonomy and

102 Engels 2013.
103 For the title, see Wiesehöfer 1991. For Baktrian examples, see Naveh and Shaked 2012: A1, line 8; A5, line 4; Tavernier 2008: 60.

limited privileges, such as the right to mint.[104] Most compelling is the evidence offered by the use of an official obverse die on an imitative coin (5.A1), proving a connection between the official mint at Susa and an imitative mint. The limited independence may have continued until the Seleukid Empire disintegrated at its eastern edge in the mid-second century. The Persid rulers then transferred their allegiance to the Parthians.[105]

The drastic reduction of the estimated output of the victory coinage (Table 2, above) does not support the hypothesis that the Susian coins were issued to finance large military operations to secure the eastern satrapies, particularly against Persid unrest. The coinage was certainly destined to pay troops and still represents an important production. However, fewer than 30 dies do not represent a dramatic increase in production at Susa as proposed by Kritt. Although this is conjectural, the victory coinage may have been produced after 301 to pay the veterans who had served at Ipsos, including the important Persian contingent. According to Diodoros (20.113.4), Seleukos's cavalry—which played a crucial role in the battle— was 12,000-men strong, most of whom were of Iranian origin.[106] At an estimated average of 20,000 coins per obverse die—using the number for comparative purpose only—28 dies would have produced over 2.2 million drachms, nearly enough to pay 12,000 men for a year.[107] This estimate only provides a framework for comparison, not an exact scenario. We do not know what cavalry men were paid exactly, although evidence from Egypt show that they received three times the acreage of regular *katoikoi*.[108] And payment for the veterans of Ipsos certainly came from several mints. Nevertheless, we should remember that Susa had been the easternmost mint in the early days of the Seleukid Empire. Interestingly, Seleukos felt the need after Ipsos to reorganize his minting operations in the East with the creation of the mint at Seleukeia on the Tigris and produce new coinages of Persian weight at Babylon, Susa, and Ekbatana.[109]

If approached as a type conceived with an awareness of local populations, which is supported by the numismatic evidence, the victory coinage offers a glimpse into Seleukid policies of conciliation with the Persid elite and their success. This understanding can resolve the long-standing contradiction between disruptions perceived by numismatists and continuity seen by historians and archaeologists in Persis. The intended audience of the victory coinage explains the innovations of the type, while its short life in the official Susian mint under direct Seleukid control could be explained by the transfer of some administrative powers including the right of minting to local dynasts such as the Frataraka rulers. A strict *interpretatio*

104 For a second-century parallel for such minting privileges, see Hoover 2005.
105 Strab. 15.3.3.
106 Olbrycht 2005: 232–233.
107 Callataÿ 2011. We must also account for the fractional coinage.
108 Bingen 2007: 124.
109 *SC* 101, 183, 219.

graeca of the trophy type, singling out Alexandrine and Dionysiac symbolism, impoverishes the complexity of a polysemous coinage cleverly incorporating elements of Persian iconography of power into a royal portrait of Greek style and format. Shifting the interpretive lens provides new, promising perspectives to approach Seleukid imagery. The reverse of the victory coinage reminded military veterans, both Greek and Persian, of Seleukos's legitimate claim to kingship, that is his crushing victory at Ipsos. Although the individual understanding of the potent imagery may be irretrievable in its complexity, the popularity of the type, used and imitated locally, testifies to the success of Seleukid policies in the early days of the empire.

Catalogue[110]

Tetradrachms

Obverse: Head of Seleukos I Nikator to right, wearing panther-spotted helmet with bull's ear and horns, and panther skin tied around the neck, dotted border.

Reverse: ΒΑΣΙΛΕΩΣ counterclockwise at right, ΣΕΛΕΥΚΟΥ counterclockwise at left, Nike standing to right, crowning trophy, dotted border.

Group 1.1. ΒΕ (lower left); Boeotian shield (between Nike and trophy); ₧ (lower right).

1.	A1	P1	17.12	12	CNG 87 (18 May 2011), lot 615.
2.	A1	P1	16.97	5	Saint Louis Art Museum, 319:1991. CNG XIV (20 Mar. 1991), lot 187; CNG XII (26 Sep. 1990), lot 406; Christie's, NY (13 Mar. 1990), lot 100. *ESMS* Tr.3; Houghton 1983, no. 1022; Spaer 1975, 38, no. 21. From Qazvin Hoard.
3.	A1	P1	17.02	4	US commerce (2008).
4.	A1*	P2	17.23	1	Nomos 2 (18 May 2010), lot 129.
5.	A1*	P2	16.97	3	Helios 6 (9 Mar. 2011), lot 71; Pars Coins (29 Jan. 2010), PCW-G2795.
6.	A1*	P3*	17.01	6	Stack's Bowers & Ponterio 173 (8 Jan. 2013), lot 242; Najaf (2012).
7.	A1	P3	16.48	10	ANS 1948.19.2304. *ESMS* Tr.1.
8.	A1	P4	16.95	9	London, British Museum, 2002.0101.1350; ex C. Hersh coll. *ESMS* Tr.2.

110 * indicates a tooled coin; # indicates that no image was available; weight in *italics* indicates a silver plated coin.

9.	A1	P5	17.06	11	Künker 216 (8 Oct. 2012), lot 485; Roma 3 (31 Mar. 2012), lot 348; Roma 2 (2 Oct. 2011), lot 356; Heritage, NY 3012 (2 Jan. 2011), lot 24494; V Auction 249 (15 Jul. 2010), lot 15.
10.	A2	P5	17.10	10	US commerce (2008).
11.	A3	P6	16.90		Auctiones 16 (1-2 Oct. 1986), lot 230. *ESMS* Tr.4.

Group 1.2. 𐤋; AI; BE (from left to right).

| 12. | A3 | P7 | 16.58 | 6 | London, British Museum, 1988.0912.2. Giessener 33 (3 Jun. 1986), lot 216. *ESMS* Tr.5. |

Group 1.3. 𐤀; Boeotian shield; AX (from left to right).

| 13. | A3 | P8 | 17.01 | | Vinchon (14 Apr. 1984), lot 197. *ESMS* Tr.6. |

Group 1.4. 𐤀 (lower left); 𐤓 (between Nike and trophy).

14.	A3	P9	17.22	11	Heritage, NY 3030 (6 Jan. 2014), lot 23796.
15.	A4	P9	17.04	8	CNG 87 (18 May 2011), lot 616.
16.	A4	P9	16.66		CNG 66 (19 May 2004), lot 665.
17.	A4	P9	16.00		Glendining (9 Jun. 1993), lot 88.
18.	A4	P10	17.44	8	Roma 8 (28 Sep. 2014), lot 705.
19.	A4	P10	17.10		Peus 332 (23-28 Oct. 1991), lot 230; Superior (11-12 Jun. 1986), lot 1234; Numismatic Fine Arts V (23-24 Feb. 1978), lot 191. *ESMS* Tr.19.
20.	A4	P10	17.38	9	Triton XV (3 Jan. 2012), lot 1281.
21.	A4	P10	17.36		Numismatica Ars Classica 88 (8 Oct. 2015), lot 601; Baldwin's, NY Sale 34 (6 Jan. 2015), lot 174.
22.	A4	P11			Münchner Münzhandlung 164 (13-14 Nov. 1975), lot 567. *ESMS* Tr.32.
23.	A4	P12	16.87	11	London, British Museum BNK, G.810. *ESMS* Tr.10; *ESM* 426 A13/P17.

24.	A5	P13	16.94	5	Numismatica Ars Classica 77 (26 May 2014), lot 77; Freeman & Sear MBS 5 (14 May 1999), lot 277; Sotheby's, Zurich (26 Oct. 1993), lot 64; Numismatic Fine Arts XXVII (5 Dec. 1991), lot 70; Numismatic Fine Arts XXII (1 Jun. 1989), lot 338; Stack's (Dec. 1987), lot 3293; Historical Coin Review XI, 4 (25 Jul. 1986), lot 490. *ESMS* Tr.29. From "Frataraka" Hoard.
25.	A5	P13	17.01	4	Leu 83 (6 May 2002), lot 371; CNG 36 (5-6 Dec. 1995), lot 2047. *ESMS* Tr.30.
26.	A5	P13	16.99	5	Bru 6 (9 Dec. 2011), lot 88.
27.	A5	P13	16.69	5	Leu 2 (25 Apr. 1972), lot 272. *ESMS* Tr.20.
28.	A5	P13	16.65		Boston, Museum of Fine Arts, anonymous gift in memory of Zoe Wilbour (1864–1885), 35.155. Naville X (15-18 Jun. 1925), lot 795; Sotheby's, Benson coll. (Feb. 1909), lot 754; Sotheby's, Late Collector (1900), lot 418. *ESMS* Tr.24; *ESM* 426 A12/P16β; *WSM* 26.
29.	A5	P13	16.68		Naville X (15-18 Jun. 1925), lot 796; Hess (Oct. 1907), lot 1136. *ESMS* Tr.25; *ESM* 426 A12/P16α.
30.	A5	P14	17.06		Naville XIV (Jul. 1929), lot 408; Naville I, Pozzi coll. (Mar. 1921), lot 2921. *ESMS* Tr.23; *ESM* 426 A14/P18.
31.	A5	P15	17.10	3	Freeman & Sear, Manhattan I (5 Jan. 2010), lot 87.
32.	A5	P15			US commerce (2008).
33.	A5	P15	16.77	6	Kovacs (1986). *ESMS* Tr.21. From "Frataraka" Hoard.
34.	A5	P16	17.06	12	Triton IX (10 Jan. 2006), lot 1008; Morton & Eden (25-26 May 2005), lot 1083.
35.	A6	P17	16.81	2	Freeman & Sear, Manhattan II (4 Jan. 2011), lot 68; Hess-Divo 307 (7 Jun. 2007), lot 1298; Monnaies et Médailles 76 (19-20 Sep. 1991), lot 828. *ESMS* Tr.28.
36.	A6	P17	17.06	3	Nomos 1 (6 May 2009), lot 117; Leu 81 (16 May 2001), lot 323.

37.	A6	P17	16.69	2	Gorny & Mosch 159 (8 Oct. 2007), lot 240; Giessener 58 (Apr. 9, 1992), lot 457; Giessener 55 (14 May 1991), lot 329. *ESMS* Tr.27.
38.	A6	P17	17.09		Giessener 46 (30 Oct. 1989), lot 360. *ESMS* Tr.26.
39.	A6	P17	16.97		Künker 270 (2 Oct. 2015), lot 8363; Baldwin's, NY Sale 29 (5 Jan. 2012), lot 1033.
40.	A7	P18	17.12	7	Triton XVI (8-9 Jan. 2013), lot 545.
41.	A7	P18	17.02	9	Berlin, Münzkabinett, C.R. Fox 1873, 18203076. *ESMS* Tr.22; *ESM* 426 A12/P16γ.
42.	A7	P18	16.60		Cederlind 105 (Sep. 1996), 375; Spink America (3 May 1995), lot 303; Vecchi FPL II (1973), lot 11. *ESMS* Tr.31/33.
43.	A7	P19	17.09		Spink 9008 (19 Mar. 2009), lot 283; Gemini II (11 Jan. 2005), lot 130.
44.	A7	P20	17.05		US commerce (2008).
45.	A8	P19	16.89	8	Hess-Divo 328 (22 May 2015), lot 65; CNG 88 (14 Sep. 2011), lot 451.
46.	A8	P20	17.07	11	CNG 97 (17 Sep. 2014), lot 280.
47.	A8	P21	17.08	10	Numismatic Fine Arts XXVI (14 Aug., 1991), lot 96; Numismatic Fine Arts XVIII (31 Mar. 1987), lot 276. *ESMS* Tr.7; Houghton 1983, 1023.
48.	A8	P21	16.90	8	CNG 94 (18 Sep. 2013), lot 722.
49.	A8	P21	16.96		Pars Coins (2012), PCW-G3667.
50.	A8	P21	16.91	4	Roma 10 (27 Sep. 2015), lot 579.
51.	A9	P22	16.97	7	Leu 52 (15 May 1991), lot 109; Superior (9-10 Dec. 1989), lot 2745. *ESMS* Tr.15.
52.	A10	P23	16.53	6	Hess-Leu 36 (17 Apr. 1968), lot 313. *ESMS* Tr.13
53.	A10	P24	15.77	3	Kurpfälzische Münze 43 (Dec. 1992), lot 159; Auctiones 22 (16-17 Jun. 1992), lot 348. *ESMS* Tr.12.
54.	A11	P25	16.99		Triton I (2-3 Dec. 1997), lot 556.
55.	A11	P25	17.00		Münzen & Medaillen FPL 555 (June 1992), lot 24. *ESMS* Tr.14.
56.	A11	P25	16.33		Peus 382 (26 Apr. 2005), lot 227.

57.	A12	P26	16.69	3	Baldwin's NY Sale 27 (4 Jan. 2012), lot 607; Spink Australia (2-3 May 1989), lot 1167; Spink (Feb. 1989).
58.	A13	P27	16.84		Gorny & Mosch 199 (10 Oct. 2011), lot 528.
59.	A14	P28	16.89	9	Lanz 160 (15 Jun. 2015), lot 283.
60.	A14	P28	16.57	1	Kern (23 Jul. 2012); Superior (9-10 Dec. 1989), lot 2746; Numismatic Fine Arts XI (8 Dec. 1982), lot 211. *ESMS* Tr.18.
61.	A15	P28	17.04		Cederlind 162 (21 Dec. 2011), lot 78; Hirsch 275 (22 Sep. 2011), lot 3984; Peus 318 (7-8 May 1987), lot 1264; Peus 315 (28-30 Apr. 1986), lot 139. *ESMS* Tr.17.
62.	A15	P29	17.16	3	Peus 348 (2 May 1996), lot 196; Peus 334 (4 Nov. 1992), lot 490; CNG V (9 Dec. 1988), lot 158. *ESMS* Tr.16.
63.	A15	P29	17.05		US commerce (2008).
64.	A15	P30	16.99	5	CNG 96 (14 May 2014), lot 532.

Group 1.5. ♠ (lower left); ♔ (between Nike and trophy).

65.	A15	P31	17.00	9	Numismatica Ars Classica 54 (24 Mar. 2010), lot 134.
66.	A15	P31	16.70		CNG 118 (13 Jul. 2005), lot 76.
67.	A16	P31	17.08	9	Künker 216 (8 Oct. 2012), lot 486; Helios 3 (29 Apr. 2009), lot 62.
68.	A16	P31	16.87	7	Berlin, Münzkabinett, Imhoof-Blumer 1900. *ESMS* Tr.37; *ESM* 424 A11/P14.
69.	A16	P31	17.14		Münzen & Medaillen 42 (3 Jun. 2015), lot 89; Münzen & Medaillen 32 (26 May 2010), lot 171.
70.	A16	P32	16.88		Peus 323 (1-4 Nov. 1988), lot 870. *ESMS* Tr.34.
71.	A16	P33	16.86	2	ANS 1944.100.74108. *ESMS* Tr.38; *ESM* 424 A11/P13.
72.	A16	P33	17.03	3	CNG 97 (17 Sep. 2014), lot 282; US commerce (2008).
73.	A16	P34	16.83		Freeman & Sear FPL 1 (Winter/Spring 1994), lot 225. *ESMS* Tr.35.

74.	A16	P35	16.64		Numismatic Ars Classica 4 (27 Feb. 1991), lot 158; Niggeler Coll. I (1965), lot 421; Münzen & Medaillen 19 (5-6 Jun. 1959), lot 521; Hess 208 (Dec. 1931), lot 680; Hirsch XXI (Nov. 1908), lot 4030. *ESMS* Tr.36; *ESM* 424 A11/P15.
75.	A16	P35	16.78	7	Heritage 3020 (6-11 Sep. 2012), lot 25010.
76.	A16	P35	16.96	6	Triton XVIII (6 Jan. 2015), lot 710.
77.	A16	P36	17.00	1	CNG 97 (17 Sep. 2014), lot 281; Peus 395 (7 May 2008), lot 188; Münzen & Medaillen FPL 514 (Sep. 1988), lot 17. *ESMS* Tr.39.
78.	A16	P36	16.58	2	Paris, Cabinet des médailles, DeClercq 17. *ESMS* Tr.41.
79.	A16	P36	16.63		Superior (29 Oct. 1993), lot 1326; Kovacs XI (19 Jun. 1993), lot 85. *ESMS* Tr.40.
80.	A17	P36	16.38		CNG MBS 53 (15 Mar. 2000), lot 594; Peus 353 (29–31 Oct. 1997), lot 197.
81.	A17	P37	16.14	7	Roma 9 (22 Mar. 2015), lot 426.
82.	A17	P38	16.31	12	Oxford, Ashmolean Museum; British Institute, Tehran, PAS/62/149. *ESMS* Tr.42; Jenkins 1965, no. 13. From the Pasargadae I Hoard.
83.	A17	P39	17.12		Goldberg 74 (2-5 Jun. 2013), lot 3465; Ebay, Victoram (Oct. 2012); Heritage, Long Beach 3015 (7 Sep. 2011), lot 23141.

Group 1.6. Ǝ (lower left); ΔI (between Nike and trophy).

84.	A17	P40	16.10		*ESMS* Tr.61; Jenkins 1965, no. 28. From Pasargadae II Hoard.
85.	A17	P40	16.93	10	Leu 45 (26 May 1988), lot 254; Münzen & Medaillen 52 (19-20 Jun. 1975), lot 208. *ESMS* Tr.58.
86.	A17	P40	16.96		Peus 349 (30 Oct.-1 Nov. 1996), lot 162. *ESMS* Tr.59.
87.	A17	P40	17.05	9	Swiss Bank Corp (20 Sep. 1989), lot 128. *ESMS* Tr.53.
88.	A17	P41	16.50		*ESMS* Tr.60; Jenkins 1965, no. 29. From Pasargadae II Hoard.

89.	A17	P42	17.07	12	Roma 6 (29 Sep. 2013), lot 692.
90.	A17	P42	16.40	10	Leu 79 (31 Oct. 2000), lot 713.
91.	A17	P43	16.70	12	Münzen & Medaillen 40 (3 Jun. 2014), lot 284; Numismatic Fine Arts VII (6 Dec. 1979), lot 255; Glendining (11 Dec. 1974), lot 87. *ESMS* Tr.52.
92.	A17	P44	15.89	1	Cambridge, Fitzwilliam Museum, 5508. *ESMS* Tr.51.
93.	A17	P44	16.87	10	London, British Museum, 1850.0412.16. *ESMS* Tr.55; *ESM* 413; *BMC* 36.
94.	A17	P44	17.07	2	Triton XVIII (6 Jan. 2015), lot 129. Nelson 2011, no. 174.
95.	A17	P44	17.04	3	CNG 97 (17 Sep. 2014), lot 283.
96.	A17	P44	17.07		Giessener 48 (2 Apr. 1990), lot 543. *ESMS* Tr.54.
97	A17	P44	17.10	1	Roma 9 (22 Mar. 2015), lot 427.
98.	A17	P44	16.99	11	Peus 320 (3-4 Nov. 1987), lot 1181.
99.	A17	P44	16.96		Sincona 10 (27 May 2013), lot 183.
100.	A17	P44	17.09	6	Leu 30 (18 Apr. 1982), lot 202. *ESMS* Tr.57.
101.	A17	P44	17.12		St James 17 (24 May 2011), lot 15.
102.	A17#	P44#	16.79	2	*ESMS* Tr.56.
103.	A18	P44	17.12	8	Gemini VIII (14 Apr. 2011), lot 99; Heritage 3010 (12 Aug. 2010), lot 20074.
104.	A18	P45	16.40	8	London, British Museum, 2002.0101.1357; ex Hersh coll. *ESMS* Tr.49.
105.	A18	P46	17.04	5	CNG 38 (6-7 Jun. 1996), lot 398; Peus 343 (26-28 Apr. 1995), lot 182. *ESMS* Tr.50.

Group 1.7. $\overline{N}$ (lower left); ΔI (between Nike and trophy).

106.	A18	P47	16.64	2	ANS 1968.183.8. *ESMS* Tr.48.

Group 1.8. ⚘ (lower left); MI (between Nike and trophy).

107.	A18	P48	16.97	4	Triton XVI (8-9 Jan. 2013), lot 546.
108.	A18	P48	16.92	1	Heritage 3009 (22 Apr. 2010), lot 20056.

109.	A18	P48	16.96	Goldberg 74 (2-5 Jun. 2013), lot 3466; Ebay, Victoram (2012); Berk 151 (1 Nov. 2006), lot 195; Berk 148 (29 Mar. 2006), lot 155.
110.	A18	P49	17.01 5	Paris, Cabinet des médailles, Babelon 42. *ESMS* Tr.47; *ESM* 422 A10/P12.
111.	A18	P49	17.03 7	Jacquier 37 (7 Sep. 2012), lot 162; Gorny & Mosch 200 (10 Oct. 2011), lot 1997; Triton XIV (4 Jan. 2011), lot 355.
112.	A18	P50	16.98 3	Triton XVII (7-8 Jan. 2014), lot 368.
113.	A18	P50	16.22 7	ANS 1944.100.74107. *ESMS* Tr.46; *ESM* 422 A10/P11.
114.	A18	P51	16.27	Münz Zentrum XLVII (10 Nov. 1982), lot 217.

Group 1.9. H (lower left); AX (between Nike and trophy).

115.	A19	P52	16.10 5	Berlin, Münzkabinett, 225/1993; Schulten (27-29 Mar. 1990), lot 410; Auctiones 18 (21-22 Sep. 1989), lot 827. *ESMS* Tr.72.
116.	A19	P52	16.96	Los Angeles, J. Paul Getty Museum, 77.NB.35; Superior (24-26 Sep. 1970), lot 93; Numismatic Fine Arts 2 (25-26 Mar. 1976), lot 281; Glendining (17-18 May 1967). *ESMS* Tr.63.
117.	A19	P52	16.95	Peus 316 (1-3 Sep. 1989), lot 313. *ESMS* Tr.69.
118.	A19	P53	17.05	Münzen & Medaillen 88 (17 May 1999), lot 262; Bourgey (4 Feb. 1960), lot 98. *ESMS* Tr.64.
119.	A19	P53	15.89 11	London, British Museum, *BMC* 37. *ESMS* Tr.62; *ESM* 417 A4/P4.
120.	A19	P53	16.57	Numismatica Ars Classica 23 (19 Mar. 2002), lot 1283; Swiss Bank Corp 21 (24-26 Jan. 1989), lot 89. *ESMS* Tr.71.
121.	A19	P53	16.87 2	Numismatica Ars Classica 66 (17 Oct. 2012), lot 69; Sotheby's, NY (21-22 Jun. 1990), lot 579; Leu 15 (4-5 May 1976), lot 341. *ESMS* Tr.70.
122.	A19*	P53*	6	US commerce (2008).
123.	A19	P54	16.48	Hirsch 178 (12-14 May 1993), lot 454. *ESMS* Tr.65.

124.	A19	P55	16.76		Pegasi XXIV (5 Apr. 2011), lot 191; Vecchi I (1-2 Feb. 1996), lot 357; Kricheldorf XIX (June 28-29, 1968), lot 306. *ESMS* Tr.67.
125.	A19	P55	16.93		Peus 380 (3 Nov. 2004), lot 588; Peus 328 (2-4 May 1990), lot 247. *ESMS* Tr.68.
126.	A19	P56	16.77	10	CNG 73 (13 Sep. 2006), lot 442.
127.	A19	P57	17.06		Spink 13012 (26 Mar. 2013), lot 9.
128.	A20	P58	16.69	6	Copenhagen, Danish National Museum. *ESMS* Tr.86; *SNG Copenhagen*, part 34, 22.
129.	A21	P59	16.80		*ESMS* Tr.73; Jenkins 1965, no. 30. From Pasargadae II Hoard.
130.	A21	P59	17.04	6	Triton XVIII (6 Jan. 2015), lot 711; Lanz 72 (29 May 1995), lot 292. *ESMS* Tr.66.
131.	A21	P60	16.88	12	Auctiones 15 (18-19 Sep. 1985), lot 177. *ESMS* Tr.74.
132.	A21	P60	16.76		Münzen & Medaillen FPL 276 (May 1967), lot 3. *ESMS* Tr.75.
133.	A21	P60	16.57	2	Paris, Cabinet des médailles, DeClercq 16. *ESMS* Tr.81.
134.	A21	P61	16.00		*ESMS* Tr.76; Jenkins 1965, no. 31. From Pasargadae II Hoard.
135.	A21	P62	16.93		The Numismatic Auction 2 (12 Dec. 1983), lot 168; Münzen & Medaillen 54 (26 Oct. 1978), lot 353; Leu & Münzen & Medaillen, Niggeler I (3-4 Dec. 1965), lot 452; Schlessinger 13 (4 Feb. 1935), lot 1422. *ESMS* Tr.77; *ESM* 417 A7(?)/P8β.
136.	A21	P63	17.07	2	Sotheby's, Zurich (27-28 Oct. 1993), lot 821; Numismatic Fine Arts XXVIII (23 Apr. 1992), lot 720; Kovacs X (18 May 1990), lot 140. *ESMS* Tr.78.
137.	A21*	P64	17.05	10	Art Coins Roma 15 (27 Apr. 2015), lot 194; Numismatic Ars Classica 59 (4 Apr. 2011), lot 640.
138.	A21*	P65	17.01	9	Heritage 3032 (10 Apr. 2014), lot 23284.
139	A21	P66	17.18	6	Triton XVIII (6 Jan. 2015), lot 712.
140.	A21	P66	15.39	10	Paris, Cabinet des médailles, fond général 44. *ESMS* Tr.79; *ESM* 417 A6(?)/P7α.

141.	A21#	P66#			Riza Khan Pahlevi coll. *ESMS* Tr.80; *ESM* 417 A6(?)/P7β. From Persepolis Hoard.
142.	A21	P67	16.87		Sotheby's (9 Oct. 1992), lot 1115; Sotheby's (29 Sep. 1988), lot 385.
143.	A21	P67	16.73	12	Cambridge, McLean coll. 9244; Sotheby's, Carfrae coll. (May 1894), lot 296. *ESMS* Tr.82; *ESM* 417 A7 (?)-P8α.
144.	A21	P68	16.66		Macridi Pacha (1895). *ESMS* Tr.83; *ESM* 417 A5/P6.
145.	A21	P69	16.79		Naville X (15-18 Jun. 1925), lot 794; Sotheby's, Headlam coll. (May 1916), lot 432b. *ESMS* Tr.84; *ESM* 417 A5/P5.
146.	A21	P70	16.49	5	*ESMS* Tr.85; Ramage 1994, no. 21.
147.	A22	P70	16.63	9	Leu 20 (25-26 Apr. 1978), lot 158. *ESMS* Tr.79.
148.	A22	P70	17.13		Spink 12026 (26 Sep. 2012), lot 354.
149.	A22	P70	16.96		CNG 41 (19 Mar. 1997), lot 649; Numismatic Fine Arts MBS (14 Dec. 1989), lot 627; Sotheby's (29 Sep. 1988), lot 385. *ESMS* Tr.88.
150.	A22	P70	16.79		Morton & Eden (25-26 May 2005), lot 1084.
151.	A22	P70	16.88	11	Berlin, Münzkabinett, C.R. Fox 1873. *ESMS* Tr.90; *ESM* 417 A3/P3.

Group 1.10. M (lower left); AX (between Nike and trophy).

152.	A22	P71	16.53	12	ANS 1944.100.74104. *ESMS* Tr.89; *ESM* 417 A2/P2.
153.	A22	P71	16.37	12	London, British Museum 1973.1210.2. *ESMS* Tr.97; Jenkins 1965, no. 33. From Pasargadae II Hoard.
154.	A22?*	P72	16.77	2	CNG 354 (1 Jul. 2015), lot 210; Gemini XII (11 Jan. 2015), lot 178; Roma 4 (30 Sep. 2012), lot 1870.
155.	A23	P73		8	Stockholm, Royal Coin Cabinet. *ESMS* Tr.105; *ESM* 420 A8/P9; Appelgren 1931, no. 257.
156.	A23	P73	16.64		Sotheby's (22-23 Mar. 1990), lot 47.

157.   A23   P74   16.87   10   London, British Museum 1969.0525.1. *ESMS* Tr.98; Jenkins 1965, no. 12. From Pasargadae I Hoard.

158.   A23   P74   16.00   Stack's Bowers & Ponterio 185 (12 Aug. 2014), lot 30143; Coin Galleries MBS (14 Apr. 1993), lot 353; Christie's (9 Oct. 1984), lot 19; Sotheby's (12 Nov. 1980), lot 217; Sotheby's (16 Apr. 1980), lot 21. *ESMS* Tr.93.

159.   A23   P74   16.08   Kölner Münzkabinett 31 (2-3 Nov. 1981), lot 72.

160.   A23   P74   16.74   6   Paris, Cabinet des médailles, Chandon de Briailles 611.

161.   A23* P74   16.93   3   Heritage 3032 (10 Apr. 2014), lot 23283; Goldberg 70 (4 Sep. 2012), lot 3134; Freeman & Sear, Manhattan 3 (3 Jan. 2012), lot 145; Heritage 3010 (12 Aug. 2010), lot 20075.

162.   A23   P74   16.99   Freeman & Sear MBS 1 (10 Mar. 1995), lot 186; Münzen & Medaillen 37 (5 Dec. 1968), lot 228; Numismatic Fine Arts 28 (23 Apr. 1992), lot 719. *ESMS* Tr.94.

163.   A23   P74   16.94   10   Gorny & Mosch 180 (12 Oct. 2009), lot 219; Numismatic Fine Arts Fall MBS (12 Oct. 1988), lot 381. *ESMS* Tr.92; Houghton 1983, no. 1025.

164.   A23   P75   17.05   V Auctions 245 (22 Apr. 2010), lot 21.

165.   A23   P75   16.60   *ESMS* Tr.101; Jenkins 1965, no. 34. From Pasargadae II Hoard.

166.   A23* P75   15.88   2   Roma 10 (27 Sep. 2015), lot 580.

167.   A23   P75   16.20   11   Paris, Cabinet des médailles, Delepierre 3015. *ESMS* Tr.102.

168.   A23   P76   17.00   *ESMS* Tr.99; Jenkins 1965, no. 32. From Pasargadae II Hoard.

169.   A23   P76   17.02   Gemini V (6 Jan. 2009), lot 145; Berk 55 (19 Oct. 1988), lot 129. *ESMS* Tr.96.

170.   A23   P76   16.82   9   Numismatica Genevensis 5 (2-3 Dec. 2008), lot 135; Peus 376 (29 Oct. 2003), lot 506. *ESMS* Tr.95. From "Frataraka" Hoard.

171.	A23	P76	17.35		*ESMS* Tr.100; Jenkins 1965, no. 11. From Pasargadae I Hoard.
172.	A23	P76	17.05		Gemini V (6 Jan. 2009), lot 657.
173.	A23	P76	17.04		Baldwin's, NY Sale 25 (5 Jan. 2011), lot 111; Ponterio 154 (18 Jun. 2010), lot 8063.
174.	A23	P77	17.06	10	Lanz 125 (28 Nov. 2005), lot 443; Hirsch 206 (24-26 Nov. 1999), lot 193.
175.	A23*	P78	16.94	9	Heritage 3033 (8 Aug. 2014), lot 23040; Heritage 3019 (26 Apr. 2012), lot 23174.
176.	A24	P78	17.03	7	London, British Museum 1996.1002.1. *ESMS* Tr.103.
177.	A24	P78	16.92		Gorny & Mosch 181 (13 Oct. 2009), lot 1553; Ponterio 148 (9 Jan. 2009), lot 379.

Group 1.11. AP (lower left); ⋈ (between Nike and trophy).

178.	A25	P79	16.90		*ESMS* Tr.106; Jenkins 1965, no. 27. From Pasargadae II Hoard.
179.	A25	P79	16.95		Spink 12009 (18-29 Mar. 2012), lot 112.
180.	A25	P80	16.63		CNG 172 (5 Sep. 2007), lot 53; Glendining (23 Apr. 1970), lot 201.

Group 1.12. AP; Helios head; ⋈ (from left to right).

181.	A25	P81	15.40		CNG 47 (16 Sep. 1998), lot 531; Superior (11-12 Jun. 1986), lot 1235; Meyers 12 (4 Dec. 1975), lot 231. *ESMS* Tr.108.
182.	A25	P81	17.18	10	Gemini XI (12 Jan. 2014), lot 197; CNG MBS 51 (15 Sep. 1999), lot 498; Giessener 50 (24 Sep. 1990), lot 406. *ESMS* Tr.109.
183.	A25	P82	16.66	12	Künker 236 (7 Oct. 2013), lot 112; Triton XI (8 Jan. 2008), lot 288.
184.	A25	P83	17.11		Kirk Davis (2014), lot 6355.
185.	A25	P83	15.92	7	Gitta Kastner 6 (26-27 Nov. 1974), lot 173. *ESMS* Tr.110.
186.	A25	P83	17.15	2	CNG 72 (14 Jun. 2006), lot 921.
187.	A25	P83	16.94		Hirsch 269 (23 Sep. 2010), lot 2598.
188.	A25	P83	17.11	7	CNG 321 (26 Feb. 2014), lot 179.

189.	A25	P84	15.76	5	London, British Museum, 1956.0710.8; Glendining (19 Jul. 1950), lot 154; Laughlin Sale (Dec. 1933), lot 245; Naville X (15-18 Jun. 1925), lot 797. *ESMS* Tr.107; *ESM* 301.
190.	A26	P85	17.10		Goldberg 91 (7 Jun. 2016), lot 1754; Cederlind 180 (14 Sep. 2015), lot 55.
191.	A26	P85	17.08		Gemini III (9 Jan. 2007), lot 229.

Drachms

Group 2.1. Ⱥ (lower left); Ṗ (between Nike and trophy).

| 192. | A1 | P1 | 3.34 | | Sotheby's (30 Apr. 1958), lot 117; Hirsch XXV, Philipsen coll. (Nov. 1909), lot 2857. *ESM* 427α. |

Group 2.2. Φ (lower left); Ṗ (between Nike and trophy).

193.	A2	P2	4.58	8	Triton XVIII (6 Jan. 2015), lot 130; Triton IX (10 Jan. 2006), lot 1009; Sotheby's, Hunt coll. (19-20 Jun. 1991), lot 6147; Numismatic Fine Arts X (17-18 Sep. 1981), lot 218; Sotheby's (21 Jan. 1981), lot 75. Nelson 2011, no. 175.
194.	A2	P2	2.78	6	Paris, Cabinet des médailles, fond général 43. *ESM* 425α.
195.	A2	P2	3.25	4	Berlin, Münzkabinett, Löbbecke 1906. *ESM* 425β.
196.	A3	P3	4.12	3	Triton II (1-2 Dec. 1998), lot 466; Sotheby's, Zurich (27-28 Oct. 1993), lot 823; Peus 328, (2-4 May 1990), lot 248.
197.	A3	P3	4.23	5	Leu 33 (3 May 1983), 411. *SNG Israel* I, 151.

Group 2.3. Ⱥ (lower left); ΔI (between Nike and trophy).

| 198. | A4 | P4 | 3.63 | 8 | Brisbane, LWT coll. Ancient Resource Vcoins (2011). |

Group 2.4. Ɛ (lower left); ΔI (between Nike and trophy).

| 199. | A4 | P5 | 4.13 | 4 | Elsen 46 (21 Sep. 1996), lot 324; Lanz 72 (29 May 1995), lot 293. |
| 200. | A4 | P5 | 4.13 | 4 | London, British Museum, IOC.387. |

201.	A5	P6	3.16		Gorny & Mosch 156 (5 Mar. 2007), lot 1518; Gorny & Mosch 152 (10 Oct. 2006), lot 1453.
202.	A6	P7	4.05		Naville X (15-18 Jun. 1925), lot 798; Sotheby's, Late collector (1900), lot 419. *ESM* 414.
203.	A7	P8	4.16		Copenhagen. Spaer 1975: 38, no. 22. From Qazvin Hoard.
204.	A7	P8	3.85		Schulman (14-15 Nov. 1994), lot 2046.
205.	A8	P9	4.14	7	ANS 1944.100.74103. *WSM* 25.
206.	A8	P9	3.92		Peus 320 (3-4 Nov. 1987), lot 1182.
207.	A9	P10	4.07	3	CNG 348 (8 Apr. 2015), lot 315.

Group 2.5. H (lower left); AX (between Nike and trophy).

208.	A10	P11	4.22	6	Sotheby's (27-28 Oct. 1993), lot 822.
209.	A10	P11	4.10	12	Peus 340 (2 Nov. 1994), lot 476.
210.	A10	P11	3.91	1	Numismatic Fine Arts (18 Dec. 1987), lot 409. Houghton 1983, no. 1024.
211.	A10	P11	4.05		Jenkins 1965, no. 9. From Pasargadae Hoard I.
212.	A10	P11	4.12		Münzen & Medaillen FPL 276 (May 1967), lot 4.
213.	A10	P11	3.98		Pozzi coll. (1921), lot 2922. *ESM* 418ε.
214.	A11	#	3.89	1	Paris, Cabinet des médailles, R2318.
215.	A12	P12	4.12	2	Baldwin's, NY Sale 32 (8 Jan. 2014), lot 178; Credit Swiss FPL (Spring 1993), lot 89.
216.	A12	P12	4.18	10	Triton XVIII (6 Jan. 2015), lot 131. Nelson 2011, no. 176.
217.	A13	P13	4.02		Numismatic Fine Arts (14 Dec. 1989), lot 628.
218.	A14	P13	4.02	10	Brisbane, LWT coll. Roma (2011); CNG 47 (16 Sep. 1998), lot 533; Giessener 33 (3 Jun. 1986), lot 217; Naville X (15-18 Jun. 1925), lot 799. *ESM* 418γ.
219.	A14	P14	4.15	3	Leu 2 (25 Apr. 1972), lot 273.
220.	A14	P14	3.77		Pegasi XIX (18 Nov. 2008), lot 164.
221.	A14	P15	3.85	11	London, British Museum, 2002.0101.1359.
222.	A14	P15	3.85		Jameson coll. I, 1656; *ESM* 418δ.

223.	A14	P15	4.18	7	Gorny & Mosch 207 (15 Oct. 2012), lot 401; CNG 88 (14 Sep. 2011), lot 452.
224.	A14	P15	4.20		Numismatic Fine Arts XVIII (31 Mar. 1987), lot 277. *ESMS*, "Frataraka" C.
225.	A14	P15	4.16	9	Ex New York, Metropolitan Museum of Art, Ward coll., 770. Sotheby's, Zurich (4-5 Apr. 1973), lot 656. *ESM* 418f.
226.	A14	P16	4.24		Spink 14006 (22 Sep. 2014), lot 656; Spink 14005 (25 Jun. 2014), lot 90; Spink 13012 (26 Mar. 2013), lot 10.
227.	A14	P17	4.24		Peus 378 (28 Apr. 2004), lot 297; Spink 3014 (8 Oct. 2003), lot 83.
228.	A14	P17	3.96		Helios 2 (25 Nov. 2008), lot 183; Peus 398 (28 Apr. 2005), lot 304.
229.	A14	P17	4.16		Pegasi XXI (24 Nov. 2009), lot 155; Spink 9008 (19 Mar. 2009), lot 284. *ESMS*, "Frataraka" B.
230.	A14	P17	4.02	2	CNG 96 (14 May 2014), lot 533.
231.	A14	P17	4.17	4	Heritage 3032 (10 Apr. 2014), lot 23285; CNG 93 (22 May 2013), lot 492.
232.	A14	P17	4.05		Jenkins 1965, no. 10. From Pasargadae I Hoard.
233.	A14	P17	4.14	10	Berlin, Münzkabinett, Imhoof-Blumer 1900.*ESM* 418a.
234.	A14	P17	4.11		Ritter Vcoins 49341 LG (July 2014), lot 119.
235.	A14	P17	4.20	5	Aberdeen, Newnham Davis coll. *SNG Great Britain* I, 353; *ESM* 418ζ.
236.	A15	P18	3.96	7	London, British Museum, 2002.0101.1358.
237.	A16	P19	4.13		CNG XXVII (29 Sep. 1993), lot 710; Hirsch 158 (4-6 May 1988), lot 135.
238	*	*	4.00	6	CNG 313 (23 Oct. 2013), lot 82.
239.	A17	P20	3.13	9	Helios 1 (17 Apr. 2008), lot 167; Leu 77 (11 May 2000), lot 364; Leu 53 (21-22 Oct. 1991), lot 121. *ESMS*, "Frataraka" A.

Group 2.6. M (lower left); Boeotian shield (between Nike and trophy).

240.	A17	P21	3.36	6	Triton XIV (4 Jan. 2011), lot 356; Ponterio 146 (25 Apr. 2008), lot 1286.
241.	A18	P22	4.21		Gemini I (11 Jan. 2005), lot 193.
242.	A18*	P22	3.98	5	Roma 8 (31 May 2014), lot 344.
243.	A18	P22	3.98	12	Berlin, Münzkabinett, Graf Prokesch-Osten 1875. *ESM* 300β .
244.	A19	P23	4.66	9	London, British Museum, 2002.0101.1352; Sotheby's (29 Sep. 1988), lot 385.
245.	#	#	4.00		St Petersburg. *ESM* 300α; *JIAN* XIII (1911): 133, no. 39.

Group 2.7. M (lower left); AX (between Nike and trophy).

246.	A20	P24	2.45	Peus 334 (4 Nov. 1992), lot 491; Superior (17-23 Jun. 1974), lot 297.
247.	A21	P25	4.04	Peus 314 (30 Oct.-1 Nov. 1985), lot 135.
248.	A22	P26	4.16	CNG 103 (14 Sep. 2016), lot 355; Heritage, Orlando (11 Jan. 2003), lot 14277; Classical Numismatic Review XIX/4 (1994), lot 90.

Group 2.8. AP (lower left); Ⱶ (between Nike and trophy).

249	A23	P27	3.07	8	Paris, Cabinet des médailles, Babelon 45. *ESM* 302α.
250.	A24	P28	3.13	3	Berlin, Münzkabinett, C.R. Fox 1873. *ESM* 302β.
251.	A25	P29	4.21		Gorny & Mosch 147 (7 Mar. 2006), lot 1515.

Group 2.9. AP; Helios head; Ⱶ (from left to right).

252.	A25	P30	3.76	CNG 355 (15 Jul. 2015), lot 172; CNG 99 (13 May 2015), lot 322; CNG IX (7 Dec. 1989), lot 109.

Unknown control marks/symbol.

253.	#	#	4.10	Jenkins 1965, no. 14. From Pasargadae I Hoard.

Hemidrachms

Group 3.1. ⋔ (lower left); ℙ (between Nike and trophy).

| 254. | A1 | P1 | 1.25 | 10 | ANS 1977.158.637. |

Group 3.2. Ɛ (lower left); ΔΙ (between Nike and trophy).

255.	A2	P2	2.10		Glendining, Lock coll. (21-23 Feb. 1961), lot 2556; Pozzi coll. (1921), lot 2923. *ESM* 415β.
256.	A2	P2	2.10	6	Berlin, Münzkabinett, C. R. Fox 1873. *ESM* 415α.
257.	A3	P3	1.84		Cahn 66 (9 May 1930), lot 363; Helbig (8 Nov. 1928), lot 4057; Naville X (15-18 Jun. 1925), lot 801; Egger XLI (1912), lot 634; *ESM* 415γ.

Group 3.3. Η (lower left); ΑΧ (between Nike and trophy).

258.	A4	P4	1.98	5	Berlin, Münzkabinett, Konsul Strauss 1091/ 1912. *ESM* 419β.
259.	A4	P4	2.00	3	Triton IX (10 Jan. 2006), lot 1010; CNG 42 (29 May 1997), lot 554; Hirsch 192 (27-29 Nov. 1996), lot 293; Spink 114 (9 July 1996), lot 65.
260.	A4	P5	1.90	7	Roma 8 (28 Sep. 2014), lot 706.
261.	A5	P6	1.66		Freeman & Sear MBS 11 (23 Nov. 2004), lot 141.
262.	A6	P7	1.12	9	ANS 1944.100.74106.
263.	A7	P8	1.41	6	ANS 1944.100.74105.
264.	A7	P8	1.25	6	Cambridge, Fitzwilliam Museum. *SNG Fitzwilliam* IV, 5509.

Obols

Group 4.1. [Ꜣ or ⋔?] (lower left); ℙ (between Nike and trophy).

| 265. | A1 | P1 | 0.67 | 11 | Copenhagen, Andersen coll; Pasargad Vcoins (Jan. 2012), lot 25003. |

Group 4.2. Ͱ (lower left); ΔΙ (between Nike and trophy).

266.	A2	P2	0.70		Allotte de la Fuÿe (1925), lot 737; *ESM* 416.

Group 4.3. ⚒ (lower left); ΜΙ (between Nike and trophy).

267.	A3	P3	0.53	6	Copenhagen, Royal National Museum. Naville X (15-18 Jun. 1925), lot 802. *SNG Copenhagen*, part 34, 24; *ESM* 423a.

Group 4.4. Η (lower left); ΑΧ (between Nike and trophy).

268.	A4	P4	0.63		Gorny & Mosch 152 (10 Oct. 2006), lot 1457.
269.	A4	P4	0.69		Gorny & Mosch 147 (7 Mar. 2006), lot 1517; Gorny & Mosch 138 (7-8 Mar. 2005), lot 140.
270.	A4	P4	0.50	1	London, British Museum, G.952.
271.	A5	P5	0.63	11	Triton XII (6 Jan. 2009), lot 359.
272.	A6	P6	0.63	10	Triton XVIII (5 Jan. 2015), lot 132. Nelson 2011, no. 177.

Group 4.5. ⚒? (lower left); Μ (between Nike and trophy).

273.	A7	P7	0.56	11	CNG 354 (1 Jul. 2015), lot 211; Najaf (2012).

Group 4.6. Boeotian shield (between Nike and trophy); ΑΡ (lower right).

274.	A8	P8	0.56		CNG 72 (14 Jun. 2006), lot 922; Hirsch 158 (4-5 May 1988), lot 136.
275.	A9	P9	0.54	9	London, British Museum, 1917.1103.1.
276.	A9	P9	0.67		Gorny & Mosch 142 (10 Oct. 2005), lot 1620.

Imitations

Tetradrachms

Group 5.

A1	⍙; MI (vertical inscription)	Same as A18 from Groups 1.6-1.8	P1	16.66	2	Washington, Arthur Houghton coll. Hoover 2007, no. 81; *SC* 196.
B1	AP (reversed); AX; ⍙	A1	P1	14.73		Goldberg 36 (29-30 May 2006), lot 3525; Gorny & Mosch 141 (10 Oct. 2005), lot 161; Gemini I (11 Jan. 2005), lot 192.
B2	⍙; ⍰	A1	P2	16.99		Feuardent, Jameson coll. III (1924), 2342. *ESMS* Tr.11; *ESM*, 156, n. 4.
B3	⍙; ⍰	A1	P3	14.04		Berk 107 (18 Mar. 1999), lot 203.
C1	⍙; ⍰	A1	P1			Münchner Münzhandlung 158 (8-9 Nov. 1973), lot 483; Oswald (16-17 Nov. 1972), lot 51. *ESMS* Tr.8.
C2	⍙; ⍰	A2	P1	16.57		Freeman & Freeman, Manhattan I (5 Jan. 2010), lot 86.
C3	⍙; ⍰	A2	P1	16.80		Goldberg 59 (30 May 2010), lot 2166.
D1	H; MI?	A1	P1	16.55	9	Munich. *ESMS* Tr.45; *ESM* 421 A9/P10
E1	H; AX	A1	P1	14.41		Münzen & Medaillen VIII (8-10 Dec. 1949), lot 859.
F1	⍙; ⍰	A1	P1	16.35		Drouot Montaigne (13 Apr. 1991), lot 19.
F2	⍙; ⍰	A1	P1	16.02	2	CNG 69 (8 Jun. 2005), lot 515.
G1	M; AX	A1	P1	14.71	6	Brussels, Bibliothèque royale de Belgique, Hirsch coll. 1640; Bompois (20 Jan. 1882), lot 706. *WSM* 26.

G2	♠; 𐍂	A1	P2	14.36		Peus 368 (25-28 Apr. 2001), lot 271; Peus 366 (25 Oct. 2000), lot 219.
H1	[ ]; AX	A1	P1	14.15	1	Heritage 3020 (6-11 Sep. 2012), lot 25011.
I1	H; ר५	A1	P1	14.60	7	Paris, Cabinet des médailles, 1968.215.
J1	H; ר५	A1	P1	16.58	2	Numismatica Ars Classica 74 (18 Nov. 2013), lot 294; Peus 376 (29 Oct. 2003), lot 507; Washington, Arthur Houghton coll., 455; Superior (11-12 Dec. 1992), lot 2150.
K1	M; AX	A1	P1	12.79	6	Triton VIII (11 Jan. 2005), lot 526; Gorny & Mosch 112 (17 Oct. 2001), lot 4163.
K2	M; AX	A1	P1	13.85		Baldwin's 68 (28 Sep. 2010), lot 3434.
K3	M; AX	A1	P2			Commerce, Münzen & Medaillen (1971). *ESMS* Tr.104.
L1	M; 𐍂	A1	P1	16.45	3	Numismatic Fine Arts MBS (Spring 1994), lot 270; Kovacs XI (19 Jun. 1993), lot 84. *ESMS* Tr.43. From "Frataraka" Hoard.
M1	♠; 𐍂	A1	P1	15.71	7	ANS 1944.100.74109; Hirsch XXV, Philipsen coll. (Nov. 1909), lot 2856; Egger Sale I (Jan. 1908), lot 565. *ESM* 424, n. 3.
N1	禾; 𐍂	A1	P1	17.52	7	Paris, Cabinet des médailles, 1973.1.196. *ESMS* Tr.9.
O1	H; AX	A1	P1	14.31	2	ANS 1977.158.636; Leu 3 (27 Mar. 1959), lot 321. Jameson coll. I, 1653; *ESM*, 154, n. 2.
O2	H; AX	A1	P1	16.27	12	Paris, Cabinet des médailles, Valton 478. *ESM*, 154, n. 2.

P1	[ ]; Ⱥ	A1	P1	14.53	7	Colin E. Pitchfork coll.; Spink 3014 (8 Oct. 2003), lot 82. Wright 2011, no. 54; *SC* 2, P29.
Q1	[ ]; ⋈I	A1	P1	16.72	6	Copenhagen, Danish National Museum. *ESMS* Tr.44; *SNG Copenhagen*, part 34, 23; *WSM* 421A
R1	H; AX	A1	P1	17.05	12	Triton IX (10 Jan. 2006), lot 1011; Waddell FPL 28 (16 Mar. 1988), lot 136.
S1	H; Boeotian shield; ⋔	A1	P1	13.20	11	Glendining, Knoepke coll. (10 Dec. 1986), lot 325; Glendining, Lock coll. (21-23 Feb. 1961), lot 2555; Naville VII (23-24 Jun., 1924), lot 1667.
T1	EBH (in the name of Antiochos)	A1	P1			Private coll.

Drachms

Group 6.

A1	ꓶy	A1	P1	3.33	1	Colin E. Pitchfork coll. Wright 2011, no. 55.
B1	E; ΔI	A1	P1	3.52	8	Brussels, Bibliothèque royale de Belgique, Hirsch 1641; Hoffman (16 May 1879). *WSM* 25.
C1	H; AX	A1	P1	2.66		Pars Coins (2012), lot PCW-G3354; Ebay, Victoram (2012).
C2	H; AX	A1	P1	3.20	9	Oxford, Ashmolean Museum. Oman (1947).
D1	NI (reversed inscription)	A1	P1	4.10	11	CNG 91 (19 Sep. 2012), lot 352; CNG 41 (19 Mar. 1997), lot 650.

E1	ʯ	A1	P1	4.20	12	Washington, Arthur Hough-ton coll. *SC* 197; Hoover 2007, no. 82.
F1	[ ]	A1	P1	3.00	8	Oxford, Keble College.
G1	[ ]; Λ+; ΚΛΕ	A1	·P1	2.74	10	London, British Museum, 1938.0725.1.
H1	H; AX	A1	P1	2.96	6	London, British Museum, *BMC* 39. *ESM* 418β.
I1	⅏ (in the name of Antiochos)	A1	P1	3.97	12	Washington, Arthur Hough-ton coll., 461. *SC* 198; Hough-ton 1983, no. 1037; Houghton 1980, 11, pl. I, 10.
J1	A (in the name of Antiochos)	A1	P1	4.20	11	Künker 115 (25 Sep. 2006), lot 224; CNG IX (10 Jan. 2006), lot 1014.
K1	(in the name of Antiochos)	A1	P1	3.79	11	ANS 1984.117.8. Houghton 1983, no. 1103; Houghton 1980: 12, no. 1, pl. 2, 1.
K2	(in the name of Antiochos)	A2	P1	3.75		Numismatic Fine Arts MBS (14 Dec. 1989), lot 634.
L1	A (in the name of Antiochos)	A1	P1	4.15		Peus 313 (13-15 May 1985), lot 192.
M1	AΛ	A1	P1	3.94	11	ANS 1984.117.11. Houghton 1983, no. 1106; Houghton 1980: 12, no. 8, pl. 2, 5.
N1	IΛ	A1	P1	4.09	1	ANS 1984.117.12. Houghton 1983, no. 1107; Houghton 1980: 12, no. 9, pl. 2, 6.
O1	CI (barbarous inscription)	A1	P1	4.11	12	ANS 1984.117.10. Houghton 1983, no. 1105; Houghton 1980: 12, no. 7, pl. 2, 4.
O2	[ ] (barbarous inscription)	A2	P1	4.06	12	ANS 1984.117.13. Houghton 1983, no. 1108; Houghton 1980: 12, no. 10, pl. 2, 7.

P1	(in the name of Antiochos)	A1	P1	3.80	12	ANS 1984.117.9. Houghton 1983, no. 1104; Houghton 1980, 12, no. 3, pl. 2, 3.
P2	(barbarous inscription)	A1	P2	3.66		Baldwin's (19 Nov. 2011), lot 15.
Q1	(barbarous inscription)	A1	P1	3.72	9	Jerusalem, Arnold Spaer coll. *SNG Israel* I, 313; Houghton 1980, 12, no. 2, pl. 2, 2.
R1	(barbarous inscription)	A1	P1	4.27		Spink 3014 (8 Oct. 2003), lot 158; Spink 60 (Oct. 1987), lot 140.
S1	(barbarous inscription)	A1	P1	2.89	12	Nomos 7 (14 May 2013), lot 144; Leu 83 (6 May 2002), lot 377.
T1		A1	P1	4.25	6	CNG 343 (28 Jan. 2015), lot 302.
#		#	#	4.60	11	Houghton 1980, 12, no. 4.
#		#	#	4.22	3	Houghton 1980, 12, no. 5.
#		#	#	2.92	12	Houghton 1980, 12, no. 6.

Hemidrachms

Group 7.

A1	H; AX	A1	P1	1.64	10	London, British Museum, 1969.1206.1. *BMC* 40.
A2	H; AX	A1	P1	1.30	3	Washington, Arthur Houghton coll. Hoover 2007, 860.
B1	[ ] (in the name of Antiochos)	A1	P1	1.83		CNG MBS 51 (15 Sep. 1999), lot 499.
B2	[ ] (in the name of Antiochos)	A2	P1	2.00		CNG 37 (20 Mar 1996), lot 622.
B3	[ ] (in the name of Antiochos)	A2	P2	2.00		Peus 345 (1-3 Sep. 1995), lot 142.

C1	[ ]; AX	A1	P1	1.58		Naville X (15-18 Jun. 1925), lot 800.
D1	EB?	A1	P1	1.90	9	ANS 1984.117.14. Houghton 1983, no. 1109; Houghton 1980, 12, no. 11, pl. 2, 8.
E1	(in the name of Antiochos)	A1	P1	1.91	1	ANS 1984.117.15. Houghton 1983, no. 1110; Houghton 1980, 12, no. 15, pl. 2, 9.
F1	P or V	A1	P1	2.06	3	ANS 1984.117.16. Houghton 1983, no. 1111; Houghton 1980, 12, no. 16, pl. 2, 10.
#		#	#	2.16	9	Houghton 1980, 12, no. 12.
#	Λ	#	#	2.09	12	Houghton 1980, 12, no. 13.
#		#	#	2.08	12	Houghton 1980, 12, no. 14.

Obols

Group 8.

A1	٦५	A1	P1	0.53	3	Berlin, Münzkabinett, 593/1909. Hirsch XXV, Philipsen coll. (Nov. 1909), 2858. *ESM* 416, note 1.
B1	CA?	A1	P1	0.60		CNG 37 (20 Mar 1996), lot 623.
C1		A1	P1	0.59	9	ANS 1984.117.22. Houghton 1983, no. 1117; Houghton 1980, 12, no. 24, pl. 2, 16.
C2		A1	P2	0.57		CNG XXVII (29 Sep. 1993), lot 711; Münz Zentrum 68 (25 Apr. 1990), lot 378.
D1	CA?	A1	P1	0.56	10	Jerusalem, Arnold Spaer coll. *SNG Israel* I, 314; Spink (Dec. 1987), lot 6967.
E1		A1	P1	0.60		Naville X (15-18 Jun. 1925), lot 803.
F1		A1	P1	0.46	2	Malter 4 (29 Oct. 1978), lot 263.

G1		A1	P1	0.54	Künker 193 (26 Sep. 2011), lot 281; CNG 47 (16 Sep. 1998), lot 533.
H1		A1	P1	0.64	Hirsch 260 (12 Feb. 2009), lot 1812; Hirsch 256 (5 May 2008), lot 345.
I1		A1	P1	0.65	2	ANS 1984.117.17. Houghton 1983, no. 1112; Houghton 1980, 12, no. 17, pl. 2, 11.
J1		A1	P1	0.43	11	ANS 1984.117.18. Houghton 1983, no. 1113; Houghton 1980, 12, no. 20, pl. 2, 12.
K1		A1	P1	0.61	6	ANS 1984.117.19. Houghton 1983, no. 1114; Houghton 1980, 12, no. 21, pl. 2, 13.
L1		A1	P1	0.66	7	ANS 1984.117.20. Houghton 1983, no. 1115; Houghton 1980, 12, no. 22, pl. 2, 14.
M1		A1	P1	0.61	7	ANS 1984.117.21. Houghton 1983, no. 1116; Houghton 1980, 12, no. 23, pl. 2, 15.
N1		A1	P1	0.60	10	ANS 1984.117.23. Houghton 1983, no. 1118; Houghton 1980, 12, no. 25, pl. 2, 17.
O1		A1	P1	0.35		CNG MBS 47 (16 Sep. 1998), lot 534.
P1	CA	A1	P1	0.79	2	ANS 1984.117.24. Houghton 1983, no. 1119.
Q1		A1	P1	0.41	12	CNG 357 (12 Aug. 2015), lot 148.
#	Λ	A1	P1	0.73	11	Houghton 1980, 12, no. 18.
#	(in the name of Antiochos)	#	#	0.72	12	Houghton 1980, 12, no. 19.

Anomalous Tetradrachms

Group 9.

A1	⋈; AX	Same as A5 from Group 1.4	P1	16.41	11	Triton VIII (11 Jan. 2005), lot 525.
A2	⋈; AX	Variant of A22 from Group 1.10	P1	16.74	12	Burtonsville, Brian Kritt coll. *ESMS* Tr.91.
A3	⋈; AX	Variant of A22 from Group 1.10	P1	17.01		Goldberg 84 (27 Jan. 2015), lot 3061.
A4	H; AX	Variant of A22 from Group 1.10	P1*	16.54	1	Baldwin's, NY Sale 27 (4 Jan. 2012), lot 608.
B1	⋈; Æ	A1	P1	17.00		Pars Coins (2012); Rauch 89 (5 Dec. 2011), lot 1222.
C1	H; AX	A1	P1	16.79		Elsen 24 (Mar. 14, 1992), lot 150.

Concordance

Control marks and symbols (from l. to r.)	Marest-Caffey	SC	ESMS
Tetradrachms			
BE; Boeotian shield; ⟨sym⟩	1.1	173.1	I
⟨sym⟩; AI; BE	1.2	173.2	J
⟨sym⟩; Boeotian shield; AX	1.3	173.3	JA
⟨sym⟩; ⟨sym⟩	1.4	173.4	ESM 426
⟨sym⟩; ⟨sym⟩	1.5	173.5	ESM 424
⟨sym⟩; ΔI	1.6	173.11	ESM 413
⟨sym⟩; ΔI	1.7	173.10	N
⟨sym⟩; MI	1.8	173.9	ESM 422
H; AX	1.9	173.12	ESM 417
M; AX	1.10	173.14	ESM 420
AP; ⟨sym⟩	1.11	173.15	Q
AP; Helios head; ⟨sym⟩	1.12	173.16	ESM 301
Drachms			
⟨sym⟩; ⟨sym⟩	2.1	174.1	ESM 427
⟨sym⟩; ⟨sym⟩	2.2	174.2	ESM 425
⟨sym⟩; ΔI	2.3		
⟨sym⟩; ΔI	2.4	174.4	ESM 414
H; AX	2.5	174.5	ESM 418
M; Boeotian shield	2.6	174.7	ESM 300
M; AX	2.7	174.6	P
AP; ⟨sym⟩	2.8	174.8	ESM 302
AP; Helios head; ⟨sym⟩	2.9	174.9	R
Hemidrachms			
⟨sym⟩; ⟨sym⟩	3.1	175.1	K
⟨sym⟩; ΔI	3.2	175.2	ESM 415
H; AX	3.3	175.3	ESM 419

Obols			
[Ā or 𐤀 ?]; 𐊕	4.1		
Ɛ; ΔI	4.2	176.2	*ESM* 416
𐤀 ; MI	4.3	176.1	*ESM* 423
H; AX	4.4	Ad87	
𐤀 ?; M	4.5		
Boeotian shield (middle); AP	4.6	Ad86	
Imitative tetradrachms			
𐊅; MI	5.A	196	
H; MI?	5.D	173.8	*ESM* 421
H; ꛍɥ	5.I–J	195	
M; 𐊕	5.L	173.6	L
𐤍I	5.Q	173.7	*WSM* 421A
H; AX	5.R	Ad92	
Imitative drachms			
NI	6.D	174.3	M
Ұ	6.E	197	
Λ+; KLE	6.G	199.2	
𐊦	6.I	198	
Various	6.J–#	226	
Imitative hemidrachms			
Various	7.D–#	227	
Imitative obols			
Various	8.I–#	228	
Anomalous tetradrachms			
Ͷ, M, or H; AX	9.A, ad16–17	173.13	O

Addendum

New specimens of the victory coinage have come to my attention since the submission of this study. Although all denominations are concerned, this addendum will only discuss seventeen new tetradrachms since they are most relevant to the arguments presented above.

First, none of the new tetradrachms present a new obverse die. These additions support the revised estimate of the original number of dies with an even higher coverage.

Second, two tetradrachms Ad16-17 are related to the anomalous Group 9A, now raising the number of specimens to six. They present the same variant of obverse A22 from Group 1.10 with its elegant carving and the same reverse die P1 unique to Group 9A with its singularities. However, Ad17 introduces a change in control marks. The same die struck the reverses of Group 9A and Ad16-17, as evidenced in the gouge between the Σ and Ε of ΣΕΛΕΥΚΟΥ. But on Ad17 the monogram Ⱨ has now lost its horizontal bar to become Ⲙ, just as it had been recut into Ⲏ on 9A4. The scenario of a reverse die, whose continued use spanned three control mark combinations with remarkably little signs of wear or refurbishing (apart from the recutting of the monogram), is otherwise unparalleled in the victory coinage. Obverse dies alone (such as A3 and A18) were used for any such length of time.

Tetradrachms

Group 1.1.

Ad1.	A3	P6	17.01		Lanz 162 (6 Jun. 2016), lot 171.

Group 1.4.

Ad2.	A5	P13	17.09	11	Nomos, Obolos 5 (26 Jun. 2016), lot 465; Heritage 3046 (14 Apr. 2016), lot 29132.
Ad3.	A6	P17	16.84		Gorny & Mosch 236 (7 Mar. 2016), lot 572.
Ad4.	A6	P17	16.81		Gorny & Mosch 224 (13 Oct. 2014), lot 276.
Ad5.	A7	new	16.44	5	Heritage 3046 (14 Apr. 2016), lot 29131.
Ad6.	A10	P24	16.70		Gorny & Mosch 219 (10 Mar. 2014), lot 264.
Ad7.	A11	new	16.76		Gorny & Mosch 215 (14–15 OCt. 2013), lot 904.

Group 1.6.

| Ad8. | A18 | new | 16.91 | | Lanz 161 (7 Dec. 2015), lot 153. |

Group 1.9.

Ad9.	A19	P57	17.03		Lanz 159 (8 Dec. 2014), lot 265.
Ad10.	A21	new	17.03	3	Heritage 3046 (14 Apr. 2016), lot 29134.
Ad11.	A22	new	17.04		Lanz, Ebay (Oct. 2015), 231714508853.

Group 1.10.

| Ad12. | A22 | P72 | 16.84 | | Pegasi 29 (6 Nov. 2013), lot 186. |
| Ad13. | A23 | P73 | 15.8 | | B.J.'s, Numismall (Aug. 2012), G0016. |

Group 1.12.

| Ad14. | A25 | P82 | 17.14 | 9 | Heritage 3046 (14 Apr. 2016), lot 29133. |
| Ad15. | A25 | new | 17.10 | | Lanz, Ebay (27 Aug. 2015), 301715864990. |

Anomalous Tetradrachms

Group 9.

| Ad16. | M̧; AX | Variant of A22 from group 1.10 | P1 | 16.80 | Lanz 159 (8 Dec. 2014), lot 264. |
| Ad17. | M; AX | Variant of A22 from group 1.10 | P1* | 17.04 | Hirsch 300 (24 Sep. 2014), lot 110. |

ACKNOWLEDGMENTS

I would like to thank all the participants of the 2012 Eric P. Newman Graduate Seminar in Numismatics and Stephanie Pearson for their comments at the early stage of this project and continued support. I especially want to acknowledge the late Rick Witschonke, who first taught us about die studies. I have benefitted from discussions and electronic exchanges with Carmen Arnold-Biucchi, Oliver Hoover, Catharine Lorber, Panagiotis Iossif, Paul Kosmin, Brian Kritt, and Andrew Meadows. Lloyd Taylor and Scott VanHorn were kind enough to share with me early drafts or discoveries about "Uncertain Mint 6A" and Persid overstrikes—respectively. I am indebted to the curators who granted me access to collections and answered my questions—particularly Frédérique Duyrat at the Cabinet des médailles in Paris, Johan van Heesch at the Bibliothèque royale de Belgique in Brussels, and Bernhard Weisser at the Münzkabinett in Berlin—and the numismatists—Morten Andersen, Frank Kovacs, Mary Lannin, and Adrian Popescu—who sent me images and/or references. Peter van Alfen, François de

Callataÿ, Arthur Houghton, and Andrew Stewart read early drafts of this paper and made insightful comments. I have however not always followed their suggestions, and any error remains entirely my own.

References

Alram, M. 1986. *Nomina propria Iranica in nummis: Materialgrundlagen zu den iranischen Personennamen auf antiken Münzen.* Iranisches Personennamenbuch 4. Wien: Österreichische Akademie der Wissensehaften.

Aperghis, G. G. 2004. *The Seleukid royal economy: The finances and financial administration of the Seleukid empire.* Cambridge/New York: Cambridge University Press.

Appelgren, T. G. 1931. *Doktor Otto Smiths Münzensammlung in Kgl. Münzkabinett Stockholm.* Stockholm: Akademien.

Askari Chaverdi, A., and P. Callieri. 2010. "Preliminary report on the Irano-Italian stratigraphic study of the Toll-E Takht, Pasargad: Investigations on the material culture of the Achaemenid and post-Achaemenid periods in Fars." In *Ancient and Middle Iranian Studies: Proceedings of the 6th European Conference of Iranian Studies, Held in Vienna, 18-22 September 2007,* edited by M. Macuch, D. Weber, and D. Durkin-Meisterernst, 11–28. Wiesbaden: Harrassowitz.

————. 2013. "Media, Khuzestan and Fars between the end of the Achaemenids and the rise of the Sasanians." In *The Oxford Handbook of Ancient Iran,* edited by D. Potts, 690–717. Oxford/New York: Oxford University Press.

Babelon, E. 1890. *Catalogue des monnaies grecques de la Bibliothèque nationale: Les rois de Syrie, d'Arménie et de Commagène.* Paris: C. Rollin & Feuardent.

Bingen, J. 2007. *Hellenistic Egypt: Monarchy, society, economy, culture.* University of California Press.

Briant, P. 2006. "L'Asie mineure en transition." In *La transition entre l'empire achéménide et les royaumes hellénistiques (vers 350-300 av. J.-C.),* edited by P. Briant and F. Joannès, 309–351. Paris: de Boccard.

Callataÿ, F. de. Forthcoming. Vaillant, Frölich and the others (Spanheim, Beger, Haym, Liebe, Pellerin, Eckhel, Duane, Etc.): "The remarkable interest in Seleucid coinages in the 18th century." *Numismatische Zeitschrift.*

————. 2011. "Quantifying monetary production in Greco-Roman times: A general frame." In *Quantifying monetary supplies in Greco-Roman times,* edited by F. de Callataÿ, 7–29. Pragmateiai 19. Bari: Edipuglia.

————. 2012. "Control marks on Hellenistic royal coinages: Use, and evolution toward simplification?" *Revue Belge de Numismatique* 158: 39–62.

Callieri, P. 2007. *L'Archéologie du Fārs à l'époque hellénistique: Quatre leçons au Collège de France, 8, 15, 22 et 29 mars 2007.* Persika 11. Paris: Boccard.

Capdetrey, L. 2007. *Le pouvoir séleucide: Territoire, administration, finances d'un royaume hellénistique, 312-129 avant J.-C.* Rennes: Presses universitaires.

Chaniotis, A. 2007. "La divinité mortelle d'Antiochos III à Téos." *Kernos* 20: 153–171.

Cohen, G. 2013. *The Hellenistic settlements in the East from Armenia and Mesopotamia to Bactria and India*. Hellenistic Culture and Society 54. Berkeley: University of California Press.

Curtis, V. S. 2010. "The Frataraka coins of Persis: Bridging the gap between Achaemenid and Sasanian Persia." In *The world of Achaemenid Persia: History, art and society in Iran and the Ancient Near East*, edited by J. Curtis and S. J. Simpson, 379–394. London; New York: Tauris.

Dahmen, K. 2007. *The Legend of Alexander the Great on Greek and Roman Coins*. London/New York: Routledge.

Debord, P. 2003. "Le culte royal chez les Séleucides." *Pallas* 62: 281–308.

Duyrat, F. 2005. "La circulation monétaire dans l'Orient séleucide (Syrie, Phénicie, Mésopotamie, Iran)." *Topoi Orient Occident Suppl.* 6: 381–424.

Engels, D. 2013. "A new Frataraka chronology." *Latomus* 72 (1): 28–80.

Erickson, K. 2013. "Seleucus I, Zeus and Alexander." In *Every Inch a King: Comparative Studies on Kings and Kingship in the Ancient and Medieval Worlds*, edited by L. Mitchell and C. Melville, 109–127. Rulers and Elites 2. Boston: Brill.

ESMS = Kritt, B. 1997. *The early Seleucid mint of Susa*. Classical Numismatic Studies 2. Lancaster: Classical Numismatic Group.

Fleischer, R. 1991. *Studien zur seleukidischen Kunst*. Vol. I. Mainz am Rhein: Philipp von Zabern.

Gardner, P. 1878. *Catalogue of Greek coins: The Seleucid kings of Syria*. London: British Museum.

Grainger, J. D. 2014. *The rise of the Seleukid Empire (323-223 BC)*. Barnsley, UK: Pen & Sword.

Hadley, R. 1974. "Seleucus, Dionysus, or Alexander?" *Numismatic Chronicle* 14: 9–13.

Heckel, W. 2006. "Mazaeus, Callisthenes and the Alexander Sarcophagus." *Historia* 55.4: 385–396.

Hölscher, T. 2009. *Herrschaft und Lebensalter: Alexander der Grosse: politisches Image und anthropologisches Modell*. Basel: Schwabe.

Hoover, O. 2002. "The identity of the helmeted head on the 'victory' coinage of Susa." *Schweizerische Numismatische Rundschau* 81: 51–60.

———. 2005. "Ceci n'est pas l'autonomie: The coinage of Seleucid Phoenicia as royal and civic power discourse." *Topoi Orient Occident Suppl.* 6: 485–507.

———. 2007. *Coins of the Seleucid Empire from the collection of Arthur Houghton*. Ancient Coins in North American Collections 9. New York: American Numismatic Society.

———. 2008a. "Overstruck Seleucid coins." In *Seleucid Coins: A comprehensive catalogue. Part 2, Seleucus IV through Antiochus XIII*, by A. Houghton, C. Lorber, and O. Hoover, 209–230. New York: American Numismatic Society.

———. 2008b. "Plated Seleucid-type coins." In *Seleucid Coins: A Comprehensive Catalogue. Part 2, Seleucus IV through Antiochus XIII*, by A. Houghton,

C. Lorber, and O. Hoover, 241–263. New York: American Numismatic Society.

———. 2011. "Never mind the bullocks: Taurine imagery as a multicultural expression of royal and divine power under Seleukos I Nikator." In *More than men, less than gods: Studies on royal cult and imperial worship: Proceedings of the international colloquium organized by the Belgian School at Athens (November 1-2, 2007)*, edited by P. Iossif, C. Lorber, and A. Chankowski, 197–228. Studia Hellenistica 51. Leuven; Walpole, Mass.: Peeters.

Houghton, A. 1980. "Notes on the early Seleucid victory coinage of 'Persepolis.'" *Schweizerische Numismatische Rundschau* 59: 5–14.

———. 1983. *Coins of the Seleucid empire from the collection of Arthur Houghton.* Ancient Coins in North American Collections 4. New York: American Numismatic Society.

———. 1986. "A colossal head in Antakya and the portraits of Seleucus I." *Antike Kunst* 29: 52–62.

Houghton, A., and A. Stewart. 1999. "The equestrian portrait of Alexander the Great on a new tetradrachm of Seleucus I." *Schweizerische Numismatische Rundschau* 78: 27–35.

Iossif, P. 2004. "Les monnaies de Suse frappées par Séleucos Ier: Une nouvelle approche." *Numismatica e Antichità Classiche* 33: 249–271.

———. 2012. "Les 'cornes' des Séleucides: Vers une divinisation 'discrète.'" *Cahiers des études anciennes* 49: 43–147.

Jenkins, G. K. 1965. "Coin hoards from Pasargadae." *Iran* 3: 41–52.

Joannès, F. 1994. "Métaux précieux et moyens de paiement en Babylonie achéménide et hellénistique." *Transeuphratène* 8: 137–144.

———. 2005. "Quelques traits de l'économie babylonienne des Achéménides à Séleucos Ier." *Topoi Orient Occident Suppl.* 6: 291–302.

Klose, D., and W. Müseler. 2008. *Statthalter, Rebellen, Könige: die Münzen aus Persepolis von Alexander dem Grossen zu den Sasaniden.* München: Staatliche Münzsammlung.

Kosmin, P. 2014. *The land of the elephant kings: Space, territory, and ideology in the Seleucid empire.* Cambridge, Mass./London: Harvard University Press.

Kritt, B. 2016. *The Seleucid Mint of Aï Khanoum.* Classical Numismatic Studies 9. Lancaster: Classical Numismatic Group.

Le Rider, G. 1965. *Suse sous les Séleucides et les Parthes: des trouvailles monétaires et l'histoire de la ville.* Paris: P. Geuthner.

———. 1999. "Histoire économique et monétaire de l'Orient hellénistique." In *Etudes d'histoires monétaire et financière du monde grec: Ecrits 1958-1998*, edited by E. Papaefthymiou, F. de Callataÿ, and F. Queyrel, 3: 1037–1133. Athènes: Société Hellénique de Numismatique.

———. 2003. *Alexandre le Grand: Monnaie, finances et politique.* Paris: Presses universitaires de France.

Le Rider, G., and F. de Callataÿ. 2006. *Les Séleucides et les Ptolémées: L'héritage monétaire et financier d'Alexandre le Grand.* Monaco: Rocher.

Lindström, G. 2003. *Uruk: Siegelabdrücke auf hellenistischen Tonbullen und Tontafeln.* Mainz am Rhein: P. von Zabern.

Ma, J. 1999. *Antiochus III and the cities of western Asia Minor.* London/New York: Oxford University Press.

Marest-Caffey, L. Forthcoming. "Images of power in Seleukid Persis: A new study of the victory coinage from Susa." In *Proceedings of the XV International Numismatic Congress.*

Miller, R., and K. Walters. 2004. "Seleucid coinage and the legend of the horned Bucephalas." *Schweizerische Numismatische Rundschau* 83: 45–56.

Mørkholm, O. 1982. "The Attic coin standard in the Levant during the Hellenistic period." In *Studia Paulo Naster Oblata,* edited by P. Naster, S. Scheers, and J. Quaegebeur, 139–149. Orientalia Lovaniensia Analecta 12. Leuven: Peeters.

Naveh, J., and S. Shaked. 2012. *Aramaic documents from ancient Bactria from the Khalili Collections.* London: Khalili Family Trust.

Nelson, B. 2011. *Numismatic Art of Persia: The Sunrise Collection. Part I, Ancient—650 BC to AD 650.* Lancaster: Classical Numismatic Group.

Olbrycht, M. J. 2005. Creating an Empire: Iran and Middle Asia in the Policies of Seleukos I. In *Central Asia from the Achaemenid to the Timurids: Archaeology, history, ethnology, culture: Materials of an international conference dedicated to the centenary of Aleksandr Markovich Belenitsky, St Petersburg, November 2-5, 2004,* edited by V. P. Nikonorov, 231–234. St Petersburg: Institute of the History of Material Culture of the Russian Academy of Sciences.

Ramage, A., ed. 1994. *Emblems of authority: Greek and Roman coins from two alumni collections.* Ithaca, NY: Herbert F. Johnson Museum of Art, Cornell University.

Robert, L. 1937. *Études anatoliennes: Recherches sur les inscriptions grecques de l'Asie Mineure.* Études orientales 5. Paris: de Boccard.

Selz, G. 2008. "The divine prototypes. "In *Religion and power: Divine kingship in the ancient world and beyond,* edited by N. Brisch, 13–31. University of Chicago Oriental Institute Seminars 4. Chicago: Oriental Institute of the University of Chicago.

Sherwin-White, S., and A. Kuhrt. 1993. *From Samarkhand to Sardis: A new approach to the Seleucid empire.* Hellenistic Culture and Society 13. Berkeley: University of California Press.

Smith, R. R. R. 1988. *Hellenistic royal portraits.* Oxford: Clarendon Press/Oxford University Press.

Spaer, A. 1975. "A hoard from the Qazvin area." In *Coin Hoards* I, 36–41. London: The Royal Numismatic Society.

Stewart, A. 1993. *Faces of power: Alexander's Image and Hellenistic politics.* Berkeley: University of California Press.

Stronach, D. 1978. *Pasargadae: A report on the excavations conducted by the British*

Institute of Persian Studies from 1961 to 1963. Oxford: Clarendon Press.

Tavernier, J. 2008. Multilingualism in the Fortification and Treasury Archives. In *L'archive des fortifications de Persépolis: Etat des questions et perspectives de recherches*, edited by P. Briant, W. Henkelman, and M. Stolper, 59–86. Paris: De Boccard.

Taylor, L. 2015. "From Triparadeisos to Ipsos: Seleukos I Nikator's Uncertain Mint 6A in Babylonia." *American Journal of Numismatics* 27

Van Nuffelen, P. 2004. "Le culte royal de l'empire des Séleucides: Une réinterprétation." *Historia* 53.3: 278–301.

Veneri, A., and C. Gasparri. 1986. "Dionysos." In *Lexicon Iconographicum Mythologiae Classicae*. Zürich; München: Artemis.

Virgilio, B.. 2003a. "Epigraphica e culti dei re seleucidi." In *Atti dell'Incontro di studio sul tema: Epigrafia e storia delle religioni: dal documento epigrafico al problema storico-religioso: Roma, Escuela española de historia y arqueologia en Roma, 28 maggio 2002*, edited by P. Xella and J.-Á. Zamora, 39–50. Verona: Essedue.

———. 2003b. *Lancia, diadema e porpora : Il re e la regalità ellenistica*. Pisa: Giardini editori e stampatori.

Wiesehöfer, J. 1991. "PRTRK, RB HYL' und MR'." In *Achaemenid history VI: Asia Minor and Egypt: Old cultures in a new empire: Proceedings of the Groningen 1988 Achaemenid History Workshop*, edited by H. Sancisi-Weerdenburg and A. Kuhrt, 305–309. Leiden: Nederlands Instituut voor het Nabije Oosten.

———. 1994. *Die "dunklen Jahrhunderte" der Persis: Untersuchungen zu Geschichte und Kultur von Fārs in frühhellenistischer Zeit (330-140 v. Chr.)*. Zetemata 90. München: Beck.

———. 2007. "Fars under Seleucid and Parthian rule." In *The age of the Parthians*, edited by V. S. Curtis and S. Stewart, 37–49. London/New York: Tauris.

———. 2011. "Frataraka rule in early Seleucid Persis: A new appraisal." In *Creating a Hellenistic World*, edited by A. Erskine and L. Llewellyn-Jones, 107–121. Oakville, CT: Classical Press of Wales.

———. 2013. "Fratarakā and Seleucids." In *The Oxford Handbook of Ancient Iran*, edited by D. Potts, pp. 718–727. Oxford; New York: Oxford University Press.

Winter, I. 2008. "Touched by the gods: Visual evidence for the divine status of rulers in the ancient Near East." In *Religion and power: Divine kingship in the ancient world and beyond*, edited by N. Brisch, 75–101. University of Chicago Oriental Institute Seminars 4. Chicago: Oriental Institute of the University of Chicago.

Wright, N., ed. 2011. *Coins from Asia Minor and the East: Selections from the Colin E. Pitchfork Collection*. Ancient Coins in Australian Collections 2. Sydney: Australian Centre for Ancient Numismatic Studies.

AJN Second Series 28 (2016) pp. 65–104
© 2016 The American Numismatic Society

The Reactions of Mint Workers to the Tumultuous Second Reign of Demetrius II Nicator

Plates 22–35   David Schwei[*]

The coins struck for Demetrius II Nicator provide an insight into how mint officials reacted to Alexander II Zabinas's challenge to the throne. While literature reveals the royal response, a die study of the coins from Antioch and Damascus demonstrates that production at these mints was little affected by the war. Mint administrators relied on loyal workers, such as the two engravers whose movements can be traced. Although the production of coinage seems to have continued at a normal pace, the weight standard at Damascus dropped slightly.

Brother fights brother. The phrase conjures up horrible images of civil war in our minds, but this was the goal of the Parthian king Phraates II (132–126 BC). He allowed Demetrius II Nicator (145–138 and 129–125 BC) to return to his kingdom and challenge his brother Antiochus VII Sidetes (138–129 BC) for the throne of the Seleucid empire. Even though Antiochus VII died before he could face Demetrius II in battle, Demetrius soon confronted a challenge to his throne from the pretender Alexander II Zabinas and his supporter Ptolemy VII Euergetes II. Modern scholars often view this tumultuous second reign of Demetrius II and the last half of the second century as part of a general decline of the once great Seleucid empire.[1] Numismatic evidence from the silver coins minted during Demetrius II's second

*University of Ohio (david.schwei@gmail.com).

1 Shipley 2000: 320–325; Ramsey and Erickson 2011: 13–14

reign provides some insight into the administration of Seleucid mints and into the reaction of various mint workers to the power struggle between Demetrius II and his enemies during this period of decline.

Historical Background

This reign was not the first time that foreign powers intervened in Seleucid politics and the succession of a Seleucid king. Following the disastrous battle of Magnesia (190 BC) and under the terms of the Treaty of Apamea (188 BC), the Romans required Antiochus III the Great (222–187 BC) to forfeit much of Asia Minor.[1] Rome continued to be involved in Seleucid affairs after the treaty. Roman ambassadors dictated terms to both Antiochus IV Epiphanes (175–164 BC) and Antiochus V Eupator (164–162 BC), whose reign the Romans supported while he was still an infant.[2] Demetrius I Soter, the father of Demetrius II, rose to power and executed Antiochus V. Subsequently, Rome, Pergamum, and the Ptolemies undermined Demetrius I and helped Alexander I Balas (152–145 BC), a supposed son of Antiochus IV, oust him from power.[3]

Demetrius II Nicator began his first reign (146–138 BC) during a two-year campaign to obtain the throne with the support of Ptolemy VI Philometor. His reign came to an abrupt end in 138 BC, during his campaign against the Parthians. Amid the fighting he was captured and held at the Parthian court after he married a daughter of the Parthian king Mithridates I.[4] Ten years later, Demetrius's brother Antiochus VII Sidetes was also fighting the Parthians and Demetrius was released to challenge his brother while the new Parthian king Phraates II tried to acquire some Seleucid territory. The Parthian king's plan was foiled when Antiochus died in battle and Demetrius began a second reign over the Seleucid empire (129–125 BC).[5]

In response either to Syrian discontent with Demetrius II or to his attempt to meddle in Ptolemaic politics, Ptolemy VII Euergetes II sent Alexander II Zabinas with an army to challenge Demetrius's position in Syria in 128 BC.[6] Alexander II claimed a dubious connection to the Seleucid royal family, but he still provided a sufficient challenge to Demetrius II.[7] This was perhaps most apparent when, in 128 BC, Antioch on the Orontes stopped minting coins for Demetrius II and began minting them for Alexander II.[8] After Alexander II overcame Demetrius II in battle, the defeated Seleucid king fled to Ake-Ptolemaïs where his queen,

2 Shipley 2000: 291
3 Shipley 2000: 292 and 320
4 Shipley 2000: 320.
5 App. *Syr.* 67–68.
6 App. *Syr.* 68; Jos. *AJ* 13.254; Just. *Epit.* 38.10.7; Newell 1939: 52.
7 Joseph., AJ 13.267–8; Just., Epit. 39.1.4–5; Bagnall 1984.
8 Ehling 1998, 144.
9 Newell 1918: 84; Ehling 1998: 145; *SC* 2.1: 409–410

Cleopatra Thea, sent him away due to his Parthian marriage.[10] Demetrius then sailed to Tyre where he was killed in 125 BC.[11]

After the death of Demetrius II, the Seleucid kingship continued to be contested. Cleopatra Thea was killed by her son Antiochus VIII Grypos (125–96 BC). Seleucid territory was temporarily split between Antiochus VIII and Antiochus IX Cyzicenus (115–95 BC). Their deaths launched another phase of disputes for the throne and loss of territory. The people of Antioch invited Tigranes of Armenia to take up the kingship in 83, but the Seleucids temporarily regained the throne in 69. Finally, the Roman general Pompey ended the Seleucid dynasty in 63 BC.[12]

CHRONOLOGY OF THE ANTIOCH COINS

Late Seleucid kings preserved their power by winning civil wars and maintaining the loyalty of their subordinate officials. Literary and epigraphic evidence suggests this personal nature of the Seleucid kingship as it relates to members of the Seleucid court.[13] Some mint workers' reactions to these historical events, as well as their relationship to the Seleucid king, can be determined from a relative chronology of the mints' coins, as established by a die study. In this study, the tetradrachms and drachms from Antioch on the Orontes and the tetradrachms from Damascus were examined, but the small emission of Damascene drachms was not. At Antioch, 13 obverse dies were observed from a sample of 163 tetradrachms. Most of these dies can be placed in a relative chronology based on die links, die wear, the location of the control marks on the reverse, and the style used to portray Demetrius's hair. Four of these obverse dies—A2, A5, A6, and A9—are linked to two reverse dies—P17 and P42 (Fig. 1, below). Die wear on the coins suggests that the earliest obverse die in this sequence depicts Demetrius with more neatly combed hair than the latest die. The earliest coin in the series has both control marks in the exergue; however, all other coins in this group have the primary control mark in the inner or outer left field, and the secondary control mark under Zeus's throne. These two observations suggest that another die, A1, was used first. The hair on this die is very neatly combed. Additionally, this die was used first with reverse dies on which the controls are both in the exergue and, then, with reverse dies on which the controls are both in the outer left field. The chronology of the other dies cannot be determined precisely. They all must fall after A1 because the hair on the portraits is tousled and because they all exhibit the stubby horn of a young cow. This stubby horn rises out of the temple and barely passes over the diadem, if at all. Niklaus Dürr has suggested that this attribute may have been intended to associate Demetrius II with the mythical Io,

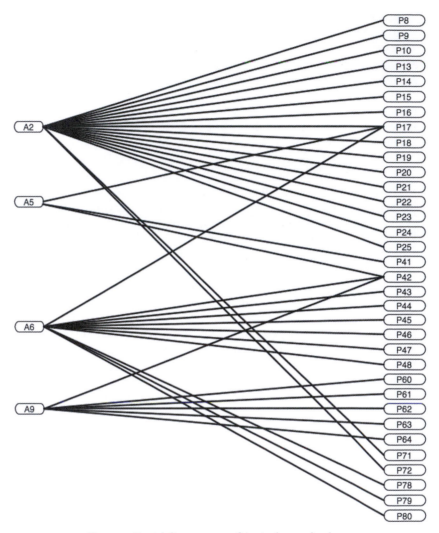

Figure 1. Partial die sequence of Antioch tetradrachms.

who was honored at Antioch because she was said to have died nearby at the end of her European wandering.[14]

The drachms follow a similar pattern. The 38 drachms examined were struck from only four obverse dies. Only one reverse die, p17, was used with multiple obverse dies. Die wear and this die link confirm that the drachms follow a similar order to the tetradrachms. The earlier obverse dies, a1 and a2, also have portraits

14 Bouchier 1921: 21 and 60; Dürr 1979: 8.

with smoothly combed hair, but the later portraits on a3 and a4 have tousled hair. On the reverse, the control marks are in the exergue at the beginning of the reign. Later, the primary control mark is in the inner left field and the secondary control mark is under Zeus's throne.

Chronology of the Damascus Coins

While the Antioch mint only produced coins for Demetrius during years 183 (130/29 BC) and 184 (129/8 BC) of the Seleucid Era (SE), the dates on the Damascus coins show that this mint produced coins for Demetrius until the end of his reign in SE 187 (126/5 BC). The first obverse die at Damascus depicted Demetrius without a beard until it was recut to include the beard that he began wearing in Parthia. As at Antioch, this first obverse die has a portrait of the king with smoothly-combed hair. The remaining dies feature a portrait with tousled hair. The reverse dies provide more information about the coins' relative chronology, in part because they contain dates in the exergue. The control marks begin under Zeus's arm, and then move beneath his throne. In SE 185 (128/7 BC), a control mark in the outer left field was added to the control mark beneath the throne. Another control mark in the outer left field was added to the other two controls during SE 187 (126/5 BC). The changes in the control marks and the one reverse die link between A5 and A6 allow the coins to be placed in order. The small issue of drachms during SE 186 (127/6 BC) was not examined for this study.[15]

The young cow's horn of Demetrius II's portrait is also relevant to the order in which the coins were struck at Damascus. The horn is not present on A1, the first die used at Damascus, but appears for part of SE 184 on dies A2–A5. The horn then disappears from the portrait of Demetrius II, but there are hints of it on a few other dies: A10, A16, and A17. It is difficult to differentiate the possible horn on these three dies from a curl of hair. Dürr's connection of the horn to the cult of Io at Antioch helps to explain the disappearance of this aspect of the portrait during SE 184. Since Demetrius II lost Antioch during SE 184, the Damascus mint workers may have found it unnecessary to continue courting the favor of the Antiochene public with a portrait designed to please the people of that city.

Engravers

This chronology and die study clarify the mint workers' reaction to the power struggle for the Seleucid throne. Throughout the second reign of Demetrius II, some mints looked to engravers from other mints in order to obtain dies rather than seeking out new engravers. Arthur Houghton noticed this phenomenon in his die study of Tarsus's royal mint. He determined that the "smooth haired engraver" of Antioch's A1 moved to Tarsus early in Demetrius II's reign and

---

15 *SC* 2182.

engraved Tarsus A2–A4.[16] Since the engraver made three dies for Tarsus and only this one die for Antioch, it seems more probable that the engraver moved to Tarsus after producing Antioch A1 than that he sent dies from Antioch to Tarsus. Upon his arrival in Tarsus, the "smooth haired engraver" modified the portrait of Demetrius II to include the beard that the king began to wear during his time among the Parthians.[17] The style of the dies made by the "smooth haired engraver" is very similar to Damascus A1, which was recut to include the king's beard, and which was made by an engraver in the circle of the "smooth haired engraver."

Like the "smooth haired engraver," the "tousled hair engraver" moved between mints controlled by Demetrius II. At Antioch, this engraver produced three obverse dies bearing portraits with tousled hair: A3, A4, and A7. In 128 BC, Antioch stopped minting coins for Demetrius II and the "tousled hair engraver" moved to Damascus where, in SE 185 (128/7 BC), he cut die A9. This die is the only representative of the "tousled hair engraver" at Damascus, and the die is represented by two unusual coins: a double-struck coin (Cat. No. 56) and an anomalous coin with a unique placement of the legend on the reverse (Cat. No. 136). In order to say that the engraver moved to Damascus, ideally, more dies produced by the engraver would have been used at this mint, but this mint was not very active during SE 185. Four known dies were used during the year, and two of these were used during other years. Obverse die A7 was used in SE 184 (129/8 BC), 185 (128/7 BC), and 186 (127/6), while A11 was used in SE 185 and 186. It is safe, therefore, to say that the "tousled hair engraver" worked at Damascus during a year of relatively low production.

The "tousled hair engraver's" work is not represented by other dies used at Damascus because he soon moved to Ake-Ptolemaïs. This mint worker produced at least three dies for the mint at this southern Phoenician city. Since, contrary to normal practice at the Ake-Ptolemaïs mint, these three coins do not bear a date, they can be dated to SE 186.[18] Interestingly, the engraver added a lock of hair at the back of Demetrius II's head when he produced the dies for the Ake-Ptolemaïs mint.[19] The movements of the "smooth haired engraver" and the "tousled hair engraver" are not the only connection between mints at this time.

The Mallus mint also exhibits the interaction between mints during Demetrius II's second reign. The engraver of Antioch A2 produced the first tetradrachm die that was used at Mallus during this reign.[20] Even though *Seleucid Coins* mentions a die link between Mallus A1 and Antioch A2,[21] the lock of hair at the height of the king's eye on Mallus A1[22] extends much further across the diadem than on the

16 Houghton 1979: 116.
17 Houghton 1979: 112–116.
18 *SC* 2202.
19 Naville 10 (15 Jun. 1925), lot 1353; Berk 19 (30 Mar. 1982), lot 89; Paris, inv. 1219bis.
20 Houghton 1984.
21 *SC* 2.1: 417 with no. 2159.
22 Naville 10 (15 Jun. 1925), lot 1357.

Antioch die, indicating that it is only the work of the same engraver and not the same die. The other tetradrachm die used at Mallus, A2,[23] is stylistically similar to three Damascus dies—A2, A3, and A4—especially with regard to the hair above the eye. The dies are not similar enough to be the work of the same engraver, but they could have been produced by an engraver who carved the die based on the image produced from a Damascus die.

Throughout Demetrius II's second reign, some mints relied on engravers from other mints instead of new engravers. The "tousled hair engraver" produced at least four dies for other mints after leaving Antioch. The extent of his oeuvre and the importance of his dies to the Ake-Ptolemaïs mint can only be known after a die study of that mint is completed. The Mallus mint was also dependent on other mints. One of its two dies was from an Antioch engraver and the other die was an imitation of a Damascene die. Two engravers produced very similar portraits for both Antioch A1 and Damascus A1. One of these engravers, then, traveled to Tarsus where his die A2 initiated the production of coins with a bearded portrait of Demetrius II.[24] This "smooth haired engraver" replaced the engraver at Tarsus.

The "tousled hair engraver" and his work may provide an explanation for this practice. After Demetrius II lost control over Antioch, the engraver chose to leave Antioch and work for another mint that remained loyal to his king. The loyalty of the engraver probably helped him obtain his appointment at the mints in Damascus and Ake-Ptolemaïs. Other evidence suggests that a mint official's loyalty may have been an important factor in the engravers' employment. At Antioch, the secondary control marks remain the same as those used during the preceding reign of Antiochus VII. The primary control mark, however, changes abruptly to Ξ, indicating that the chief mint official was replaced by someone more loyal or friendly to Demetrius II.[25] Furthermore, Gillian Ramsey's analysis of the historical sources suggests that a rebellious official's success, or king's ability to maintain power, depended upon the loyalty of the administration and upon the politician's self-promotion.[26] The need to rely on loyal workers must have intensified during the dispute over the Seleucid throne in 129–125. The mints, therefore, drew on a relatively small group of loyal engravers to obtain dies and staff the mints.

Size of Issue

While the power struggle affected the means by which the mints obtained dies, the conflict does not seem to have affected the number or the weight standard of Demetrius II's coins. E. T. Newell proposed that the Antioch mint produced a rather large output during Demetrius II's second reign in order to finance his military operations against Ptolemy VII who was supporting Alexander II

23 CSE 508.
24 Houghton 1979: 112–116.
25 SC 2.1: 418.
26 Ramsey 2011.

Zabinas.[27] However, the reattribution of several issues to different mints now requires this proposal to be reevaluated in light of the present die study. Table 1 shows the basic coin statistics for the tetradrachms and drachms from Antioch as well as the tetradrachms from Damascus. Table 2 shows the die frequencies for each denomination at both mints. The die frequency is the number of dies represented in the sample by one coin, two coins, three coins, etc.

Table 1. Die statistics and estimates.[28]

	Antioch		Damascus
	Tetradrachms	Drachms	Tetradrachms
Coins in Total	163	38	135
Coins assigned to dies	163	38	134
Number of dies	13	4	17
Number of singletons	1	1	3
Mean number of coins per die	12.53	9.50	7.88
Estimated coverage	99.4%	97.4%	97.8%
Estimated total number of dies	14	5	19
95% confidence interval	13–14	4–6	17–21

As noted above, 13 obverse dies were observed in a sample of 163 coins, and one of these dies was represented by only one coin. Warren Esty's formulae suggest that, with 95% confidence, 13 to 14 obverse dies were used to strike the Antioch tetradrachms.[29] This sample has a very high estimated coverage of the mint's production (i.e. the probability that a new coin will have been made from a die already included in the sample) because there is only one die represented by only one coin. The sample, however, may not have been very random in the sense that each coin could have entered the sample with equal likelihood. Two dies are represented by 30 or more coins, which might suggest that the coins made by these dies stayed together after production, as in a hoard, until they were found and entered collections and the modern coin market. Esty's estimator of coverage then should be used with a little caution.

The rate of 13 or 14 tetradrachm obverse dies used per year is not high for the time period. Houghton compared the estimated number of dies used each year by the major mints of the Seleucid empire, and found that the mints were generally striking new coins in order to maintain the current coin supply. As time progressed, Antioch began striking more and more of the coinage. The mint used

27 Newell 1918: 84.

28 As noted above, the small issue of drachms from Damascus are not part of this study. The coins listed under the heading "Anomalous" in the catalogs are also not included in these figures.

29 Esty 2006.

approximately 15 dies per year under Demetrius I (162–150 BC) and more than 25 dies per year under Antiochus VII.[30] Demetrius II's Antioch issue, then was not struck in order to finance a war with Ptolemy VII, but was part of a routine effort to maintain the size of the coin supply.

Table 2. Die frequencies.

	Antioch		Damascus
Frequency	Tetradrachms	Drachms	Tetradrachms
1	1	1	3
2	1		4
3			2
4	2	1	
5	1		
6		1	1
9	1		1
10			2
12	1		1
13	1		
14	1		
15	1		
19	1		1
24			1
27		1	1
30	1		
34	1		

The Damascus mint also seems to have focused on maintaining the coin supply during Demetrius II's reign. According to Newell, Antiochus VII opened a mint at Damascus in order to supply the surrounding region of Coele Syria with coinage.[31] Newell also thought that the mint was very active under Demetrius and focused on financing the king's army after Antioch started minting coins for Alexander II.[32] However, this die study suggests that Damascus did not increase production to finance Demetrius II's army. Seventeen obverse dies were observed from 134 coins, and three of these dies are represented by only one coin. Esty's formulae suggest that, with 95% confidence, 17 to 21 obverse dies were used to strike this

30 Houghton 2002.
31 Newell 1939: 48
32 Newell 1939: 55.

issue over five years.[33] The yearly average use of three to four dies—four to five, if the short year of SE 183 (130/29 BC) in which only one die was partially used is excluded—certainly would not replace the loss of Antioch's 13 dies per year.

Indeed, the pattern of dies observed for each year seems not to respond to Demetrius's need for money. The one die used in SE 183 (130/29 BC) was reused in SE 184 (129/8 BC), during which year six other dies were also used. One of these dies—A7—is among the five dies used during SE 185 (128/7 BC). This same die, and another from SE 185—A11—was reused the following year when three new dies were also employed. Finally, only one die from SE 186 (127/6 BC) was reused alongside three new dies during the final year of Demetrius II's second reign, SE 187 (126/5 BC). The production was highest during the first year of Demetrius's reign when he also controlled Antioch, and slowed down to a steady level in which three or four new dies were used. This steady use of dies suggests that Damascus was maintaining the current coin supply, not making up for the loss of Antioch.

It is worth noting that the estimation of the coverage of the Damascus tetradrachm sample is very high, so it is unlikely that a new coin will affect this interpretation of the mint's behavior.

METROLOGY

Instead of increasing the number of coins produced, the Damascus mint reacted to Demetrius II's loss of Antioch by lowering the weight standard slightly. This new Damascus standard was not the same as the Antiochene Attic standard but a version of a lighter standard that had been used at Damascus under Antiochus VII. In order to compare the coins struck under Demetrius II to the coins minted before his second reign, a provisional list was assembled of 37 coins minted at Damascus under Antiochus VII, who opened the mint in this southern Syrian city (Table 3). For the purpose of weight analyses, all weights over 17.00 g and under 15.50 g were excluded. These are: at Damascus under Antiochus VII, Table 3, Nos. 4 (15.21 g) 10 (15.01 g); at Antioch under Demetrius II, Cat. Nos. 54 (15.13 g), 80 (14.88 g), 96 (15.42 g), 106 (17.17 g), 111 (15.46 g), and 129 (15.43 g); and at Damascus under Demetrius II, Cat. Nos. 9 (15.03 g), 29 (14.19 g), 88 (15.33 g), 95 (15.06 g), 97 (15.13 g), 126 (10.70 g), and 127 (11.82 g). Table 4 (below) presents a summary of various statistical characteristics of the coins examined for this die study. Demetrius II's Damascene tetradrachms have been divided by year and there is a subgroup for all the coins from SE 185–187 (128–125 BC) after he had lost Antioch. Table 5 (below) shows the weight frequencies for each of the tetradrachm issues analyzed in Table 4, and Figure 2 shows the weight frequencies from Table 5 charted as line graphs. Figure 2 plots the years SE 185–187 as a group instead of individually for reasons that will become clear in the discussion below.

33 Esty 2006.

Table 3. Provisional list of Damascus tetradrachms of Antiochus VII.

	Year	Weight (g)	Collection
1.	138–129	16.71	ANS 1978.64.216.
2.	137/6	16.48	*SNG Berry* 1385.
3.	137/6	16.78	*LSM* 55.
4.	135/4	15.21	ANS 1944.100.77933; *LSM* 56b.
5.	135/4	15.80	*LSM* 56a.
6.	135/4	16.17	Jerusalem, *SNG Spaer* 2128.
7.	135/4	16.50	*LSM* 56c.
8.	135/4	16.55	Jerusalem, *SNG Spaer* 2129.
9.	135/4	16.64	*CSE* 1, 835.
10.	134/3	15.01	*LSM* 57b.
11.	134/3	15.82	Jerusalem, *SNG Spaer* 2130.
12.	134/3	16.20	*LSM* 58.
13.	134/3	16.45	*LSM* 57d.
14.	134/3	16.50	*CSE* 2, 640.
15.	134/3	16.52	*LSM* 57c.
16.	134/3	16.54	*CSE* 2, 640.
17.	133/2	15.65	*LSM* 60.
18.	133/2	16.29	ANS 1944.100.77934; *LSM* 59a.
19.	133/2	16.40	ANS 1944.100.77935; *LSM* 59b.
20.	132/1	15.77	ANS 1944.100.77937; *LSM* 61a.
21.	132/1	16.02	CNG e-auction 215 (29 July 2009), lot 241.
22.	132/1	16.05	ANS 1944.100.77936; *LSM* 61b.
23.	132/1	16.09	*LSM* 61c.
24.	132/1	16.46	*LSM* 62.
25.	132/1	16.58	Jerusalem, *SNG Spaer* 2131.
26.	131/0	16.03	*LSM* 63b.
27.	131/0	16.45	*CSE* 1, 836.
28.	131/0	16.45	*LSM* 64b.
29.	131/0	16.55	*LSM* 63a.
30.	131/0	16.58	*SNG Berry* 1386.
31.	131/0	16.65	*LSM* 64c.
32.	130/29	16.24	CNG E-auction 153 (29 Nov. 2006), lot 68.

	Year	Weight (g)	Collection
33.	130/29	16.24	CNG E-auction 224, 19 Dec. 2009, 274.
34.	130/29	16.33	CSE 1, 837.
35.	130/29	16.48	Jerusalem, SNG Spaer 2132.
36.	130/29	16.53	ANS 1944.100.77940; LSM 66.
37.	130/29	16.53	LSM 65.

Statistical analyses suggest that, during Demetrius II's second reign, the Damascus mint changed its weight standard. A Kruskal-Wallis test, which compares multiple data sets to determine if they are statistically the same, was used to compare the weights of the coins from each year. It suggests, with a p-value of 0.03998, that the weight standards are statistically significantly different during Demetrius II's reign (the Kruskal-Wallis statistic is 8.3122.). Following the procedure outlined by Viv Bewick, Liz Cheek, and Jonathan Ball, further statistical comparisons show that the coin weights from SE 184 are statistically different from the coin weights from both SE 186 and SE 187.[34] It is, therefore, safe to say that the weight standard changed sometime during SE 185, after Demetrius II lost Antioch.

Table 4. Resume of data sample and statistical characteristics.

	Antioch		Damascus						
	Tetradrachms	Drachms	Antiochus VII*	Demetrius II Total	SE 183–184	SE 185–187	SE 185	SE 186	SE 187
Total no. of coins	163	38	37	135	47	88	26	39	23
Weight Unknown	23	2	0	6	4	2	0	2	0
Excluded	6	0	2	7	2	5	0	3	2
No. of coins analyzed	134	36	35	122	41	81	26	34	21
Mean	16.52	3.99	16.34	16.38	16.46	16.29	16.37	16.32	16.31
Standard deviation	0.26	0.18	0.29	0.28	0.25	0.36	0.30	0.30	0.29
Interquartile range	0.35	0.18	0.36	0.29	0.26	0.31	0.39	0.39	0.22
Minimum	15.72	3.55	15.65	15.52	15.85	15.06	15.54	15.54	15.66
25th Percentile	16.38	3.94	16.19	16.29	16.38	16.21	16.18	16.18	16.25
Median	16.55	4.02	16.45	16.43	16.51	16.40	16.40	16.40	16.39
75th Percentile	16.72	4.11	16.55	16.58	16.64	16.52	16.57	16.57	16.47
Maximum	16.95	4.29	16.78	16.89	16.89	16.73	16.68	16.68	16.67

34 Bewick, Cheek, and Ball 2004.

Table 5. Weight frequencies.

Weight (g)	Antioch	Damascus						
	Demetrius II	Antiochus VII*	Demetrius II Total	SE 183–184	SE 185–187	SE 185	SE 186	SE 187
Above 17.00	1							
16.95–16.99	1							
16.90–16.94	1							
16.85–16.89	6		1	1				
16.80–16.84	4		0	0				
16.75–16.79	14	1	1	1				
16.70–16.74	16	1	3	2	1	1		
16.65–16.69	9	1	10	6	4	1	1	2
16.60–16.64	8	1	11	5	6	2	4	0
16.55–16.59	9	5	11	3	8	3	5	0
16.50–16.54	14	4	10	4	6	1	3	2
16.45–16.49	8	6	10	1	9	4	1	4
16.40–16.44	8	1	15	6	9	4	3	2
16.35–16.39	5	0	10	3	7	1	4	2
16.30–16.34	6	1	9	3	6	3	0	3
16.25–16.29	6	1	3	0	3	1	1	1
16.20–16.24	6	3	6	1	5	1	3	1
16.15–16.19	0	1	4	0	4	2	2	0
16.10–16.14	2	0	2	0	2	0	1	1
16.05–16.09	4	2	2	1	1	0	1	0
16.00–16.04	0	2	1	1	0	0	0	0
Below 16.00	11	4	17	4	13	2	5	3

A comparison of the weight standards used at Damascus shows that the new weight standard for the later portion of Demetrius II's reign was probably the same standard that was used at Damascus under Antiochus VII. Another Kruskal-Wallis test, with a p-value of 0.02286, finds that the Damascene weight standards are statistically different for three time periods: under Antiochus VII, during SE 183–184 under Demetrius II, and during SE 185–187 under Demetrius II (the

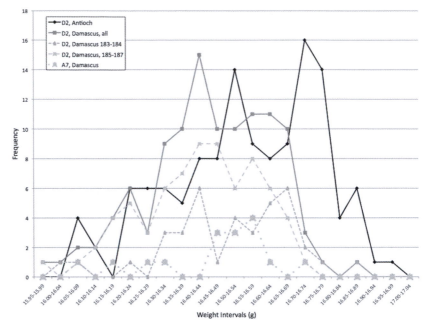

Figure 2. Weight distributions.

Kruskal-Wallis statistic is 7.5567). Further statistical comparisons suggest that the SE 183–184 weight standard is different from that used under Antiochus VII and that used later in Demetrius II's reign. The comparisons also reveal that the same standard was used under Antiochus VII and during the years SE 185–187. Therefore, as Figure 2 helps illustrate, the Damascus mint raised the weight standard at the beginning of Demetrius II's reign, but lowered the standard back to the Antiochus VII weight standard after Demetrius II suffered the loss of Antioch.

While it is clear that the Damascus mint lowered the standard in order to save money after the loss of Antioch, it is uncertain why the mint raised the standard at the beginning of the reign. Figure 2 shows that the Damascene standard during SE 183–184 was not much heavier than the standard under Antiochus VII. A Kolmogorov-Smirnov test, which tests to see if two data sets are statistically the same, was used to compare the weights of coins struck at Damascus during SE 183–184 and the weights of coins struck at Antioch during the same time period. It shows, with a p-value of 0.075, that the weight standards are statistically the same (the Kolmogorov-Smirnov statistic is 0.2233). This test suggests that the Damascus mint raised its standard in SE 183 in order to strike coins with weights closer to the standard of the Antioch mints.

This change did not respond to or seek to alter the coin circulation patterns. The lighter Damascus coins of Antiochus VII still circulated alongside the Antioch coins of Demetrius II, as is shown by the presence of coins from both groups in a hoard found at Kessab.[35] The lower standard of Antiochus VII also did not prevent that king's Damascus coins from reaching Asia Minor.[36] More probably, the Damascus mint was meant to strike coins on a standard closer to other mints, like Antioch or Ake-Ptolemaïs, for the sake of consistency among the mints. This hypothesis would best be tested with a die study of the Ake-Ptolemaïs mint under Demetrius II, and a comparison of the weight standards used at the mint with attention to chronological change throughout Demetrius II's reign. The Ake-Ptolemaïs mint is geographically much closer to Damascus than Antioch, and the coins from Ake-Ptolemaïs and Damascus probably circulated in the same areas to a greater extent than did coins from Antioch with coins from either of the other two cities. However, one should also remember that the set of weights used for the analysis of Antiochus VII's reign was only provisional, so a larger sample from Damascus under this king could also clarify matters.

Conclusion

This die study of the coins struck at two mints under Demetrius II augments our knowledge of how the ancient Syrians responded to the political struggles of the Seleucid kings at the end of the second century BC. Demetrius II fought wars and fled to find safety after military defeat, only to be rejected by his wife Cleopatra Thea. The inhabitants of Antioch switched their allegiance to Alexander II Zabinas after he challenged Demetrius II's position. While the political turmoil caused upheaval in the lives of Demetrius II and other rulers, the administration of the empire largely conducted business as usual. This discord further encouraged mint administrators to rely on loyal engravers to provide dies for striking coins just like the kings who relied on loyal administrators to govern. The number of dies used by the mints continued at the typical levels necessary to maintain the Syrian coin supply. The Damascus mint, furthermore, did lower its weight standard due to Demetrius II's misfortunes in the power struggle. Even this lower standard appears to have revived an earlier Damascene standard which was temporarily abandoned during SE 183–184. These conclusions may be improved and further clarified by studies of the coinage struck at Damascus under Antiochus VII and at Ake-Ptolemaïs under Demetrius II.

35 *IGCH* 1568.
36 *SC* 2.1: 377–378.

CATALOG: DEMETRIUS II AT ANTIOCH[37]

Tetradrachms

Obverse: Diademed head of Demetrius II r., bearded, with hair combed smooth on crown of head, diadem ends falling straight behind, fillet border.

Reverse: ΒΑΣΙΛΕΩΣ ΔΗΜΗΤΡΙΟΥ in two lines on r., ΘΕΟΥ ΝΙΚΑΤΟΡΟΣ in two lines on l., Zeus enthroned l., resting on scepter and holding Nike, inside legend, facing r. offering wreath to Zeus.

Group 1: ΞΔ in exergue. *SC* 2164

Die A1

(Obverse link to P5–P7, below)

1.*	A1	P1	No Wt.	Lanz 62 (26 Nov. 1992), lot 418; Lanz 44 (16 May 1988), lot 271.
2.	A1	P1	16.22	GM 46 (30 Oct. 1989), lot 366; GM 36 (8 Apr. 1987), lot 285.
3.	A1	P1	16.77	*SNG Berry* 1394.
4.	A1	P2	No Wt.	GM 69 (18 Nov. 1994), lot 432.
5.	A1	P2	16.47	Naville 10 (15 Jun. 1925), lot 1348.
6.	A1	P3	16.58	*CSE* 286; NFA 16 (2 Dec. 1985), lot 252.
7.	A1	P4	16.68	GM 40 (7 Apr. 1988), lot 324.

Obverse: Diademed head of Demetrius II r., bearded, *with hair combed smooth on crown of head*, diadem ends falling straight behind, fillet border.

Reverse: ΒΑΣΙΛΕΩΣ ΔΗΜΗΤΡΙΟΥ in two lines on r., ΘΕΟΥ ΝΙΚΑΤΟΡΟΣ in two lines on l., Zeus enthroned l., resting on scepter *and extending r. hand through legend*, holding Nike, *who faces l., extending wreath towards edge of coin.*

Group 2: Ξ above Δ in outer l. field. *SC* 2165

Die A1

(Obverse die link to P1–P4, above)

8.	A1	P5	15.93	New York, ANS 1944.100.76708.
9.	A1	P5	No Wt.	Seyrig, *Trésors*, 30.190. The same cast was used for 30.334, so no weight is given here.
10.*	A1	P5	16.85	Leu 42 (12 May 1987), lot 355.

37 The coins are placed in order based on the progression of die wear. Die axes are 12 o'clock.

11.   A1   P6   16.20   Copenhagen, *SNG Copenhagen* 346.

12.   A1   P7   16.39   Vinchon (14 Apr. 1984 [de Béhague]), lot 202.

13.   A1   P7   16.72   GM 84 (13 Oct. 1987), lot 5399.

Obverse: Diademed head of Demetrius II r., bearded, *with tousled locks on crown of head and stubby horn at temple,* diadem ends falling straight behind, fillet border.

Reverse: ΒΑΣΙΛΕΩΣ ΔΗΜΗΤΡΙΟΥ in two lines on r., ΘΕΟΥ ΝΙΚΑΤΟΡΟΣ in two lines on l., Zeus enthroned l., resting on scepter *and extending r. hand through legend,* holding Nike, *who faces l., extending wreath towards edge of coin.*

Group 3: ΞΛ in exergue. No *SC* number

Die A2

(Obverse die link to P9–P10, P13–25, and P71–72, below)

14.*   A2   P8   16.92   MuM 88 (17 May 1999), lot 296.

Group 4: Ξ in outer left field; ⋔ under throne. *SC* 2166.2b

Die A2

(Obverse die link to P8 above, P13–25 and P71–72, below)

15.*   A2   P9   16.68   New York, ANS 1944.100.76710.

16.   A2   P10   16.26   CNG 55 (13 Sep. 2000), lot 684.

Die A3

(Obverse die link to P26–P29, P89–P90, and P92, below)

17.   A3   P11   No Wt.   Sotheby's (3 May 1984), lot 147.

18.   A3   P11   16.75   Superior (11 Dec. 1992), lot 2157; Peus 257 (12 Oct. 1967), lot 39.

19.*   A3   P11   16.32   CNG E-auction 112 (13 Apr. 2005), lot 74.

Die A4

(Obverse die link to P30–P40, P73–P77, P91, and P93 below)

20.*   A4   P12   16.85   Seyrig, *Trésors,* 30.106.

21.   A4   P12   16.73   Europea (Horde) Market, Sep. 1991.

Group 5: Ξ in outer left field; Σ under throne. *SC* 2166.2f

Die A2

(Obverse die link to P8–P10, above, P14–P25 and P71–P72, below)

22.*   A2   P13   16.76   *CSE* 2, 663.

Group 6: Ξ in inner left field; Δ under throne. *SC* 2166.1

Die A2

(Obverse die link to P8–P10 and P13, above, P18–P25 and P71–P72, below;
Reverse die link to A5–A6, below)

23.*	A2	P14	16.65	New York, ANS 1944.100.76709.
24.	A2	P15	16.51	Peus 314 (30 Oct. 1985), lot 162.
25.	A2	P15	16.65	CNG 63 (21 May 2003), lot 644.
26.	A2	P16	16.74	GM 40 (7 Apr. 1988), lot 323.
27.	A2	P16	No Wt.	GM 73 (11 Oct. 1996), lot 217.
28.	A2	P17	No Wt.	Kastner 4 (28 Nov. 1973), lot 193.
29.*	A2	P17	16.45	MuM GmbH 32 (26 May 2010), lot 193; MuM Deutschland 12 (2003), lot 118.
30.	A2	P17	16.66	GM 130 (8 Mar. 2004), lot 1291; Lanz 26 (5 Dec. 1983), lot 291.
31.	A2	P17	16.85	Peus 351 (25 Apr. 1997), lot 303.
32.	A2	P17	No Wt.	Peus 315 (24 Apr. 1986), lot 162; Peus 313 (13 May 1985), lot 221.
33.	A2	P17	16.43	CNG 61 (25 Sep. 2002), lot 846.
34.	A2	P17	16.58	Berk 115 (2 Aug. 2000), lot 300.
35.	A2	P17	16.78	Hirsch 171 (25 Sep. 1991), lot 430; Hirsch 166 (16 May 1990), lot 490.

Die A5

(Obverse die link to P41–P42, below; Reverse die link to A2, above, and A6, below)

36.*   A5   P17   16.70   GM 101 (6 Mar 2000), lot 386.

Die A6

(Obverse die link to P42–P48 and P78–P80, below; Reverse die link to A2 and A5, above)

37.*   A6   P17   16.71   CNG 88 (14 Sep. 2011), lot 487.

Group 7: Ξ in outer left field; O under throne. *SC* 2166.2c

Die A2

(Obverse die link to P8–P10 and P13–P17, above, P71-P72, below)

38.	A2	P18	16.74	Hess-Leu 9 (2 Apr. 1958), lot 248.
39.	A2	P19	16.75	*CSE* 2, 662; Spink 87 (9 Oct. 1991), lot 71.
40.	A2	P20	16.54	CNG E-auction 229 (10 Mar. 2010), lot 214.
41.	A2	P18	15.77	Naville 10 (15 Jun. 1925), lot 1352.
42.	A2	P18	16.64	Peus 386 (26 Apr. 2006), lot 284.
43.	A2	P21	16.44	Copenhagen, *SNG Copenhagen* 345.
44.	A2	P22	No Wt.	M. Platt (4 Dec. 1970), lot 146.
45.	A2	P22	16.67	Aufhauser 2 (21 Oct. 1985), lot 158.
46.	A2	P22	16.44	Aberdeen, *SNG Newnham Davis* 431.
47.	A2	P22	16.84	Peus 308 (19 Oct. 1983), lot 186; Naville 12 (18 Oct. 1926), lot 1977.
48.*	A2	P23	16.55	CNG E-auction 264 (21 Sep. 2011), lot 192; Sotheby's (15 Feb. 1972), lot 275.
49.	A2	P23	16.87	Berk 146 (29 Nov. 2005), lot 137.
50.	A2	P24	No Wt.	Malloy FPL (Dec. 1971), lot 315.
51.	A2	P25	16.64	MuM 19 (5 Jun. 1959), lot 548.
52.	A2	P25	16.69	Hirsch 10 (20 Sep. 1956), lot 39.

Die A3

(Obverse die link to P11, above, P89–P90 and P92, below)

53.	A3	P26	16.70	CNG 87 (18 May 2011), lot 641.
54.	A3	P26	15.13	Stack's (5 Mar. 1971), lot 282.
55.	A3	P26	16.70	GM 89 (5 May 1981), lot 273.
56.*	A3	P27	16.50	Stack's and Ponterio 163 (6 Jan. 2012), lot 301.

57.	A3	P27	16.65	Auctiones 13 (23 Jun. 1983), lot 367; SBC (27 Oct. 1977), lot 373.
58.	A3	P28	15.71	Lanz 141 (26 May 2008), lot 217.
59.	A3	P29	16.61	Münz Zentrum 56 (21 Apr. 1982), lot 135.

Die A4

(Obverse die link to P12 above, P73–P77, P91, and P93 below)

60.*	A4	P30	16.47	New York, ANS 1944.100.76707.
61.	A4	P31	16.06	Sotheby's (30 Apr. 1958 [Haughton]), lot 238.
62.	A4	P32	15.78	Munich.
63.	A4	P33	16.05	Hirsch 75 (22 Nov. 1971), lot 244.
64.	A4	P34	16.42	CNG E-auction 269 (30 Nov. 2011), lot 166.
65.	A4	P34	No Wt.	GM 20 (1 Dec. 1981), lot 66.
66.	A4	P35	16.41	Lanz 125 (26 Nov. 2005), lot 472.
67.	A4	P30	16.76	Sternberg 27 (7 Nov. 1994), lot 193; MuM FPL 542 (Apr. 1991), lot 59.
68.	A4	P36	No Wt.	Schulman 92 (26 Feb. 1973), lot 644.
69.	A4	P37	16.73	CNA FPL 17.3 (1992), lot 152.
70.	A4	P37	No Wt.	Glendining, (11 Dec. 1974), lot 116.
71.*	A4	P38	16.95	CSE 288; CNG 61 (25 Sep. 2002), lot 845. Secondary control mark O cut over Δ.
72.	A4	P39	16.83	New York, ANS 1977.158.679.
73.	A4	P39	16.73	CSE 2, 661; Spink 87 (9 Oct. 1991), lot 71.
74.	A4	P37	16.41	Argenor Numismatique FPL 7 (13 Apr. 2005), lot 84.
75.	A4	P40	16.60	A. Hess 230 (28 Apr. 1936), lot 738.
76.	A4	P30'	No Wt.	Hirsch 84 (27 Jun. 1973), lot 142. Zeus's drapery was recut at the back of the throne.

Die A5

(Obverse die link to P17, above; Reverse die link to A6 and A9, below)

| 77.* | A5 | P41 | 16.53 | CNG 60 (22 May 2002), lot 921. Secondary control mark O cut over inverted Δ. |
| 78.* | A5 | P42 | 16.20 | Berk 137 (31 Mar. 2004), lot 195. |

79.	A5	P42	16.40	CNG 50 (23 Jun. 1999), lot 914.
80.	A5	P42	14.88	Elsen E-auction 114 (15 Sep. 2012), lot 139.

Die A6

(Obverse die link to P17, above, and P78–P80, below; Reverse die link to A5, above, and A9, below)

81.	A6	P43	16.62	Copenhagen, *SNG Copenhagen* 344.
82.	A6	P42	16.29	Berk 122 (6 Sep. 2001), lot 247.
83.	A6	P42	15.73	CNG 43 (24 Sep. 1997), lot 734.
84.	A6	P44	16.54	Leu 86 (5 May 2003), lot 436.
85.	A6	P44	16.71	Sotheby's (9 Oct. 1995), lot 224; *SNG von Post* 593.
86.	A6	P42	16.39	Tkalec (29 Feb. 2008), lot 425.
87.	A6	P45	16.53	Superior (3 Oct. 1977), lot 1010.
88.	A6	P42	16.68	Paris, Babelon 1212.
89.	A6	P42	16.70	*Collectors' Journal of Ancient Art* 3.2–4 (Winter 1981), lot 27.
90.	A6	P42	15.92	Egger (1 July 1908), lot 628.
91.	A6	P46	16.46	Peus 329 (31 Oct. 1990), lot 235.
92.*	A6	P47	16.31	New York, ANS 1948.19.2385.
93.	A6	P48	16.35	Glendining (18 Apr. 1955), lot 589; Glendining (10 Oct. 1951), lot 322.
94.	A6	P47	16.25	Sotheby's (9 Oct. 1995), lot 436.

Die A7

(Obverse die link to P81–P84, below)

95.*	A7	P49	16.60	Triton V (15 Jan. 2002), lot 1502.
96.	A7	P50	15.42	Vienna.
97.	A7	P51	16.78	MuM 79 (28 Feb. 1994), lot 405.
98.	A7	P51	16.58	Egger 41 (18 Nov. 1912 [Fenerley Bey]), lot 733.
99.	A7	P52	16.54	Hirsch 53 (26 July 1967), lot 3252.
100.	A7	P53	16.59	Stack's FPL (Fall 1991), lot 72.

Die A8

(Obverse die link to P85–P86, below)

101.	A8	P54	16.27	Ratto (4 Apr. 1927), lot 2516.
102.	A8	P56	16.60	Peus 287 (3 Apr. 1979), lot 120.
103.	A8	P57	16.07	Stack's (19 Jun. 1969), lot 197.
104.	A8	P58	15.98	Cambridge, Grose, Fitzwilliam, 9329.
105.*	A8	P59	16.26	Berk FPL 3 (Summer 1975), lot 110.
106.	A8	P60	17.17	Leu 83 (6 May 2002), lot 390.
107.	A8	P60	16.05	Hirsch 63 (1 July 1979), lot 2395.

Die A9

108.	A9	P61	16.13	Bourgey (4 Nov. 1960), lot 168.
109.	A9	P62	No Wt.	Berk FPL 2 (Fall 1974), lot 131.
110.	A9	P61	16.74	Kricheldorf 7 (12 Nov. 1959), 101; Sotheby's (30 Apr. 1958 [Haughton]), lot 237.
111.	A9	P61	15.46	CNG E-auction 216 (12 Aug. 2009), lot 187.
112.	A9	P63	No Wt.	MuM 8 (8 Dec. 1949), lot 861.
113.	A9	P63	16.46	London.
114.	A9	P63	No Wt.	Barcelona ANE (26 Jun. 1973), lot 163.
115.	A9	P42	16.55	Tradart (12 Dec 1991), lot 201.
116.*	A9	P64	No Wt.	Berk 19 (30 Mar. 1982), lot 91.
117.	A9	P64	16.84	Cahn 66 (4 May 1930), lot 159.
118.	A9	P61	16.50	Kovacs 10 (18 May 1990), lot 159.
119.	A9	P64	No Wt.	Berk 63 (29 Aug. 1990), lot 121.

Die A10

120.*	A10	P65	16.32	Paris, Armond-Valton 504.

Die A11

121.	A11	P66	16.52	Monetaria FPL 49 (Spring 1988), lot 74.
122.*	A11	P66	16.77	CNG 87 (18 May 2011), lot 640.

Die A12

123.	A12	P67	16.23	Jerusalem, *SNG Spaer* 2162.
124.	A12	P68	16.56	*SNG Australia* 2, 76.
125.	A12	P69	No Wt.	Lanz 117 (24 Nov. 2003), lot 416.
126.*	A12	P70	16.29	Peus 309 (2 May 1984), lot 81.

Group 8: Ξ in outer left field; Δ under throne. *SC* 2166.2a

Die A2

(Obverse die link to P8–P10 and P13–P25, above)

127.	A2	P71	16.35	Schulman Gallery 62 (14 Mar. 1969), lot 361.
128.*	A2	P72	16.47	Lanz 40 (25 May 1987), lot 389; MuM FPL 316 (Sep. 1970), lot 389.

Die A4

(Obverse die link to P12 and P30–P40, above, P91 and P93, below)

129.*	A4	P73	15.43	NFA 24 (18 Oct. 1990), lot 933.
130.	A4	P74	16.51	Coin Galleries 37 (19 Nov. 1973), lot 255.
131.	A4	P75	No Wt.	MuM FPL 186 (Jan. 1959), lot 28.
132.	A4	P76	16.50	Peus 400 (22 Apr. 2010), lot 189.
133.	A4	P75	16.37	GM 78 (13 Jan. 1996), lot 280.
134.	A4	P73	16.71	Peus 380 (3 Nov. 2004), lot 601.
135.*	A4'	P77	16.69	Paris 1973.1.232 (Seyrig's). Obverse die was extensively recut where the hair meets the neck.

Die A6

(Obverse die link to P17 and P42–48, above)

136.	A6	P78	16.53	Stack's (Apr. 2010), lot 161.
137.	A6	P79	16.54	Freeman & Sear FPL 7, lot 170; Coin Galleries (19 Nov. 1971), lot 143.
138.	A6	P79	16.53	CNG 53 (15 May 2000), lot 633; CAN 21 (26 Jun. 1992), lot 138.
139.*	A6	P80	16.22	New York, ANS 1978.64.219.

Die A7

(Obverse die link to P47–P53, above)

140.	A7	P81	16.78	Hess-Leu 19 (12 Apr. 1962), lot 353.
141.	A7	P81	16.78	*SNG Berry* 1390; CNG 73 (13 Sep. 2006), lot 459.
142.*	A7	P82	16.80	Superior (9 Dec. 1989 [Heitetz]), lot 2770; Sternberg 12 (18 Nov. 1982), lot 295.
143.	A7	P82	16.21	Paris, Babelon 1216.
144.	A7	P83	16.48	Superior (8 Dec. 1993 [Abramowitz]), lot 363.
145.	A7	P83	16.59	Credit de la Bourse (Paris) FPL (Oct. 1992), lot 393.
146.	A7	P84	16.79	London Market (Baldwin), Nov. 1991.
147.	A7	P84	16.72	Myers/Adams 6 (6 Dec. 1973), lot 232; Superior (24 Sep. 1970), lot 1692; Peus 270 (10 Jun. 1969), lot 93.

Die A8

(Obverse die link to P54–P59, above)

148.	A8	P85	16.53	*SMA* 321.
149.*	A8	P86	16.58	*CSE* 2, 660.

Die A13

150.	A13	P87	16.34	Peus 291 (30 Mar. 1977), lot 291; Peus 282 (30 Oct. 1973), lot 176.
151.	A13	P87	No Wt.	Malloy 2 (28 Mar. 1973), lot 227.
152.	A13	P88	16.41	Coin Galleries (17 Apr. 1975), lot 288; Glendining (21 Jun. 1972), lot 298.
153.*	A13	P87	16.45	Hirsch 169 (20 Feb. 1991), lot 541.
154.	A13	P87	16.30	Paris, Babelon 1215bis (Seyrig coll.).

Group 9: Ξ in outer left field; Φ under throne. *SC* 2166.2d

Die A3

(Obverse die link to P11 and P26–P29, above, P92, below)

155.*	A3	P89	16.87	MuM 37 (5 Dec. 1968), lot 259.
156.	A3	P90	No Wt.	Berk 12 (2 Feb. 1981), lot 104.
157.	A3	P90	16.75	MuM Deutschland 11 (7 Nov. 2002), lot 773.

Die A4

(Obverse die link to P12, P30–P40, and P73–P77, above, P93, below)

158.*   A4   P91   16.73   *SNG Berry* 1391.

Group 10: Ξ in outer left field; Ɑ under throne. *SC* 2166.2e

Die A3

(Obverse die link to P11, P26–P29, and P89–P90, above)

159.   A3   P92   16.85   Seyrig, *Trésors*, 30.105.

160.*   A3   P92   16.78   CNG 87 (18 May 2011), lot 642.

Die A4

(Obverse die link to P12, P30–P40, P73–P77, and P91, above)

161.   A4   P93   16.10   Stack's (27 Aug. 1940), lot 135.

162.   A4   P93   16.80   GM 195 (7 Mar. 2011), lot 292.

163.*   A4   P93   16.62   New York, ANS 1967.152.640.

Anomalous

164.*   A5   15.86   NFA 27 (4 Dec. 1991), lot 75. (Also listed as Damascus tetradrachm, Cat. No. 138) The obverse die is from Antioch and the reverse is from Damascus. The mule was most likely made from casts of coins, and the letters near the spear and hand of Zeus were poorly transferred.

165.*   A6   16.16   Hirsch 281 (2 May 2012), lot 466; Hirsch 272 (4 May 1991), lot 376 (Also listed as Damascus tetradrachm, Cat. No. 139). The obverse die is from Antioch and the reverse die is from Damascus. A modern mule was made from casts of coins, and the Nike was not well transferred.

166.*   P17   16.33   GM 55 (14 May 1991), lot 344; GM 50 (24 Sep. 1990), lot 422 (Also listed as Damascus tetradrachm, Cat. No. 137). The obverse die is from Damascus and the neck does not extend as far below the fillet border as it should. The mule was made from a Damascus coin struck off-center and an Antioch coin.

167.*   16.75   Edward J. Waddel FPL 42, lot 21. The flan is too
                              oblong for this mint, and the engraving of the
                              dies is of inferior quality.

Drachms

Obverse: Diademed head of Demetrius II r., bearded, *with hair combed smooth on
crown of head,* diadem ends falling straight behind, fillet border.

Reverse: ΒΑΣΙΛΕΩΣ ΔΗΜΗΤΡΙΟΥ in two lines on r., ΘΕΟΥ ΝΙΚΑΤΟΡΟΣ in two
lines on l., Zeus enthroned l., resting on scepter and holding Nike, *inside
legend, facing r. offering wreath to Zeus.*

Group 1: ΞΟ in exergue. *SC* 2167c

Die a1

(Obverse die linked with p3–p13 and p15–17, below)

| 1. | a1 | p1 | 4.03 | Hauch and Aufhauser 18 (5 Oct. 2004), lot 362. |
| 2.* | a1 | p2 | 3.97 | Copenhagen, *SNG Copenhagen* 347. |

Group 2: ΞΑ in exergue. No *SC* number

Die a1

(Obverse die linked with p1–p2, above, p5–p13 and p15–p17, below)

3.*	a1	p3	3.67	CNG E-auction (17 Aug. 2011), lot 154.
4.	a1	p3	3.97	Boston, *MFA Supp.* 288.
5.	a1	p4	3.65	Jerusalem, *SNG Spaer* 2163.

Group 3: Traces of letters in exergue. No *SC* number

Die a1

(Obverse die linked with p1–p4, above, p6–p13 and p15–p17, below)

| 6.* | a1 | p5 | 3.94 | Copenhagen, *SNG Copenhagen* 348. |

Group 4: ΞΜ in exergue. *SC* 2167b

Die a1

(Obverse die linked with p1–p5, above, p9–p13 and p15–p17, below)

| 7. | a1 | p6 | 4.10 | CNG E-auction (2 Feb. 2005), lot 92; Elsen 73 (15 Mar. 2003), lot 127. |
| 8. | a1 | p6 | 4.04 | Superior, (10 Dec. 1988 [Moreira]), lot 2032. |

9.   a1   p6   4.13   Paris, inv. R2254 (Henri Seyrig).

10.*   a1   p7   3.55   CNG E-auction (21 Sep. 2011), lot 194; Kovacs
                            IX (21 Nov. 1988), lot 123.

11.   a1   p7   3.96   Paris, De Clercq, 203.

12.   a1   p8   4.15   Auctiones 29 (13 Jun. 2003), lot 748; Aufhauser 9
                            (Oct. 1992), lot 223.

Group 5: Ξ ℛ in exergue. *SC* 2167d

Die a1

(Obverse die linked with p1–p8, above, p15–p17, below)

13.   a1   p9   3.96   Egger 41 (18 Nov. 1912 [Fenerley Bey]), lot 734.

14.   a1   p10   4.02   *SNG Australia* 2 (Pitchfork coll.), 77.

15.   a1   p11   4.05   CNG E-auction 260 (20 July 2011), lot 285.

16.   a1   p12   4.16   Freeman & Sear FPL 7 (Spring 2003), lot 171.

17.*   a1   p12   3.62   New York, ANS 1977.158.682.

18.   a1   p12   4.02   NFA 5 (23 Feb. 1978), lot 207.

19.   a1   p12   4.24   New York, ANS 1944.100.76711.

20.   a1   p12   No Wt. GM 46 (30 Oct. 1989), lot 367.

21.   a1   p12   4.06   CNG E-auction 246 (15 Dec. 2010), lot 123.

22.   a1   p13   3.93   Jerusalem, *SNG Spaer* 2164.

Die a2

23.*   a2   p14   4.01   Paris, De Clercq, 201.

Group 6: ΞΑΙ in exergue. *SC* 2167a

Die a1

(Obverse die linked with p1–p13, above, p17, below)

24.   a1   p15   4.13   Paris, Babelon 1224.

25.   a1   p16   3.91   Paris, De Clercq, 202.

26.*   a1   p16   4.15   CNG E-Auction 264 (21 Sep. 2011), lot 193;
                            CSE 287.

Obverse: Diademed head of Demetrius II r., bearded, *with hair combed smooth on crown of head*, diadem ends falling straight behind, fillet border.

Reverse: ΒΑΣΙΛΕΩΣ ΔΗΜΗΤΡΙΟΥ in two lines on r., ΘΕΟΥ ΝΙΚΑΤΟΡΟΣ in two lines on l., Zeus enthroned l., resting on scepter and *extending r. hand outside inscription, holding Nike, who faces l., extending wreath toward edge of coin.*

Group 7: Ξ inner l., A under throne. *SC* 2168.1a

Die a1

(Obverse die linked with p1–13 and p15–p16, above; Reverse die linked with a3, below)

27.*	a1	p17	4.12	Paris, inv. R2256 (Seyrig coll.).
28.	a1	p17	4.17	Auctiones 25 (Jul.–Aug. 1995), lot 521; NAC "C" (11 Mar. 1993), lot 1459.

Obverse: Diademed head of Demetrius II r., bearded, *with tousled locks on crown of head and stubby horn at temple*, diadem ends falling straight behind, fillet border.

Reverse: ΒΑΣΙΛΕΩΣ ΔΗΜΗΤΡΙΟΥ in two lines on r., ΘΕΟΥ ΝΙΚΑΤΟΡΟΣ in two lines on l., Zeus enthroned l., resting on scepter and *extending r. hand outside inscription*, holding Nike, *who faces l., extending wreath toward edge of coin.*

Group 7: Ξ inner l., A under throne. *SC* 2168.1a

Die a3

(Obverse die linked with p14, below; Reverse die linked with a1, above)

29.	a3	p18	3.99	*SNG von Post* 594.
30.	a3	p18	3.88	Berk 139 (4 Aug. 2004), lot 192.
31.	a3	p18	No Wt.	Berk 43 (28 May 1986), lot 145.
32.*	a3	p17	4.29	*CSE* 2, 664.

Group 8: Ξ inner l., O under throne. *SC* 2168.1b

Die a3

(Obverse die linked with p14 and p17–p18, above)

33.*	a3	p19	3.66	MuM FPL 256 (Jul.–Aug. 1965), lot 32.
34.	a3	p20	3.84	Berk 97 (7 Oct. 1997), lot 168.

Group 9: Ξ inner l., Δ under throne. *SC* 2168.2a

Die a4

35.*	a4	p21	3.94	New York, ANS 1944.100.76712.
36.	a4	p22	4.06	New York, ANS 1944.100.76713; *SMA* 323.
37.	a4	p23	4.11	Hirsch 199 (6 May 1998), lot 234; Hirsch 197 (26 Nov. 1997), lot 375.
38.	a4	p23	3.99	Peus 351 (25 Apr. 1997), lot 304; NFA 20 (9 Nov. 1988), lot 790.

CATALOG: DEMETRIUS II AT DAMASCUS[38]

Tetradrachms

Obverse: Diademed head of Demetrius II r., *clean-shaven cheeks with hints of a moustache, with hair combed smooth on crown of head,* diadem ends falling straight behind, fillet border.

Reverse: ΒΑΣΙΛΕΩΣ ΔΗΜΗΤΡΙΟΥ in two lines on r., ΘΕΟΥ ΝΙΚΑΤΟΡΟΣ in two lines on l., Zeus enthroned l., resting on scepter and holding Nike, *inside legend, facing r. offering wreath to Zeus.*

SE 183

Group 1: Inner l., below Zeus's arm, ΔN; in exergue, ΓΠΡ. No *SC* number

Die A1

(Obv. link to P2–P6, below)

1.*	A1	P3	15.88	Sotheby (7 Dec. 1896 [Bunbury]), lot 545.

Obverse: Diademed head of Demetrius II r., bearded, *with hair combed smooth on crown of head,* diadem ends falling straight behind, fillet border.

Reverse: ΒΑΣΙΛΕΩΣ ΔΗΜΗΤΡΙΟΥ in two lines on r., ΘΕΟΥ ΝΙΚΑΤΟΡΟΣ in two lines on l., Zeus enthroned l., resting on scepter and holding Nike, *inside legend, facing r. offering wreath to Zeus.*

SE 183

Group 1: Inner l., below Zeus's arm, ΔN; in exergue, ΓΠΡ. *SC* 2179

Die A1'

(Obverse die link with P4–P6, below)

---

38 The coins are placed in order based on style, control marks, and dates. Die axes are 12 o'clock.

2.	A1	P1	16.68	Hirsch 21 (16 Nov. 1908 [Consul Weber]), lot 4110.
3.	A1	P1	16.43	Naville 10 (15 Jun. 1925), lot 1341.
4.	A1	P1	16.43	Superior (11 Jun. 1986 [Grove-Grover]), lot 1343.
5.*	A1	P2	16.50	New York, ANS 1944.100.77941; *LSM* 67d.
6.	A1	P2	16.77	Paris, inv. 1210A.
7.	A1	P3	16.60	Berlin, Lobbecke.

Group 2: Inner l., below Zeus's arm, ΝΔ; in exergue, ΓΠΡ. *SC* 2179

Die A1

(Obverse die link with P1–P3, above, and P5–P6, below)

| 8.* | A1 | P4 | No Wt. | Kricheldorf 34 (24 Jan. 1980), lot 205. |

SE 184

Group 1: Inner l., below Zeus's arm, ΝΔ; in exergue, ΔΠΡ. *SC* 2180

Die A1

(Obverse die link with P1–P4, above)

| 9.* | A1 | P5 | 15.03 | CNG E-auction 249 (9 Feb. 2011), lot 179. |
| 10. | A1 | P6 | 16.67 | Schulman 56 (26 Sep. 1904 [White-King]), lot 606; NFA 11 (8 Dec. 1982), lot 232; Naville 10 (15 Jun. 1925). |

Obverse: Diademed head of Demetrius II r., bearded, with tousled locks on crown of head and stubby horn at temple, diadem ends falling straight behind, fillet border.

Reverse: ΒΑΣΙΛΕΩΣ ΔΗΜΗΤΡΙΟΥ in two lines on r., ΘΕΟΥ ΝΙΚΑΤΟΡΟΣ in two lines on l., Zeus enthroned l., resting on scepter and extending r. hand through legend, holding Nike, who faces l., extending wreath toward edge of coin.

Group 1: Inner l., below Zeus's arm, ΝΔ; in exergue, ΔΠΡ. *SC* 2181.1

Die A2

(Obverse die link with P8, below)

| 11.* | A2 | P7 | 16.55 | Copenhagen, *SNG Copenhagen* 350. |
| 12. | A2 | P7 | 16.89 | NFA 21 (12 Oct. 1988), lot 501. |

Group 2: Under throne, ᚼ; in exergue, ΔΠΡ. *SC* 2181.2a

Die A2

(Obverse die link with P7, above)

13.*	A2	P8	No Wt.	Aurea (19 May 2012), lot 1373; CAN (7 Nov. 1987), lot 181.

Die A3

14.	A3	P9	16.60	Leu 83 (6 May 2002), lot 391.
15.	A3	P10	16.64	New York, ANS 1944.100.77942.
16.*	A3	P11	16.24	Glendining 12 (3 Oct. 1988), lot 770; Sotheby (30 Apr. 1956 [Haughton]), lot 236; Sotheby (19 Jan. 1914 [Cumberland Clark]), lot 280.

Die A4

(Obverse die link with P18, below)

17.	A4	P12	16.30	*LSM* 68d; London, *BMC* 12.
18.	A4	P12	16.63	Merzbacher (15 Nov. 1910), lot 829.
19.	A4	P12	16.51	Künker 182 (14 Mar. 2011), lot 346.
20.	A4	P13	16.58	Argenor (2 May 2006), lot 172.
21.*	A4	P13	15.89	New York, ANS 1908.115.10.
22.	A4	P14	15.85	Brussels, De Hirsch 1707.
23.	A4	P15	16.71	CNG E-auction 250 (23 Feb. 2011), lot 125.
24.	A4	P16	16.67	Freeman & Sear 9 (16 July 2003), lot 156.
25.	A4	P17	16.66	Peus 301 (25 May 1981), lot 477; Peus 300 (28 Oct. 1990), lot 158.

Group 3: Under throne, ᚼ̄; in exergue, ΔΠΡ. *SC* 2181.2b

Die A4

(Obverse die link with P12–P17, above)

26.	A4	P18	16.43	NFA 19 (18 Dec. 1987), lot 445.
27.	A4	P18	16.38	NFA 21 (12 Oct. 1988), lot 502.
28.*	A4	P18	16.43	NFA 31 (18 Mar. 1993), lot 284.

Die A5

(Reverse die link with A6, below)

29.	A5	P19	14.19	Leu 79 (31 Oct. 2000), lot 751; Hess-Leu 19 (12 Apr. 1962), lot 354.
30.*	A5	P19	16.69	Jerusalem, *SNG Spaer* 2266; MuM 32 (20 Oct. 1966), lot 148.
31.	A5	P19	16.00	Lanz Ebay (3 Nov. 2011), item 370553188222.
32.	A5	P20	16.63	GM 190 (11 Oct. 2010), lot 350; CNG 53 (15 Mar. 2000), lot 636; Spink America (7 Dec. 1995), lot 2181; Superior (11 Jun. 1986 [Grove-Grover]), lot 1341.
33.	A5	P20	16.32	New York, ANS 1944.100.77943.
34.	A5	P21	16.44	Berlin, inv. 84 1873.
35.	A5	P22	16.45	CNG 51 (15 Sep. 1999), lot 542.
36.	A5	P23	16.36	Hirsch 186 (10 May 1995), lot 528.
37.	A5	P24	16.69	GM 71 (3 May 1995), lot 409; GM 64 (11 Oct. 1993), lot 218.

Obverse: Diademed head of Demetrius II r., bearded, *with tousled locks on crown of head*, diadem ends falling straight behind, fillet border.

Reverse: ΒΑΣΙΛΕΩΣ ΔΗΜΗΤΡΙΟΥ in two lines on r., ΘΕΟΥ ΝΙΚΑΤΟΡΟΣ in two lines on l., Zeus enthroned l., resting on scepter and *extending r. hand through legend*, holding Nike, *who faces l., extending wreath toward edge of coin.*

Die A6

(Reverse die link with A5, above)

38.	A6	P24	16.30	Hirsch 177 (10 Feb. 1993), lot 423; Tkalec (23 Oct. 1992), lot 164.
39.*	A6	P25	16.68	CNG 87 (18 May 2011), lot 644.

Die A7

(Obverse die link with P29–P32 and P43–P45, below)

40.*	A7	P26	16.54	CNG 90 (23 May 2012), lot 685; NFA 23 (14 Dec. 1989), lot 682; Auctiones 5 (2 Dec. 1975), lot 205.
41.	A7	P26	16.52	*CSE* 2, 668.
42.	A7	P26	16.73	Hess Leu, 28 (5 May 1965), lot 277.

43.   A7   P26   16.05   Hirsch 184 (23 Nov. 1994), lot 345.

44.   A7   P26   No Wt.   Tartous Hoard, 16.

45.   A7   P27   16.59   GM 44 (3 Apr. 1989), lot 460; Hirsch 159 (21 Sep. 1988), lot 424.

46.   A7   P27   16.44   VCoins, NB Numismatics (12 July 2012), item GR1913.

47.   A7   P28   No Wt.   Tartous Hoard, 9.

SE 185

Group 1: Under throne, $\underset{\Delta}{N}$; in exergue, ΕΠΡ. *SC* 2181.3a

48.   16.46   Borrell, *NC* (1853): 43, no. 5.1 (No image).

Group 2: Under throne, $\underset{\Delta}{\bar{\bar{x}}}$; in exergue, ΕΠΡ. *SC* 2181.3b

Die A7

(Obverse die link with P26–P28, above, and P43–P45, below)

49.   A7   P29   16.42   Cambridge, McClean 9330.

50.   A7   P30   16.34   Naville 10 (15 Jun. 1925), lot 1344.

51.*   A7   P31   16.39   CNG 42 (29 May 1997), lot 563.

52.   A7   P31   16.21   Hirsch 195 (5 May 1997), lot 471; Hirsch 191 (24 Sep. 1996,) lot 701.

53.   A7   P32   16.32   CNG 87 (18 May 2011), lot 643. No date is on the coin, but the reverse die was engraved by the same engraver as P30 and P42.

54.   A7   P32   16.59   GM 107 (2 Apr. 2001), lot 267. No date is on the coin, but the reverse die was engraved by the same engraver as P30 and P42.

Die A8

55.*   A8   P33   16.50   New York Sale 17 (9 Jan. 2008), lot 110.

Die A9

56.*   A9   P34   16.49   Hirsch 157 (24 Feb. 1988), lot 182. Double-struck on the reverse only.

Group 3: Outer l., ⧉; under throne, ⧈; in exergue, ΕΠΡ. *SC* 2181.4

Die A10

(Obverse die link with P36–P39, below)

57.* A10 P35 16.65 Egger 46 (11 May 1914), lot 2464; *LSM* 71.

Group 4: Outer l., ⧉; under throne, ⧈; in exergue, ΕΠΡ. *SC* 2181.5

Die A10

(Obverse die link P35, above)

58. A10 P36 16.63 CNG 64 (29 Sep. 2003), lot 399.

59. A10 P36 16.40 Antikpat Ebay (22 July 2012), item 190703373832; CNG 85 (15 Sep. 2010), lot 496.

60.* A10 P36 16.49 CNG 90 (23 May 2012), lot 686.

61. A10 P36 16.28 Lanz 138 (26 Nov. 2007), lot 454.

62. A10 P36 15.52 Lancashire, *SNG Blackburn* (Hart Collection) 1066.

63. A10 P37 16.62 GM 58 (9 Apr. 1992), lot 475.

64. A10 P37 16.42 Cederlind 132 (4 Oct. 2004), lot 86; Peus 283 (14 May 1974), lot 143.

65. A10 P38 16.55 Hess-Divo 307 (8 Jun. 2007), lot 1323.

66. A10 P39 16.33 New York, ANS 1977.158.686.

Die A11

67. A11 P40 16.47 *SNG Berry* 1392.

68.* A11 P40 15.55 Künker 204 (12 Mar. 2012), lot 349; Hirsch 245 (4 May 2006), lot 253; Hirsch 220 (21 Feb. 2002), lot 1439.

69. A11 P40 16.73 MuM FPL 322 (Apr. 1971), lot 15.

70. A11 P41 16.56 *CSE* 839; *Numismatic Art and Ancient Coins* 2 (15 May 1981), lot 98.

71. A11 P41 16.44 GM 190 (11 Oct. 2010), lot 351; Cederlind 154 (3 Mar. 2010), lot 124.

72. A11 P42 16.15 Munch, DEM II, 19562M.

73. A11 P42 16.19 Paris, inv. 1206ay.

SE 186

Group 1: Under throne, $\bar{\bar{\Delta}}$; in exergue, ϚΠΡ. No *SC* number

Die A7

(Obverse die link with P26–P32)

74.	A7	P43	15.95	Berlin, inv. 238 1993 (Dpavel).
75.	A7	P43	15.89	Hirsch 175 (23 Sep. 1992), lot 510.
76.*	A7	P43	16.42	Peus 301 (25 May 1981), lot 478; Peus 297 (3 Apr. 1979), lot 118.
77.	A7	P44	16.53	CNG E-auction 129 (21 Dec. 2005), lot 161; CNG E-auction 22 (11 Feb. 2001), lot 61555.
78.	A7	P45	16.63	Tkalec Rauch (25 Apr. 1989), lot 174.

Group 3: Outer l., ⊠; under throne, ⋈; in exergue, ϚΠΡ. *SC* 2181.6

Die A11

(Obverse die link with P50–P56, below)

79.	A11	P46	15.54	Hirsch 196 (24 Sep. 1997), lot 420; Hirsch 191 (24 Sep. 1996), lot 702.
80.	A11	P46	16.21	Cederlind 145 (18 Dec. 2007), lot 94.
81.	A11	P47	16.60	Naville 7 (23 Jun. 1924), lot 1699.
82.	A11	P47	16.50	Sotheby (4 Apr. 1973 [Ward]), lot 680.
83.*	A11	P48	16.59	Künker 97 (7 Mar. 2005), lot 930; Glendining (21 Feb. 1961 [Lockett]), lot 2626; *SNG Lockett* 3171; Naville 10, 15 Jun. 1925, 1346.
84.	A11	P48	16.21	Paris, inv. Babelon 1210.
85.	A11	P49	16.09	New York, ANS 1944.100.77945.

Group 4: Outer l., ⋈; under throne, ⋈; in exergue, ϚΠΡ. *SC* 2181.7a

Die A11

(Obverse die link with P46–P49, above)

86.	A11	P50	16.58	Berk 115 (2 Aug. 2000), lot 302.
87.	A11	P50	16.55	CNG 72 (14 Jun. 2006), lot 953; Gemini I (11 Jan. 2005), lot 215; Superior 58 (11 Jun. 1986 [Grove-Grover]), lot 1342.

88.*	A11	P50	15.33	NAC "N" (26 Jun. 2003), lot 1384.
89.	A11	P51	16.17	Berlin, Lobbecke.
90.	A11	P51	No Wt.	Sotheby (3 July 1911), lot 265.
91.	A11	P52	16.36	Berlin, Lobbecke.
92.	A11	P53	16.51	Egger 20 (7 Jan. 1908), lot 627.
93.	A11	P54	16.39	Hirsch 172 (27 Nov. 1991), lot 330.
94.	A11	P55	16.68	Naville 10 (15 Jun. 1925), lot 1345.
95.*	A11	P56	15.06	Jerusalem, *SNG Spaer* 2267; Obverse obviously retooled in modern times (Newell, *LSM*, p. 50).

Die A12

96.*	A12	P57	16.61	*CSE* 840.
97.	A12	P57	15.13	Paris, DeClerq 206.
98.	A12	P58	No Wt.	Tartous Hoard, 1.
99.	A12	P58	16.59	Triton VII (13 Jan. 2004), lot 352; Triton V (15 Jan. 2002), lot 1503; Cons. 15 (4 May 1955), lot 174.
100.	A12	P59	16.58	New York, ANS 1944.100.77944.
101.	A12	P60	16.10	Manchester, *SNG Manchester* 1346; Naville 10 (15 Jun. 1925), lot 1347.

Group 5: Outer l., Ϻ; under throne, Ϯ; in exergue, ϚΠΡ. *SC* 2181.7b

Die A13

| 102.* | A13 | P61 | 16.24 | CNG 53 (15 Mar. 2000), lot 637; Palladium 18 (21 Aug. 1998); Palladium 10 (22 Nov. 1995), lot 133; Palladium 8 (7 Apr. 1995), lot 65. |

Die A14

(Obverse die link P65–P72, below)

103.	A14	P62	16.35	CNG 66 (19 May 2004), lot 692.
104.	A14	P62	16.36	NAC "B" (25 Feb. 1992), lot 1523; GM 52 (6 Nov. 1990), lot 377; MuM FPL 356 (May 1974), lot 12.
105.	A14	P62	16.40	New York, ANS 1948.19.2453.
106.	A14	P62	16.48	Jerusalem, *SNG Spaer* 2268.
107.	A14	P63	16.41	CNG 38 (6 Jun. 1996), lot 425.

108.   A14   P63   16.61   Gemini 6 (10 Jun. 2010), lot 234.

109.   A14   P63   16.15   MuM 36 (30 May 2012), lot 481.

110.   A14   P63   16.29   *SNG Von Post* 595.

111.   A14   P63   15.80   Sternberg 7 (24 Nov. 1977), lot 168.

112.*   A14   P64   15.59   Pegasi 8 (29 Apr. 2003), lot 181.

SE 187

Group 1: Outer l., ᛡ; under throne, Ᾰ; in exergue, ΖΠΡ. *SC* 2181.8

Die A14

(Obverse die link with P62–P64, above, and P71–P72, below)

113.   A14   P65   15.66   CNG 29 (30 Mar. 1994), lot 268.

114.*   A14   P65   16.54   Freeman & Sear 7 (22 Feb. 2002), lot 189.

115.   A14   P65   16.42   Paris, inv. 1210B, y601.

116.   A14   P66   16.35   MuM Deutschland 16 (19 May 2005), lot 996; Sotheby NY (21 Jun. 1990), lot 598.

117.   A14   P66   15.80   Paris, DeClerq 208.

118.   A14   P66   16.43   Pegasi 5 (4 Jun. 2001), lot 173.

119.   A14   P67   16.34   Naville 1 (4 Apr. 1921 [Pozzi]), lot 3005.

120.   A14   P67   16.45   Peus 299 (6 May 1980), lot 204; Peus 297 (3 Apr. 1979), lot 119.

121.   A14   P68   16.47   Brussels, De Hirsch 1708.

122.   A14   P69   16.48   New York, ANS 1948.19.2454.

123.*   A14   P70   16.21   Pegasi 11 (19 Oct. 2004), lot 193.

Group 2: Outer l., ⚹ above ᛡ; under throne, Ᾰ; in exergue, ΖΠΡ. *SC* 2181.9

Die A14

(Obverse die link with P65–P70, above, and P72, below)

124.*   A14   P71   16.33   CNG 79 (17 Sep. 2008), lot 422.

125.   A14   P71   16.52   *LSM* 76; London, *BMC* 16.

126.   A14   P71   10.70   New York, ANS 1977.158.687.

127.   A14   P71   11.82   Peus 304 (16 Mar. 1982), lot 157.

128.   A14   P71   16.67   Spink FPL (Oct. 2003), lot 1562.

Group 3: Outer l., ✣; under throne, Ĥ; in exergue, ZΠP. No *SC* number

Die A14

(Obverse die link with P65–P71)

129.* A14 P72 16.32 Auctiones 11 (30 Sep. 1980), lot 210.

Group 4: Outer l., ✣; under throne, H; in exergue, ZΠP. No *SC* number

Die A15

130.* A15 P73 15.66 CNG 32 (9 Dec. 1994), lot 204.

131. A15 P73 16.10 Lanz 52 (14 May 1990), lot 277.

Group 5: Outer l., ✣ above ; under throne, ✤;in exergue, ZΠP. *SC* 2181.10

Die A16

132. A16 P74 16.47 VCoins, NB Numismatics (July 2012), item GR1866; CNG 53 (15 Mar. 2000), lot 638; Palladium 9 (9 Aug. 1995), lot 161.

133.* A16 P74 16.25 Paris, DeClerq 209.

Die A17

134. A17 P75 16.39 *LSM* 77; Sotheby (15 Jun. 1896 [Bunbury]), lot 548.

135.* A17 P75 16.65 NAC "Q" (6 Apr. 2006), lot 1444.

Anomalous

136.* A9 16.50 Hirsch 171 (25 Sep. 1991), lot 431. ΘΕΟΥ is below Zeus's arm.

137. A10 16.33 GM 55 (14 May 1991), lot 344; GM 50 (24 Sep. 1990), 422 (Also listed as Antioch tetradrachm, Cat. No. 166). The obverse die is from Damascus and the neck does not extend as far below the fillet border as it should. The mule was made from a Damascus coin struck off-center and an Antioch coin.

| 138.* | | P12 | 15.86 | NFA 27, 4 Dec. 1991, 75. (Also listed as Antioch tetradrachm, Cat. No. 164). The obverse die is from Antioch and the reverse die is from Damascus. The mule was most likely made from casts of coins, and the letters near the spear and hand of Zeus were poorly transferred. |
| 139. | | P36 | 16.16 | Hirsch 281, 2 May 2012, 466; Hirsch 272, 4 May 291, 376 (Also listed as Antioch tetradrachm, Cat. No. 165). The obverse die is from Antioch and the reverse die is from Damascus. A modern mule was made from casts of coins, and the Nike was not well transferred. |

Annex: Inner l., below Zeus's legs, Δ; under throne, Ω; in exergue, ϚΠΡ *SC* 2173

Die A1

| 140.* | A1 | P1 | 16.71 | *CSE* 842. |
| 141. | A1 | P1 | 16.57 | *LSM* 73; London, *BMC* 15. |

Previous scholars have assigned this set of control marks to the Damascus mint for the year SE 186.[39] The obverse portrait is abnormal for the Damascus mint in that the hair is more neatly combed than is typical for the Damascus dies. A few locks of hair run along the top of the head in a manner that disqualifies the die as a work of the "smooth hair engraver." The reverse die is also inconsistent with the other Damascus dies. The primary control mark, Δ, is attested at Damascus, but it is also well attested at Antioch. This control mark is under the legs of Zeus, and this location is not used for control marks on any other die. The secondary control mark, Ω, is completely unknown at either the Antioch or Damascus mint under Demetrius II. *Seleucid Coins* tentatively attributes these coins to Seleucia in Pieria.[40]

ACKNOWLEDGEMENTS

I am very thankful to Oliver Hoover and Arthur Houghton, who helped me gather images of coins for the study and provided excellent, kind advice, encouragement, and guidance; Petr Vesely, who provided excellent guidance about statistics; Mary Lannin and Morten Andersen, who also helped gather images of coins; and the late Getzel Cohen, who read an earlier draft of this paper. Without their help, this project would not have been possible. I am responsible for any remaining mistakes and errors.

39 Newell 1939: 52; *CSE*: 83.
40 *SC* 2.1: 421.

REFERENCES

Bagnall, R. S. 1984. "An unrecognized date by the rebellion of 131 B.C." *ZPE* 56: 58–60.

Beweick, V., L. Cheek, and J. Ball. 2004. "Statistics review 10: Further nonparametric methods." *Critical Care* 8.3: 196–199.

Bouchier, E. S. 1921. *A short history of Antioch, 300 B.C.–A.D. 1268*. Oxford: Basil Blackwell.

Dürr, N. 1979. "Das Horn des Demetrios II." *SM* 29 (113): 7–9.

Ehling, K. 1998. "Seleukidische Geschichte zwischen 130 und 120 v. Chr." *Historia* 47.2: 141–151.

Esty, W. 2006. "How to estimate the original number of dies and the coverage of a sample." *NC* 166: 359–364.

Houghton, A. 1979. "The second reign of Demetrius II of Syria at Tarsus." *ANSMN* 24: 111–116.

———. 1984. "The Seleucid mint of Mallus and the cult figure of Athena Magarsia." In *Festschrift für Leo Mildenberg: Numismatik, Kunstgeschicte, Archäologie/ Studies in honor of Leo Mildenberg: Numismatics, art history, archaeology*, edited by A. Houghton, S. Hurter, P. Erhart Mottahedeh, and J. Ayer Scott, 91–110. Wetteren: Editions NR.

———. 2002. "The production of money by mints of the Seleucid core." In *Les monnayages syriens: Quell apport pour l'histoire du proche-orient hellénistique et Romain? Actes de la table ronde Damas, 10–12 novembre 1999*, edited by C. Augé and F. Duyrat, 5–9. Bibliothèque Archéologique et Historique 162. Beyrouth: Institut Francais d'Archéologie du Proche-Orient.

Newell, E. T. 1918. *The Seleucid mint of Antioch*. New York: American Numismatic Society.

———. 1939. "Late Seleucid mints in Ake-Ptolemais and Damascus." ANS NNM 84. New York: American Numismatic Society.

Ramsey, G. C. 2011. "Seleucid administration: Effectiveness and dysfunction among officials." In *Seleucid dissolution: The sinking of the anchor*, edited by K. Erickson and G. C. Ramsey, 37–49. Philippika 50. Wiesbaden: Harrassowitz.

Ramsey, G. C. and K. Erickson. 2011. "Introduction: The sinking of the anchor?" In *Seleucid dissolution: The sinking of the anchor*, edited by K. Erickson and G. C. Ramsey, 13–18. Philippika 50. Wiesbaden: Harrassowitz.

Shipley, G. 2000. *The Greek world after Alexander, 323–30 B.C.* London: Routledge.

AJN Second Series 28 (2016) pp. 105–158
© 2016 The American Numismatic Society

The Koinon of Athena Ilias and its Coinage

Plates 36–46   Aneurin Ellis-Evans*

This article presents the first die study of the coinage of the koinon of Athena Ilias, the evidence for which has doubled since the series was last catalogued in Alfred Bellinger's *Troy: The Coins* (1961). The new evidence confirms the longevity of the series (late 180s/early 170s–60s/50s BC) and suggests that the series was minted continually but at a low level of production throughout this period. It also provides an opportunity to revisit the question of the identity of the magistrate named on the reverse of the coins and the length of time they were in office, questions which have primarily been discussed in relation to the epigraphic evidence. It is argued that the purpose of the coinage was twofold: to provide the *agonothetai* who ran the festival with cash with which to make external payments and to act as a status symbol for the koinon's festival. The early dating of the series proposed here contributes to our understanding of the development of the phenomenon of civic spread-flan coinages in the mid-second century, while the late end date combined with the results of the die study provide an opportunity to look at the impact of the Mithradatic Wars on the finances of the koinon's cities.

* aneurin.ellis-evans@classics.ox.ac.uk.

1. INTRODUCTION

The koinon of Athena Ilias was a confederation of cities centred on the Troad which collectively administered the annual *Panathenaia* festival in honor of Athena Ilias form the last decade of the fourth century down to at least the late first century AD.[1] This major regional festival has left no trace whatsoever in the surviving literary sources for the Hellenistic period and is instead only known to us through a rich epigraphic dossier and an impressive silver coinage. The epigraphic evidence illuminates particular moments in the koinon's history, for example the circumstances of its creation in the last decade of the fourth century, its institutions and finances in the late third century, and the same in the very different circumstances of the first century BC. Cumulatively, these documents illustrate a high degree of continuity in the institutional structure of the koinon throughout the Hellenistic period. The koinon's coinage of silver tetradrachms (the drachms and didrachms of the series are late and few) were minted throughout most of the second century and in the first half of the first century BC and have the potential to provide us with a continuous narrative of the koinon's fortunes in the mid- to late Hellenistic period.

It has been over fifty years since Alfred Bellinger's *Troy: The Coins* (1961) catalogued the coins minted by the koinon of Athena Ilias.[2] Since then, our understanding of the institutions of the koinon has been significantly advanced first by Louis Robert's book-length review of Bellinger, more recently in a wide-ranging article by Denis Knoepfler, and now by a new contribution on the finances of the koinon by François Lefèvre and William Pillot.[3] In all three cases, the focus has been on reinterpreting the epigraphy in order to better understand the koinon's institutions. This approach has made a substantial contribution to our understanding of the coins, in particular regarding the identification of the minting authority (the koinon of Athena Ilias, not the city of Ilion) and the identity of the magistrate named in the exergue on the reverse (the Ilian president of the koinon's board of *agonothetai*). More generally, this approach has succeeded in embedding the production of the coinage in its institutional context, as well as suggesting potential prosopographical links with literary and epigraphic texts.

The progress which has been made in understanding the epigraphic evidence has not, however, been matched by a reevaluation of the numismatic evidence, which in the time since Bellinger's publication has increased significantly. To the 56 examples of the series known to Bellinger we can now add 55 more which have either appeared since 1961 or were overlooked in the original publication,

1 All dates are BC unless otherwise stated. For the shift to the administration of the *Panathenaia* by Ilion alone in the second/third century AD see n. 59.

2 For earlier treatments see von Fritze (1902: 2.481–482, 505–506) and Regling (1928: 118–123).

3 Robert 1966; Knoepfler 2010; Lefèvre and Pillot 2015.

doubling the total number of specimens to 111. As a result, whereas Bellinger catalogued 33 magistrates (and was aware of a possible 34th), 47 are now attested (and possibly a 48th).[4] We can also add six hoards to the two known to Bellinger which help us date ten of the magistrates (16 if we include the magistrates die linked to these). In addition, there are of course numerous new die links which help with the establishment of a relative chronology. This substantially enlarged body of numismatic evidence provides an opportunity to test, critique, and build upon the arguments of those who have primarily approached the koinon from the perspective of its epigraphic evidence.

2. CATALOGUE[5]

Obverse: Head of Athena r. in wreathed, triple-crested helmet.

Reverse: Athena Ilias advancing r. on ground line, distaff in l. hand, spear held above shoulder in r. hand (fillets sometimes attached to distaff, more often to spear), wearing a kalathos on her head and dressed in a peplos; <LF and RF> ΑΘΗΝΑΣ | ΙΛΙΑΔΟΣ written vertically; <EX> magistrate's name in the genitive.[6]

Hegesidemos (1)

Ref. None.
Rev. <EX> ΗΓΗΣΙΔΗΜΟΥ, <RF> owl.

O1	R1	16.48	GM 207 (15/10/2012), lot 289.
O1	R1	16.39	Pecunem 26 (14/12/2014), lot 192—Poor condition.

Antiphanes (1)

Ref. Regling 1, Bellinger T 37, Knoepfler 2.
Rev. <EX> ΑΝΤΙΦΑΝΟΥ, <RF> owl.

---

4 I am counting Philokles and Philon as a single magistrate on the assumption that they served a single term of office together. The 34th magistrate would have been Hermippos son of Menophanes: Bellinger 1961: 35; Robert 1966: 58, n. 1; Knoepfler 2010: 53, n. 89. For the possible 48th magistrate see n. 13.

5 Abbreviations: Von Fritze = 1902: 2.481–482; Regling = 1928: 119–123; Bellinger = 1961; Knoepfler = 2010: 52–53. It is a pleasure to thank the following curators for their help: Ute Wartenberg (New York), Bernhard Weisser (Berlin), Amelia Dowler (London), Klaus Vondrovec (Vienna), Helle Horsnaes (Copenhagen), Julien Olivier (Paris), Stefan Krmnicek (Tübingen), and Dimitra Tsangari (Alpha Bank). In addition, Catharine Lorber kindly provided photos of *CH* X 301.136–139. In compiling the catalogue I made use of the auction catalogue collection in the Sackler Library (Oxford) and the photo files of sale catalogues at the Institut für Numismatik und Geldgeschichte (Vienna), the British Museum (London), and the American Numismatic Society (New York).

6 Lacroix 1949: 103–112.

O2   R2   13.45   [*IGCH* 1774.71 (Babylon, Iraq, 1900), c. 155–150] Berlin,
                     18252144—Poor condition.

O2   R3   16.69   Coll. Gulbenkian (1989) 962 = Coll. Jameson (1924) 3.
                     2231.

O2   R4   16.77   *SNG Ashmolean* 1159 = Glendining (21/2/1961) 2212 =
                     SNG Lockett 2738 = Naville 1 (4/4/1921), lot 2275 (S. Pozzi)

Athenokles[7]

Ref. None.
Rev. <EX> ΑΘΗΝΟΚΛΕΟΥΣ, <RF> owl.

O2   R5   16.45   *CH* X 301.136 ('Demetrius I', Commerce, 2003; pre-151).

O2   R5   16.81   [*CH* IV 55 (Near East, Commerce, 1977), pre-160] BM
                     1977,0704.2.

Iphiades[8]

Ref. None.
Rev. <EX> ΙΦΙΑΔΟΥ, <RF> owl.

O2   R6   16.84   Tübingen, Inv. 16248 = Brandt & Sonntag (Oct. 1996) =
                     UBS 41 (10/9/1996), lot 67 = UBS 26 (22/1/1991), lot 11.

Thersandros

Ref. Bellinger T 38, Knoepfler 3.
Rev. <EX> ΘΕΡΣΑΝΔΡΟΥ, <RF> owl.

O2   R7   16.83   Adolph Hess 253 (8/3/1983), lot 224 = Bourgey (5/12/
                     1932), lot 213 (H. Gallice).

Xanthippos

Ref. Regling 11, Bellinger T 36, Knoepfler 1.
Rev. <EX> ΞΑΝΘΙΠΠΟΥ, <RF> owl.

7 Otherwise unattested at Ilion, but a possible restoration of *I. Ilion* 64.41–42 (third/
second century list of new citizens): Μητρόδ[ωρος | —]νοκλείους. Frisch (*I. Ilion*, p. 162)
instead suggests [Agath]okles.

8 This rare name is attested five times at Abydos between the mid-fifth and early first
century (*LGPN VA*, s.v. 1–5) and once at Parion in a recently discovered Hellenistic epitaph
(P. Hamon, *BE* [2015], no. 593). The individuals from Abydos may all belong to the same
family: Robert 1967: 24–25. The magistrate named on this issue of the koinon could be
related to the Iphiades who was one of two ambassadors sent to negotiate with Philip V
during the siege of Abydos in 200: Plb. 16.30.7. Since the magistrate named in exergue
was always an Ilian citizen (see section 4.6), this would imply intermarriage between elite
families of Ilion and Abydos.

O2   R8   15.32   [*IGCH* 1544.42 (Latakia, Syria, 1759), pre-160] BNF Fonds
Général 683 (Mionnet 2.658, no. 190)—Poor condition,
part of flan chipped off.

Metriketes

Ref. Regling 10, Bellinger T 39, Knoepfler 4.
Rev. <EX> MHTPIKETOY, <LF> ⋈, <RF> owl.

O2   R9   16.87   CNG 102 (18/5/2016), lot 399 = Cederlind 181
(16/12/2015), lot 80 = GM 207 (15/10/2012), lot 287.

O2   R9   16.78   GM 207 (15/10/2012), lot 288.

O2   R10   16.84   Gerhard Hirsch 275 (22/9/2011), lot 3736 = GM 104
(9/10/2000), lot 370.

O2   R10   16.77   BNF Fonds Général 688 = Coll. Waddington 1150.

O3   R11   16.71   Gemini 11 (12/1/2014), lot 165 = LHS Numismatik 95 (25/10/2005), lot 657 = H. J. Berk Buy or Bid 118
(17/1/2001), lot 175 = Bank Leu 79 (31/10/2000), lot 633 =
Gitta Kastner 10 (18/5/1976), lot 50.

O?   R?   15.35   (not illustrated) Sotheby, Wilkinson & Hodge (7/12/1896),
lot 124 (E. Bunbury)—"Much oxydized".[9]

Akkos[10]

Ref. Regling 4, Bellinger T 45, Knoepfler 7.
Rev. <EX> AKKOY, <LF> ⋈, <RF> owl.

O3   R12   16.95   GM 224 (13/10/2014), lot 229.

O3   R12   13.52   [*IGCH* 1774.73 (Babylon, Iraq, 1900), c. 155–150] Berlin,
18252272—Poor condition.

O4   R13   15.64   CNG 53 (15/3/2000), lot 434 = CNR 19.4 (1994), lot 67.

O5   R14   16.28   Coll. Norman Davis (1969), 202 = Hesperia Art Bulletin
11 (1959), lot 45.

9 The catalogue entry reads: "Ilium, Tetradrachm, similar type to the preceding coin
[= see under Menephron son of Menephron below], but of more spread fabric [the Paris
example of Metriketes is 37 mm, whereas the Menephron son of Menephron coins are 28–
34 mm], and on rev. owl before Athena, and magistrate's name . . THKETOY, wt. 237 grs.
[= 15.35 g], much oxydized, rare." The two unread letters will be MH. Mistakenly reading H
for PI is an understandable error to make on a poorly preserved coin.

10 Previously read as Ἀ[ρέ]ου on the severely degraded example in the Babylon Hoard,
but rightly doubted by Robert (1966) 78 n. 3, 121 n. 3, and 133. Correct reading and
discussion of name in Robert (1967: 119-123). Still "très incertaine" and "indéchiffrable" in
Knoepfler (2010) 52 n. 84, 55.

Metrodoros

Ref. C. Boehringer, *SNR* 54 (1975): 46–47, no. 95.
Rev. \<EX\> ΜΗΤΡΟΔΩΡΟΥ, \<LF\> ⊠, \<RF\> owl.

O6	R15	15.63	ANS 1977.158.305 (R. F. Kelley, acq. Istanbul, 1952).[11]
O6	R15	16.63	NAC 54 (24/3/2010), lot 109.
O6	R15	16.75	Ponterio & Associates (16/8/2011), lot 21525 = Stack's (18/8/2009), lot 4132 = idem (22/4/2009), lot 1114 = Numismatica Genevensis 5 (2/12/2008), lot 111 = Christie's, New York 7718 (12/6/1993), lot 43 = MM Basel Liste 432 (Apr. 1981), lot 10—Obverse double struck.

Rev. \<LF\> ⊠.

O6	R16	16.85	[*CH* IX 530 (Ordu, Turkey, 1970), c. 150] MM Basel 53 (29/11/1977), lot 93.
O6	R17	16.16	MM Basel 37 (5/12/1968), lot 210.[12]

Eudemos

Ref. None.
Rev. \<EX\> ΕΥΔΗΜΟΥ, \<LF\> ⊠, \<RF\> owl.

O6	R18	16.78	Lanz 158 (5/6/2014), lot 239.[13]

Phoinix

Ref. None.
Rev. \<EX\> ΦΟΙΝΙΚΟΣ, \<LF\> ⧉ (above), eight-pointed star (below), \<RF\> owl.

O6	R19	16.69	Künker 236 (7/10/2013), lot 81 = Triton 11 (7/1/2008), lot 215.

11 In a letter dated 28/9/1952, the Istanbul dealer Nicolas Avgheris offers Kelley this and five other coins, writing, "Je viens de retourné d'un petit voyage d'Anatolie, où j'ai acheté quelques pièces rares qui peuvent vous intéresser je vous remets ci-joint les empreintes" (Kelley Correspondence, ANS).

12 This may have appeared earlier in the year as the unidentified coin in E. Bourgey FPL (March 1968), lot 124.

13 Between EY and MOY a longer series of about four letters has been incompletely scratched out and replaced with ΔH. In the upper left space of the line after EY there is the beginning of a letter, and the efforts to conceal what comes to its right suggests there may have been a crossbar here. Before MOY, there are traces of an epsilon that bear comparison with the one at the name's beginning. Considering the options listed in *LGPN*, I would suggest that the name which ΕΥΔΗΜΟΥ replaced may have been ΕΥΠ[ΟΛ]ΕΜΟΥ. A Eupolemos son of Poseidonios is the Ilian *agonothetes* in *I. Ilion* 5 (late third century). If correct, we should expect an issue of Eupolemos with the O6 die to turn up in the future.

Dionysodoros

Ref. Regling 6–7, Bellinger T 41–42, Knoepfler 5.
Rev. <EX> ΔΙΟΝΥΣΟΔΩΡΟΥ, <LF> ⋈, <RF> owl.

| O7 | R20 | 14.35 | [*IGCH* 1774.74 (Babylon, Iraq, 1900), c. 155–150] Berlin, 18252273–Poor condition, reverse double struck. |

Rev. <LF> ⋈.

| O8 | R21 | 13.01 | [*IGCH* 1774.75 (Babylon, Iraq, 1900), c. 155–150] Berlin, 18252274–Poor condition. |

Apemantos

Ref. Regling 2, Bellinger T 43–44, Knoepfler 6.
Rev. <EX> ΑΠΗΜΑΝΤΟΥ, <LF> ⋈, <RF> owl.

| O8 | R22 | 16.82 | The Hague. |

Rev. <LF> ⋈.

O8	R23	16.72	BNF Fonds Général 680 (Mionnet 2.657, no. 186).
O9	R24	16.90	[CH X 308.C222 (Gaziantep, Turkey, 1994), pre-Aug./ Oct. 143] Alpha Bank, Inv. 5128 = *NCirc* 103.2 (Mar. 1995), lot 882 = Spink 106 (11/10/1994), lot 62.
O10	R24	16.89	UBS 55 (16/9/2002), lot 1731.

Rev. <LF> ⋈.

| O11 | R25 | 16.95 | MM Basel Liste 525 (Sep. 1989), lot 16 = Auctiones Basel 17 (7/6/1988), lot 212 = MM Basel Liste 483 (Nov./ Dec. 1985), lot 34. |

Antiphanes (2)

Ref. Bellinger T 53, Knoepfler 16.
Rev. <EX> ΑΝΤΙΦΑΝΟΥ, <LF and RF> ΚΛΕ–ΩΝΟΣ, <RF> owl.

| O12 | R26 | 16.38 | Védrines (29/12/1984), lot 53 = Auctiones Basel 8 (27/6/1978), lot 233 = *SNG von Aulock* 1521. |
| O12 | R27 | 16.85 | Künker 262 (13/3/2015), lot 7168. |

Zoilos

Ref. von Fritze 16, Regling 8, Bellinger T 52, Knoepfler 15.
Rev. <EX> ΖΩΙΛΟΥ, <LF and RF> ΚΛΕ–ΩΝΟΣ, <LF> winged caduceus (below), <RF> owl (below).

O12   R28   16.02   [*CH* X 301.138 ('Demetrius I', Commerce, 2003), pre-151] Stack's (11/10/2010), lot 150 (C. Vermeule) = CNG 66 (19/5/2004), lot 429.

O12   R29   16.79   [*CH* X 301.139 ('Demetrius I', Commerce, 2003), pre-151] Gemini 1 (11/1/2005), lot 153.

O12   R29   17.03   CNG 91 (19/9/2012), lot 249 = CNG 70 (21/9/2005), lot 205.

O12   R30   16.69   NAC, Auction P (12/5/2005), lot 1505.

O12   R30   16.60   BM BNK,G.1153 (*BMC Troas* 58,10; acq. 1877).

Soterides

Ref. Regling 12, Bellinger T 50, Knoepfler 14.
Rev. <EX> ΣΩΤΗΡΙΔΟΥ, <LF> ⊠ (above), Gorgon's head (below), <RF> owl.

O13   R31   15.89   BM 1979,0101.281 = *SNG von Aulock* 1520.

O13   R31   16.78   Spink 196 (24/9/2008), lot 11 = Bank Leu 15 (4/5/1976), lot 284.

O13   R31   15.47   NAC, Auction H (30/4/1998), lot 1354.

Rev. <LF> ⊠ (above).

O13   R32   15.89   Berlin, 18252275 (A. Löbbecke, 1906)—Poor condition.

Apollodoros

Ref. Regling 3, Bellinger T 48, Knoepfler 8.
Rev. <EX> ΑΠΟΛΛΟΔΩΡΟΥ, <LF> ⊠ (above), caduceus (below), <RF> owl.

O14   R33   16.69   *CH* X 301.137 ('Demetrius I', Commerce, 2003; pre-151).

O14   R34   14.90   Berlin, 18252271 (F. Imhoof-Blumer, 1900)—Poor condition.[14]

O15   R35   15.04   [*IGCH* 1774.72 (Babylon, Iraq, 1900), c. 155–150] Berlin, 18252160–Poor condition.

O16   R36   16.81   Bank Leu 36 (7/5/1985), lot 148.

Demetrios (1)

Ref. None.
Rev. <EX> ΔΗΜΗΤΡΙΟΥ, <LF> ⊠, owl, <RF> ship's prow.

14 Counted twice by Bellinger (the second time as T 49a).

O17 R37 16.74 CGB.fr 47 (19/3/2011), lot 103.

Euboulides

Ref. Bellinger T 49, Knoepfler 9.
Rev. <EX> ΕΥΒΟΥΛΙΔΟΥ, <LF> 🐂 (above), caduceus (below), <RF> owl.

O18 R38 16.87 ANS 1945.33.5.

O19 R39 16.85 GM 164 (17/3/2008), lot 178 = Lanz 123 (30/5/2005),
lot 225 = CNG 67 (22/9/2004), lot 651 = NFA 29
(13/8/1992), lot 130 = Sotheby's New York (21/6/1990),
lot 474 = Bank Leu 20 (25/4/1978), lot 121.

O19 R40 16.74 Triton 1 (2/12/1997), lot 523.

Lysikles

Ref. Bellinger T 51, Knoepfler 12.
Rev. <EX> ΛΥΣΙΚΛΕΙΟΥ, <LF> $\widehat{\Sigma Y}$ (above), small eight-pointed star (below), <RF>
crested helmet (above), owl (below).

O20 R41 15.90 CGB.fr 51 (17/11/2011), lot 178 = Giessener
Münzhandlung 46 (30/10/1989), lot 229 = Leu 45
(26/05/1988), lot 205 = Hess-Leu 45 (12/5/1970), lot
251 = *SNG von Aulock* 1522—Poor condition.

O20 R41 16.00 BNF 1984.1053 = Banque Populaire du Nord &
Nomisma 32 (June 1984), lot 114 = Kircheldorf 14
(7/7/1964), lot 105 = Hesperia Art Bulletin 23 (1962),
lot 53 = MM Basel Liste 131 (Jan. 1954), lot 36—Poor
condition.[15]

Protokleides

Ref. Bellinger T 46, Knoepfler 11.
Rev. <EX> ΠΡΩΤΟΚΛΕΙΔΟΥ, <LF> $\widehat{\Sigma Y}$, <RF> palm branch (above), owl (below).

O20 R42 16.68 BNF 1973.1.142 (H. Seyrig)—Poor condition.

Rev. <LF> $\widehat{\Sigma Y}$ (above), small eight-pointed star (below).

O20 R43 16.34 Coll. Zhuyuetang (2004) 42 = Leu Numismatik 83
(6/5/2002), lot 292 = NAC 7 (1/3/1994), lot 236 = idem
4 (27/2/1991), lot 138.

O20 R43 16.86 NFA 32 (10/6/1993), lot 69.

15 Presumably, this is the "other specimen in a dealer's hands" referred to in Bellinger
1958: 13 and 1961: 25.

O20   R44   16.48   Boston, MFA 1988.257 = NFA 20 (9/3/1988), lot 715.

Dionysios

Ref. von Fritze 17, Regling 5, Bellinger T 40, Knoepfler 30.
Rev. <EX> ΔΙΟΝΥΣΙΟΥ, <LF> ⋈, <RF> winged Nike holding palm branch facing r.

O21   R45   16.71   BNF Fonds Général 686 = Coll. Waddington 1148.

Hermokreon

Ref. None.
Rev. <EX> ΕΡΜΟΚΡΕΟΝΤΟΣ, <LF> ⏃ (above), Athena Ilias with spear and distaff (below), <RF> owl.

O22   R46   16.93   [Malko   Tarnovo,   Bulgaria,   1968?][16]   UBS   33 (20/9/1993), lot 284 = Poindessault (30/5/1979), lot G23 = MM Basel Liste 404 (Sep. 1978), lot 8.

Melantas

Ref. Regling 9, Bellinger T 47, Knoepfler 10.

Rev. <EX> ΜΕΛΑΝΤΟΥ, <LF> ⌗ (above), caduceus (below), <RF> owl.

O23   R47   16.44   BM 1936,0504.1 (*NC* [1937] 245, no. 19; T. O. Mabbott) = Leo Hamburger 92 (11/6/1930), lot 311 (Niklovitz, Budapest) = Coll. Jameson (1913) 1.1456 = Feuardent (9/6/1913), lot 274.

Prytanis

Ref. None.
Rev. <EX> ΠΡΥΤΑΝΙΔΟΣ, <LF> winged thunderbolt, <RF> ⍒.

O24   R48   16.73   Peus 332 (23/10/1991), lot 187.

Menephron[17]

Ref. von Fritze 18, Regling 15, Bellinger T 79, Knoepfler 18.
Rev. <EX> ΜΕΝΕΦΡΟΝΟΣ, <LF> ⋈, <RF> palm branch.

---

16 For this possibility see n. 33.
17 Very likely to be the father of Menephron son of Menephron (see below): Kraft 1962: 240; Guépin 1969: 212; Knoepfler 2010: 56.

O25   R49   16.76   Berlin, 18252277 (F. Imhoof-Blumer, 1900) = Rollin & Feuardent (27/5/1889), lot 81 (M. le Comte de Duchâtel).

Melanippides

Ref. von Fritze 19, Regling 14, Bellinger T 80–81, Knoepfler 19.
Rev. <EX> ΜΕΛΑΝΙΠΠΙΔΟΥ, <LF> ⋈ (above), palm branch (below), <RF> bull suspended from post.[18]

O25   R50   16.37   Winterthur 2.2744 (O. Bernhard, F. Imhoof-Blumer, 1952) = A. Ladé 19 (Apr. 1902), lot 1359.

Rev. <LF> owl (below).

O26   R51   16.23   Berlin, 18252276 (A. von Prokesch-Osten, 1875)— Center of reverse chipped away.

O27   R52   16.10   BNF Fonds Général 687 = Coll. Waddington 1149— Pierced.

Diopeithes son of Zenis

Ref. Regling 19–20, Bellinger T 93, Knoepfler 21.
Rev. <EX> ΔΙΟΠΕΙΘΟΥΣ | ΤΟΥ ΖΗΝΙΔΟΣ, <LF> ⋈, <RF> winged Nike holding wreath facing r. above ship's prow.

O27   R53   16.67   Künker 94 (27/9/2004), lot 1028 = Müller 18 (23/9/1976), lot 99—Poor condition.

O27   R53   16.45   Berlin, 18252281 = Schlessinger 13 (4/2/1935), lot 1205 (Hermitage) = Yakunovich 1909: 33, pl. 5.66.[19]

Rev. <RF> Athena facing r.

O27   R54   16.61   *SNG Munich* 218 (Mionnet 2.658, no. 187; E.-M. Cousinéry).

18 For this method of sacrifice in the cult of Athena Ilias and its representation on Ilion's Roman provincial coinage see von Fritze (1902: 2, 514-516), Brückner (1902: 2, 563–566), and Bellinger (1961: 31, 54).

19 Regling (1928: 122) has a reference to "Jakuntschikoff, Zapisok imp. russ. arch. obsch. 1908, Taf. V 66". As Kienast (1959–1960: 239) and Robert (1966: 80 n. 6) noticed, this is missing from Bellinger 1958 and 1961. Robert thought the coin might be the Munich example. In fact, Regling's reference is to a lecture given to the Russian Archaeological Society in 1908 by Boris Mihailovich Yakunovich (1859–after 1917) about his private collection. It was published in St. Petersburg as a pamphlet, *Neizdannye i redkie drevne-grecheskie monety* [*Unpublished and Rare Ancient Greek Coins*], and as an article in *Zapiski*

Kallisthenes

Ref. None.
Rev. <EX> ΚΑΛΛΙΣΘΕΝΟΥΣ, <LF> ⨎, <RF> ear of corn.

O28   R55   16.78   Giessener Münzhandlung 97 (11/10/1999), lot 350 = Gerhard Hirsch 204 (5/5/1999), lot 334.

Metronax son of Hippodamas

Ref. None.
Rev. <EX> ΜΗΤΡΩΝΑΚΤΟΣ ΤΟΥ | ΙΠΠΟΔΑΜΑΝΤΟΣ, <LF> ⨎, <RF> Tyche facing l. holding cornucopia.

O29   R56   16.86   CNG 97 (17/9/2014), lot 163.

Sostratos

Ref. Regling 16, Bellinger T 95, Knoepfler 23.
Rev. <EX> ΣΟΣΤΡΑΤΟΥ, <LF> ⨎, <RF> wreath.

O29   R57   16.40   BNF Fonds Général 684 (Mionnet 2.658, no. 191).

Hermippos son of Menophanes

Ref. Bellinger p. 35, Knoepfler 24.
Rev. <EX> ΕΡΜΙΠΠΟΥ ΤΟΥ | ΜΗΝΟΦΑΝΟΥ, <LF> ⨎, <RF> wreath.

O29   R58   –   *Hesperia Art Bulletin* 16 (June 1961), lot 35—Weight not given.

Theokydes

Ref. Regling 13, Bellinger T 94, Knoepfler 22.
Rev. <EX> ΘΕΟΚΥΔΟΥ, <LF> ⨎, <RF> horse facing r.

O29   R59   17.04   ANS 1944.100.43909 (E. T. Newell) = Naville 5 (18/6/1923), lot 2486 = Rodolfo Ratto (26/4/1909), lot 3687 (W. Fröhner)—Poor condition.

numizmaticheskogo otdeleniya Russkogo arkheologicheskogo obshchestva [*Notes of the Numismatic Department of the Russian Imperial Archaeological Society*] 1.2–3 (1909): 7–59. The publication cross-references the example in Mionnet from Cousinéry's collection, confirming that it is not the same coin. Yakunovich was shot and his collection confiscated sometime after being dismissed from his government post by the Bolsheviks on December 14, 1917. His collection ended up at the Hermitage before parts of it (including this coin) were sold off at the Schlessinger sale in Berlin. I am grateful to Georgy Kantor for helping me track down this publication and for translating the Russian.

Menephron son of Menephron

Ref. Regling 21–23, Bellinger T 96–99, Knoepfler 25.
Rev. <EX> ΜΕΝΕΦΡΟΝΟΣ ΤΟΥ | ΜΕΝΕΦΡΟΝΟΣ, <LF> ᛗ, <RF> spider.[20]

O29	R60	16.25	BM 1841,B.2596 (*BMC Troas* 58,13; T. Burgon).
O29	R60	16.24	BNF Fonds Général 689 (Mionnet 2.658, no. 189).
O29	R61	–	Malloy 9 (9/5/1977) 122—Broken and worn, weight not given.

Rev. <LF> ᛗ, <RF> winged horse drinking l.

O29	R62	15.72	BM RPK,p130A.1.Ili (*BMC Troas* 58,12; R. Payne Knight, 1824).
O29	R62	16.66	Kölner Münzkabinett 87 (25/4/2007), lot 16 = idem 85 (10/5/2006), lot 35 = Sotheby's Zurich (27/10/1993), lot 602 = MM Basel Liste 427 (Nov. 1980), lot 16 = Seaby 723 (Nov. 1978), lot C1094 = MM Basel 53 (29/11/1977), lot 94 = *SNG von Aulock* 7604.
O29	R62	16.54	ANS 1944.100.43910 (E. T. Newell).
O29	R62	16.67	BNF Fonds Général 682 (Mionnet 2.658, no. 188).
O29	R62	16.58	Berlin, 18252294 (C. R. Fox, 1873) = S. Leigh Sotheby (31/7/1848), lot 893 (Earl of Pembroke; cf. *Numismatum Antiquorum in Musaeo Pembrochiano* [1746] II, Table 45).
O29	R62	16.62	Berlin, 18252289 (acq. from Rollin & Feuardent, 1872).
O29	R62	16.62	*SNG Copenhagen* 363 = Katalog. *Auktionen i Brygger Dr. phil. Carl Jacobsens Dødsbo* (26/11/1914), lot 112.
O29	R62	16.70	A. E. Cahn 60 (2/7/1928), lot 795 (Osman Nouri Bey).
O29	R62	16.35	Coll. McClean 3.7828 = Jacob Hirsch 14 (27/11/1905), lot 510 (F. Merkens).

20 There is a long history of misidentifying the animal on T 96 as a fly (Wroth, *BMC Troas* p. 58, no. 13), an ant (Bellinger 1961: 33), or even a bee (de Callataÿ 1997: 291). However, it is quite clearly a spider: it has no wings, eight legs (not six), and two *tagmata* (not three). The choice of image perhaps alludes to Arachne, a particularly appropriate myth for this cult of Athena given its focus on weaving. The cult image of Athena Ilias which appears on both the coins and stamped onto loom weights and spindle whorls dedicated in the sanctuary in the fourth century show her holding a distaff and spindle in her left hand: Wallrodt 2002; Rose 2014: 56, 153.

O29 R62 16.72 Triton 8 (11/1/2005), lot 389 = NFA 25 (29/11/1990), lot 128 = NFA 20 (10/3/1988), lot 716 = Sternberg 9 (15/11/1979), lot 36.

O29 R62 16.13 Boston, MFA 1.1629 (E. P. Warren, 1901).

O?   R?   16.39 (not illustrated) Sotheby, Wilkinson & Hodge (7/12/1896), lot 123 (E. Bunbury)—Perhaps the same as Coll. McClean 3.7828?

Rev. <LF> ⫙, <RF> wreath.

O30 R63 15.93 *SNG Copenhagen* 362 = Sotheby, Wilkinson & Hodge (11/7/1877), lot 261 (D. Dundas)—Pierced.

Demophon son of Dionys[?]

Ref. Regling 18, Bellinger T 92, Knoepfler 20.
Rev. <EX> ΔΗΜΟΦΩΝΤΟΣ | ΤΟΥ ΔΙΟΝΥΣ[?], <LF> ⫙, <RF> wreath.

O30 R64 16.77 Berlin, 18252280 (A. Löbbecke, 1906).[21]

Demetrios (2)

Ref. Bellinger T 119, Knoepfler 29.
Rev. <EX> ΔΗΜΗΤΡΙΟΥ, <LF> ⫙.

oA   rA   2.50 Berlin, 18252278 = Jacob Hirsch 25 (29/11/1909), lot 1917 (G. Philipsen)—Top and one side of flan missing.

Philokles and Philon

Ref. Bellinger T 55, Knoepfler 17.
Rev. <EX> ΦΙΛΟΚΛΕΟΥΣ | ΚΑΙ ΦΙΛΩΝΟΣ, <LF> ⫙, <RF> ΥΛΛ . Ν (?).[22]

O31 R65 15.33 ANS 1953.54.14—Large crack obscures legend in right field.

Hegesidemos (2) son of Diophanes

Ref. Bellinger T 54, Knoepfler 34.
Rev. <EX> ΗΓΗΣΙΔΗΜΟΥ | ΤΟΥ ΔΙΟΦΑΝΟΥ, <LF> ⫙, <RF> owl above palm branch.

21 The die link with Bellinger's T 99 was first spotted by Kraft (1962: 240). It is difficult to see in Bellinger's plates, but perfectly clear on the coins themselves (the shared die faults, e.g., across the bottom of the helmet plume and leading away from the chin, clinch it).

22 Robert 1966: 79 n. 1: "Je ne les lis ni ne les comprends". Bellinger (1961: 25, 27) read the penultimate letter as *omega*, but this does not fit the traces. The other readings are secure. A solution to what is written in the right field will have to await a second example of the issue.

O32   R66   13.83   Paunov 2013: 282–285 (Georgi Dobrevo, Bulgaria, 2000;
                        c. 55–40)—Bottom corner of flan broken.

Rev. <LF> 𐅆.

O32   R67   16.26   ANS 1967.152.422 (E. T. Newell).

Hippodamas

Ref. Bellinger T 58, Knoepfler 28.
Rev. <EX> ΙΠΠΟΔΑΜ|ΑΝΤΟΣ, <LF> 𐅆, <RF> tripod.

oB   rB   3.37   Berlin, 18252300.

Philodromos son of Tychandros

Ref. Regling 25, Bellinger T 104, Knoepfler 31.
Rev. <EX> ΦΙΛΟΔΡΟΜΟΥ | ΤΟΥ ΤΥΧΑΝΔΡΟΥ, <LF> 𐅆, <RF> winged Nike hold-
ing wreath r.

O33   R68   16.62   BNF Fonds Général 681 = Coll. Waddington 1152.

Mnaseas son of Demetrios

Ref. Regling 24, Bellinger T 103, Knoepfler 30.
Rev. <EX> ΜΝΑΣΕΟΥ ΤΟΥ | ΔΗΜΗΤΡΙΟΥ, <LF> 𐅆, <RF> prize amphora and
torch.

O34   R69   16.42   Auctiones Basel 6 (1/10/1976), lot 204 (W. Giesecke).

Hermias

Ref. Bellinger T 57, Knoepfler 27.
Rev. <EX> ΗΡΜΙΟΥ, <LF> 𐅆, <RF> owl.

oC   rC   3.30   Gotha = Brüder Egger 46 (11/5/1914), lot 653 (T.
                        Prowe).

Opsigonos

Ref. None.
Rev. <EX> ΟΨΙΓΟΝΟΥ, <LF> 𐅆, <RF> palm branch.

ooAA   rrAA   8.32   ANS 1967.152.423 (E. T. Newell).

Pylades

Ref. Bellinger T 56, Knoepfler 26.
Rev. <EX> ΠΥΛΑΔΟΥ, <LF> 𐅆, <RF> palm branch.

oD   rD   3.94   BNF Fonds Général 690 = Coll. Waddington 1151—
                        Pierced and repaired.

Zmithinas

Ref. F. Imhoof-Blumer, *SNR* 19 (1913): 29–30.
Rev. Not illustrated. According to catalogue, "i[m] F[eld] ΠΥ-ΛΟ."

o?   r?   4.02   Jacob Hirsch 13 (15/5/1905), lot 3472 (A. Rhousopou-
                        los).

Agathes son of Menophilos

Ref. Regling 17, Bellinger T 102, Knoepfler 33.
Rev. <EX> ΑΓΑΘΟΥ | ΤΟΥ ΜΗΝΟΦΙΛΟΥ, <LF> 𝔛, <RF> palm branch.

O35   R70   16.58   BM G.4422 (*BMC Troad* 58,11).

O35   R70   16.59   BNF Fonds Général 685 (Mionnet 2.657, no. 185).

O35   R70   13.11   BNF AA.GR.502

O35   R70   16.62   Naples, 7972.

O35   R71   16.54   Coll. Hunterian (1901) 2.301, pl. XLIX 14

O35   R71   15.72   Vienna, Gr 33870 = Jacob Hirsch 21 (16/11/1908), lot
                        2584 (Consul Weber).

Euthydikos[23]

Ref. Bellinger T 105, Knoepfler 32.
Rev. <EX> ΕΥΘΥΔΙΚΟΥ, <LF> 𝔛, <RF> owl.

oE   rE   3.72   *SNG Ashmolean* 1163 (acq. 1924) = Naville 4
                        (17/6/1922), lot 804 = Coll. Weber 5382 = Sotheby,
                        Wilkinson & Hodge (2/2/1891), lot 216 (C. Babington)

oE   rE   3.60   Winterthur 2.2746 (F. Imhoof-Blumer, *SNR* 19 [1913]: 29–
                        30, no. 77; F. Imhoof-Blumer 1910, A. O. van Lennep
                        1908).

Forgeries

Rev. <EX> ΑΓΑΘΟΥ, <LF> 𝔛, <RF> palm branch.

–   –   15.50   MM Basel 41 (18/6/1970), lot 159.

23 Name not read in Bellinger (1961: 36), missing from Robert (1966: 78–79), read as
]ΥΛΑ in *SNG Ashmolean* (2007), still considered illegible in Knoepfler (2010: 53). See,
however, Imhoof–Blumer 1913: 29–30, no. 77, Robert 1967: 123–124, and Winterthur 1997
ad loc.

The coin is obviously trying to copy the issue of Agathes son of Menophilos (e.g., palm branch control mark, similar monogram, magistrate's name). However, many details are wrong. On the obverse, the helmet strap covering the ear is unparalleled in the series and the chin protrudes unnaturally beyond the lips. On the reverse, the patronymic is missing, the crossbars of the *alphas* are not broken, and the monogram has been incompletely copied.

3. Metrology

Table 1 compares the distribution of weights in the Athena Ilias coinage to 1) the Apollo Smintheus tetradrachms of Alexandreia Troas which were produced over a similar time span (mid-170s–65), 2) three well-attested series of wreathed tetradrachms from the 150s–140s (Herakleia, Smyrna, Kyme), and 3) two wreathed coinages from the Troad dating to c. 100–70 (Tenedos, Abydos).[24]

The widespread phenomenon of civic tetradrachms minted on a gradually lighter standard between the mid-second and early first century is illustrated here by the contrast between the mode and median of the wreathed tetradrachms of Herakleia, Smyrna, and Kyme and those of Abydos and Tenedos.[25] This trend can likewise be observed in the precisely dated Apollo Smintheus coinage. From its beginning in the mid-170s down to 86 there are only three years (163, 157, and 135) in which coins below 16.00 g appear, whereas between 85 and the final emission in 65 coins below this weight appear six times in just 20 years (85, 80, 79, 78, 68, 65).[26] By contrast, the Athena Ilias coinage appears to have maintained its weight standard relatively well even in the late second and early first centuries, with coins below 16.00 g encountered as commonly in the first half of the series as in the second, even after one discounts damaged specimens.

---

24 The single didrachm and seven drachms in the Athena Ilias series are too few for a metrological analysis to be worthwhile. The data for the Apollo Smintheus coinage is based on a die study I have prepared. The data for the other five coinages is taken from de Callataÿ (1998: 112). It should be noted that two examples of the Tenedian series have now appeared in a hoard which closed in 151/0 (*CH* X 301.140–141), half a century earlier than the c. 100 start date de Callataÿ (1998) proposed. However, the evidence of die links and overstrikes indicates that the overwhelming majority of these coins were indeed minted c. 100–70, and therefore that this coinage was a revival of an earlier and much smaller issue from the mid-second century.

25 See in general Thonemann 2015: 124–127.

26 De Callataÿ 1997a: 153.

Table 1. Metrology.

Weight	Athena Ilias	Apollo Smintheus	Herakleia	Smyrna	Kyme	Tenedos	Abydos
X>17.09	0	0	4	1	0	2	2
17.00–9	2	0	12	0	1	0	1
16.90–9	4	5	12	1	19	0	2
16.80–9	14	6	29	5	37	4	6
16.70–9	18	7	45	24	68	7	7
16.60–9	15	11	23	22	56	13	14
16.50–9	5	7	19	8	47	7	14
16.40–9	7	3	14	2	41	8	11
16.30–9	6	3	8	3	27	7	12
16.20–9	5	3	9	5	24	8	7
16.10–9	3	1	1	1	32	6	11
16.00–9	2	3	3	4	19	5	10
15.90–9	3	2	(X<16.00) 21	(X<16.00) 19	(X<16.00) 62	(X<16.00) 17	(X<16.00) 24
15.80–9	1	0					
15.70–9	2	2					
15.60–9	2	2					
15.50–9	0	0					
15.40–9	1	0					
15.30–9	3	0					
15.20–9	0	0					
15.10–9	0	1					
15.00–9	1	1					
X<15.00	7	4					
N/A	2	2					
Total	103	64	200	95	433	83	121
Mode	16.70–9	16.60–9	16.70–9	16.70–9	16.70–9	16.60–9	16.50–69
Median	16.61	16.59	16.70	16.62	16.52	16.37	16.37

4. Dating

4.1 Hoards and Dating Principles

There are eight relevant hoards, six buried in the period c. 160–143 and two in c. 90 and c. 55–40 respectively. These hoards contain a total of 16 tetradrachms representing 10 magistrates and two cases where the magistrate was not recorded before the coin was dispersed in trade, but the identity of whom can in one case be deduced with some confidence:

1) *IGCH* 1544 (Latakia, Syria, 1759).[27]
   Burial: c. 160 BC.
   Magistrates: Xanthippos

2) *CH* IV 55 (Near East, Commerce, 1977).
   Burial: c. 160 BC.
   Magistrates: Athenokles

3) *IGCH* 1774 (Babylon, Iraq, 1900).[28]
   Burial: c. 155–150 BC.
   Magistrates: Akkos,[29] Antiphanes (1), Apollodoros, x 2 Dionysodoros

4) *CH* X 301 ('Demetrius I', Commerce, 2003).
   Burial: 151/0 BC.[30]
   Magistrates: Apollodoros, Athenokles, x2 Zoilos

5) *CH* IX 530 (Ordu, Turkey, 1970).
   Burial: c. 150 BC.[31]
   Magistrates: Metrodoros

6) *CH* X 308 (Gaziantep, Turkey, 1994).
   Burial: August/October 143 BC.[32]
   Magistrates: Apemantos, Unknown

27 Seyrig (1973: 49–56) argued for c. 169 BC, but Mattingly (1993) 85–6 has now argued for c. 160 BC on the basis of the Maʾaret En-Nuʾman Hoard (Syria), 1980 (= *CH* VIII 433). Kinns (1999: 55–60) provides independent validation of this lower date for the hoard with his study of the Ephesian drachms.

28 For arguments favoring 155 over 150 see Regling 1928: 98 and Meadows and Houghton 2010: 179 n. 13.

29 For this reading instead of Ἀ[ρέ]ου see n. 10.

30 Lorber 2010: 125.

31 *CH* IX 530 follows Arslan and Lightfoot (1999: 42–43) in dating this hoard c. 140–120, but Boehringer (1975: 51–52) and Meadows and Houghton (2010: 179 n. 13) rightly prefer 150.

32 Meadows and Houghton 2010: 179.

7) Gerasimov (1979) 138 (Malko Tarnovo, Bulgaria, 1968).
    Burial: c. 90 BC.[33]
    Magistrates: Hermokreon (?)

8) *CH* X 165 (Georgi Dobrevo, Bulgaria, 2000).[34]
    Burial: c. 55–40 BC.[35]
    Magistrates: Hegesidemos (2) son of Diophanes

Five of the magistrates from hoards dated c. 160–150 are obverse die linked to six further magistrates.[36] With 16 magistrates predating August/October 143, two features of these issues from the beginning of the series become apparent which help with dating. First, a monogram first appears in left field with Metriketes. This magistrate is die linked to five magistrates who do not have a monogram, of which three (Xanthippos, Antiphanes (1), Athenokles) appear in hoards from c. 160–150. By contrast, once a monogram does appear in the left field with Metriketes it then always appears here except in three cases: the issue of Prytanis instead places it in right field and those of Antiphanes (2) and Zoilos spell out the name referred to by the monogram (ΚΛΕ–ΩΝΟΣ). Since the examples of Hegesidemos (1) lack a monogram, they belong at the very beginning of the series. Second, the only control mark used is an owl in the right field until the issue of Phoinix, which adds an eight-pointed star in the left field below the monogram. From Zoilos onwards, two or three control marks become the norm.[37] Since Hegesidemos (1) has only the owl in the right field, this again argues for it belonging at the beginning of the series.

    In the rest of the series, three general trends can be observed which contribute to establishing a relative chronology. First, the magistrate's patronymic first appears on the coins of Diopeithes son of Zenis. Thereafter, it is included by eight of the remaining twelve magistrates who produce tetradrachms (the six issues of drachms and the didrachm issue can be excluded from consideration since their flans are too small).[38] This distinctive feature of the later issues is not only a useful dating criterion, but also allows us to start making prosopographical links with

---

33 Paunov 2013: 289–290. The coin of Apollo Smintheus (Year 208 = 93 BC) found in this hoard first appeared in GM 15 (17/12/1978), lot 68. I therefore wonder whether the unidentified coin of Athena Ilias in this hoard is in fact the coin of Hermokreon which first appears in MM Basel Liste 404 (Sep. 1978), lot 8 and belongs to the right part of the series.

34 See now Paunov 2013.

35 Paunov 2013: esp. 291–292.

36 Die links: Xanthippos, Antiphanes (1), Athenokles (Hoards 1, 2, 3) to Iphiades, Thersandros, and Metriketes; Metrodoros (Hoard 5) to Eudemos, Phoinix; Zoilos (Hoard 4) to Antiphanes (2).

37 Unlike with the monograms, I see no reliable pattern in the control marks and so have not used them for dating.

38 See e.g., the drachm issue of Hippodamas where just the magistrate's name on its own has to be split over two lines because of lack of space.

epigraphic and literary texts.[39] Second, if one compares the issues from Hoards 1–6 (c. 160–143) with the issue of Hegesidemos (2) son of Diophanes from Hoard 8 (c. 55–40) it is immediately clear that significant stylistic changes have occurred in the intervening century and that, generally speaking, the types have become much cruder.[40] Third, if we look at the monograms on sets of magistrates which are die linked or which we know belong together for other reasons it becomes clear that this is often a good indication that two coins belong together, or at least near to one another. Caution is needed, however, since there is at least one die linked sequence where minor variations of two different monograms are used alternately (Phoinix, Dionysodoros, Apemantos).

4.2 Relative Chronology

Hegesidemos (1) to Akkos. The position of these eight magistrates at the beginning of the series is guaranteed by hoard finds, die links, and diagnostic features such as monograms and control marks. The order of the five magistrates only using O2 cannot currently be determined, so I have ordered them alphabetically.

Metrodoros to Soterides. The presence of magistrates from hoards dated c. 155–150 (Dionysodoros), 151/0 (Zoilos), 150 (Metrodoros), and August/October 143 (Apemantos) indicate that these four magistrates and the three magistrates to which they are die linked belong soon after the Hegesidemos (1) to Akkos sequence. The three magistrates sharing O6 are placed first because Metrodoros (⊠, ⊠) and Eudemos (⊠) display variations of the same monogram as Metriketes (⊠) and Akkos (⊠) which come before and some of the examples of Dionysodoros (⊠) and Apemantos (⊠, ⊠) which follow, whereas Phoinix (⊠) introduces the monogram that will be used on the other examples of Dionysodoros and Apemantos. Metrodoros is placed before Eudemos because the monogram on two of this magistrate's reverse dies adds a crossbar at the top that will then appear on Eudemos. Soterides is included in this group of eight magistrates because the obverse die is exceptionally close to that of Antiphanes (2) and Zoilos and it shares a monogram (⊠) with Eudemos.

Apollodoros to Hermokreon. These nine magistrates can be split into three groups which, for lack of good dating criteria, I have arranged alphabetically: 1) Three examples of Apollodoros have appeared in hoards dated c. 155–150 and 151/0. They share a monogram (⊠, ⊠) with Demetrios (1) and Euboulides and

---

39 The approach is exemplified by Robert (1966: 58–82) and Knoepfler (2010: 47–59). For harsh (and only occasionally justified) criticism of Robert's prosopographical approach see Guépin 1969: 207–212.

40 Kraft 1962: 240. The assertion to the contrary of Guépin (1969: 211) is difficult to understand. For example, delicate work on the obverse, such as the streaming plumes of Athena's helmet and the wavy hair which tumbles down the back of her neck, are increasingly executed in a blocky style or avoided altogether from Melanippides onwards. Likewise, the

the dies of all three magistrates display strong stylistic affinities with earlier issues. 2) Lysikles and Protokleides are die linked and share a monogram.[41] The dies display the beginnings of stylistic developments typical of the second half of the series (e.g., Athena's dress billowing out behind her on the reverse). 3) There are then four magistrates (Dionysios, Hermokreon, Melantas, Prytanis) which display even clearer stylistic affinities with the coins in the next sequence (especially with the first two magistrates, Menephron and Melanippides). If the Athena Ilias coin in the Malko Tarnovo hoard (buried c. 90) is indeed the issue of Hermokreon as I have speculated (see n. 33 above), then these four magistrates will date to the late second/very early first century.

Menephron to Demetrios (2). These 10 magistrates can be ordered with some confidence since all but one (Kallisthenes) are die linked to other magistrates in this group. Kallisthenes shares a monogram (⍓) with some of these issues (cf. ⍓ on Menephron son of Menephron, O29/R62) and is stylistically similar. The order of the five magistrates sharing O29 (Metronax son of Hippodamas to Menephron son of Menephron) can be determined by a worsening fault on the left side of the obverse die.[42]

Philokles and Philon to Euthydikos. Since six of the 10 magistrates in this sequence chose to mint drachms and one magistrate didrachms instead of tetradrachms, the chances of identifying obverse die links between the issues of tetradrachms are greatly reduced, and indeed none has so far appeared. Consequently, we must instead rely on monograms. 1) Philokles and Philon and the example of Hegesidemos (2) son of Diophanes in the Georgi Dobrevo hoard (c. 55–40) share a monogram (⍓) with Demetrios (2) who dates to 77 (see sections 4.5 and 4.6) and ends the previous sequence. 2) The other example of Hegesidemos (2) son of Diophanes and Hippodamas share a monogram (⍐). 3) Philodromos son of Tychandros, Mnaseas son of Demetrios, Opsigonos, and Hermias all share variations of the same monogram (⍓, ⍓). 4) I see no good way to determine the position of Pylades and Zmithinas, and so have placed them before the pair of magistrates most likely to have come last. 5) Agathes son of Menophilos and Euthydikos share variations of a monogram (⍓, ⍓) and probably come latest in the series given the prosopographical evidence (see section 4.5).

---

depiction of the drapery of Athena Ilias's dress on the reverse becomes increasingly poor. In particular, the back of her dress goes from falling naturally to the floor to billowing out behind her (e.g., Lysikles, Protokleides) to becoming a blocky protrusion (e.g., Melantas, Prytanis).

41 Kraft 1962: 240.
42 De Callataÿ 1997a: 291 n. 80.

4.3 The Beginning of the Series

The hoard evidence indicates that the series had begun by c. 160, and it is generally agreed that autonomous, spread-flan tetradrachms are an innovation of the post-Apameia period.[43] Unfortunately, we cannot tell from the hoard evidence or the coins whether the series began over two decades earlier in the mid-180s or just a few years earlier in the mid-160s. However, it has long been recognized that the spread-flan tetradrachms which Alexandreia Troas minted in the name of Apollo Smintheus bear a striking similarity to the Athena Ilias series and were therefore probably minted in imitation of them.[44] Since the Apollo Smintheus coins can be precisely dated because they feature an era date on the reverse, we can therefore use them to infer a *terminus ante quem* for the Athena Ilias series. The earliest example known to Bellinger was from Year 137. Bellinger assumed that this was an era which began in 301 when Lysimachos changed the city's name from Antigoneia to Alexandreia, and so he dated the coin to 164 BC.[45] Consequently, Boehringer, for example, argued for a date not long before this for the beginning of the Athena Ilias coinage.[46] However, in 2005 an example appeared in trade from Year 130 which would therefore date to 171 BC. To this we can now add an example which is die linked to the Year 130 issue and shares a monogram with Year 130 and Year 137, but lacks an era date and so should probably be placed first in the series.[47] The beginning of the series may now be described as follows:

43 For a recent overview see Thonemann 2015: 45–65 and for the chronological development of coinages with broader flans in the 3rd and 2nd c. see Mørkholm (1991: 12) and de Callataÿ (2006: 148-152).

44 E.g., Bellinger 1961: 93-94.

45 Knoepfler (2010: 60) has recently revived the suggestion that the era on the coins may be the Seleukid Era which would make a Year 137 coin date to 176 instead of 164 BC. However, Paul Kosmin (pers. comm.) reminds me that Seleukid Era dates always go from smallest to largest (i.e., ZΛP—7-30-100) not largest to smallest (i.e., PΛZ—100-30-7) as we find in all other contexts and, indeed, on the Apollo Smintheus coins. On this phenomenon, see (e.g.) J. and L. Robert, *BE* (1967): 557, no. 651.

46 Boehringer 1972: 15.

47 Another example without an era date has appeared in trade: Elsen 92 (9/6/2007), lot 125 = Elsen 88 (10/6/2006), lot 113 = Triton 8 (11/1/2005), lot 388 = Triton 1 (2/12/1997), lot 522 (16.65 g), Rev. <EX> AΛEΞAN, <LF> ⚏, <RF> ⚏. If this were genuine it would be the earliest example. However, I am relatively sure it is a forgery: 1) On the obverse, the three locks of Apollo's hair on his neck are tightly braided until Year 183, whereas here they are loose; the forger's model may be Year 185 (*SNG Copenhagen Suppl.* 320 = Bank Leu 13 (29/4/1975), lot 209 = *SNG von Aulock* 7548); 2) On the reverse, Apollo always holds a recurved bow (pulled in at the grip, each limb a half-moon, bends back at the tips), but on this coin he instead has a longbow with its distinctive half-moon shape; 3) The bow also lacks the decorative recurve on the upper limb curving back on itself (a prominent feature until Year 144 and still common thereafter) and the arrow is notched implausibly high, a

Obverse: Head of Apollo l. wearing laurel wreath with ties floating behind; hair rolled above forehead, falling in three braided locks on neck (tightly braided until Year 183 [= 118 BC], loosely braided thereafter).

Reverse: Apollo Smintheus standing r. on ground line, recurved bow with arrow notched in l. hand, patera in r. hand, quiver over l. shoulder, head wreathed, dressed in himation; <LF and RF> ΑΠΟΛΛΩΝΟΣ | ΖΜΙΘΕΩΣ written vertically, in exergue the city ethnic above (ΑΛΕΞΑΝ, lengthened to ΑΛΕΞΑΝΔΡΕΩΝ between Year 166 and Year 173[48] (135–128 BC) and the magistrate's name in the genitive below (introduced between Year 144[49] and Year 148[50] (157–153 BC).

Earliest Issue 1

Ref. None.
Rev. <EX> ΑΛΕΞΑΝ, <LF> ⧄, <RF> ⧉.

     O1   R1   16.68   MM DE 40 (4/6/2014), lot 221 = Bank Leu 28 (5/5/1981), lot 138.

Year 130

Ref. None.
Rev. <EX> ΑΛΕΞΑΝ, <LF> ⧉ (above), ⧄ (below) <RF> ΡΛ (130).

     O1   R2   16.94   NAC 29 (11/5/2005), lot 198.

Year 137

Ref. Bellinger A 134.
Rev. <EX> ΑΛΕΞΑΝ, <LF> ⧈ (above), ⧄ (below) <RF> ΡΛΖ (137).

     O2   R3   16.44   BNF Fonds Général 117 = Coll. Waddington 1081.

Rev. <LF> ⧄ (below).

     O2   R4   16.71   Lanz 158 (5/6/2014), lot 235.

Since Earliest Issue 1 is die linked to Year 130, it probably dates to the late 170s BC. It may also be significant that these three early issues are the only ones in the Apollo Smintheus series to share monograms with issues in the Athena Ilias

stylistic infelicity typical of late issues (e.g., Year 216); 4) While the left field monogram is plausible, the one in right field looks to be a misdrawn version of a monogram which appears on Lampsakene Lysimachi: Thompson 1968: 171, nos. 49–52.

48 Not in Bellinger: CNG 99 (13/5/2015), lot 194 (16.85 g).

49 Not in Bellinger: Künker 236 (7/10/2013), lot 80 = GM 207 (15/10/2012), lot 284 (16.91 g); BM 1998,1007.1 = Spink 128 (7/10/1998), lot 170 (15.64 g).

50 Not in Bellinger: Roma Numismatics 9 (3/22/2015), lot 269 = Lanz 158 (5/6/2014), lot 236 (16.98 g).

series. Earliest Issue 1, Year 130, and the example of Year 137 in Paris share a monogram (🅀) which is almost identical to that on the Metriketes issue of the Athena Ilias series (🅀). Likewise, the new Year 137 specimen has an almost identical monogram (🅀) to the Akkos issue (🅀) which followed Metriketes. In both cases, the only difference is that the hasta descending from right to left meets the crossbar at its middle rather than at its left hand end. Finally, it should be noted that whereas the five issues which follow Akkos only lightly modify its monogram, from Year 138 onwards the monograms on the Apollo Smintheus issues bear no relation to those on the Athena Ilias coinage.

Monograms on coins are notoriously difficult to interpret, but some progress can perhaps be made with this one. On the Apollo Smintheus coinage there are always two monograms down to Year 144. However, after the magistrate's name first appears written in full in Year 148, there is only ever one monogram, implying that the second monogram was previously referring to this magistrate. This hypothesis is supported by the fact that in the issues we currently know of prior to Year 148 one of the monograms changes from year to year whereas the other can remain for longer periods. For example, later in the series the 🅀 monogram lasts from Year 183 to Year 236 (= 118–65 BC) and so cannot represent a single living individual.[51] It also seems likely that the monogram which does not refer to the magistrate on the Apollo Smintheus coinage served the same function as the lone monogram on the Athena Ilias coinage. First, the Athena Ilias monogram cannot be concealing the magistrate's name because this is spelled out in exergue from the very beginning of the series. Second, of the two monograms on the early issues of Apollo Smintheus, the Athena Ilias coins share the monogram that lasts for several years at a time, not the annually changing one. Finally, the monogram on the Athena Ilias series lasts for extended periods (albeit often with minor variations over time).

Bellinger thought that these monograms recorded individuals who had given money towards the cost of minting the coins, a theory Louis Robert long ago cast doubt on.[52] An alternative explanation would be that the monogram refers to the workshop which produced these coins.[53] The shared monograms would then reflect the fact that, when Alexandreia Troas decided to begin the Apollo Smintheus series, the city hired the same workshop the koinon used for the Athena Ilias coinage, perhaps in order to make sure that its coinage was of a similar artistic quality.[54] After about a decade (i.e., Earliest Issue 1–Year 137), the city decided to bring the work of die engraving in house. As a result, whereas the monogram

51 Bellinger 1961: 98; de Callataÿ 1997a: 155 n. 2.

52 Bellinger 1961: 30 n. 94 with L. Robert, *OMS* 6:125–35.

53 As noted, the monograms can last beyond a single person's career, so they are less likely to refer to individual die engravers.

54 For an experienced workshop cutting dies for other mints see Marinescu (1996: 334–372) on the 'Bosporus Workshop' of die engravers at Byzantion and Kalchedon which in the third and second centuries produced Lysimachi dies for mints throughout the region.

mostly stays the same for the five magistrates after Akkos in the Athena Ilias series, it completely changes for the Apollo Smintheus coinage. If correct, this has two implications for the Athena Ilias series. First, it would confirm the longstanding assumption that the Apollo Smintheus series imitated the Athena Ilias series and not vice versa. Second, if on this basis we date the end of Metriketes's magistracy to 165/4 and assume that the term of office was one year, then the remaining six magistrates without a monogram would date the beginning of the series to 171/0 at the earliest. However, as we shall see, the koinon's epigraphy strongly suggests that the magistrate named in exergue (the Ilian president of the board of *agonothetai*, as shall be argued in section 4.6 below) could serve for up to four years. As a result, the remaining six magistrates could suggest a date as early as 189/8.

4.4 A Gap in the Middle of the Series?

If we split the series into three roughly dateable periods—1) c. 185–c. 150 (beginning to Babylon hoard), 2) c. 150–c. 100 (Babylon hoard to Malko Tarnovo hoard), and 3) c. 100–c. 50 (Malko Tarnovo hoard to end)—and divide the length of each period by the number of magistrates attested for that period, we see that the average length of a magistracy for periods 1 and 3 is just above two years, whereas that for period 2 (the Apollodoros to Hermokreon sequence described in section 4.2 above) is about five years.[55] There are two possible explanations for this discrepancy: either there was a gap in production in the second half of the second century or the magistrates for period 2 are underrepresented in our sample. Bellinger preferred the first explanation, arguing on stylistic grounds that there was a break in production 119–95. While the specific argument he made can now be disproved (it involves assigning the die linked magistrates Melanippides and Diopeithes son of Zenis to two different periods), a gap at this point nevertheless remains a possibility.[56]

However, it is worth noting that Bellinger likewise posited a break in the Apollo Smintheus series 135–118 which new examples from 128 and 127 have now shown to be illusory.[57] As will be argued in section 5.4, the Apollo Smintheus coinage is by far the best comparandum for the Athena Ilias coinage, and so this new evidence suggesting unbroken production of the series is a strong argument in favor of the Athena Ilias series likewise having been produced continually. Moreover, it is well known that hoards containing civic tetradrachms primarily appear in the mid-second century in relation to the Seleukid dynastic wars and in the first half of the first century in relation to the Mithradatic Wars, a pattern

55 1) c. 185–c. 150 (35 years/16 magistrates = 2.2 years per magistrate); 2) c. 150–c. 100 (50/9 = 5.5), 3) c. 100–c. 50 (50/22 = 2.3).

56 Bellinger 1961: 30, 32–33.

57 Bellinger 1961: 98, most recently followed by Thonemann (2015: 180). Year 173 = 128 BC: see n. 48. Year 174 (Anaxikrates) = 127 BC: Roma Numismatics 9 (22/3/2015), lot 270 (16.89 g).

we see in the Athena Ilias coins from Hoards 1–6 (dating to c. 160–143) and 7–8 (dating to c. 90–c. 55/40) respectively. We would therefore expect period 2 (the second half of the second century) to be quite poorly represented by comparison with periods 1 and 3. In addition, as I will argue in section 4.6, the die study of the series suggests that we do not yet have a representative sample of the series: we should therefore be looking to identify areas of potential 'growth' in the series, and this is the most obvious one.

While the existence of a gap in production in the second half of the second century cannot be ruled out, this argument from silence should not be viewed as the safer hypothesis. Comparison with the Apollo Smintheus coinage shows that continual production is perfectly possible and also illustrates the evidence problem: the two examples disproving Bellinger's argument only appeared in 2015 and can only be used to disprove his argument because they bear era dates which the Athena Ilias coins lack. Likewise, if we viewed the Athena Ilias series in isolation we might imagine that six magistrates sharing a single obverse die (O2) must indicate the compactness of production. Yet the die study I have prepared of the Apollo Smintheus series attests an obverse die lasting from Year 138 to Year 153 (and perhaps as late as Year 165) = 163–c. 148/136. Were it not for the era dates of these coins we would not have imagined that these obverse dies lasted so long, yet this is the situation we find ourselves in with the Athena Ilias series. In sum, underrepresentation at this point in the series is to be expected given the nature of the hoard evidence, and the die study of the Athena Ilias series provides grounds for believing that new examples will in time appear to fill this gap.

4.5 The End of the Series

The koinon continued to exist as a multi-state confederation well into the first century AD,[58] and it was only in the second or early third century AD that the Panathenaia of Athena Ilias came to be organized by Ilion alone.[59] However, long before this the number of Greek mints producing autonomous silver coinage dropped precipitously in the middle decades of the first century BC, and by the

---

58 Ilion honours Licinnius Proclus Themison as τὸν φιλ[όπατ]ριν καὶ προστάτην καὶ κόσμον τοῦ συνεδρί[ου] τῶν ἐννέα δήμων καὶ εὐεργέτην τοῦ δήμου (*I. Ilion* 107.4–8, first century AD). Since the synedrion was the executive body of the koinon, the nine demoi will be the member states, and the demos of which he is a benefactor will be Ilion itself. Also relevant is *I. Perge* 272.16–17 (first century AD?) in which L. Robert, *OMS* 2: 1096 restored [Πανα | θήναια ἐ]ν Εἰλίῳ π[αῖδας].

59 *I. Alex. Troas* 50 (post-AD 212) honors an Ilian athlete who competed at the νέα Παναθ[ήναια] and *I. Alex. Troas* 51 is a fragment of a similar text. Frisch (followed by Ricl) wrongly attributed these texts to Alexandreia Troas when in fact they belong to Ilion: J. and L. Robert, *BE* (1974): no. 458, (1976): no. 567. An unpublished text found in the recent excavations of Ilion (by the gift shop when I saw it in July 2013) helps confirm the attribution of all three texts to Ilion and will be published by Reyhan Körpe.

reign of Augustus only a handful continued to do so.[60] In the Troad, the silver tetradrachms issued by Abydos and Tenedos ended in c. 70 and the Apollo Smintheus coinage in 65. Bellinger had assumed that the Athena Ilias series ended in 85, but it has been persuasively argued that the Demetrios (2) on an issue of drachms is in fact the Demetrios son of Hippodamas who is the Ilian *agonothetes* in *I. Ilion* 10 (77 BC; for the argument in detail see section 4.6).[61] In addition, an example of Hegesidemos (2) son of Diophanes has now appeared in a hoard dated to c. 55–40 (Hoard 8). The coin in the hoard has a monogram ($\frac{1}{4}$) which is different from the other example of the issue ($\overline{\mathcal{A}}$), but is the same as that on the issues of Demetrios (2) and Philokles and Philon, whose obverse types are also stylistically similar.[62] This brings the series down to the late 70s/early 60s and supports Robert's identification of Hegesidemos (2) as the Ilian *epistates* mentioned in *I. Ilion* 59 (c. 70–50) and the father of Diophanes and Hipparchos, sons of Hegesidemos, listed as debtors in *I. Ilion* 65 (c. 30–20), with Hipparchos appearing again as an Ilian *synedros* of the koinon who honors Augustus with a statue in *I. Ilion* 81 (c. 25).[63] After this, the series continues under nine more magistrates. Among these are Agathes son of Menophilos, who is praised in an honorific decree of the koinon (*I. Ilion* 12, mid-first century) for his service as *agonothetes* and *agoranomos*,[64] and Euthydikos, who is probably the father of the Melanippides son of Euthydikos who hosted Augustus in Ilion, set up a statue to him in 12 BC (*I. Ilion* 83), and became high priest of the Imperial cult and a Roman citizen (*I. Ilion* 85, 85a).[65] The issues of Agathes son of Menophilos and of Euthydikos share a monogram, and if, as I have supposed on the basis of these prosopographical arguments, they come last in the series, then they may date to the 50s. As with the beginning of the series, the unknown variable is the length of time these magistrates were in office.

60 Kinns 1987: 111–113; Thonemann 2015: 177–182.

61 Knoepfler 2010: 58. Bellinger (1961: 39–40) instead thought this was an Augustan issue ("19 B.C.–A.D. 14"), presumably influenced by the bronzes of Ilion with Obv. Bare head of Augustus l., Rev. Head of Athena in crested helmet l., IΛI (l.), ΔΗΜΗΤ (below) which are a similar weight and size (*RPC* I 2309).

62 See already Kinns (1987: 111 n. 52) making some of these points.

63 Robert 1966: 68–70. Contrast Bellinger 1961: 25–27 (mid-second century); Guépin 1969: 211 (same, *contra* Robert); Knoepfler 2010: 59 n. 121 (c. 120–100, thinks style rules out post-Mithridatic period).

64 L. Robert, *OMS* 2: 1027; Robert 1966: 73–75; Knoepfler 2010: 59. Possible descendants include Menophilos son of Menophilos, *panegyrikos agoranomos* of the koinon (*I. Ilion* 4, first century AD) and L. Stlaccius Menophilos (*I. Ilion* 181, first/second century AD). However, the name is extremely common (at Ilion: *LGPN VA*, s.v. Μηνόφιλος nos. 341–351, s.v. Μηνόφιλα no. 19).

65 Robert 1966: 75–78; Robert 1967: 123–124.

4.6 Dating the Magistrates

Denis Knoepfler has recently argued that there is the possibility of being able to precisely date this series on the basis of the magistrates named in exergue on the reverse. This suggestion combines two earlier insights: Louis Robert's identification of this magistrate as the Ilian president of the board of *agonothetai* and John Ma's suggestion that the Panathenaia was a penteteric festival.[66] Knoepfler has argued that the *agonothetai* were in office for the whole penteteric cycle and therefore that each magistrate's name should represent a four-year period in the chronology of the series. If correct, this would suggest that we could precisely date every magistrate once a relative chronology of the series was established and a chronological fixed point within the series identified. Knoepfler's assumption is that the series ran from the Peace of Apameia in 188 to the Battle of Actium in 31 and therefore covered a period of about 39 penteteric cycles. Given that his catalogue (based on Bellinger) contained 34 magistrates, his assumption was that we were relatively close to having the full series.[67]

However, it is now clear that this argument must be either abandoned or significantly modified. At least 47 magistrates are now attested which, at four years per magistrate, would equate to a 188-year period. If we follow Knoepfler's assumption that the series began in 188, then this would lead to the unlikely conclusion that the koinon was still producing autonomous silver coinage by the middle of Augustus's reign. Conversely, if we adopt his end date of 31, then we would have to imagine that the koinon began minting an autonomous spread-flan coinage in 219 almost four decades before this innovation appeared anywhere else in the Greek world. Moreover, these already problematic chronological arrangements do not account for the fact that hoard finds and obverse die links mean that in practice there is even less flexibility than this. For example, the first quarter of the series from Hegesidemos (1) down to Apollodoros in the Babylon hoard (c. 155–150) includes 17 magistrates who, if they had all served for four years, would have begun the series in c. 223–218.

Knoepfler assumed that the body of evidence collected by Bellinger was fairly representative.[68] However, it can be shown that even after more than doubling the number of specimens known from the series there are still quite a few more examples to come. Table 2 below shows the progress in our knowledge of this series by comparing the die study which could have been done with the coins available to Regling and Bellinger with my own die study. When the ratio between the number of specimens (n) and the number of obverse dies observed (d) is above 3 it becomes possible to estimate the original number of obverse dies (D) with

---

66 Robert 1966: 58–59, 67–94, with the objections of Guépin (1969: 208–209) answered by Le Rider (1973: 77–79); Ma 2007: 55.

67 Knoepfler 2010: 50.

68 Knoepfler 2010: 50.

some confidence using the calculations of Carter and Esty.[69] Since the number of drachms currently falls well below this threshold ($n = 7$, $d = 6$, $n/d = 1.16$) and only one didrachm is so far known, I have not likewise applied these calculations to these other denominations. Finally, I give $n = 101$ rather than $n = 103$ since I have been unable to check the obverse dies of two tetradrachms.

Table 2. Progress in knowledge of the Athena Ilias series.

	n	d	n/d	singletons	D (Carter)[70]	D (Esty)[71]
Regling	41	18	2.27	12	26.5 ±3.42	32.0 ±12.53
Bellinger	51	22	2.31	12	32.0 ±3.63	38.6 ±13.34
Ellis-Evans	101	35	2.89	20	45.3 ±3.05	53.6 ±10.97

The first thing to note is that in all three data sets the obverse die (O29) shared by the issues of Metronax son of Hippodamas, Sostratos, Hermippos son of Menophanes, Theokydes, and Menephron son of Menephron is substantially overrepresented (12/41 for Regling, 14/51 for Bellinger, 19/101 for Ellis-Evans). This artificially inflates the n/d figure, giving the impression that we know the series better than we really do. Table 3 excludes the examples of this die to see how well we know the series when this outlier is set aside.

Table 3. Progress in knowledge of the Athena Ilias series (excluding O29).

	n	d	n/d	singletons	D (Carter)	D (Esty)
Regling	29	17	1.71	12	32.1 ±6.51	41.1 ±25.68
Bellinger	37	21	1.76	12	38.4 ±6.60	48.6 ±25.86
Ellis-Evans	82	34	2.41	20	48.4 ±4.15	58.1 ±15.26

This much greater degree of uncertainty is what we should expect given that more than half of the obverse dies are known from only one example ("singletons"). It is therefore a certainty that new examples of the series will continue to appear. Some of these new specimens will be further examples of dies already known to us, some will be new dies of already attested magistrates, and a small number will be new magistrates. In sum, Knoepfler's argument that each magistrate should represent a four-year period is only likely to become less tenable as new evidence appears.

In a recent article, Johannes Nollé has likewise noted that too many magistrates exist for Knoepfler's argument to work.[72] However, he has concluded from this that, since the numismatic evidence appears to contradict the epigraphic arguments of

69 For discussion of these two methodologies and the advantages of Esty's see de Callataÿ 2006: 28–39.

70 Carter 1983.

71 Esty 2011.

72 Nollé 2014: 301 n. 75, citing the 40 magistrates listed in Leschhorn (2002–2009: 2, 1015) which, unfortunately, contains a number of significant errors.

Knoepfler, they must also invalidate the epigraphic arguments of Robert on which Knoepfler's arguments are built. As a result, he not only argues that Knoepfler is wrong to conclude that the magistrates named in exergue on the coins were in office for a full penteteric cycle, but more fundamentally that the coins were not even minted by the koinon of Athena Ilias but rather by the city of Ilion.[73] This sweeping rejection of the carefully constructed epigraphic arguments of Robert and Knoepfler is somewhat rash. While the numismatic evidence now shows that Knoepfler's argument about the dating of the magistrates cannot be completely right, it does not necessarily follow that it is completely wrong.

If we reexamine the epigraphic evidence, we see that the fundamentals of the case built by Robert and Knoepfler are strong. Robert originally argued that the koinon was the minting authority for these coins because they were minted in the name of Athena Ilias (Ἀθηνᾶς Ἰλιάδος) and lacked a city ethnic. By contrast, the bronze and silver coinage of Ilion always bore the ethnic Ἰλι(έων) and the coins minted at Alexandreia Troas in the name of Apollo Smintheus and at Parion in the name of Apollo Aktaios bore the ethnics Ἀλεξανδρέων and Παριανῶν respectively.[74] Nollé objects to Robert's argument on several grounds. First, he emphasizes that the word κοινόν is never used on the Athena Ilias coinage.[75] However, this is an unreasonable expectation since no koinon calls itself a koinon on its coinage before the Imperial period. More substantively, he notes that Robert used the example of Athena Ilias to formulate the maxim that coinages in the name of a god which lack a city ethnic were produced by religious koina. This led to the conclusion that the Athena Nikephoros and Artemis Pergaia coinages were not minted by Pergamon and Perge respectively, but rather by religious koina similar to the koinon of Athena Ilias.[76] As Nollé notes, there is no epigraphic evidence for the existence of these confederations, only numismatic arguments which in recent years have been overturned.[77] In both cases, therefore, it seems that a city rather than a koinon produced these coinages, and therefore that while Robert's maxim may hold true for the Troad, it does not elsewhere. However, Nollé takes

73 Nollé 2014: 300–301 (esp. n. 75) and 310.

74 Robert 1966: 36–46.

75 Nollé 2014: 300.

76 Robert 1966: 45–46.

77 Nollé 2014: 291–295, 299–308. Athena Nikephoros: The monograms on the reverse of the bronzes have been interpreted as referring to the cities which contributed to the koinon and participated in the festival: von Fritze 1910: 28–30, 32; Robert 1966: 46; Le Rider 1973: 77; Psoma 2007: 240; Psoma 2008: 234. However, Marcellesi (2012: 125–127) identifies a number of problems with this argument and more plausibly explains these coins as quasi-royal issues. Artemis Pergaia: Seyrig (1963: 38–51) argued that the dates on the Alexanders issued by Perge, Aspendos, Phaselis, and Sillyon referred to a common era of Pamphylia, which Robert (1966: 46) (followed by Psoma 2007: 240; Psoma 2008: 235) took as evidence for the existence of a koinon perhaps centred on Artemis Pergaia. See, however, Meadows (2009) for evidence that all these cities (as well as Magydos and Termessos) used their own individual eras.

his critique one step further and argues that since the Athena Nikephoros and Artemis Pergaia coinages were minted by cities but lack an ethnic, then the Athena Ilias coinage must likewise have been minted by a city.[78]

This does not follow. As Nollé acknowledges, unlike with Athena Nikephoros and Artemis Pergaia, abundant epigraphic evidence attests a religious koinon of Athena Ilias. The idea that the koinon could have minted its own coinage is therefore an *a priori* possibility in a way that it is not for these two cults whose putative koina are otherwise unattested. Moreover, what Nollé's discussion of the Athena Nikephoros and Artemis Pergaia coinage surely illustrates is not that we need a different hard and fast rule for interpreting these coin legends, but rather that we should not be reducing the interpretation of coins to an analysis of their legends. Discussions of coinages in the name of a god often begin by repeating Robert's mantra that coinages with an ethnic need to be kept quite separate from those without an ethnic.[79] But what are the numismatic arguments for that being so? As we have seen, as a rule of thumb it does not necessarily help us with identifying the minting authority—it works for Athena Ilias, but not for Athena Nikephoros and Artemis Pergaia. More importantly, it is not self-evident that (for example) the coinage of Alexandreia Troas in the name of Apollo Smintheus *was not* minted for reasons to do with the running of the Smintheia simply because it *was* minted by the city that controlled that sanctuary rather than by a religious koinon of cities administering that sanctuary (see further section 5.4). To answer questions of this sort, we need to look to the numismatic evidence: Was the series minted continually or in fits and starts? What do the number of obverse dies tell us about the volume of production? What do the metal, weight standard, and denomination tell us about the transactions these coins were intended to facilitate?

Insofar as we can draw legitimate inferences about a coinage from its choice of legend, the comparanda should be local. In the case of the Athena Ilias coinage, this means not Pergamon or Perge but rather the Apollo Smintheus and Apollo Aktaios coinages of Alexandreia Troas and Parion respectively. Both cities were members of the koinon and the style of these coinages clearly emulates that of the Athena Ilias coinage. The fact that both cities include their ethnics suggests that this was the norm in the Troad. As such, the onus is on those who want to attribute the Athena Ilias coinage to Ilion to explain why Ilion placed its ethnic on all its other coinage but not on this series. A better explanation is that, in a regional context where a confederation of cities was minting coins in the name of a god *without* an ethnic, Alexandreia Troas and Parion felt obliged to include their ethnic on their similar looking coinages in a way which (for example) Pergamon and Perge, in their very different regional contexts, did not. Furthermore, in light of what we know about the general character of the koinon, the decision not to place an ethnic on the coinage makes good sense. The member states were represented

78 Nollé 2014: 300–301.

79 E.g., Le Rider 1973: 75–77, Gauthier 2011: 178–183; Psoma 2007: 240; Psoma 2008: 228.

in its two key bodies (the *synedrion* and the board of *agonothetai*) by equal rather than proportional representation. It would therefore have run counter to the spirit in which the koinon's institutions had been designed to place one city's ethnic (i.e., Ilion's) on the coinage. In addition, there is the basic but important point that the wealth being used to mint the coinage belonged not to the city of Ilion, but rather to all the cities of the koinon which collectively managed the confederation and its funds on an equitable basis. Apart from anything else, it would therefore have simply been inaccurate to put any one city's ethnic on the coinage. In sum, while the particular arguments Robert used to identify the minting authority as the koinon of Athena Ilias are open to question, the conclusion itself is not in doubt.

The clearest indication that the name of the magistrate in exergue on the coins is, as Robert argued, that of the Ilian *agonothetes* is provided by the decree concerning the reorganization of the koinon's finances from 77 (*I. Ilion* 10). While two other inscriptions give us a full list of *agonothetai*,[80] we cannot use them to compare the names they mention with the names on the coins because they date to the third century when the coinage had not yet begun.[81] After its dating formula, *I. Ilion* 10 lists the individuals from each of the seven member states then belonging to the koinon who met with L. Julius Caesar to come to an agreement about how to cut the festival's costs (lines 6–13):

> ἐξ Ἰλίου μὲν Δημήτριος Ἱπποδάμαντος, Θεοκύδης Ἑρμίου,
> Ποσειδώνιος Ἀπελλείους, ἐγ Δαρδάνου δὲ Δίφιλος Ἀριζήλου, Ἀπολλοφάνης Διφίλου,
> 8 Ἡρακλείδης Ἡρώδου· ἐξ Σκήψεως δὲ Κλέανδρος Πυθοδώρου, Κόνων Βακχίου·
> ἐξ Ἄσσου δὲ Ἀνόδικος Ἀριστολόχου νεώτερος, Λάδικος Ἀνοδίκου, Βόμβος Λυσι-
> θέμιδος· ἐξ Ἀλεξανδρείας δὲ Φιλίτας Σίμωνος, Ζωῖλος Λεοντίσκου, Καλλισ[θέ]-
> νης Κλεόμμιδος· ἐξ Ἀβύδου δὲ Ἀπολλωνικέτης Ἀναξαγόρου, Θέσπις Λαερτ[ι]-
> 12 άδου, Ἑκαταῖος Καλλιππίδου· ἐκυ Λαμψάκου δὲ Πυθογένης Φιλίσκου, Κλεότ[ι]-
> μος Ἀρχεδήμου.

While the official roles of these individuals are not explicitly stated, they can be easily inferred. Five of the cities have three representatives, while two (Skepsis and Lampsakos) only have two. The first of the three individuals from Ilion is also the

---

80 *I. Ilion* 5.1–6, SEG LIII 1373.1–4.
81 Knoepfler 2010: 53–54.

Ilian *agonothetes* named in the dating formula, Demetrios son of Hippodamas.[82]
We know that the koinon had a board of five *agonothetai*,[83] that each city provided
two *synedroi*,[84] and that later in the decree it speaks of the *agonothetai* and *synedroi*
on this occasion taking decisions jointly.[85] It is therefore clear that in the five cases
where a city has three representatives, one is their *agonothetes*. Furthermore,
we can infer from the case of Ilion that the *agonothetes* is the first individual
named. Of the five individuals named first in these three-person delegations,
only the name Demetrios also appears on the Athena Ilias coinage: once on an
issue of tetradrachms and once on an issue of drachms. As discussed earlier,
there are numismatic arguments independent of the epigraphy which indicate
that the magistrates responsible for these two issues are two different people: the
tetradrachms of Demetrios (1) date soon after c. 150, whereas the drachms of
Demetrios (2) date to the 70s. It is therefore fairly certain that the Demetrios (2)
on the drachms is in fact the Demetrios son of Hippodamas in *I. Ilion* 10. This
should not surprise us. Documents of the koinon are dated by naming the board
of *agonothetai* in office beginning with the Ilian *agonothetes*, and it was sufficient
to name the Ilian *agonothetes* alone.[86] Moreover, the president of the board of
agonothetai was also an appropriate person to name on the coins, first, because
it was the *agonothetai* who were responsible for contracting out all work for the
koinon and thus who would have been responsible for having the coins minted
and, second, because it was the *agonothetai* who would have been spending these
coins on behalf of the koinon.[87] This, of course, does not make the *agonothetai*
"mint magistrates"—they very obviously did a great deal more than just mint
coins—but I think it does explain why the koinon would have found it appropriate
to name the president of the board of *agonothetai* on the coins, thus vindicating
Robert's arguments for the identification of this individual.

Finally, the case for the Panathenaia of Athena Ilias being a penteteric festival
and for the board of *agonothetai* (and therefore the Ilian *agonothetes* on the coins)
serving for a full term is also strong. Inscriptions from all periods of the koinon's
history attest to the existence of a Great and a Little Panathenaia.[88] The four-
year length of this cycle is indicated by the honorific decree for Agathes son of
Menophilos, which describes him as ἀγωνοθετήσαντα τῆς κοινῆς τῶν πόλεων

---

82 *I. Ilion* 10.2: ἐπὶ ἀγωνοθετῶν τῶν περὶ Δημήτριον Ἱπποδάμαντος Ἰλιέα.

83 *I. Ilion* 5.1–6, *SEG* LIII 1373.1–4.

84 *I. Ilion* 2.53–9, 64–66.

85 *I. Ilion* 10.28–29, 32–36, 41.

86 Named first: *I. Ilion* 5.1–2, 7.1–2, 10.6–7; *SEG* LIII 1373.1–2. Named alone: *I. Ilion*
3.8–10, 10.2–3.

87 Contracting out work: *I. Ilion* 1.41–6, 52–3, 2.40–2, 5.27–31; *SEG* LIII 1373.39–44.

88 *I. Ilion* 2.5–6, 45–46, 50–51 (last third of the third century); *SEG* LIII 1373.5–6, 11–12
(last third of the third century), *I. Ilion* 3.7–8 (third century; μεγάλα or μικρά are the likely
restorations), *I. Ilion* 5.8 (third century), *I. Ilion* 12.12–13 (first century), *I. Ilion* 9.1–2 (first
century; μεγάλων or μικρῶν Παναθηναίων is the likely restoration), *I. Ilion* 10.31–32
(77 BC).

πανηγύρεως ἐπὶ ἔτη τρία εὐσεβῶς καὶ φιλοδόξως καὶ ἀγορανομήσαντα ὑπὸ τὰ μεγάλα [Πα]ναθήναια φιλοδόξως καὶ μεγαλομερῶς ("having acted as *agonothetes* of the common panegyris of the cities for three years in a pious and glory-loving manner and having served as *agoranomos* during the Great Panathenaia in a glory-loving and munificent manner").[89] As Lefèvre and Pillot have recently pointed out, it is not clear whether he held these offices cumulatively (*agonothetes* for four years and *also agoranomos* in the fourth year) or consecutively (*agonothetes* for three years and *then agoranomos* in the fourth year).[90] In either case, the conclusion is the same: the Panathenaia of Athena Ilias ran on a four-year cycle and was therefore a penteteric festival, just like its Athenian model.[91] Bellinger thought that Agathes was unusual in serving for more than one year.[92] However, the evidence for a Great and a Little Panathenaia (and, by implication, for the existence of a penteteric cycle) comes from all periods of the koinon's history, and in fact the *gymnasiarchoi* are explicitly said to have served τά τε μικρὰ καὶ τὰ μεγάλα Παναθήναια ("at both the Little and Great Panathenaia") in inscriptions from the late third century.[93] There is therefore no reason to think that the length of Agathes's term of office was exceptional.

The epigraphic arguments for concluding that the coinage was minted by the koinon of Athena Ilias and not Ilion, that the magistrate named in the exergue was the Ilian president of the board of *agonothetai*, and that the festival was organized on a penteteric basis are therefore all strong. The two debatable assumptions which Knoepfler makes are instead, first, that the Ilian *agonothetes* always remained in office for the full four years of the penteteric cycle and, second, that the coins were only issued in the year of the Great Panathenaia. My reasons for thinking that coins were also issued in the other years of the penteteric cycle will be set out in the next section. Regarding the first assumption, however, it should be noted that if, for whatever reason, the Ilian *agonothetes* did not complete the full four years of his term of office, then a new president of the board of *agonothetai* would need to have taken up his duties. We would surely expect coins minted under this new *agonothetes* to bear his name rather than his predecessor's, thus creating a situation in which more magistrates would be attested on the coins than the number of penteteric cycles.

We can imagine this coming about in one of three main ways. First, the *agonothetes* could have become ill or died in office: it would be extremely surprising if this did not happen on at least a few occasions in almost a century and a half of minting. Second, the *agonothetes* could have been ejected from office

89 *I. Ilion* 12.9–13 (first century BC). For bibliography on the identification of this Agathes son of Menophilos with the magistrate on the coins see n. 64.
90 Lefèvre and Pillot 2015: 22.
91 Knoepfler 2010: 59 with n. 120.
92 Bellinger 1961: 36.
93 *I. Ilion* 2.5–6, 45–46, 50–51; *SEG* LIII 1373.5–6, 11–12.

for corruption. The *agonothetai* were handling considerable sums of money, and so the temptation to use their office to enrich themselves through graft would have been considerable. While, as is so often the case, corruption is not directly attested by the surviving inscriptions, it would strain credulity to infer from this silence that it never happened. Certainly, we know that the *agonothetai* were expected to keep careful accounts, and there are indications that, as we would expect, their conduct in office was subject to oversight by the *synedrion*.[94] We could therefore imagine, for example, an annual *euthyna* following the year's festival which would provide an opportunity for allegations of corruption to be levelled and thus for *agonothetai*, if found guilty, to be removed from office.[95] Finally, Lefèvre and Pillot's suggestion that Agathes could have held the offices of *agonothetes* and *agoranomos* consecutively rather than cumulatively opens up the possibility of *agonothetai* choosing to move sideways into roles such as *agoranomos* or *gymnasiarchos*. The advantage of doing so would have been that these magistracies offered opportunities for making benefactions and thus for receiving honors which, by contrast, were unavailable to *agonothetai*. Perhaps, as in the case of Agathes, this was particularly common in the year of the Great Panathenaia when the opportunities for displaying one's liberality and the rewards for doing so were correspondingly greater.

In conclusion, while we have good reason to think that the Ilian *agonothetes* named in exergue could in theory serve for up to four years, it is clear from the number of magistrates attested that many must have served for less than this. We would therefore need an extremely fine-grained knowledge of the koinon's history to be able to date the magistrates on the coins precisely, and this is unlikely to be forthcoming. Currently, we have no inscriptions of the koinon from the second century and only a handful from the first half of the first century, of which just the honorific decree for Agathes sheds any light on the problem, and then only in passing. While we therefore cannot hope to date the magistrates on the coins precisely, we can say that each magistrate could represent a period of up to four years and that they were minting coins throughout the penteteric cycle, not just in the year of the Great Panathenaia. On current evidence, however, it would seem that, *on average*, an Ilian *agonothetes* was only in office for about two years.[96] If more magistrates belonging to the already well-represented beginning (c. 185– c. 150) and end (c. 100–c. 50) of the series appear or if strong arguments are put forward for pushing the start of the series down to the late 170s and bringing the end up into the 60s, then this average will drop to a point where we will have to reassess the validity of the arguments put forward in this section. Alternatively, if new magistrates instead primarily appear in the underrepresented middle of the series (c. 150–c. 100) then this will bring the average length of office for magistrates

94 Lefèvre and Pillot 2015: 16–17, 21–2.
95 For such procedures in the Hellenistic period see in general Fröhlich (2004).
96 See n. 55.

in this period into line with the rest of the series and provide independent support for the epigraphic arguments discussed here.

5. The Purpose of the Coinage

5.1 Panegyris Coinages

Bellinger thought that the individuals named on the coins were wealthy benefactors who, out of a sense of civic pride and a desire to advertise their liberality and patriotism, donated the money to produce these handsome coins.[97] Robert put paid to this by demonstrating that these individuals were in fact magistrates whose reason for appearing on the coinage had to do with their portfolio of responsibilities within the koinon's institutions rather than euergetism.[98] More recently, Selene Psoma has interpreted the Athena Ilias series as an example of what she terms a "panegyris coinage." She compares it to other bronze and silver coinages in the name of a god whose use, she argues, was imposed on all transactions at the festival market in order to turn a profit for the sanctaury through money-changing charges.[99]

There are a number of problems with this interpretation of the coinage's purpose. First, if its purpose were to take a cut of as great a proportion as possible of the economic activity at the festival market, the best way to do this would have been to provide a variety of large and small denomination coins in both silver and bronze so that the coinage could be used in transactions of all sizes. Instead, there is no bronze coinage and the silver coins are only minted as tetradrachms until 77, and thereafter on occasion as drachms and didrachms, but always in place of tetradrachms rather than as part of the same issue. This suggests that these smaller denominations were not an attempt to expand the range of denominations (see further section 5.5). Second, perhaps anticipating this criticism, Psoma suggested that the coins were only meant to be used in large transactions.[100] However, it is not clear what the definition of a large transaction would be, nor how the *agoranomoi* would effectively police this even if an arbitrary figure were fixed upon. In any case, even large transactions require denominations below a tetradrachm, as indeed we see in the financial inscriptions of the koinon. In addition, given what a large role the *agoranomoi* would play in such an arrangement, it is a little surprising that it

97 Bellinger 1958: 15–24; Bellinger 1961: 26–27.

98 Robert 1966: 58–59, 67–93; cf. L. Robert, *OMS* 6: 125–135.

99 Psoma 2007 and 2008. Endorsed by Thonemann (2011: 118) but now rejected in 2015: 82–84.

100 Psoma 2007: 243: "The coinage issued in the name and types of the god in whose honour the fairs were organized by the corresponding association of cities was the only legal currency (*dokimon nomisma*) for large payments during this event, and all large-scale transactions had to be made with that currency." This caveat about the size of the transaction does not feature in Psoma 2008, in which case the fact of only silver tetradrachms being minted becomes even more problematic for her argument.

is instead the *agonothetai* who get named on the coinage. Finally, if the idea were
to create a mini-closed currency system for the duration of the festival, it would
make more sense to use an underweight and overvalued coinage (as the Ptolemies,
Attalids, and Byzantines did) which would lose its value outside the context of the
festival.[101] Instead, the koinon minted a full weight Attic coinage which, unlike
other large denomination silver coinages of the late Hellenistic period, maintained
its weight rather well right down to the mid-first century and would therefore have
been acceptable in international commerce (see section 3).

Nollé has recently attempted to deconstruct the notion of panegyris coinages
in general, and it is in this context that he formulates a new interpretation of the
purpose of the Athena Ilias coinage in order to establish that it is not, as Psoma
supposes, an example of a panegyris coinage at all.[102] He argues that Ilion was
attempting to provide coinage for the whole Troad and therefore imagines that the
city was exercising its financial hegemony over the Troad via this coinage.[103] Since
we now have a die study of the series, we can test the validity of this argument by
using quantitative methods to estimate the coinage's original size.

5.2 The Size of the Coinage

Nollé argues that the Athena Ilias coinage was a large series which served the needs
of the Troad as a whole, but does not provide any quantitative data to back up this
assertion. Rather, he comes to this conclusion on analogy with his interpretation
of the Artemis Pergaia coinage which he likewise interprets as a large coinage
serving the needs not just of the sanctuary, but also of Perge and of Pamphylia in
general.[104] However, the quantitative arguments he makes in support of this claim
are somewhat puzzling. As proof of its size, he cites the 44 (actually 42) obverse
and 268 reverse dies of the silver coinage and 470 obverse and 1,675 reverse dies
of the bronze coinage.[105] In order to compare like with like, I shall only discuss the
silver coinage, since there is no bronze coinage in the name of Athena Ilias and
Ilion's bronze coinage (which, on Nollé's view, would have been produced by the
same minting authority as the Athena Ilias coinage) has not received a die study.

---

101 Thonemann 2015: 83–84.

102 Psoma 2007: 240–241; Psoma 2008: 235–236; Nollé 2014.

103 Nollé 2014: 301 n. 75: "Feststeht aber meines Erachtens auch bei diesen Prägungen
die Dominanz von Ilion, auf dessen Territorium das Heiligtum der prägenden Göttin lag.
Eine Situation ähnlich der in Perge scheint mir gut möglich zu sein; dass die Städte der
Kultgemeinschaft sich für ihre Geldwirtschaft der Prägungen des Heiligtums bedienten, ist
wahrscheinlich"; 310: "In seltenen Fällen scheinen Heiligtümer die alleinigen oder zumind-
est wichtigsten Träger der städtischen Geldwirtschaft gewesen zu sein, wie etwa das Athe-
naheiligtum von Ilion oder das Artemision von Perge. Charakteristisch dafür sind mengen-
mäßig ins Gewicht fallende Emissionen von Wertgeld (insbesondere Tetradrachmen und
Drachmen) über längere Zeiträume."

104 Nollé 2014: 291–295.

105 Nollé 2014: 292, drawing on the die study of Colin 1996.

Because reverse dies wear out more quickly than obverse dies their usefulness for quantification is limited and so we can set them aside for the moment.[106] In order to reach this figure of 42 AR obverse dies Nollé adds together the tetradrachms, drachms, and hemidrachms from two separate series dated 260–230 and c. 48/7–c. 39/8.[107] There are several problems here. First, the number of obverse dies is only impressive relative to the period of time over which they were used (42 dies in a year is impressive; 42 dies in a century is not) and we need to establish whether the sample of obverse dies we have is representative (i.e., $n/d = >3$) before we can draw any further conclusions. The number of obverse dies is therefore a figure which has to be contextualized before it can become meaningful. More fundamentally, though, it makes no sense to add together different denominations in this way. If the aim is to calculate the number of obverse dies as a proxy for production and by extension the amount of silver being minted and therefore spent, then a tetradrachm die obviously cannot be given the same weighting as a drachm die or a hemidrachm die given that it is four and eight times larger than these respectively.

Table 4 therefore breaks these 42 dies down into their respective denominations and series. In the right-hand column I have converted the number of dies attested in each case into drachm die equivalents to make the figures comparable to one another (i.e., a tetradrachm = 4 drachm dies, so 7 tetradrachm dies = 28 drachm die equivalents) and then divided these figures by the length of time each series was minted to arrive at a rate of annual production. For comparison, I have also included the posthumous Alexanders struck at Perge which were minted following the first Artemis Pergaia series.[108]

Table 4. A comparison of the annual production in drachm die equivalents of the Artemis Pergaia and Perge Alexanders coinages.[109]

Series 1 = 260–230 Series 2 = 48/7–39/8	n	d	n/d	Drachm Die Equivalents	Annual Production
Tetradrachm (Series 1)	42	7	6.00	28	1.07
Tetradrachm (Series 2)	41	20	2.05	80	8.89
Drachm (Series 1)	14	3	4.66	3	0.10
Drachm (Series 2)	8	4	2.00	4	0.44
Hemidrachm (Series 1)	17	6	2.83	3	0.10
Hemidrachm (Series 2)	10	2	5.00	1	0.11
Alexanders (223/2–191/0)	361	73	4.94	292	9.13

106 For the uses which can be made of them see de Callataÿ 2006: 131–143.

107 For this downdating to c. 48/7–c. 39/8 from Colin's dates of c. 170–c. 100 see Meadows 2014.

108 For dating and interpretation of the Perge Alexanders (a coinage probably minted from royal rather than civic funds) see Meadows 2009.

109 Sources: Colin 1996.

The figures for Series 1 certainly do not justify Nollé's claims about the size and importance of the Artemis Pergaia coinage. Moreover, the downdating of Series 2 to the 40s BC and Meadows's argument that it is an imitative series produced on a weight standard compatible with the Roman *denarius* in the context of Antony's campaigns all suggest that this is a series which has very little to do with the civic finances of Perge and therefore needs to be excluded from consideration.[110] However, what the Series 2 Artemis Pergaia coinage along with the posthumous Alexanders do demonstrate is what genuinely sizeable coinages look like by comparison with the very low volume of production we see in the Series 1 Artemis Pergaia coinage. Table 5 places the Series 1 Artemis Pergaia tetradrachms, the Perge Alexanders, and the Athena Ilias and Apollo Smintheus tetradrachms in the broader context of several wreathed tetradrachm coinages for which we have die studies and a representative sample of the series. Since only tetradrachms are represented in this table, annual production represents tetradrachm dies per year rather than drachm die equivalents.

Table 5. A comparison of the annual production of i) the Series 1 Artemis Pergaia and Perge Alexander tetradrachms, ii) the Athena Ilias and Apollo Smintheus tetradrachms, iii) wreathed tetradrachm series with n/d = >3.[111]

Mint	*n*	*d*	*n/d*	Dates	Annual Production
Apollo Smintheus	62	18	3.44	175–65	0.16
Artemis Pergaia (Series 1)	42	7	6.00	260–230	0.23
Athena Ilias	101	35	2.89	180–50	0.27
Tenedos	86	21	4.10	100–70	0.70
Abydos	126	35	3.60	100–70	1.16
Lebedos	53	8	6.63	140–135?	1.60
Smyrna (Tyche/ΣΜΥΡΝΑΙΩΝ)	71	13	5.46	150–143	1.85
Aigai	36	4	9.00	151–143	2.00
Perge Alexanders	361	73	4.94	221–189	2.28
Magnesia	242	36	6.72	150–140	3.60
Herakleia	117	25	4.68	140–135?	5.00
Myrina	415	97	4.28	160–143	5.70
Kyme	537	79	6.80	155–143	6.58

110 See Meadows (2014) and his forthcoming paper on the penetration of the *denarius* and *quinarius* standards into Asia Minor in the first century BC which he was kind enough to share with me in an early draft.

111 Sources: Apollo Smintheus = Ellis-Evans work in progress; Perge = Colin (1996); Tenedos = de Callataÿ (1998); Abydos = de Callataÿ (1996); other wreathed tetradrachm series = de Callataÿ (2013) 233, Table 6.10.

The rates of production for the Athena Ilias, Apollo Smintheus, and Series 1 Artemis Pergaia coinages are very substantially below that of all the other mints. Even if we use Esty's estimated original number of dies for Athena Ilias (53.6), which is higher than Carter's estimate (45.3), and we then contract the time period to the most conservative estimate possible (175–65), we end up with a figure of 0.49 for annual production which is still well below even Tenedos at 0.70. Finally, it is worth noting that one of the assumptions made by both Carter and Esty is that mints were using dies until they broke. However, the Athena Ilias series has a ratio of obverse to reverse dies of 1:2 which is very low (compare e.g., Artemis Pergaia's tetradrachms at 1:6) which suggests that the Athena Ilias mint frequently discarded obverse dies before they were used up. The already low production figures suggested by Carter and Esty's estimates are therefore, if anything, slightly optimistic.[112] While, as established earlier, our knowledge of the Athena Ilias series is certain to grow, there is no realistic possibility that it will grow by the orders of magnitude necessary to put it on a par with any of the other mints in Table 5. The mints producing the Athena Ilias, Apollo Smintheus, and Series 1 Artemis Pergaia coinages therefore appear to have been minting only to meet their own rather modest needs, not those of other cities throughout their region as Nollé supposes.

5.3 Festival Coins and Festival Expenditure

Another possible explanation of the coinage's purpose is that the coins were minted to meet the organization's expenditure, in this case the cost to the koinon of running the festival.[113] Many of these costs are detailed in the epigraphic evidence, while others can be inferred from what we know about the running of festivals more generally. Occasional expenses included things such as the construction of new buildings and diplomatic activity (e.g., Malousios paying for a new theatre and for embassies to be dispatched to Antigonos Monophthalmos).[114] Regular expenses partly consisted of costs incurred by the *synedrion* (e.g., publishing decrees, making proclamations, conferring crowns, setting up bronze statues, and attending meetings of the *synedrion*), but mostly came from running the festival itself.[115] We are well informed about the nature of these expenses by *I. Ilion* 10 (the decree from 77 discussed in section 4.6), since the inscription's second half lists some of the expenses incurred at the Great and Little Panathenaia and how they will be decreased in order to alleviate the financial pressure on the koinon. These included the procession, sacrifice, victim for sacrifice, provision of oil, and musical, athletic, and horse-racing competitions.[116] Further expenses are mentioned in passing elsewhere in the inscriptions, for example the erection

---

112 I am grateful to Ute Wartenberg for drawing my attention to this point.
113 On state expenditure and coins see Howgego 1990 and 1995: 33–38.
114 Lefèvre and Pillot 2015: 6–7 and *I. Ilion* 1.
115 Lefèvre and Pillot 2015: 7–8.
116 *I. Ilion* 10.21–31.

of temporary structures during the festival or the extras for which benefactors provided the funds, for example the doctor paid for by a Parian *agoranomos* or the beast fight put on at the expense of Agathes son of Menophilos.[117] In addition to all this, Thonemann notes that our evidence for Hellenistic festivals in general shows that hiring theatrical troupes and star athletes to perform at one's festival could be extremely expensive, and so the coins may in part have gone towards their fees and the prize money for which they competed.[118] The anonymous athlete whose string of victories at international competitions—including one at the Panathenaia at Ilion—were celebrated at Perge in the first century AD may have been just such an individual.[119]

The inscriptions make clear that the magistrates responsible for making all these payments were the *agonothetai*. It is therefore entirely appropriate that the president of the board of *agonothetai* should be named on the coins: this was the individual who would ultimately be held accountable for the use of these funds. Presumably, a basic budget existed of the regular expenses always incurred in putting on the festival to which the occasional expenses were added as necessary—we get a sense of what this might have looked like from the savings listed in *I. Ilion* 10. Based on this, the *synedrion* released the relevant funds to the *agonothetai* (the procedure which we see them follow with, for example, Malousios's donation), who then had part or all of this sum minted as high value silver tetradrachms in order to have cash on hand with which to make external payments. The choice to mint only high value coinage is consistent with the fact that many of these expenses will have been large lump-sum payments for which silver tetradrachms were the most convenient method of payment. The *agonothetai* therefore did not bother to mint a wide variety of lower value denominations which would be suited to market exchange because this was never the intended purpose of the coinage (the drachms and didrachm which appear to be an exception to this will be discussed in section 5.5). This explanation has the advantage of accounting for both the salient characteristics of the coinage (i.e., continual production, low die count, the coinage keeping its weight, the choice of a high value denomination) and what we know from the coins and the inscriptions about the procedures and institutions of the koinon.

5.4 The Coinage of Athena Ilias and Regional Dynamics

While this economic explanation of the purpose of the coinage accounts for the physical characteristics of the coins (i.e., size, weight, metal), it cannot be the whole story since it does not also account for the choice to mint a coinage with civic types. The running of all festivals required cash to make payments, but only a small number of festivals are associated with coinages minted specially for that

---

117 *I. Ilion* 1.4–5 (temporary structures), 3.16–18 (doctor), 12.14–18 (beast fights).
118 Thonemann (2015) 84.
119 See n. 58.

purpose. In the case of the koinon of Athena Ilias, the need for coins in which to make payments was just as great before the Athena Ilias coinage was introduced in the late 180s/early 170s, and it will have continued to be important after the coinage ended in the mid-first century.[120] Presumably, in the third century the koinon made use of the Attic-weight royal and posthumous coinages which possessed the same key characteristics as the Athena Ilias coinage of being high value and internationally acceptable. Indeed, in third century inscriptions the *agonothetai* use Ἀλεξανδρέαι δραχμαί as their unit of account.[121] As Peter Thonemann has recently emphasized, the koinon was therefore *choosing* to make its payments in its own coinage, which suggests that the koinon was just as concerned with the visual impression these coins would make as with their ability to fulfil their economic function.[122]

As has long been recognized, the Athena Ilias coinage is typical of a much broader transformation in Greek coinage which took place in the middle decades of the second century and can be seen at more than 40 mints in and around the Aegean basin.[123] In terms of types, the obverses are elaborate, often virtuoso portraits of deities, while the reverses feature full-figure depictions of local gods. The reverse figure is framed either with legends or, as in the case of the "stephanephoric" coinages, with wreaths, and the iconography and legends make prominent reference to distinctively local traditions about the deities depicted. In terms of physical characteristics, the coins are typically minted on broad, thin flans and use the Attic weight standard. In addition to the artistic accomplishment of the dies, care for the aesthetic appearance of the coins can also be detected in the rarity of worn dies (suggesting they were being discarded well before reaching this point, something which a low ratio of obverse to reverse dies also points to) and, it has been argued, from the practice of hammering the edges of the flan.[124] These coins were therefore not just a means of making payments, they were also status symbols which advertised the distinctive civic identity and local traditions of the minting authority.

However, alongside these striking similarities, there are also significant differences, in particular in terms of the overall size of the coinages, the tempo at which they were minted, and the longevity of the series. At one end of the spectrum we have very small issues known from only a handful of specimens: for example, the Athena Nikephoros tetradrachms of Pergamon are only known from

120 For discussion of the epigraphic evidence attesting continuity in how the koinon was run from the third–first century see section 4.6.

121 *I. Ilion* 5 (passim), 6.1, 18.6.

122 Thonemann 2015: 84.

123 For recent overviews see Matthaei 2013; Thonemann 2015: 56–64; Meadows (forthcoming).

124 Thonemann 2015: 59 (rarity of worn dies); Mørkholm 1991: 12 (development of broad flans); de Callataÿ 2006: 148–152 (hammering edges).

three specimens preserving two obverse dies.[125] At the other end of the spectrum, we have extremely large issues which were intensively minted over a period of just a few years: for example, the stephanephoric tetradrachms of Kyme are known from 537 specimens, preserving 79 dies, all of which were minted 155–143.[126] The Athena Ilias and Apollo Smintheus coinages are therefore of particular interest since they do not fit either model: they were minted continually, over a long period of time, and at a low volume of production. Moreover, as I have argued above, the Athena Ilias series probably began in the late 180s/early 170s and the Apollo Smintheus series in the mid-170s. This makes these two coinages the earliest examples of this new style of autonomous spread-flan coinage, placing them almost a decade earlier than the adopters of the 160s (mostly from mainland Greece and from Thrace, the Propontis, and the Black Sea), and two decades earlier than the stephanephoric coinages of Aiolis, Ionia, and Karia to the south.

It would seem, therefore, that, at some point in the late 180s/early 170s, the member states of the koinon took a collective decision to start making their payments with a coinage which would celebrate Athena Ilias and raise the international profile of the Panathenaia. Reminting the perfectly acceptable coinage already in the koinon's treasury as an artistically beautiful and carefully produced spread-flan series will have incurred extra expense for the koinon. This decision therefore indicates that this coinage was not just a means of payment, but also a status symbol. The Apollo Smintheus coinage which Alexandreia Troas began to produce soon afterwards has a strikingly similar numismatic profile: in addition to the visual similarities, it was continually minted from the mid-170s–65, production remained at a low volume throughout, the denominations were limited to high value tetradrachms until late in the series, and great care was taken for the appearance of the coins (e.g. hammered flan edges, a low obverse to reverse die ratio of 1:2.5). I would therefore suggest that Alexandreia Troas may have been using the Apollo Smintheus coinage to cover expenditure on the Smintheia, and was therefore producing a coinage which was not just a means of making payments, but also a mark of prestige for the festival which, particularly within the Troad, sent the message that the Smintheia was on a par with the Panathenaia of Athena Ilias. Alain Bresson has recently argued that Hamaxitos, in whose territory the sanctuary of Apollo Smintheus stood, was only synoikized into Alexandreia Troas following the Peace of Apameia.[127] Soon after this, Alexandreia began to publish its public decrees in the sanctuary, and in the mid-second century a grand new temple was built there.[128] The Apollo Smintheus coinage may therefore belong

---

125 Le Rider 1973; Mørkholm 1984: 187–192; Le Rider 1989: 175–176; Marcellesi 2012: 125–127; Meadows 2013: 175.

126 Oakley 1982; de Callataÿ 1997b: 198–199; Meadows and Houghton 2010: 180–181.

127 Bresson 2007: esp. 154–155.

128 Public decrees published in the Smintheion: *I. Alex. Troas* 4 (early second century) and 5 (c. 165). Temple: Özgünel 2003.

to this broader context of Alexandreia laying claim to the sanctuary and vigorously promoting its festival.[129]

5.5 The Coinage of Athena Ilias and the Finances of the Koinon

A further implication of arguing that the Athena Ilias coins were being minted to cover expenditure for the festival is that it should therefore be possible to use the coins as a proxy for the health of the koinon's finances. The assumption here is that during periods of prosperity the koinon will have had more money to spend on the festival and therefore more funds will have been released to the *agonothetai*. Consequently, there will have been more silver to mint and so they will have gone through a larger number of obverse dies. To an extent, the first two-thirds of the series conform to this picture, much as we would expect given the general prosperity of the cities of western Asia Minor in the second century. However, since the only way to track increased expenditure in this way is through the number of obverse dies used and we still lack a truly representative sample of the series (i.e., ideally an n/d of >5), it would be rash to speculate further on this. By contrast, periods of financial difficulty for the koinon should be somewhat easier to identify because this should manifest itself not just in obverse dies lasting longer or remaining in use long after they should have been retired, but also in the minting of smaller denominations to reflect the smaller volumes of silver being minted. This is precisely what we see happening in the last third of the series which dates to the first half of the first century. We know both from the parallel and dated Apollo Smintheus series and from the koinon decree of 77 (*I. Ilion* 10) that it was in precisely this period that the koinon's cities experienced severe financial hardship and that this resulted in decreased expenditure on the festival.

One of the more important pieces of evidence for a slowdown in the koinon's minting activity has instead been misinterpreted as evidence for a spike in minting. With sixteen specimens, the issue of Menephron son of Menephron is by some margin the best attested in the series.[130] Twelve of these 16 coins have as their control mark a Pegasus facing left and drinking water, a symbol which has naturally been connected to Mithradates VI and the events of 88–85. As Bellinger puts it: "The size of [Menephron's] output shows a substantial effort to convince the Pontic king that Ilium would be of service to him … These are the sinews of war produced in quantity for a crisis."[131] Even when the connection with Mithradates

---

129 In light of this argument, Parion's Apollo Aktaios (Group 1: mid-160s; Group 2: 140s/130s?) and Lampsakos's Priapos tetradrachms (last third of the second century) may need to be reinterpreted as short-lived attempts by other members of the koinon to emulate the Athena Ilias and Apollo Smintheus coinages. I will present my die studies of these two short series and my arguments for dating them as I do here in the near future.

130 Others: Agathes son of Menophilos, Metriketes (6); Apemantos, Metrodoros, Zoilos (5); Akkos, Soterides (4).

131 Bellinger 1961: 34. Accepted by (e.g.) Healy (1962: 218) and Kinns (1987: 110).

is doubted, it is still assumed that this is an unusually large issue and that it must therefore be linked to an episode of increased expenditure.[132]

However, it seems to have been misunderstood that it is not the number of specimens but rather the number of obverse dies which indicates the original size of a coinage.[133] The issue of Menephron son of Menephron is represented by only two obverse dies, putting it on a level with Metrodoros, Dionysodoros, and Euboulides and below Akkos, Apollodoros, and Melanippides (on three) and Apemantos (on four). Moreover, Menephron son of Menephron is represented by two to three times as many coins as these other issues, so whereas new obverse dies might well turn up for these and other magistrates, that is much less likely to be the case for Menephron son of Menephron. What is more, the obverse die used for 15 of the 16 Menephron son of Menephron coins is shared with four of the previous magistrates. Worsening die faults allow us to show both that the die was being used well beyond its natural life and that Menephron son of Menephron was the last to use it and did not immediately retire it (he went through three more reverse dies first).[134]

In sum, the inference to draw from this magistrate's issue is not that coin production was speeding up in this period, but rather that it was slowing down. Given that a single reverse die is substantially overrepresented (12 of the 16 coins), that 12 of the coins either certainly or very probably have pre-1900 provenances, and that four have pre-1800 (in one case pre-1750) provenances, it seems likely that a significant number of these Menephron son of Menephron coins came from an early unrecorded hoard find which has led to Menephron son of Menephron being substantially overrepresented within the series.[135] While the most straightforward explanation of the Pegasus control mark remains that it was a reference to Mithradates, it should perhaps be interpreted simply as a show of support for the Pontic king, since the coins themselves certainly do not support the hypothesis that the issue of Menephron son of Menephron was an especially large issue minted to meet military expenditure. In support of this distinction we

132 E.g., Knoepfler 2010: 56-57.

133 Already observed in this case by de Callataÿ 1997a: 291, esp. n. 79.

134 Bellinger (1961: 33–34) also lists a further reverse die, T 97. On this basis, Knoepfler (2010: 56–57) has argued that Menephron son of Menephron was unusual in issuing tetradrachms not just in the year of the Great Panaethnaia, but also in the three years of the Little Panathenaia. However, of the two coins Bellinger lists, the one at Winterthur does not exist, while "Mionnet II, p. 658, No. 189" is in fact an example of Bellinger's T 96 in Paris (BNF Fonds Général 689).

135 For a comparable argument (proposed with all due caution) regarding the wreathed tetradrachms of Tenedos see de Callataÿ 1998: 109–110, and for an example of such a hoard Seyrig 1973: 49–56 (*IGCH* 1544, Latakia, Syria, 1759). It is perhaps suggestive that the catalogue entry for the Menephron son of Menephron specimen in the Earl of Pembroke's collection (acquired in the first half of the eighteenth century) remarks: "Since the discovery of hoards, which furnished specimens to the principal cabinets of Europe, above a century ago, these coins are scarcely ever seen" (S. Leigh Sotheby [31/7/1848], p. 191).

can compare the appearance of this same control mark on an issue of "New Style" Athenian tetradrachms from 97/6. One of the magistrates, Aristion, was later a partisan of Mithradates at Athens and led the doomed resistance to Sulla in 87/6, so the political interpretation of the control mark seems secure. However, the issue is dated almost a decade before the Mithradatic Wars and so obviously cannot be linked to Mithradates's military expenditure.[136]

One magistrate later we get the first issue of drachms instead of tetradrachms. As I argued in section 4.6, the Demetrios named on this issue is the Demetrios son of Hippodamas mentioned in the koinon decree of 77 in which the cities refer to αἱ τῶν πόλεων θλίψεις ("the afflictions of the cities") which have forced them to severely reduce expenditure on the festival.[137] It has sometimes been argued that the issues of drachms should be grouped together in a period of poverty for the koinon, and Knoepfler has suggested the immediate aftermath of the Mithradatic Wars specifically, which would thus indicate the destitution of the cities in the decade or so after 85 before they began to recover.[138] However, as I argued in sections 4.2 and 4.5, criteria such as shared monograms and prosopography instead suggest a more complex picture in which, from one magistrate to the next, the koinon went back and forth between tetradrachms, drachms, and, on one occasion, didrachms. We see something similar in the contemporary Apollo Smintheus issues: a didrachm appears in 101 and drachms in 80, 78, and 73.[139] Another phenomenon worth noting in the Apollo Smintheus coinage is the introduction of the practice, first attested in 93, of coins being issued by two different magistrates in a single year. Given how frequently this is attested after 93 (it occurs again in 92, 85, 80, 79, 78, 71, 68, and 65), this would appear to have been a reform of the magistracy which may reflect the financial pressures of the time.

While the Mithradatic Wars and their aftermath undoubtedly brought enormous hardship on the cities of the koinon, it is worth noting that in the dated Apollo Smintheus coins there are signs of trouble even before 88, for example the didrachm of 101 and the reform of the magistracy in c. 93 in which the job is shared between two men. In the Athena Ilias series, it is just about possible to fit the five magistrates sharing a single obverse die (culminating in Menephron son of Menephron) and Demophon son of Dionys[?] between the beginning of the Mithradatic Wars in 88 and Demetrios son of Hippodamas in 77 and therefore attribute these first signs of financial distress to fallout from the Mithradatic Wars alone. However, it is equally possible, especially in light of the evidence of the Apollo Smintheus series, that these issues stretch back before 88 and well into the 90s, therefore pointing to underlying financial problems in the cities which predate the catastrophes of the 80s.

136 Thonemann 2015: 167–168.
137 *I. Ilion* 10.14–15.
138 Bellinger 1961: 27; Knoepfler 2010: 58.
139 Didrachm: CNG EA 235 (23/6/2010), lot 161 (Archagoras; 27 mm, 12h, 6.98 g). Drachms: Bellinger A 160 (80 BC), A 163 (78 BC), A 164 (73 BC).

6. CONCLUSIONS

In discussing the coinage of the koinon of Athena Ilias I have argued for the following four claims: 1) the coinage was minted continually from the late 180s/ early 170s down to the 60s/50s (sections 4.1–5); 2) the magistrate named on the reverse is the Ilian president of the board of *agonothetai* who could in theory be in office for an entire penteteric cycle of up to four years, but who on average was in office for closer to two years (section 4.6); 3) the coins were minted for the double purpose of covering festival expenditure, which accounts for their physical characteristics, and as a status symbol, which explains their aesthetic characteristics (sections 5.1–4); 4) the variations in output we see in issues dating to the first half of the first century independently attest the financial difficulties which we already knew about from *I. Ilion* 10 that the member cities were experiencing following the Mithradatic Wars, but also point to the existence of problems even before 88– 85 (section 5.5).

As the die study has made clear by revealing an *n/d* which barely reaches 3 even with the help of an overrepresented obverse die, the large number of obverse dies only attested by a single example, and the underrepresentation of the series in the second half of the second century, we should expect new examples of this series to continue to appear. As they do, the four main claims I have argued for will become testable hypotheses and may need to be revisited. However, if for the moment we accept these conclusions, then perhaps the most striking finding to emerge from this study is the longevity of the series, matched only by the Apollo Smintheus series of Alexandreia Troas, and its resilience in the face of the Mithradatic Wars, severe economic pressures on the region's cities, and, in particular, the sack of Ilion at the hands of Fimbria in 85.[140] This resilience should certainly be attributed in part to the member states' enthusiasm for the Panathenaia festival, evidenced by their desire in 77 to organize it "just as it had also been in the past" (καθότι καὶ πρότερον) even at a time of financial crisis.[141] Equally important, however, was the effectiveness of the koinon's communally-run institutions which helped share the burden of running this major festival in a way which seemed equitable to the member states and was therefore politically sustainable.

---

140 Liv. *Per.* 83; Julius Obsequens, *Liber de prodigiis* 56b (epitome of Livy's lost *De prodigiis*); Strabo 13.1.27; App. *Mithr.* 53; Dio 30–35.104.7. For evidence of the Ilians clearing out the treasures of Temple A in the West Sanctuary in advance of Fimbria's sack see Rose 1994: 76–80 and 1997: 92.

141 καθότι καὶ πρότερον: *I. Ilion* 10.22, 37, 39.

Acknowledgements

I am grateful to Andrew Meadows, Ute Wartenberg, Peter Thonemann, Simon Glenn, and Ben Raynor for their help with this paper. Late in the publication process François de Callataÿ alerted me to a number of new references and suggested several counterarguments to the reconstruction proposed here which helpfully prompted me to tighten up the argument in a number of places.

Bibliography

Arslan, M. and C. Lightfoot. 1999. *Greek coin hoards in Turkey: The Antalya Archaeological Museum and the C. S. Okray Collection with additional material from the Burdur, Fethiye and Sinop Museums.* Ankara.

Bellinger, A. R. 1958. "The first civic tetradrachms of Ilium." *ANSMN* 8: 11–24.

———. 1961. *Troy: The Coins.* Princeton.

Boehringer, C. 1972. *Zur Chronologie mittelhellenistischer Münzserien, 220–160 v. Chr.* Berlin.

———. 1975. "Hellenistischer Münzschatz aus Trapezunt 1970." *SNR* 54: 37–64.

Bresson, A. 2007. "Hamaxitos en Troade." In *Espaces et pouvoirs dans l'Antqiuité de l'Anatolie à la Gaule. Hommages à Bernard Rémy,* edited by J. Dalaison, pp. 139–158. Grenoble.

Brückner, A. 1902. "Geschichte von Troja und Ilion." In *Troja und Ilion: Ergebnisse der Ausgrabungen in den vorhistorischen und historischen Schichten von Ilion, 1870–1894,* edited by W. Dörpfeld, vol. 2, 549–600. Athens.

Callataÿ, F. de. 1997a. *L'Histoire des guerres mithridatiques vue par les monnaies.* Louvain.

———. 1997b. *Recueil quantitatif des émissions monétaires hellénistiques.* Wetteren.

———. 1998. "Les monnaies hellénistiques en argent de Ténédos." In *Studies in Greek numismatics in memory of Martin Jessop Price,* edited by R. H. J. Ashton et al., pp. 99–114. London.

———. 2006. *Quantifications et numismatique antique: choix d'articles (1984–2004).* Wetteren.

———. 2013. "The coinages of the Attalids and their neighbours: a quantified overview." In *Attalid Asia Minor: Money, international relations, and the state,* edited by in P. Thonemann, pp. 207–244. Oxford.

Carter, G. F. 1983. "A simplified method for calculating the original number of dies from die link statistics." *ANSMN* 28: 195–206.

Colin, H. J. 1996. *Die Münzen von Perge in Pamphylien aus hellenistischer Zeit.* Cologne.

Esty, W. W. 2011. "The geometric model for estimating the number of dies." In *Quantifying monetary supplies in Greco-Roman times,* edited by F. de Callataÿ, pp. 43–58. Bari.

Fröhlich, P. 2004. *Les cités grecques et le contrôle des magistrats (IVe–Ier siècle avant J.-C.)*. Geneva.

Gauthier, P. 2011. *Études d'histoire et d'institutions grecques: choix d'écrits*. Geneva.

Gerasimov, T. 1979. "Trésors monétaires trouvés en Bulgarie au cours de 1968, 1969 et 1970." *Bulletin de l'Institut archéologique bulgare* 35: 134–141.

Guépin, J. P. 1969. *"De novis libris iudicia* [Robert (1966)]." *Mnemosyne* 22: 207–212.

Healy, J. F. 1962. "*Troy: The Coins* by Alfred Bellinger." *Gnomon* 34.2: 218–219.

Howgego, C. J. 1990. "Why did ancient states strike coins?" *NC* 150: 1–25.

———. 1995. *Ancient history from coins*. London.

Imhoof-Blumer, F. 1913. "Antike griechische Münzen." *SNR* 19: 5–134.

Kienast, D. 1959–1960. "Buchbesprengungen [Bellinger (1958)]." *JNG* 10: 239–240.

Kinns, P. 1987. "Asia Minor." In *The coinage of the Roman world in the Late Republic*, edited by A. M. Burnett and M. H. Crawford, pp. 105–119. Oxford.

———. 1999. "The Attic weight drachms of Ephesus: a preliminary study in the light of recent hoards." *NC* 159: 47–97.

Knoepfler, D. 2010. "Les agonothètes de la Confédération d'Athéna Ilias: une interpretation nouvelle des données épigraphiques et ses conséquences pour la chronologie des émissions monétaires du Koinon." *Studi Ellenistici* 24: 33–62.

Kraft, K. 1962. "Buchbesprechungen [Bellinger (1961)]." *JNG* 12: 239–240.

Lacroix, L. 1949. *Les reproductions de statues sur les monnaies grecques: la statuaire archaïque et classique*. Liège.

Le Rider, G. 1973. "Un tétradrachme d'Athéna Niképhoros." *RN*[6] 15: 66–79.

———. 1989. "La politique monétaire du royaume de Pergame après 188." *Journal des savants*: 163–189.

Lefèvre, F. and Pillot, W. 2015. "La confederation d'Athéna Ilias: administration et pratiques financières." *REG* 128.1: 1–27.

Leschhorn, W. 2002–2009. *Lexikon der Aufschriften auf griechischen Münzen*. 22 vols. Vienna.

Lorber, C. C. 2010. "Commerce ('Demetrius I' Hoard), 2003 (*CH* 10.301)." In *Coin Hoards* X: *Greek Hoards*, edited by in O. Hoover, A. R. Meadows, and U. Wartenberg, pp. 153–172. New York.

Ma, J. 2007. "Dating the new decree of the Confederation of Athena Ilias." *EA* 40: 55–57.

Marcellesi, M.-C. 2012. *Pergame: de la fin du Ve au début du Ier siècle avant J.-C.: pratiques monétaires et histoire*. Studi Ellenistici 26. Pisa.

Marinescu, C. A. 1996. *Making and spending money along the Bosporus: The Lysimachi coinages minted by Byzantium and Calchedon and their socio-cultural context*. PhD diss. Columbia University, New York.

Matthaei, A. 2013. *Münzbild und Polisbild: Untersuchungen zur Selbstdarstellung kleinasiatischer Poleis im Hellenismus*. Munich.

Mattingly, H. B. 1993. "The Ma'aret En-Nu'man Hoard, 1980." In *Essays in Honour of Robert Carson and Kenneth Jenkins*, edited by M. Price, A. Burnett, and R. Bland, pp. 69–86. London.

Meadows, A. R. 2009. "The eras of Pamphylia and the Seleucid invasions of Asia Minor." *AJN* 21: 51–88.

———. 2013. "The closed currency system of the Attalid kingdom." In *Attalid Asia Minor: Money, international relations, and the state*, edited by P. Thonemann, pp. 149–205. Oxford.

———. 2014. "Imitative coinage in first-century Pamphylia." In *Proceedings of the First International Congress of the Anatolian Monetary History and Numismatics*, edited by K. Dörtlük, pp. 409–422. Istanbul.

———. Forthcoming. "The Great Transformation. Civic coin design in the second century BC." In *TYPOI: Greek Coins and their Images*.

Meadows, A. R. and A. Houghton. 2010. "The Gaziantep Hoard, 1994 (*CH* 9.537; 10.308)." In *Coin Hoards* X: *Greek Hoards*, edited by O. Hoover, A. R. Meadows, and U. Wartenberg, pp. 173–223. New York.

Mørkholm, O. 1984. "Some Pergamene coins in Copenhagen." In F*estschrift für Leo Mildenberg: Numismatik, Kunstgeschichte, Archäologie*, edited by A. Houghton et al., pp. 181–192. Wetteren.

———. 1991. *Early Hellenistic coinage: From the accession of Alexander to the Peace of Apamea (336–188 BC)*. Cambridge.

Nollé, J. 2014. "«Panegyris coinages»–eine moderne Geisterprägung." *Chiron* 44: 285–323.

Oakley, J. H. 1982. "The autonomous wreathed tetradrachms of Kyme, Aeolis." *ANSMN* 27: 1–38.

Özgünel, C. A. 2003. "Das Heiligtum des Apollon Smintheus und die Ilias." *Studia Troica* 13: 261–291.

Paunov, E. I. 2013. "Georgi Dobrevo/2000 reconsidered: note on a first century BC coin hoard from Thrace." *Ancient West and East* 12: 281–294.

Psoma, S. 2007. "Profitable networks: coinages, panegyris and Dionysiac artists." *Mediterranean Historical Review* 22.2: 237–255.

———. 2008. "Panegyris coinages." *AJN* 20: 227–55.

Regling, K. 1928. "Hellenistischer Münzschatz aus Babylon." *ZfN* 38: 92–132.

Robert, L. 1966. *Monnaies antiques en Troade*. Geneva.

———. 1967. *Monnaies grecques: types, légendes, magistrats monétaires et géographie*. Geneva.

Rose, C. B. 1994. "The 1993 Post-Bronze Age Excavations at Troia." *Studia Troica* 4: 75–104.

———. 1997. "The 1996 Post-Bronze Age excavations at Troia." *Studia Troica* 7: 73–110.

————. 2014. *The Archaeology of Greek and Roman Troy*. Cambridge.

Seyrig, H. 1963. "Monnaies hellénistiques. VIII: Pergé; IX: Aspendos; X: Sidé." *RN*[6] 5: 38–64.

————. 1973. *Trésors du Levant anciens et nouveaux*. Paris.

Thompson, M. 1968. "The mints of Lysimachus." In *Essays in Greek coinage presented to Stanley Robinson*, edited by C. M. Kraay and G. K. Jenkins, pp. 163–182. Oxford.

Thonemann, P. 2011. *The Maeander Valley: A historical geography from antiquity to Byzantium*. Cambridge.

————. 2015. *The Hellenistic world: Using coins as sources*. Cambridge.

Von Fritze, H. 1902. "Die Münzen von Ilion." In *Troja und Ilion: Ergebnisse der Ausgrabungen in den vorhistorischen und historischen Schichten von Ilion, 1870–1894*, edited by W. Dörpfeld, vol. 2, 477–534. Athens.

Wallrodt, S. J. 2002. "Ritual activity in late Classical Ilion: the evidence from a fourth century BC deposit of loomweights and spindlewhorls." *Studia Troica* 12: 179–196.

Yakunovich, M. 1909. *Neizdannye i redkie drevne-grecheskie monety* (St. Petersburg).

KEY TO PLATES

Athena Ilias (Koinon of Athena Ilias)

Plate 35

1. O1: Hegesidemos (1). GM 207 (15/10/2012), lot 289.
2. O2: Antiphanes (1). Ashmolean Museum of Art and Archaeology.
3. O2: Athenokles. Trustees of the British Museum.
4. O2: Iphiades. Universität Tübingen, ZNr. 16248. Photo: Thomas Zachmann.
5. O2: Thersandros. Adolph Hess 253 (8/3/1983), lot 224.
6. O2: Xanthippos. Bibliothèque nationale de France.

Plate 36

7. O2: Metriketes. Bibliothèque nationale de France.
8. O3: Metriketes. Gemini 11 (12/1/2014), lot 165.
9. O3: Akkos. GM 224 (13/10/2014), lot 229.
10. O4: Akkos. CNG 53 (15/3/2000), lot 434 (www.cngcoins.com).
11. O5: Akkos. H. A. Troxell, *The Norman Davis Collection* (New York 1969), no. 202.
12. O6: Metrodoros. NAC 54 (24/3/2010), lot 109.

Plate 37

13. O6: Eudemos. Lanz 158 (5/6/2014), lot 239.
14. O6: Phoinix. Künker 236 (7/10/2013), lot 81.
15. O7: Dionysodoros. Münzkabinett, Staatliche Museen zu Berlin. Photo by Reinhard Saczweski.

16. O8: Dionysodoros. Münzkabinett, Staatliche Museen zu Berlin. Photo by Reinhard Saczweski.
17. O8: Apemantos. A. R. Bellinger, *Troy: The Coins* (Princeton 1961), p. 24, T 43, Plate 2.
18. O9: Apemantos. Alpha Bank Numismatic Collection.

Plate 38

19. O10: Apemantos. UBS 55 (16/9/2002), lot 1731.
20. O11: Apemantos. MM Basel Liste 525 (Sep. 1989), lot 16.
21. O12: Antiphanes (2). Künker 262 (13/3/2015), lot 7168.
22. O12: Zoilos. CNG 91 (19/9/2012), lot 249 (www.cngcoins.com).
23. O13: Soterides. Trustees of the British Museum.
24. O14: Apollodoros. Private collection.

Plate 39

25. O15: Apollodoros. Münzkabinett, Staatliche Museen zu Berlin. Photo by Reinhard Saczweski.
26. O16: Apollodoros. Bank Leu 36 (7/5/1985), lot 148.
27. O17: Demetrios (1). CGB.fr 47 (19/3/2011), lot 103.
28. O18: Euboulides. American Numismatic Society.
29. O19: Euboulides. Triton 1 (2/12/1997), lot 523 (www.cngcoins.com).
30. O20: Lysikles. Bibliothèque nationale de France.

Plate 40

31. O20: Protokleides. Museum of Fine Arts, Boston.
32. O21: Dionysios. Bibliothèque nationale de France.
33. O22: Hermokreon. UBS 33 (20/9/1993), lot 284.
34. O23: Melantas. Trustees of the British Museum.
35. O24: Prytanis. Peus 332 (23/10/1991), lot 187.
36. O25: Menephron. Münzkabinett, Staatliche Museen zu Berlin. Photo by Reinhard Saczweski.

Plate 41

37. O25: Melanippides. Münzkabinett der Stadt Winterthur.
38. O26: Melanippides. Münzkabinett, Staatliche Museen zu Berlin. Photo by Reinhard Saczweski.
39. O27: Melanippides. Bibliothèque nationale de France.
40. O27: Diopeithes son of Zenis. Münzkabinett, Staatliche Museen zu Berlin. Photo by Reinhard Saczweski.
41. O28: Kallisthenes. GM 97 (11/10/1999), lot 350.
42. O29: Metronax son of Hippodamas. CNG 97 (17/9/2014), lot 163 (www.cngcoins.com).

Plate 42

43. O29: Sostratos. Bibliothèque nationale de France.
44. O29: Hermippos son of Menophanes. Hesperia Art Bulletin 16 (June 1961), lot 35.
45. O29: Theokydes. American Numismatic Society.
46. O29, R60: Menophron son of Menophron. Bibliothèque nationale de France.
47. O29, R62: Menophron son of Menophron. Bibliothèque nationale de France.
48. O29, R63: Menophron son of Menophron. National Museum of Denmark. Photo by Helle Horsnæs.

Plate 43

49. O30: Demophon son of Dionys[?]. Münzkabinett, Staatliche Museen zu Berlin. Photo by Reinhard Saczweski.
50. oA: Demetrios (2). Münzkabinett, Staatliche Museen zu Berlin. Photo by Reinhard Saczweski.
51. O32: Philokles and Philon. American Numismatic Society.
52. O32: Hegesidemos (2) son of Diophanes. American Numismatic Society.
53. oB: Hippodamas. Münzkabinett, Staatliche Museen zu Berlin. Photo by Reinhard Saczweski.
54. O33: Philodromos son of Tychandros. © Bibliothèque nationale de France.

Plate 44

55. O34: Mnaseas son of Demetrios. Auctiones Basel 6 (1/10/1976), lot 204.
56. oC: Hermias. A. R. Bellinger, *Troy: The Coins* (Princeton 1961), p. 26, T 57, Plate 4.
57. ooAA: Opsigonos. American Numismatic Society.
58. oD: Pylades. Bibliothèque nationale de France.
59. O35: Agathes son of Menophilos. Trustees of the British Museum.
60. oE: Euthydikos. Ashmolean Museum of Art and Archaeology.
61. Forgery. MM Basel 41 (18/6/1970), lot 159.

Apollo Smintheus (Alexandreia Troas)

Plate 45

62. O1: Earliest Issue 1. MM DE 40 (4/6/2014), lot 221.
63. O1: Year 130. NAC 29 (11/5/2005), lot 198.
64. O2: Year 137. Bibliothèque nationale de France.
65. O2: Year 137. Lanz 158 (5/6/2014), lot 235. 66. Forgery. Elsen 92 (9/6/2007), lot 125.
66. Forgery. Elsen 92 (9/6/2007), lot 125.

AJN Second Series 28 (2016) pp. 159–184

The Coin Hoards of the Roman Republic Database: The History, the Data, and the Potential

Kris Lockyear*

The first part of this paper discusses the origins and development of the CHRR database as compiled by the author. The second section provides some examples of the sorts of questions the data can be used to answer by examining two assemblages: the hoard from Mainz and the possible hoard from Alésia. It stands alongside a separate paper (Gruber and Lockyear 2015) that discusses the creation of CHRR Online. It should be noted, however, that CHRR Online is derived from the author's database, and will be regularly updated by uploading the data from it.

1. Introduction

The title of this paper may remind some readers of the film *The Good, the Bad, and the Ugly*. The echo is deliberate. This paper examines the Coin Hoards of the Roman Republic (CHRR) database, from which CHRR Online hosted by the ANS, has been created.[1] A detailed discussion of the CHRR database has been published previously,[2] and the first part of this paper will summarize that discussion and then expand upon some of the issues. The second part will present two previously

---

* Institute of Archaeology, University College London (noviodunum@hotmail.com).
This paper is dedicated to the memory of Rick Witschonke.
1 Gruber and Lockyear 2015.
2 Lockyear 2007, chapter 2. Available from http://numismatics.org/chrr/pages/background.

unpublished case studies demonstrating the potential of the database and some possible methods of analysis.

2. The CHRR Database

I have previously outlined in detail the sources of data used in the construction of the CHRR database, the data manipulation strategies employed, and the structure of the database.[3] I wish here, however, to expand upon some of the wider issues which have impacted on the database.

The CHRR database began as part of an MSc dissertation and was originally implemented using the RDMS package Ingres on a network of powerful Sun workstations.[4] At that time the database only contained information about the 24 hoards published by Crawford (1974) in Table L. The database structure was based on that designed by Ryan (1988) for site finds from Roman Britain. It became clear that there was scope to expand the original dissertation into a doctoral thesis.[5] Although the data was originally moved to Ingres for PC this proved too slow and also could not be run on the only laptop available at that time. As a result the data was imported into dBase III+. A suite of programs were written to ease data entry and manipulate it for analysis. The database grew from twenty-four hoards to 617 containing information about 71,363 coins. No new data were added between 1996 and 2006 at which point the database was imported into Microsoft Access and new hoards began to be appended. The growth of the database can be seen in Figures 1–2. The CHRR database at the time of writing contains some information about 718 hoards containing 120,177 coins of which 106,771 are well identified. Of these 510 hoards have detailed information concerning their contents and 208 only have limited information included in the main FINDSPOT table of the database.

The database up to this point is what I have called a *personal research* database. It was created for my particular projects and interests with no intention, at least initially, of making the information publicly available. Conversion of the database to a *resource* database in the form of CHRR Online involved not only the technical issues in making the data available across the web, but also in meeting and managing the expectations of the target audience who may well have somewhat different interests than the creator of the database.[6] We have attempted to do this via a process of informing, enhancing and enabling. This paper, along with the information posted on the CHRR Online website[7] and the paper by Gruber and Lockyear (2015), forms part of the process of informing. Conversion of the database to an open linked data format and implementation of the webpages

---

3 Lockyear 2007: Chapter 2.
4 Lockyear 1989.
5 Lockyear 1996b.
6 Gruber and Lockyear 2015.
7 See especially http://numismatics.org/chrr/pages/background.

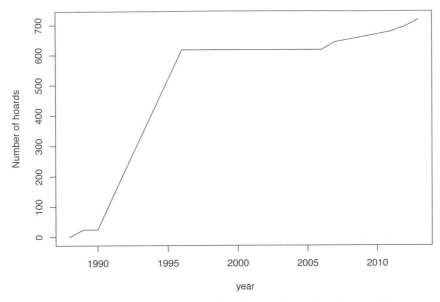

Figure 1. Growth of the CHRR database by numbers of hoards recorded.

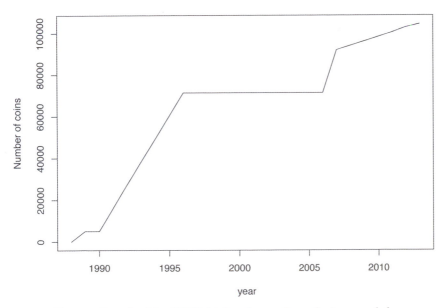

Figure 2. Growth of the CHRR database by numbers of coins recorded.

by Ethan Gruber constitutes the process of enabling. The enhancement of the database will be discussed below.

What hoards are included in the database? The intended scope of the database matches that of *Roman Republican Coin Hoards* (henceforth *RRCH*).[8] It includes hoards which (a) contain at least one Roman coin, and (b) hoards which close with or before the issues of Gaius and Lucius Caesares (c. 2 BC–AD 4). In reality, the coverage is more limited. The original research project centered on patterns in the distribution of *denarii*, and thus pre-*denarius* hoards are largely omitted. Additionally, early anonymous *denarii* are difficult to identify especially from published sources alone. Recent work is going some way to remedy this situation.[9] The need to have reasonable-sized groups of hoards with a narrow range of closing dates and good quality data led to few hoards prior to 157 BC being put into the database. The groups used varied from a maximum of 30 years to a single year and contained between eight and 25 hoards. Similarly, the difficulties in identifying early Imperial issues from older published sources, as well as the lack of hoards of silver *denarii* from Italy of that date, has led to an underrepresentation of Augustan hoards.

In general, *denarius* hoards from Italy are well represented as both Crawford (1969, 1985) and Backendorf (1998) have provided excellent information. My research interests coupled with the corpus published by Chiṭescu (1981) has led to excellent coverage for late Iron Age Dacia. Unfortunately, information from Bulgaria is less well published although the work of Evgeni Paunov is helping to improve the situation. Coverage for the late second century from the Iberian peninsula is excellent as a result of data collection for a forthcoming paper. The principal weak areas are, therefore, early hoards and non-*denarius* hoards.

There are some omissions which initially seem surprising. By way of example, the "New Italian" hoard, actually found in Sardinia and published by Hersh (1977), is currently omitted as the publication does not include the early issues within the hoard and therefore did not meet the criteria for the original analyses. Problems with the detailed data is the main reason that 208 hoards only have a summary entry in the FINDSPOT table but no detailed information concerning their contents.

One recurrent problem is the consistent identification of hoards. The usual methods used by numismatists are either to cite a corpus number, e.g., *RRCH* 234 or the find spot plus the date found, e.g., Alife 1937. The problem with the former method is that published corpora have fixed number sequences so new listings create new references, thus El Centenillo (1911) is *RRCH* 181, Blázquez (1987–1988), No. 26, Chaves Tristán (1996), No. 16, or Villaronga (1993), No. 77! Consistent identification in a database system is via a field designated as the primary key. In this case neither the corpus number (not all hoards have them) or the name plus year (some places such as Rome and Padua have multiple finds) seemed

8 Crawford 1969.
9 e.g., Debernardi 2012.

really suitable and so a simple three-letter code has been created for every entry, e.g., ALI for Alife and EL1 the El Centenillo hoard. These codes have been consistently used by the author in previous publications and are used in the online version of the database. They are also used in the second part of this article. They have the advantage over a simple number in that there is no expectation of the codes reflecting a dating sequence, and also they are generally easier to remember. By asking users of the online resource to use these codes when using the data in their own work, it is hoped they will become the standard method by which hoards are identified.

A few hoards create problems at even this level. The Ancona hoard (*RRCH* 169 and 344, AN1 and AN2) is held by the American Numismatic Society. Crawford split this assemblage into two hoards on the basis of its contents although the documentation at the ANS suggests it is one hoard.[10] The structure of this assemblage suggests that Crawford's division into two hoards is basically correct but that he has incorporated some of the tail of the second hoard in with the body of the first.[11] The La Oliva hoard (*RRCH* 197, OL1 and OL2, Chaves Tristán 1996, Nos. 24 and 32) is thought by Crawford to be two lots of the same hoard but is argued to be two separate hoards by Chaves Tristán.[12] Wherever possible, I have kept disputed hoards like this separate as it is easier to combine listings than it is to split them.

The database design includes a series of "accuracy" codes which enable one to assess the degree of confidence in the identification of individual coins. The first four codes are based on the levels created by Reece (1975). For Reece, an unqualified reference is definitely a coin of that type, "as" indicates the first possible reference that a coin may be when it cannot be precisely identified, "copy of" indicates a copy of a specific coin and "copy as" indicates a copy like the reference given. In CHRR these four levels are coded 1 to 4. There are, however, instances when a coin can be identified down to an *RRC* issue, but not down to a specific type. For example, *RRC* 408/1a and 408/1b are sometimes either published as 408/1 or 408/1a–b. To indicate coins identified to this level the database assigns the accuracy code 5 and CHRR Online uses "as issue…" in its lists. As well as coins which can be given some form of precise reference, there are a number of general categories such as "miscellaneous Republican *asses*" or "Iberian *denarii*." Coin type numbers have been created for these categories and they are assigned an accuracy code of 8. The remaining codes are explained in Table 1. There are weaknesses with this system. For example, how does one record *RRC* 408/1a–b when only presence/absence data is available? Up until now, this problem has been irrelevant as hoards with only presence/absence data are of no use in the types of analyses the database was designed to support. With its conversion from research to resource, however, some of these issues will have to be addressed.

10 Crawford pers. comm., Metcalf pers. comm.
11 Lockyear 2007: 82.
12 Chaves Tristán 1996: 245.

Table 1: Meaning of the various accuracy codes used in the CHRR database.

Code	Meaning
1	exactly identified coin.
2	inexactly identified coin ("as *RRC…*").
3	copy of a specific coin ("copy of *RRC…*").
4	copy of a general type of coin of which the reference is an example ("copy as *RRC…*").
5	Almost exactly identified coin, e.g., either RRC 408/1a or 408/1b ("as issue…").
6	Coin in a Romanian hoard which is suspected to be a copy.
7	considered extraneous, usually by Crawford.
8	a general coin type, e.g., miscellaneous Iberian *denarius*.
9	total in hoard unknown, i.e., only presence/absence of type.

The dating of Republican issues is controversial. In *Roman Republican Coinage*, Crawford (1974) offers quite precise dates for most issues, especially after 157 BC. These dates are not universally accepted and alternative dating schemes have been offered for parts of the sequence; for example those by Hersh (1977), Hersh and Walker (1984) and Mattingly (2004, chapter 13). From the point of view of creating a usable database, these partial sequences are problematic. For example, if one adopts Mattingly's (2004) scheme for the issues from *RRC* 197 down to the Social War, one ends up with an artificial gap in the dating sequence between Crawford's dates for the earlier issues and Mattingly's. The CHRR database, therefore, uses the dates from *RRC* by default. A crude but very effective way of incorporating the alternative dating schemes was to simply duplicate the COINTYPE table and then to edit the dates for the affected issues. The database now incorporates two tables with alternative dating schemes taken from Mattingly (2004) and Hersh and Walker (1984) allowing for the impact of the various schemes on the patterns in the hoards to be assessed.

The enhancement of the CHRR database is taking three forms:

1. The addition of additional hoard data to the current database.
2. Importing information from the online version of the database to enhance the "working" version.
3. The expansion of the scope of the database to include additional areas of information.

The first of these requires little explanation. Further hoards are added to the database whenever the opportunity arises, and/or hoards already included at a summary listing level have detailed data input as and when possible. At regular intervals the data included in CHRR Online will be updated from the master database held by the author. The main change is that hoards not previously prioritized, such as the early material or non-*denarius* hoards are being input in order to improve the function of the database as a general resource for scholars.

The online version of the database varied from the author's working database in that the information regarding coin types was derived from the British Museum's database which contained information regarding designs, legends, etc. taken from *RRC* as well as the basic information regarding dates and denominations which had been included in CHRR's COINTYPE table. The British Museum data were incomplete, however, and the missing information was added by the American Numismatic Society. These data were then used to enhance CHRR. The second source of data was that many of the hoard's find spots were automatically located using the Geonames system by Ethan Gruber. Although only accurate down to the level of the named settlement, this basic location information allows CHRR Online to map hoards. This information has now been incorporated into CHRR which will allow more formal spatial analyses to be undertaken if desired.

Lastly, two other hoard projects are currently underway: one team at Oxford is building a database of Roman Imperial hoards from outside the UK and a second team from the British Museum and Leicester are looking at hoards from within the UK. Both these projects are currently recording more generic information about hoards such as the vessels in which they were found, associated artefacts, circumstances of discovery etc. rather than the detailed coin-by-coin listings gathered by CHRR. The Oxford Project intends to extend its coverage to more detailed listings in the future. Much of the more generic information for Republican hoards is available in either the CHRR logbooks and archive, or Crawford's archive held by the British Museum. The two Imperial hoard projects will also be available online: the BM/Leicester project via the Portable Antiquities Scheme database (www.finds.org) and the Oxford Project via a bespoke web application (http://chre.ashmus.ox.ac.uk/).

Although the above discussion has highlighted some of the problems with the data, and has looked at how it may be enhanced, it cannot be emphasized too strongly that the database as is forms a substantial and significant body of information of enormous use to scholars investigating the coinage of the late Republic. The next section presents two sets of analyses which demonstrate just some of the ways this data may be used.

3. Using the Data: Two Examples

Many analyses using the data from the CHRR database have already been published.[13] The majority of these previous analyses examine groups of hoards in order to identify and assess patterning within them. In this section I wish to examine how the data may be used in a slightly different scenario where there are questions relating to a specific assemblage. Two examples are investigated—

---

13 e.g., Lockyear 1991, 1993, 1995, 1996a, 1999b, 2007, 2008, 2012.

the Mainz (MNZ) hoard and the assemblage from Alésia, Camp D (ALD)—in order
to illustrate the sorts of ways the data can be used to examine specific finds in their
broader context. I would like to thank Stéphane Martin for posing such interesting
questions about these two assemblages and providing the data from Alésia, Camp
D.

3.1 The Mainz Hoard

The Mainz hoard consists of only 12 *denarii* and closes in 78 BC according to
Crawford's chronology. It is of interest as it was found in Treveran territory but
closes some 20 years before the Gallic Wars. It is, however, a very small hoard and
thus the closing date is rather unreliable, but how unreliable is it? Additionally, is
there anything else exceptional about this hoard?

The data for Mainz was input to the CHRR database from Michael Crawford's
notes currently held in the British Museum. The hoard was not analyzed previously
as its small size falls considerably below the minimum of 30 coins I generally use.[14]
This is the earliest hoard from Germany in the CHRR database, and one of only
a handful from France and Austria. The late 80s–early 70s BC mark the period
of initial penetration of *denarii* into northern Europe as well as eastwards into
Romania and Greece. The period 78–75 BC is characterized by a high degree of
homogeneity in coin hoard structure. The large issues of the Social War, which
created such marked patterning in the data for the 80s BC, had circulated
sufficiently that hoards of this date are extremely similar to each other.[15]

A data set of 19 hoards with 12 or more well-identified *denarii* closing between
78–75 BC was extracted from the CHRR database (Table 2, below).[16] Of these
hoards four fall below the usual 30-coin limit including Mainz (MNZ), two French
hoards, Bompas (BOM) and Brusc (BRU) and Puerto Serrano from Spain (PSE). One
of the first things to note about this selection is their wide geographical spread.
These 19 hoards come from nine modern countries, a quite unusual distribution at
this period when usually Italy, Spain, and Romania dominate the data sets.

My usual procedure for analyzing a data set such as this is to graph the data
as cumulative percentage curves, and to perform Correspondence Analysis (CA),
a multivariate statistical technique developed to analyze tables of categorical data
such as we have here.[17] The cumulative percentage curves allows one to see the
broad patterning in the data by date and are generally easier to interpret than
an ordinary line graph with many overlapping lines, or by plotting multiple
histograms. I have discussed CA in detail previously.[18] The aim of CA is to extract

14 Lockyear 2007: 44.

15 Lockyear 2007, cf. sections 5.4.7 and 5.4.9.

16 "Good total" refers to the number of *denarii* that can be accurately identified to an *RRC*
issue, but not necessarily down to an exact *RRC* reference.

17 Greenacre 2007.

18 Lockyear 2007: 40–64.

from a large data set the underlying trends in the data and it is worth quickly recapping the major aspects of the technique.

1. CA is a technique for analyzing tables of non-negative integer data, e.g., counts of coins in hoards or site assemblages.

2. CA calculates scores for every variable and every assemblage on a series of new axes where the first axis represents the main underlying pattern in the data, the second axis represents the next most important source of variation, and so on. In coinage studies, the first axis often represents date (e.g., early to late hoards). Each axis can be said to "explain" a percentage of the variation in the data which gives an indication of how successful the analysis is in revealing the underlying patterns.

3. The results of the technique are presented as one or more scattergrams, technically called maps as both the x and y axes should be plotted to the same scale. Usually two maps are produced, both showing axes 1 *v.* 2 but the first representing the assemblages (in our case hoards) and the second representing the variables (in our case coinage issues). More subtle patterns can be observed by examining axes 3 and beyond although in hoard studies these can quickly start representing the variation in only a very small number of issues.

4. Two points on a map plotted close together are likely to be similar in some way, and two points plotted at a distance are likely to be dissimilar. In our case, two hoards plotted close together are likely to contain a similar range and proportion of coinage issues. Similarly, two issues plotted close together are likely to have a similar distribution across the hoards.

5. By comparing the two maps it is possible to see which issues are particularly related to which hoards, and *vice versa*.

6. The process of calculating the axes and plotting the scores is an attempt to simplify a complex data set. As a result, some items will not fit that simplified pattern. Consultation of the accompanying diagnostic statistics (more properly known as decompositions of inertia) enables one to identify which items (hoards and/or issues) fit the pattern well, and which should be ignored. One of the most useful of the diagnostic statistics is "quality" which scores out of 1,000 how well a point "fits" the map. The position of items with a very low quality should not be given any great meaning on that map

7. By comparing the maps and consulting the diagnostic statistics, an interpretation for each axis can be given.

Table 2: Hoards from 78–75 BC.

CHRR	Name	RRCH	Country	Closing Date	"Good" Total
ADM	Alba di Massa	289	Italy	77	82
ALX	Alexandria	295	Romania	77	32
BOM	Bompas	290	France	77	13
BRU	Brusc	284	France	77	15
COR	Cornetu (Căpreni)	296	Romania	75	128
INU	Inuri	—	Romania	77	37
KER	Kerassia	283	Greece	78	47
MNZ	Mainz	281	Germany	78	12
MAL	Maluenda	282	Spain	78	32
MBR	Mihai Bravu	—	Romania	75	56
ION	Montalbano Ionico	297	Italy	75	45
NER	Neresine, Lussino Island	—	Fmr Yugoslavia	78	42
NOY	Noyer	—	France	78	51
PSE	Puerto Serrano	—	Spain	77	28
RAN	Randazzo	287	Sicily	77	30
MAN	San Mango sul Calore	294	Italy	75	81
SDC	Santana da Carnota	—	Portugal	76	134
STE	Stejeriș	—	Romania	75	200
ZAT	Zătreni	—	Romania	75	41

A formal description of CA has been provided by Greenacre (1984) and his later work is a more practical description of the method.[19] The method has been used widely in archaeology (e.g., Pitts and Perring 2006) and coinage studies (e.g., Orton 1997). Baxter and Cool (2010) have provided a useful hands-on description.

The total number of well-identified *denarii* in the data set was only 1,106, a remarkably small number for 19 hoards. As a result, the cumulative percentage curves presented in Fig. 3 are often quite jagged. The graph does show, however, that (a) the majority of the hoards are very similar to each other with the exception of the Bompas hoard which has quite a "modern" profile; and (b) that the Mainz hoard looks very similar to the rest of the assemblage.

As a result of the small size of most of the hoards, the data set is very sparse with 77% of the cells having an entry of zero. Correspondence Analysis can be badly affected by having comparatively rare issues—by which I mean rare in the

19 Greenacre 2007.

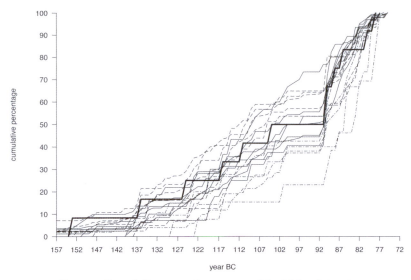

Figure 3. Cumulative percentage curves of the Mainz data set.
Bold line: Mainz; solid lines: Italy, Sicily, Spain and Portugal; dashed lines: Romania;
dash-dot lines: all other locations.

current data set—occurring in small hoards. To alleviate this problem, all issues prior to *RRC* 197 were deleted from the data set, some 19 coins. Additionally, the four smallest hoards were included in the analysis as supplementary points.[20] This means that the CA map is created without using these four hoards, and then the position of those hoards is calculated and plotted. This process highlighted the fact that four issues only occurred in these smaller hoards: *RRC* 242, 330 and 343 in the Puerto Serrano hoard (PSE; one example each) and *RRC* 365 in the Bompas hoard (BOM; two examples). The CA of the complete data set (not presented) is unsurprisingly dominated by the two examples of *RRC* 365 and the Bompas hoard. These four issues were therefore also deleted from the data set which was then reanalyzed. In the second analysis the first axis accounted for 11.9% of the variance in the data, and the second axis 10.3% giving a total of 22.2% for the maps, a very low figure but one which is to be expected given the small size of most of the hoards.

The resulting maps from this analysis (Figs. 4–5, below) do show some patterning despite the problems. The three Italian sites are plotted in the lower-left quadrant of the map, the majority of the outliers tend to be Romanian or French hoards with the exception of the hoard from Randazzo (RAN). This pattern is very similar to that reported previously.[21] As far as the Mainz hoard is concerned, it

20 Greenacre 2007: Chapter 12
21 Lockyear 2007: 91–92.

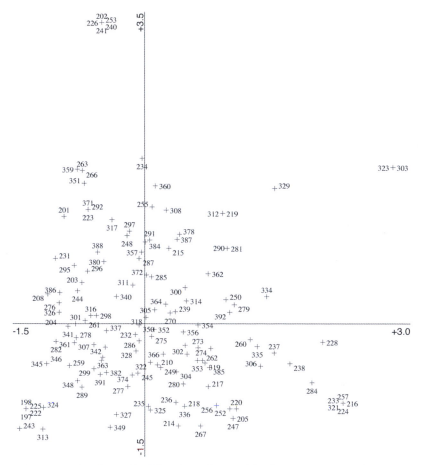

Figure 4. Map from CA of the Mainz data set. The data points are *RRC* issues.

appears to be similar to Italian, Spanish, and Portuguese hoards of this period and is rather unremarkable although the small sample size does need to be taken in consideration when making such a judgement. These maps reinforce the impression given by the cumulative percentage graph discussed above.

Although we now know that the Mainz hoard is unremarkable, structurally, it does not help us assess the problem of the probability that a small hoard closing in 78 BC may actually have been extracted from the coinage pool somewhat later. A method exists by which we may graph the probability of a later closing date.[22] This method relies on using the die estimates for *Roman Republican Coinage* as *relative issue size coefficients*,[23] i.e., indicators of relative rather than absolute issue size. By

22 Lockyear 2012: 203–206.
23 Lockyear 1999a.

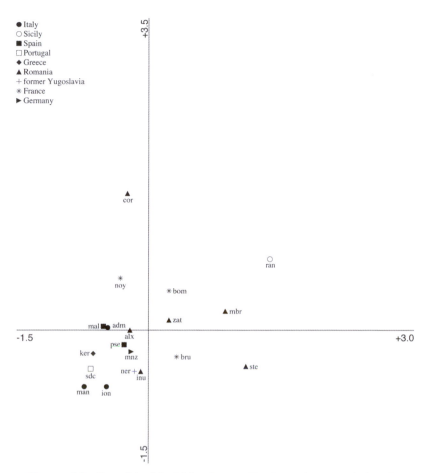

Figure 5. Map from CA of the Mainz data set. The data points are coin hoards.
Hoards BOM, BRU, MNZ and PSE have been made passive.

using the binomial formula and the coinage population figures calculated using a
2% decay rate we can calculate the probabilities for hoards of various sizes. Taking
the Mainz hoard as an example, in 77 BC coins struck in that year form 1.9% of
the coinage pool. To calculate the probability of a hoard of 12 coins collected in
77 BC *not* containing any coins of that year we use the formula $(1-p)^n$ where p is
the probability, in this case the percentage expressed as a proportion, and n is the
number of trials, i.e., the size of the hoard. In this case, therefore, we get:

$$(1-p)n = (1-0.019)^{12} = 0.98^{12} = 0.79$$

We can then calculate the probability for 76 BC using the proportion of the coinage
pool dating to 77–76 BC, and then for 75 BC using the proportion for 77–75 BC
and so on.

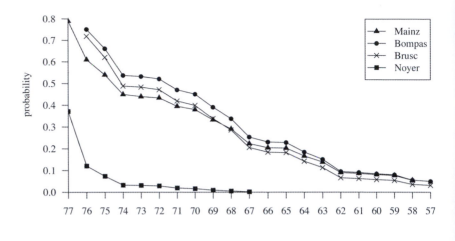

year BC

Figure 6. The probability of hoards the size of Mainz, Brusc, Bompas and Noyer closing later than the date of their newest coin.

Figure 6 shows the probabilities for coin hoards of the size of the three smallest hoards, along with a hoard of the same size as the Noyer hoard (NOY) for comparison calculated using this method. As can be seen, a hoard the size of Mainz stands a 30% chance of having been collected 10 years after its closing date, and a 14% chance of being collected 15 years later. Similar figures hold for hoards the same size as Bompas and Brusc. There is a probability of 0.055, i.e., just over 1 in 20, that the Mainz hoard was collected as late as 58 BC. This is, of course, a "best case" scenario assuming the hoards were collected from a coinage pool similar to the Italian one which from the CAs appears to be the case. There is no way of knowing precisely the gap between the closing date and the deposition/loss date. It does appear, however, that it is rather unlikely that the Mainz hoard dates to as late as the Gallic Wars, and in the light of these analyses it can be seen as further evidence of the contacts which developed between the Treverii and the Romans in the period 100–50 BC.[24]

3.2 The Alésia "Hoard"

Excavations in the nineteenth century at Alésia "Camp D" retrieved an assemblage of 99 Roman Republican coins, 98 *denarii* and one *quinarius*. The date of the final coin is 55 BC. This assemblage was found scattered along a section of ditch and comprises almost all the silver from the finds associated with the famous siege. It has been suggested by Popovitch that the assemblage could represent a dispersed hoard rather than, for example, a votive deposit.[25]

24 Martin, pers. comm.
25 Popovitch 2001: 80–83.

Table 3: Hoards from 56–54 BC.

CHRR	Name	RRCH	Country	Closing Date	"Good" Total
ALD	Alésia, camp D	—	France	55	98
AMN	Amnaş	338	Romania	56	155
AN1	Ancona	344	Italy	55	42
BUZ	Buzău	346	Romania	54	48
CLN	Calineşti	347	Romania	54	92
COM	Compito	345	Italy	55	929
DUN	Dunăreni	—	Romania	56	128
FND	Frauendorf (Axente Sever)	341	Romania	56	563
GRA	Grazzanise	349	Italy	54	257
ICN	Icland	—	Romania	56	33
KAR	Karavelovo	—	Bulgaria	54	35
MC1	Macedonia	—	Greece	54	91
SDS	Sălaşul de Sus	348	Romania	54	103
SMC	Someşul Cald	321	Romania	56	115
SUS	Sustinenza	339	Italy	56	63
THS	Thessalonica	—	Greece	54	51

The data for Alésia Camp D was uploaded to the CHRR database (ALD) and a comparative data set extracted. There are 16 hoards in the database with 30 or more well-identified *denarii* dating to the period 56–54 BC and comprising 2,803 coins (Table 3). Previous analysis of hoards of this period showed that the majority of Romanian and Bulgarian hoards were very similar in structure and had a very archaic profile.[26] The Italian hoards were slightly more varied and more modern in profile, and the most modern hoard was that from Thessalonica (THS). The current data set adds another hoard from Greece (Macedonia, MC1) as well as the Alésia assemblage.

As noted previously, there are data quality issues with the Ancona hoard (AN1), specifically the lack of early coinage. This hoard has, therefore, been omitted from the cumulative frequency graph (Fig. 7, below) although it has been retained in the correspondence analyses where it has little impact on the results. From Figure 7 the similarity between the Romanian and Bulgarian hoards can be seen clearly. The Italian and Greek hoards have more varied profiles but all are more modern in structure than the Romanian/Bulgarian hoards. The assemblage from Alésia is slightly archaic in structure but still more modern than the Romanian and Bulgarian hoards, and is quite similar to the hoard from Compito (COM).

26 Lockyear 2007: 107–112.

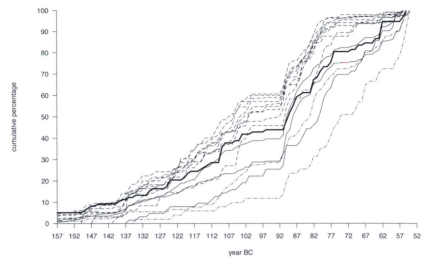

Figure 7. Cumulative percentage curves of the Alésia data set. Bold line: Alésia; solid lines: Italy; dashed lines: Romania and Bulgaria; dash-dot lines: Greece.

The CA of these 16 hoards is presented in Figures 8–9. The total variance explained by the first two axes of inertia is 28%, not a very high percentage but acceptable. As expected, the map of sites shows a tight cluster of Romanian and Bulgarian hoards, with a wider spread amongst the remaining hoards. The addition of Alésia and Macedonia has done little to change the overall configuration of the map from the previously published analysis.[27] Macedonia has a moderately high quality on this map of 319 whereas Alésia is on the low side with only 90.[28] This, however, compares favorably with the low quality of many of the small Romanian hoards such as Icland (18) or Someşul Cald (17). The Alésia assemblage appears to be very similar to the Italian hoards from Compito (COM), Grazzinese (GRA) and Sustinenza (SUS). The Ancona hoard (AN1) has had its tail artificially truncated hence its position close to the Macedonia and Thessalonica hoards. The location of the Macedonia hoard, the other new addition to this data set, in the same region of the map as Thessalonica is an interesting confirmation of the previously described patterning in the hoards.

27 Lockyear 2007: 107–112.

28 "Quality" is a measure of how well an individual point is represented on the map and is a score out of 1000. See Lockyear (2007: 57–9) for a description of how the diagnostic statistics can be interpreted.

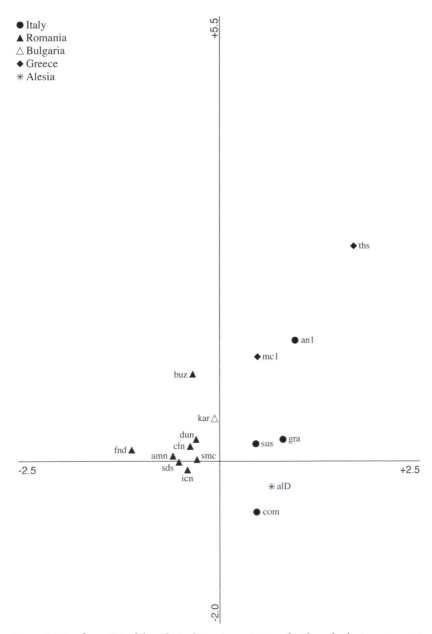

Figure 8. Map from CA of the Alésia data set consisting of 16 hoards closing 56–54 BC.

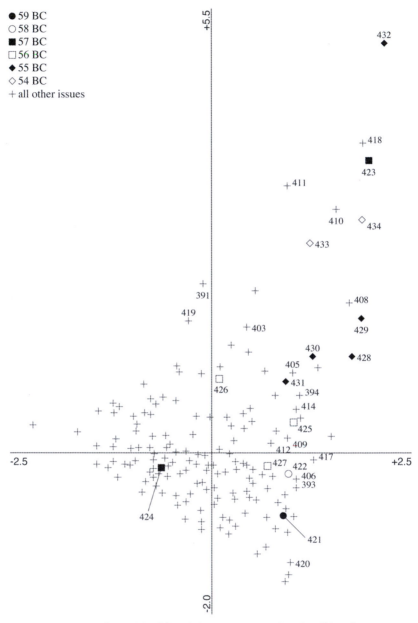

Figure 9. Map from CA of the *RRC* issues contained in the Alésia data set.

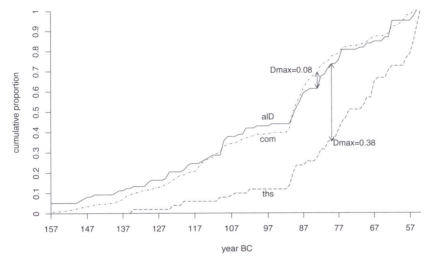

Figure 10. Cumulative percentage curves for the Alésia, Compito and Thessalonica hoards showing the calculation of the Kolmogorov-Smirnov distance, Dmax.

The map of issues (Fig. 9) generally shows the newest issues at the right-hand end of the first axis and the older issues at the left, giving a generally old to new gradient across the map. The second axis separates out most of the very newest issues towards the top of the map and the slightly older issues to the bottom right. The second axis is, therefore, highlighting the pattern in the very newest issues of coins in the data set. Comparing the two maps shows the Romanian and Bulgarian hoards with a preponderance of older issues, the Italian hoards and Alésia with more modern profiles but the two Greek hoards being associated with many of the newest issues.

One may enquire why the period 56–54 BC was chosen to select hoards to compare to Alésia. This grouping was originally used simply to create a group of hoards with as small a range of closing dates as possible but in sufficient numbers to allow for analysis.[29] It is likely, therefore, that there are hoards similar in structure to Alésia but with a different closing date. An alternative approach would be to use Dmax-based cluster analysis,[30] a technique which has been applied successfully to both hoards and site finds.[31] In this case, however, we are not trying to create groups but simply wish to see which hoards are most similar to Alésia. We can do this by calculating the Dmax value (more properly known as the Kolmogorov-Smirnov distance) between Alésia and the remainder of the hoards in the CHRR

29 Lockyear 1996b, 149–151. In *Patterns and Process* (Lockyear 2007) I divided the available hoards into 22 groups covering the period 147–2 BC. The groups varied in date range from 29 years to a single year, depending on the distribution of closing dates.
30 Lockyear 1996a.
31 Hoards: Lockyear 2007: 2008. Site finds: Lockyear 2000; Walton 2012.

database with 30 or more well-identified *denarii*. Dmax is simply the maximum difference between the cumulative proportion curves for two hoards. To illustrate this Fig. 10 presents the curves for Alésia, Compito and Thessalonica. As can be seen, Compito and Alésia are very similar with a Dmax value of 0.08 whereas Thessalonica and Alésia are very different, Dmax is 0.38.[32]

Table 4 presents all those hoards with a Dmax value of less than 0.15. A large number of these hoards are from Romania and date sometime after Alésia. This is unsurprising and reflects the pattern of coinage supply to that region.[33] Of more relevance are the hoards from Italy, France and Spain. The hoard most similar to Alésia is that from Compito included in the CAs discussed above. The rather archaic Piedmonte d'Alife hoard (PIE) is also quite similar, as is San Gregorio di Sassola (GRE) which closes in 58 BC. All in all, the Alésia assemblage looks very similar to Italian hoards of the early 50s BC or archaic profiled hoards closing a little later and would be unremarkable if it were not for the find spot.

Having determined that the Alésia assemblage looks like a perfectly ordinary hoard of the early 50s BC, there is one last possibility to examine. If we assume a hoard is a random collection of coins—in this case *denarii*—from the coinage pool, we can also expect that there will be differences between hoards which is entirely due to chance. This is, of course, why we set a minimum size of hoard for analysis; the smaller the hoard the bigger the variation caused by the random selection process. One issue with CA, however, is that it is a purely deterministic technique which represents the data set given without indicating the variation one might expect from random selection. A solution to this is to undertake a bootstrapped CA. In this method, new data sets are created by sampling with replacement from a population defined by the structure of the existing data set and then analyzed using CA. This process is then repeated, usually 10,000 times. For each hoard and issue we now have 10,000 data points instead of just one. By plotting ellipses around the points for each hoard or issue, or more usually 95% of them, we can see how much variation we could expect for hoards of that size and structure. Bootstrapped CA is a useful technique and has been used in the analysis of a variety of archaeological assemblages including site finds and Republican coin hoards.[34]

32 Some 328 hoards as of 16 June 2012.
33 Lockyear 2008.
34 Lockyear 2013.

Table 4: Hoards compared to Alésia Camp D assemblage with a Dmax value less than 0.15.

CHRR	Name	RRCH	Country	Closing Date	"Good" Total	Dmax
COM	Compito	345	Italy	55	929	0.08
VIS	Vişina	—	Romania	41	139	0.08
NAG	Nagykágya	411	Romania	42	131	0.08
PIE	Piedimonte d'Alife	406	Italy	42	191	0.09
PIA	Piatra Roşie	—	Romania	43	268	0.10
SIN	Sînvăsii	—	Romania	46	43	0.10
CAS	Casaleone	351	Italy	51	712	0.11
PRS	Poroschia	436	Romania	39	541	0.11
GRE	San Gregorio di Sassola	337	Italy	58	532	0.11
SMI	Sminja	395	Tunisia	45	912	0.12
SPR	Sprîncenata	—	Romania	46	110	0.12
BUZ	Buzău	346	Romania	54	48	0.12
PRE	Prejmer	412	Romania	42	150	0.12
ISS	Puy D'Issolu	—	France	46	39	0.12
JEG	Jegălia	—	Romania	43	453	0.13
JAE	Jaén	386	Spain	46	65	0.13
NB2	Nicolae Bălcescu II	—	Romania	42	43	0.13
ILI	Ilieni	—	Romania	46	109	0.13
BHR	"Bahrfeldt"	—	—	49	426	0.13
RAC	Răcătău de Jos II	—	Romania	39	53	0.13
TRN	"Transylvania"	369	Romania	47	36	0.13
TI2	Tîrnava	—	Romania	46	148	0.13
CNT	Conţeşti	—	Romania	15	141	0.13
FA1	Fărcaşele	420	Romania	42	81	0.14
ISL	Islaz	—	Romania	42	124	0.14
HAG	Haggen	405	Switzerland	42	61	0.14
ODS	Orbeasca de Sus	—	Romania	48	139	0.14
STP	Stupini	—	Romania	41	227	0.14
GRI	La Grajuela	—	Spain	51	523	0.14

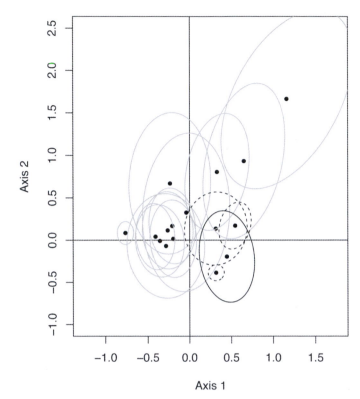

Figure 11. Bootstrapped CA of 16 hoards closing 56–54 BC.
Solid black: Alésia; dashed black: unproblematic hoards from Italy; grey: all other hoards.
For hoard labels compare this figure with Fig. 8.

Fig. 11 is the output from a bootstrapped analysis using the method and code developed by Ringrose (2012). The ellipse for Alésia, although larger than the three unproblematic hoards from Italy, clearly lies in the same general region. Comparison with some of the other ellipses, such as that from the Buzău hoard (BUZ) shows that the point for Alésia is relatively stable and we can have confidence it where it is located on the map. If the ellipse was very large we could not be able to have confidence in its location, and thus its interpretation. In this case, the bootstrapped analysis has reinforced our conclusions derived from the other analyses.

In conclusion, the Alésia Camp D assemblage has all the characteristics of a hoard withdrawn from the Italian coinage pool in the early to mid-50s BC, and although it is impossible to be definitive, it appears very likely that it is a dispersed hoard as previously suggested by Popovitch (2001) rather than a votive deposit.

4. Conclusion

This article has outlined the history of the CHRR database, and by extension CHRR Online,[35] as well as explaining the "quirks" that the database exhibits which are a result of the origin of the database as a research database, not a resource database. A program of work is underway, generously funded by the late Rick Witschonke, to enhance the database and to iron out many of the issues discussed. These enhancements will, in due course, be carried over to CHRR Online.

The second part of this paper has provided some examples of how the data contained within the database can be used to examine individual hoards against the wider background pattern as revealed by the previous extensive analyses.[36] A variety of different methods were presented, perhaps more than is needed in each case, in order to illustrate the range of techniques which can be applied to this data. The methods chosen are ones that I have found useful in my research, but other analysts may well choose different techniques. Many of the methods are not exclusive to the study of hoards but can usefully be applied to assemblages of site finds such as those collected by Reece (1991) and Walton (2012). Some of the techniques require the use of statistical packages such as R (e.g., the correspondence analyses) and even bespoke R code (e.g., Dmax-based clustering) whereas other methods such as the use of Dmax as a similarity coefficient can be calculated using a spreadsheet package.

With the current development of databases of Roman Imperial coin hoards, alongside the growing adoption of the sorts of methods discussed here as shown by the creation of *The Journal of Archaeological Numismatics*, we are entering an exciting period for numismatic research. This research will be fuelled by access to large bodies of comparative data along with ever more sophisticated methods of analysis.

Acknowledgments

I would like to thank Stéphane Martin for the stimulating questions posed by the Mainz and Alésia hoards. I would also like to thank Michael Crawford for allowing access to his records now housed in the Department of Coins and Medals, and to the many members of the Department past and present for facilitating that access. I am indebted to the late Rick Witschonke for providing the initial impetus for CHRR Online and for coordinating its development, as well as funding the current process of updating and expanding the CHRR database. I would also like to thank Ethan Gruber for creating the Online version of the database without which the data would not be so widely available.

35 Gruber and Lockyear 2015.
36 Lockyear 2007.

References

Backendorf, D. 1998. *Römische Münzschätze des zweiten und ersten Jahrhunderts v. Chr. vom italienischen Festland*. Studien zu Fundmünzen der Antike, Band 13. Berlin: Gebr. Mann Verlag.

Baxter, M. J. and H. E. M. Cool. 2010. "Correspondence Analysis in R for archaeologists: an educational account." *Archeologia e Calcolatori* 21: 211–228.

Blázquez, C. 1987–1988. "Tesorillos de moneda republicana en la península Ibérica. Addenda a Roman Republican Coin Hoards." *Acta Numismática* 17–18: 105–142.

Chaves Tristán, F. 1996. *Los Tesoros en el Sur de Hispania. Conjuntos de denarios y objetos de plata durante los siglos II y I a C*. Seville: Fundación el Monte.

Chiṭescu, M. 1981. *Numismatic aspects of the Dacian state*. Oxford: British Archaeological Reports International Series 112.

Crawford, M. H. 1969. *Roman Republican coin hoards*. Special Publication 4. London: Royal Numismatic Society.

————. 1974. *Roman Republican Coinage*. Cambridge: Cambridge University Press.

————. 1985. *Coinage and Money under the Roman Republic*. London: Methuen.

Debernardi, P. 2012. "La 'riscoperta' del ripostiglio di Orzivecchi e le sue tipologie inedite." *Panorama Numismatico* 9: 19–25.

Greenacre, M. J. 1984. *Theory and Applications of Correspondence Analysis*. London: Academic Press.

————. 2007. *Correspondence Analysis in Practice*, second edition. Boca Raton, London and New York: Chapman and Hall.

Gruber, E. and K. Lockyear. 2015. "From dBase III+ to the semantic web: twenty-five years of the Coin Hoards of the Roman Republic database." In *Across space and time. Papers from the 41st Conference on Computer Applications and Quantitative Methods in Archaeology, Perth, 25–28th March 2013*, edited by Arianna Traviglia, pp. 336–46. Amsterdam: Amsterdam University Press.

Hersh, C. A. 1977. "Notes on the chronology and interpretation of the Roman Republican coinage." *Numismatic Chronicle* 137: 19–36.

Hersh, C. A. and A. Walker 1984. "The Mesagne hoard." *ANS Museum Notes* 29: 103–134.

Lockyear, K. 1989. *A statistical investigation of Roman Republican coin hoards*. MA thesis, University of Southampton.

————. 1991. "Simulating coin hoard formation." In *Computer applications and quantitative methods in archaeology 1990* edited by K. Lockyear and S. P. Q. Rahtz, pp. 195–206. Oxford: British Archaeological Reports International Series 565.

————. 1993. "Coin hoard formation revisited…" In *Computer applications and quantitative methods in archaeology 1992*, edited by J. Andresen, T. Madsen, and I. Scollar, 367–376. Aarhus: Aarhus University Press.

————. 1995. "The supply of Roman Republican *denarii* to Romania." *Studii şi Cercetări de Numismatică* 11: 85–102.

————. 1996a. "Dmax based cluster analysis and the supply of coinage to Iron Age Dacia." In *Computer applications and quantitative methods in archaeology CAA 95*, edited by H. Kamermans and K. Fennema, pp. 165–178. Analecta Praehistorica Leidensia 28. Leiden.

————. 1996b. *Multivariate money. A statistical analysis of Roman Republican coin hoards with special reference to material from Romania.* PhD diss., Institute of Archaeology, University College London.

————. 1999a. "Coins, copies and kernals—a note on the potential of Kernal Density Estimates." In *Computer applications and quantitative methods in archaeology 1997*, edited by L. Dingwall, S. Exon, V. Gaffney, S. Laflin and M. van Leusen, pp. 85–90. Oxford: British Archaeological Reports International Series 750.

————. 1999b. "Hoard structure and coin production in antiquity — an empirical investigation." *NC* 159: 215–243.

————. 2000. "Site finds in Roman Britain: a comparison of techniques." *Oxford Journal of Archaeology* 19.4: 397–423.

————. 2007. *Patterns and process in Late Roman Republican coin hoards 157–2 BC.* Oxford: British Archaeological Reports International Series 1733

————. 2008. "Aspects of Roman Republican coins found in late Iron Age Dacia." In *Miscellanea numismatica Antiquitatis. In honorem septagenarii magistri Virgilii Mihailescu-Bîrliba oblata*, edited by V. Spinei and L. Munteanu, pp. 147–176. Honoraria 4. Bucureşti: Editura Academiei Române.

————. 2012. "Dating coins, dating with coins." *Oxford Journal of Archaeology* 31.2: 191–211.

————. 2013. "Applying bootstrapped correspondence analysis to archaeological data." *Journal of Archaeological Science* 40.12: 4744–4753.

Mattingly, H. B. 2004. *From coins to history: Selected numismatic studies.* Ann Arbor: University of Michigan Press.

Orton, C. R. 1997. "Testing significance or testing credulity?" *Oxford Journal of Archaeology* 16.2: 219–225.

Pitts, M. and D. Perring 2006. "The making of Britain's first urban landscapes: The case of late Iron Age and Roman Essex." *Britannia* 37: 189–212.

Popovitch, L. 2001. Les monnaies romaines. In *Alésia. Fouilles et recherches franco-allemandes sur les travaux militaires romains autour du Mont-Auxois (1991–1997)*, edited by M. Reddé and S. Schnurbein, pp. 69–95. Paris: Mémoire de l'Académie des Inscriptions et Belles Lettres, vol. XXII.

Reece, R. 1975. The coins. In *Excavations at Portchester Castle*, edited by B. Cunliffe, pp. 188–197. London: Society of Antiquaries.

————. 1991. *Roman coins from 140 sites in Britain, provisional edition.* Cotswold Studies IV. Cirencester: Cotswold Press.

Ringrose, T. J. 2012. "Bootstrap confidence regions for correspondence analysis." *Journal of Statistical Computation and Simulation* 82.10: 1397–1413.

Ryan, N. S. 1988. *Fourth century coin finds in Roman Britain: A computer analysis.* Oxford; British Archaeological Reports British Series 183.

Villaronga, L. 1993. *Tresors monetaris de la Peninsula Ibèrica anteriors a August: Repertori i Analisi.* Barcelona.

Walton, P. J. 2012. *Rethinking Roman Britain: Coinage and archaeology.* Wetteren: Moneta.

AJN Second Series 28 (2016) pp. 185–200
© 2016 The American Numismatic Society

Notes on the Early Medieval Numismatics
of Central Asia

Michael Fedorov*

This article discusses the early mediaeval coins with the Sogdian variant of the Turkic ram horns *tamgha*, which were minted in ancient Penjikent, and the the coins with the Turkic runic monogram *ush+j*, which were minted in Fergana.

1. More on the Coins with the Ram Horns *Tamgha*

In 1999, L. Baratova published some early mediaeval Chachian bronze coins with a royal couple on the obverse and a specific kind of *tamgha* on reverse.[1] She described these coins as "Klasse II. Gruppe d—Mit gabelartigem Zeichen" although the *tamgha* in question has nothing to do with a *Gabel* (fork). Baratova also described the trident *tamgha* as "gabelartiges Zeichen," but allocated them to "Klasse 1. Mit Herrscherdarstellungen. Gruppe C. Mit lyraförmigen Zeichen."[2] M. Fedorov defined this *tamgha* as variant of the lyre-shaped *tamgha*.[3] He subsequently realized that this *tamgha* comprised four ram horns and renamed it the ram horns *tamgha*.[4] Twin horns curving outwards are topped by two separate

---

* Ida-Dehmel-Ring 64, D-68309 Mannheim, Germany.
1 Baratova 1999: 250–253, pl. 4, 43–48.
2 Baratova 1999: 50, pl. 3, 29–30.
3 Fedorov 2003: 13.
4 Fedorov and Kuznetsov 2007: 279; Fedorov 2011: 189.

Figure 1. Chachian variants of the ram horns *tamgha*.

Figure 2. Rams in the Afrasiab murals.

horns turned back to back (Fig. 1). Rams with similar curving horns are pictured in the Afrasiab murals decorating palace of the Samarqandian king Varhuman (c. AD 655–675). The full series of ram horns *tamgha* coins has been published by Shagalov and Kuznetsov.[5]

In "Early Mediaeval Chachian Coins with Lyre and Ram Horns *Tamgas*," it was argued that the original homeland of the Turkic tribes using the ram horns *tamgha* was probably in the Talas valley (Kirghizia) on the grounds that, in 2004, the Kirghiz archaeologist K. Tabaldiev discovered petroglyphs with this particular *tamgha* at Djaltyraktash, in the Talas valley (Fig. 3).[6] G. Babayarov, M. Iskhakov, and Sh. Kamoliddin regarded them as a stylized form of the patrimonial *tamgha* of the Ashina ruling clan, to which the supreme rulers of both Turkic qaganates belonged.[7] However, the *tamghas* seem better understood as ram horns *tamghas*.

It was also suggested that the Turkic tribes using the ram horns *tamgha* migrated to Chach after they were driven out by the nomadic Turkic tribes off the Tiurgesh who fought for hegemony in Semirechie and created the Tiurgesh qaganate. After AD 657, the Western Turkic qagans became Chinese puppets. The nineteenth Western Turkic qagan was Buri Shad Hosrov. He and the Turkic tribes loyal to him were overthrown by the Tiurgesh, and in AD 699 he withdrew to China with 60–70,000 adherents.[8] After arriving in Chach, the Turkic tribes using the ram horns *tamgha* parted. Some stayed in Chach and created in the Angren

5 Shagalov and Kuznetsov 2006: 107–140, 311–312.
6 Fedorov 2011: 204.
7 Babyarov 2007: 34, 35, 50, 95; Babyarov et al. 2009: 14.
8 Bichurin 1950: 294–295.

Figure 3. Ram horns and swan-shaped *tamghas* from Djaltyraktash petroglyphs in the Talas valley (Kirghizia).

Figure 4. Khwarezmian variant of the ram horns *tamgha*.

valley a principality which minted coins with the ram horns *tamgha*. Other part of these tribes went farther to Khwarezm and created there a principality which minted coins with a Khwarezmian variant of the ram horns *tamgha* (Fig. 4). Still others turned south and eventually settled in the region of Termez. There are found local imitations of Sasanian drachms which were countermarked with a variant of the ram horns *tamgha*.[9]

After perusing an article by Baratova it became clear that there were also bronze coins with a Sogdian variant of the ram horns *tamgha*.[10]

Type 1 (Baratova 1999: 244, pl. 3, 27). 19 mm, 1.45 g (Fig. 5).

Obverse: Within a beaded circle is the head of king wearing a kind of hemispherical *kulah* and a diadem with a round medallion(?) above his forehead. He has a necklace. His face is roundish and rather full, with big almond-shaped eyes.

Reverse: Big *tamgha*, which Baratova calls *"lyraförmigen Zeichen"* (lyre-shaped sign) but which in fact is the ram horns *tamgha*. Around it is a heavily worn legend, apparently including the word *prn* on the right.

The coin is kept in the Samarqand museum.

Type 2 (Baratova 1999: 244, pl. 3, 28). 25 mm, 3.4 g (Fig. 6).

Obverse: Within a beaded circle is the head of the king in a *bashlik* (*kulah* with pointed top) with flaps leaving ears uncovered. In his left ear is an earring with a pearl. He has a necklace. His face is oblong, with round eyes. He appears to have a moustache. Over his right shoulder is a cross with broadening ends. Above this cross is an S-shaped symbol. Over his left shoulder is another, somewhat smaller cross.

Reverse: *Tamgha*, which Baratova calls *lyraförmigen*, but which is really a ram horns *tamgha*. Around it is a worn legend apparently including *prn* and *βγy*.

9 Fedorov 2011: 205.
10 Baratova 1999: 244–246, pl. 3, 27–28.

Figure 5. Coin with Sogdian variant of the ram horns *tamgha* in the Samarqand Museum.

Figure 6. Coin with Sogdian variant of the ram horns *tamgha* from Afrasiab.

The coin was found in 1968 at Afrasiab (ancient Samarqand) and, what is very important, in the same archaeological strata with coins of the Samarqandian *ikhshid* (king) Shishpir. He came to power in Samarqand no earlier than 631 and is known to have sent an embassy to China in 642. He appears to have died by 643, the year in which the Chinese imperial court accepted the embassy of *D'ung-xa* (Tongha), a new Samarqandian king.[11]

Type 3 (Baratova 1999: 245). 21 mm, 0.8 g (chipped).

Obverse: Within beaded circle is the head of a diademed king with oblong face, big almond-shaped eyes, and a moustache. His mouth is depicted as a large dot. To the left of the king is a worn symbol.
Reverse: Same *tamgha* as preceding. The word *prn* to right and *βyy* above.

The coin was found in Penjikent.

Baratova noted that the *tamgha* on coins of our Types 1–3 was also found on coins of Chach: "Die auf diesen Münzen vorkommenden Zeichen begegneten auf allen Münzen mit paariger Darstellung aus Chach."[12] She believed that only three such coins were known, but Smirnova has published several bronze coins with the same *tamgha* or its variants found in Penjikent:[13]

Type 4 (Smirnova 1981: Nos. 1472 and 1473). 21 mm and 20 mm, 1.8 g and 0.98 g (chipped) (Fig. 7).

Obverse: Within a beaded circle is a ruler in a *bashlik* with necklace and earring in the left ear.

11 Smirnova 1981: 25, 38; Fedorov 2003a: 7.
12 Baratova 1999: 245.
13 Smirnova 1981: 349–357, nos. 1472–1480.

Figure 7. Coin with slightly modified ram horns *tamgha* from Penjikent.

Figure 8. Coin with variant form of ram horns *tamgha* and cross from Penjikent.

Reverse: Ram horns *tamgha* (slightly modified). It has one short horizontal sprout on the upper left side. The word *prn* to right and *βyy* above.

Type 5 (Smirnova 1981: No. 1474). 19 mm.

Obverse: Within a linear circle is the head of a king wearing a hemispherical *kulah* with flaps leaving the ears uncovered. He has a necklace or torc. The face is roundish, with a short, straight nose and round eyes. The cheeks and chin are depicted by a broad horseshoe-shaped line.

Reverse: Partly effaced ram horns *tamgha* and heavily worn legend. Above the *tamgha* may have been the word *βyy*.

Type 6 (Smirnova 1981: Nos. 1475 and 1476). 17 mm and 18 mm, 0.61 g (chipped).

Obverse: Within a beaded circle is the head of a king in a hemispherical *kulah* with flaps leaving the ears uncovered. He has a necklace. The face is rather oblong, with a straight nose and round eyes. The cheeks and chin are depicted by a broad horseshoe-shaped line.

Reverse: Partly effaced and chipped ram horns *tamgha* and worn legend. The words *prn βy(y)* can be discerned.

Type 7 (Smirnova 1981: Nos. 1477 and 1478). 23 mm and 24 mm, 2.58 g and 2.73 g (Fig. 8).

Obverse: Within a beaded circle is the head of king wearing a hemispherical *kulah* with flaps covering the ears. He has a necklace with three pendants. The face is oblong, with a straight nose, round eyes, and small fleshy lips. The cheeks and chin are depicted by a broad horseshoe-shaped line.

Reverse: Modified ram horns *tamgha* with cross within it and two downward sprouts on the lower left side. The legend is worn, but the word *βy(y)* can be read.

Type 8 (Smirnova 1981: No. 1479). 24 mm, 1.53 g.

Obverse: Within a beaded circle is the head of king wearing a beaded diadem. In his left ear is an earring with four pearls (two horizontal topped by two vertical). The face is oblong, with a straight nose, round eyes, and small fleshy lips. The cheeks and chin are depicted by a broad horseshoe-shaped line. To the left of his chin is an uncertain symbol composed of an acute angle with apex upwards, topped by a tiny rectangle, topped by tiny crescent (or circlet?).

Reverse: A variant form of the ram horns *tamgha*. The legend *prn / βyy* can be read, but a third word is illegible.

Smirnova 1981: No.1480. 23 mm, 3.13 g.

Obverse: Within a beaded circle is the head of a king in a hemispherical *bashlik*(?) with a round and puffy Asian face, straight nose broadening downwards, lens-shaped eyes, and fleshy lips. The cheeks and chin are depicted by a broad horseshoe-shaped line. He has a necklace.

Reverse: A variant of the ram horns *tamgha* with two sprouts on the lower right and one sprout on the lower left side. The legend can be read as *prn / βyy/ n'r* or *δ'r*.

Out of 10 coins with the ram horns *tamgha* found in Samarqandian Sogd, one (Type 1) is kept in the Samarqand Museum and most probably was found in the region of Samarqand; one coin (Type 2) was found at Afrasiab; and eight (80%) coins (Types 3–8) were found in Penjikent. Six out of eight types of coins (75%) were found in Penjikent. All of this can leave little doubt that the coins with the Sogdian ram horns *tamgha* (and its variants) were minted in Penjikent.

When were these coins minted? The fact that the Type 2 coin with the Sogdian variant of ram horns *tamgha* was found in the same archaeological strata with coins of Shishpir (c. AD 631–642) allows us to date it to the second quarter of seventh century. Bearing in mind that copper and bronze coins could stay in circulation for twenty and even more years and that there were at least eight types of coins, minted by eight rulers, we can date the coins with the Sogdian variant of the ram horns *tamgha* to the first half of the seventh century AD.

The numismatic evidence and the scarce written sources allow us to infer that there were two waves of ram horns *tamgha* Turkic nomad tribes migrated to the west. The first wave took place in the beginning of seventh century and was connected to the creation of the Turkic qaganate and the campaigns of the first Turkic qagans, which reached as far west as the Black Sea and as far south as Afghanistan and northern India. At that time part of the ram horns *tamgha* tribes together with other Turkic tribes moved west and settled in Samarqandian (Western) Sogd, while other Turkic tribes settled in Chach and Fergana. In AD 605, the Turks killed the ruler of Chach and established a Turk Tegin at his place. Thereafter, at least three Turkic principalities sprang up in Chach, which minted coins with stag, trident, and lyre *tamghas*.

In the second quarter of the seventh century, Turks killed Kibi, the ruler of Fergana (*k'iei piet*). His place was taken by the Turk Ashina Shuni (*śiwo ńiek*), who was succeeded in Kasan by his son Iebochji.[14] Thus northern Fergana also came under the sway of the Turks, but local dynasties still retained their power in southern Fergana.[15] As the kingdom of Samarqand appeared to be too strong for them, part of the ram horns *tamgha* tribes that moved west with the other Turkic tribes seized Penjikent. There they created a new state and minted coins bearing the *tamgha* of their tribe. A second wave of ram horns *tamgha* Turkic migration to the west took place around 699, when the formidable Tiurgesh nomads forced them to leave their homeland.

V. Livshits wrote that the first Penjikent ruler to be named on coins was G/Hamaukian (Smirnova's Amukian/Chamukian), who ruled Penjikent in the second half of the seventh century (Fig. 9).[16] Iskhakov, Kamoliddin, and Babayarov read the name as Chamukian and associated him with the distinguished Turkic clan of Djamuk.[17] He was succeeded by Chakin Chur Bilga (Smirnova's Bidian/ Bidkan; Fig. 10), mentioned in a Sogdian document from Mount Mug. Judging by his name Chakin, honorary epithet Bilga, and title Chur, he was a Turk. After him, Penjikent was ruled by a Sogdian named Divashtich, son of Iodkhshetak,[18] who came to power c. 708, or c. 706, according to Hirano, whoshares the opinion of Marshak.[19] The name of Divashtich, however, was not placed on the coins. Instead, coins of Penjikent cite Lady Nana of Panch (Fig. 11). Livshits suggested that she was the senior wife of Divashtich. If so, she must have been the queen of Penjikent and he the prince consort.

Ilyasov wrote that the analysis of *tamghas* on Penjikent coins allows us to identify the ethnic affiliation of some rulers.[20] He agreed with Smirnova and B. Vainberg, who noticed close affinity of one *tamgha* on Penjikent coins to Göbl's *tamgha* S 60 found on Hephthalite coins.[21] However, it has been shown that this *tamgha* in fact was the ram horns *tamgha* of the Turkic nomad tribes in the Talas

14 Smirnova 1981:428–430; Bichurin 1950: 319.
15 *Istoriia* 1984: 235.
16 Livshits 1979: 60.
17 Iskhakov et al. 2009: 9.
18 Gafurov 1972: 231.
19 Hirano 2011: 356.
20 Ilyasov 2004: 54–61.
21 Smirnova 1970: 173; Vainberg 1977: 41; Göbl 1967: II, 210; IV, 289.

Figure 9. Coin of Chamukian, ruler of Panch.

Figure 10. Coin of Bilga, ruler of Panch.

Figure 11. Coin of Divashtich citing Lady Nana of Panch.

valley. Ilyasov disagreed with Smirnova that the second *tamgha* on some Penjikent coins was the Turkic rune *Oq* (arrow).[22] Ilyasov thought that it had greater affinity to the anchor-shaped *tamgha* on early medieval copper coins found near Termez. He found analogies to this *tamgha* in the *tamghas* of northern Khorezm, southern Kazakhstan, Chach, and the Sarmatian *tamghas* of the Crimea. He wrote that in the fourth century, at the time of Chionite conquest of Central Asia (in which he saw a southward advance of the southern Kazakhstan Kangüi nomads, triggered by the Huns' onset from the east), nomads using the anchor-shaped *tamgha* settled near Termez, and minted coins with this *tamgha*. In the fifth century, Hephthalite tribes, coming from the east, invaded the lands south of the Amu Darya and began the conquest of Transoxiana. The Chionite tribe (or part of it) using the anchor-shaped *tamgha* joined the Hephthalite advance and eventually settled in Penjikent. Later, some chief of this tribe seized power in Penjikent, resulting in the appearance of the anchor-shaped *tamgha* on coins of Penjikent.

This is an interesting hypothesis, but such movements back and forth seem somewhat doubtful. As for the lyre-shaped *tamgha* (which is actually a form of the ram horns *tamgha*) on Penjikent coins, regarded by Smirnova and Vainberg as

22 Smirnova 1981: 47, 230.

Hephthalite *tamgha* S 60, Ilyasov wrote that Chamaukian could have been a vassal of the Hephthalites and used the *tamgha* of his suzerain. This way or the other, old Turk dynasty, which in first half of seventh century minted in Penjikent coins with ram horns *tamgha*, was supplanted by the new dynasty, which placed on its coins two *tamghas*. These two *tamghas* could also reflect a matrimonial union between two dynasties. But as it recently transpired, Chamukian was not the first to place two *tamghas* on coins of Panch. Hirano published a bronze coin issued in Penjikent by Pēčut:[23]

30 mm. 5.5 g (four lines lower Hirano reports the weight of the coin as 5.04 g).

Obverse: Within a linear circle, around the square hole in the center: *pnčy MR'Y pyčwtt* (Pēčut Lord of Panch).

Reverse: Within a linear circle, to left of the hole is a winged human figure with javelin, staff, or sword in his right hand. To the right of the hole is a human figure holding a narrow-necked vessel(?). Both figures appear to be naked. Above the hole is a variant of the ram horns *tamgha* placed horizontally. Below the hole is an anchor-shaped *tamgha* or the Turkic rune *Oq* (arrow).

There were two Pēčuts in Penjikent. The first ruled at the beginning of the seventh century. The second one, according to the Chinese chronicle, *Tang shu*, was appointed prefect of Mi (Panch/Penjikent) in AD 658. He is considered to be the grandson of the first Pēčut. This second Pēčut (*pyčwtt*) is mentioned in a Sogdian document from Mount Mug as the father of *βylk'* (Bilga, i.e., Livshits' Chakin Chur Bilga), who ruled Panch in c. AD 691–706 (or 708).[24] In 2003, the reign of Amukian/Chamukian was dated to the second quarter of the seventh century.[25] Having discovered that in the first half of the seventh century Penjikent was ruled by the Turkic ram horns *tamgha* dynasty (numbering at least eight rulers, assuming that each new coin type represented a new ruler) and that a coin of one of their coins was found in the same archaeological strata with coins of Shishpir (no earlier than 631 and no later 642), it now seems much more likely that Amukian/Chamukian must belong to the second half of the seventh century.

If Ilyasov is right and the *tamgha* on coins of Amukian/Chamukian is the anchor-shaped Chionite *tamgha*, the historical situation could be as follows: The anchor-shaped *tamgha* belonged to a dynasty that ruled Panch before the Turkic invasion. At the beginning of seventh century the ram horns *tamgha* Turkic tribe captured Penjikent. Perhaps they killed the native king of Panch (as they did in Chach and northern Fergana) whose name may have been Pēčut (I). However, they did not exterminate the old aristocratic clan to which the native king belonged.

---

23 Hirano 2011: 355.
24 Hirano 2011: 355–356.
25 Fedorov 2003: 12.

About half a century later, kings from the ram horns *tamgha* Turkic dynasty ruled Panch. They were ousted from power by Pĕčut (II) from the clan with anchor-shaped *tamgha*, whom the Chinese emperor appointed prefect of Panch in 658. Pĕčut (II) may have retained the old ram horns *tamgha* on his coins because it had become an emblem of his capital at Penjikent, but added the anchor-shaped *tamgha* of his clan. It is not out of the question two *tamghas* on the Penjikent coins was a result of a marriage alliance.

An analogous situation occurs at Samarqand. When Shishpir, king of Kesh, captured the city, he left on his coins the old Y-shaped *tamgha*, which had become regarded more as the badge of Samarqand than as the Chionite-derived dynastic *tamgha* of ancient rulers.[26] To this Shsihpir added the triskelion *tamgha* of his clan on his Samarqandian coins.

Chamukian came to power after Pĕčut (II). It is not clear who he was, but, judging by the fact that he placed on his coins the same two *tamghas* as Pĕčut (II), he was a close relative of the latter (son, brother, or nephew). The son of Pĕčut (II), Chakin Chur Bilga, who reigned for at least 15 years, came to power in c. 691 or 693. The reigns of Pĕčut (II) and Chamukian therefore took place between 658 and 691/693, and lasted some 34–36 years. Curiously, the anchor-shaped *tamgha* of Pĕčut (II) and Chamukian disappeared from Penjikent coins under the son of Pĕčut, Chakin Chur Bilga. It is difficult to say why. Perhaps it was because Bilga incorporated a square hole in the center of the coin, which distorted the proportions and outline of the ram horns *tamgha*, leaving no space for the anchor-shaped *tamgha*. Bilga may have changed the ram horns *tamgha*'s contours purposely in order to create his own new type of *tamgha*. This new *tamgha* (slightly modified) remained on the coins of Panch minted by his successor. Shinji Hirano wrote:[27]

> this [Pĕčut's] coin poses further questions. When did *Pycwtt* issue this coin? If it was when he was a Bactrian king, why did he not call himself *βxtyk MLK'* as his son did? If this coin was issued before his enthronement in Bactria, why did he put Greek style figures on his coin? Was this coin part of the regular currency or a special memorial issue?

It is very difficult to see how *Pycwtt* could have been "king of Bactria" since in the seventh century the region of ancient Bactria was known as Tokharistan—a name that first appears in AD 385.[28] To answer Hirano's second question, the coin must have been part of an inauguration issue, otherwise it is difficult to explain its extreme rarity.

Document B-8 from Mount Mug mentions *βytyk MLK' pnčy MR'Y čk'yn čwr βylk"*. According to Hirano, Étienne de la Vaissière read the title as *βxtyk MLK' pnčy MR'Y* (King of Bactria Lord of Panch). Livshits, however, read the first word

26 Fedorov 2003a: 14; 2010: 189–190.
27 Hirano 2011: 358.
28 Gaufrov 1972: 225.

as *βytyk* and translated it as *βytian*,[29] which is far more plausible. We must also ask ourselves, if Bactria is named, then where is the letter *r*?

Finally, in 2003 it was suggested that coins with the Sogdian variant of the ram horns *tamgha* (following Smirnova, it was then described as the "lyre-shaped" or "lyre-shaped with triangular pedestal *tamgha*") could have been minted in Usrushana.[30] The evidence presented here shows now that this cannot be the case.

2. Coins with the *USH+J* Turkic Runic Monogram

There is an interesting series of bronze and copper coins with royal couple on the obverse and the Turkic runic monogram *ush+j* on the reverse (Fig. 12). The latest publication of such coins took place in 2010 in the article of M. Fedorov and A. Kuznetsov.[31]

The first coin with a royal couple and the Turkic runic monogram *ush+j* was published in 1880.[32] It was in the collection of Count Stroganoff, but its provenance and attribution were unknown. In 1952, O. Smirnova published three more such coins in the Samarqand museum, but did not read the legends or suggest an attribution.[33] In 1958, she published another two coins, found in the excavations at Penjikent, describing them as "coins of unknown ruler."[34] In 1961, she published three more coins from Penjikent, in her article about titles of early mediaeval Central Asian rulers known from Sogdian coins.[35] Smirnova noted that the coins in the Samarqand Museum were cast, while the coins from Penjikent were struck, and dated the struck coins to the middle of the eighth century.

On her coin no. 1, Smirnova read the Sogdian legend *MR'Y ...yttwn(h)*, and on coin no. 3 *MR'(?) ...ytt(w)nh*. She wrote that the Sogdian title *...yttwn(h)* corresponded to the Turkic title *qatūn* and translated it as "queen" or "wife." She mentioned the Queen-regent Khatūn who ruled Bukhara at the time of Arab conquest of Central Asia. The Arab chronicles do not give her name but only refer to her by her title, *khatūn*. Smirnova commented that "It is very enticing to see in the *yttwn(h)*, cited on these coins, the famous queen of Bukhara, but we have no data for this' since such coins had not been found in Bukharan Sogd." She interpreted the reverse type as a schematic fire altar with a triangle for the flames and an X-shaped pedestal for the altar.

In her catalogue of the coins found during the excavations of ancient Penjikent in 1949–1956, Smirnova published five such coins under the heading

29 Livshits 1962: 41, 51.
30 Fedorov 2003b: 7–8.
31 Fedorov and Kuznetsov 2010: 446–451.
32 Tiesenhausen 1880: no. 9 (24 mm, 1.54 g).
33 Smirnova 1952: 44 (22–23 mm, 2.7 g, 2.65 g, 2 g [chipped]).
34 Smirnova 1958: 226.
35 Smirnova 1961: 55–62 (23–25 mm, 1.73 g, 1.57 g, 1.16 g [broken]).

Figure 12. Coins with the royal couple and the Turkic runic monogram *ush+j*.

"Bukhara(?)."[36] In her *magnum opus*, Smirnova published 15 coins but left the question of attribution unresolved. However, she changed her opinion about the reverse and wrote that instead of the "stylized fire altar" is actually the Turkic runic monogram *ush+j*.[37] In 2010, it was suggested that the monogram *ush+j* could be interpreted as the mint name Ūsh (modern Osh), an ancient town at the eastern-most outskirts of the Ferghana valley, in the modern Kirghiz Republic.[38] However, it was pointed out that "The problem with this identification is that such coins have not yet been found in the Fergana valley."

Unfortunately, in the discussion of the Ming Tepe hoard of bronze Sogdian coins, Livshits' relevant article, "Pis'mennost' drevneī Fergany (Written language of ancient Fergana)," was overlooked.[39] In this article, Livshits read the legends on three coins in the Samarqand Museum as *βry'nk MR'Y čyš* (Ferganian Lord Chish). This legend provides direct evidence that coins with the Turkic runic monogram *ush+j* were minted in the Fergana valley and, quite plausibly, in Ūsh. Livshits dated such coins to the sixth–seventh centuries AD. Two more coins of this type are in the Hermitage Museum.[40] But Smirnova did not read the legends on them.[41] She wrote that these coins (Group 1) were cast and had good, realistic portraits. The later coins (Group 2) were struck and had schematic, degraded portraits. The coins of Group 2 were all found in Penjikent, while there was not a single coin of Group 1 found in Penjikent. Degradation of the portraits in her opinion shows that these coins were minted for a long period. There was also a Group 3, represented by one coin (No. 1497) on which the king and queen "changed places." Smirnova considered this coin to have a Turkic runic legend, but M. Iskhakov read the Sogdian letters *m*, *č*, and *š*.[42]

The coins differ by legend, portraits, form of the queen's headdress, disposition of personages, and dots in the monogram.

36 Smirnova 1963: 137–138.
37 Smirnova 1981: nos. 1482–1496.
38 Fedorov and Kuznetsov 2010: 451.
39 Fedorov and Kuznetsov 2010: 446–451; Livshits 1968: 230.
40 Smirnova 1981: nos. 1483–1484n
41 Smirnova 1981: 55, 360–361.
42 Smirnova 1981: 369; Baratova 1999: 249.

Group 1 (Samarqand Museum 10.181-183/ 226-228k; Smirnova 1981: nos. 1483–1484: 24 mm, 2.75 g, 2.46 g, 1.8 g, 1.53 g [chipped]). Legend: *βry'nk MR'Y čyš*. The queen, to the right of the king, wears a three-horned headdress. The portraits are realistic. There are no dots in the monogram turned to right.

Group 2/a (Smirnova 1981: no. 1482). Legend: *MRWY βčš' y'ttwnh*. The queen, to the right of the king, wears a three-horned headdress. Portraits are realistic. There are no dots in the monogram turned to left.

Group 2/b (Smirnova 1981: Nos. 1485 and 1493, 24 mm, 20 mm, 1.29 g, 1.02 g [chipped]). Legend: *MR'… y'tt*. The queen, to the right of the king, wears a *kolpak* (cone-shaped cap with slanting point). Portraits are somewhat schematized. In each triangle of the monogram, turned left, there is a dot.

Group 2/c (Smirnova 1981: nos. 1486–1488: 25 mm, 24 mm, 20 mm, 21 mm, 1.73 g, 1.29 g, 0.91 g [chipped], 0.85 g [chipped]). Legend: *MR'… y'tt…*. The queen, right of the king, has three-horned headdress. Portraits are somewhat schematized. There are dots in the monogram to left.

Group 2/d (Smirnova 1981: nos. 1489–1492, 25 mm, 24 mm, 25 mm, 21 mm, 2.15 g, 1.57 g, 1.16 g, 1.0 g ([chipped]). Same legend as Group 2/c, but heavily worn. The queen, to the right of the king, wears a *kolpak* contoured by pearls or beads. Portraits are more schematized. There are no dots in the monogram turned to left.

Smirnova 1981: nos. 1494–1495 (21 mm, 20 mm, 1.6 g, 0.74 g [chipped]) have dots in the monogram to left. However, since the coins are broken, it is not possible to identify the headdress worn by the queens. Smirnova 1981, no. 1496 (23 mm, 2.47 g) is worn.

Group 3 (Smirnova 1981: no. 1497, 21 mm, 0.95 g [chipped]). This coin differs from all the others in that the queen is to the left of the king. She wears a *kolpak*. There are no dots in the monogram to left. The legend is heavily worn, but the Sogdian letters *m*, *č*, and *š* are discernible.

Struck examples featuring the queen wearing a *kolpak* and monograms turned to left also appeared in the Ming Tepe hoard:[43]

Fedorov and Kuznetsov 2010: no. 7 (21 mm, 1.6 g). The contour of the queen's *kolpak* is depicted by a dotted line (representing pearls or beads). There is no dot in the lower triangle of the monogram, but there is a dot in the upper triangle. The legend is heavily worn, but …'r/k … can be discerned.

Fedorov and Kuznetsov 2010: no. 8 (22 mm, 1.2 g [chipped]). The contour of the queen's *kolpak* is shown by a line. The front of the *kolpak* is decorated with three pellets. The tip of *kolpak* is adorned by a large pellet. There is no dot in the top triangle of the monogram, but there is a dot in the lower triangle.

43 Fedorov and Kuznetsov 2010: 447–448, pl. 24, 7–10.

Fedorov and Kuznetsov 2010: no. 9 (23 mm, 2.6 g). The queen wears a kolpak without decoration and to her left is a young boy, suggesting that the queen-regent and the heir to the throne are depicted. Smirnova seems to have mistaken the double portrait for that of a "man and young boy."[44] There are two dots in the monogram. The legend is heavily worn, but ... tw...(for γ'ttwn) can be discerned.

Fedorov and Kuznetsov 2010: no. 10 (25 mm, 2.1 g). The contour of the queen's *kolpak* is shown by a dotted line. There are two dots in the monogram. It is the same type as Smirnova 1981: no. 1485 (Group 2/b). The legend can be read as *MR'Y βč... γ'ttwn*.

The coins of Group 2 were minted for a long period, as indicated by the schematization and degradation of the portraits and numerous variants of the same type. Monograms occur without dots, with one dot placed either in the upper or lower, or with two dots. The queen wears a horned headdress or a *kolpak*, which can be undecorated or edged with a beaded or simple line. The faces of different rulers can be distinguished. Small variations within the same type are not fortuitous, but instead serve to distinguish the coins of one ruler from those of another.

The individual emissions were small, suggesting that they were inauguration issues. This would explain the comparative rarity of the coins.

In the first half of the seventh century, in neighboring Chach, a Turkic dynasty minted coins bearing a stag-shaped *tamgha*.[45] A royal couple is depicted on some of these coins. The queen appears to the right of the king and also wears the same three-horned headdress as the queen on the Ferganian coins with the *ush+j* monogram (Group 1). This hints that the Ferganian coins with the *ush+ j* monogram may have been issued at about the same time. The coins of Group 2/a, featuring the queen with three-horned headdress, were closest in time to the coins of Group 1. Later issues featured the queen wearing a *kolpak*. Smirnova dated the struck coins to the middle of the eighth century. The struck coins from Ming Tepe hoard were found together with Sogdian coins of the Samitan ruler Nanaiabiat, which have been dated to the first third of the eighth century.[46]

To be objective, the bronze coins depicting the heraldic lion of Otrar on the obverse and the Turkic runic monogram *ush+n* on the reverse should be noted. Both coins were found in modern Kazakhstan, near the town Otrar and in the Keles steppe (22 mm, 20 mm, unknown weight, 2.44 g). In this case, the monogram cannot represent the mint name. It may be that the Turkic runic monogram *ush+j* on the coins minted in Fergana was the heraldic *nishan* (symbol) of a Turkic dynasty kindred to the dynasty that minted coins in Otrar, since both of them have the *ush* component in their *nishans*.

---

44 Smirnova 1981: 56.
45 Kuznetsov and Shagalov 2006: 60–106, 307–310.
46 Fedorov and Kuznetsov 2010: 450.

References

Babayarov, G. 2007. *Drevnetiurkskie monety chachskogo oazisa (VI–VIIIvv. N.E.)*. Tashkent.

Baratova, L. 1999. Alttürkishe Münzen Mittelasiens aus dem 6.–10. Jh. n. Chr. *Archäologishe Mitteilungen aus Iran und Turan* 31: 219–292.

Bichurin, N. Ja. 1950. *Sobranie svedeniĭ o narodakh,obitavshikh v Sredneĭ Azii v drevnie vremena*. Vol. 1. Moscow.

Fedorov, M. 2003. Money circulation in the early–mediaeval Chach (6th–the first half of the 8th century AD. *ONS Newsletter* 176 (Summer): 8–16.

————. 2003a. Money circulation in the early-mediaeval Sogd (6th–the first half of the 8th century AD). *Supplement to ONS Newsletter* 175: 1–26.

————. 2003b. Money circulation in the early-mediaeval Usrushana, Farghana, and Tokharistan (6th–the first half of the 8th century AD). *ONS Newsletter* 177: 6–15.

————. 2010. Chionite rulers of Chach in the middle of the fourth to the beginning of the seventh century (according to the data of numismatics). *Iran* 48: 59–67.

————. 2011. Early mediaeval Chachian coins with lyre and ram horns *tamgas*. *AJN* 23: 189–208.

Fedorov, M. and A. Kuznetsov. 2007. A hoard of early mediaeval Chach coins from Kanka. *NC* 167: 277–285.

————. 2010. A hoard of early mediaeval Sogdian bronze coins from the Ming Tepe hillfort. *NC* 170: 446–451.

Hirano, S. 2011. A new coin in the name of Pēchut Lord of Panch. *NC* 171: 355–358.

Ilyasov, J. 2004. Ob etnicheskoĭ prinadlezhnosti praviteleĭ Pendzhikenta. *Numizmatika Tsentral'noi Azii* 7: 54–61

Istoriia 1984. *Istoriia Kirgizskoĭ SSR*. Vol. 1. Frunze.

Livshits V. A. 1962. *Sogdiĭskie dokumenty s gory Mug, 2. Iuridicheskie dokumenty i pis'ma, chtenie, perevod i kommentarii V. A. Livshitsa*. Moscow.

————. 1968. Pis'mennost' drevneĭ Fergany. *Narody Azii i Afriki* 6: 230.

————. 1979. Praviteli Pancha (sogdiitsy i tiurki). *Narody Azii i Afriki* 4: 56–61.

Shagalov, V. and A. Kuznetsov. 2006. *Katalog monet Chacha III-VIII vv.* Tashkent.

Smirnova, O. I. 1952. Materialy k svodnomu katalogu sogdiiskikh monet. *Epigrafika Vostoka* 6: 3–45.

————. 1958. Monety drevnego Pendjikenta. In *Trudy Tadjikskoĭ arkheologicheskoĭ ekspeditsii*, Vol. 3, pp. 216–280. Moscow/Leningrad.

————. 1961. Zametki o sredneaziatskoi titulature (po monetnym dannym). *Epigrafika Vostoka* 14: 55–70.

————. 1963. *Katalog monet s gorodishcha Pendjikent*. Moscow.

————. 1970. *Ocherki iz istorii Sogda*. Moscow.

————. 1981. *Svodnyĭ katalog Sogdiĭskikh monet*. Moscow.

Tiesenhausen, W. 1880. *Notice sur une collection de monnaies orientales de M. le*

comte Stroganoff. St. Petersburg.
Vainberg, B. I. 1977. *Monety drevnego Khorezma.* Moscow.

AJN Second Series 28 (2016) pp. 201–230
© 2016 The American Numismatic Society

The Administration of the 'Abbāsid North and the Evidence of Copper Coins
(AH 142–218 / AD 759–833)

PLATES 47–50 ARAM VARDANYAN *

This article introduces a series of copper coins (*fulūs*) struck in the northern provinces of the 'Abbāsid caliphate (Armīniyah, Arrān, Shirwān, and Daghastān) from the early 760s AD when the first 'Abbāsid coins appeared in the region until the 830s when the provincial copper coinage came to an end. These coins are important for revealing the names of minor officials who acted as sub-governors and whose activities are not documented in the contemporary literary sources. In addition, the copper coins minted at al-Yazīdiyah and al-Bāb are important for the history of medieval Shirwān and Daghastān, especially because the region lacked any locally produced precious metal coinage after the Umayyad era. Finally, a short discussion on the nature of the regional 'Abbāsid administration in the light of copper coinage is offered.

MINOR OFFICIALS AND SUB-GOVERNORS

A. Officials involved in municipal administration

Undoubtedly, the importance of silver coinage for investigating the institute of governors who acted on behalf of the 'Abbāsid caliphs in different corners of the huge Islamic caliphate cannot be overestimated. Likewise, the early 'Abbāsid *dirhams* provide us with a clear sequence of governors appointed by the central

*Department of Arabic Studies, Institute of Oriental Studies, NAS of Republic of Armenia, Marshal Baghramyan Ave., 24/4, Yerevan 0019 (aramvardanian@yahoo.com).

authorities to the provinces of Armīniyah, Arrān (Ałuankʿ), Daghastān, and
Shirwān with administrative capitals at Dabīl (Dvin), Bardaʿah (Partav), Bāb al-
Abwāb (Darband) and Shamākhā (Shamākhī) respectively. These provinces are
conventionally described as the "'Abbāsid North."[1] This geographic term was
preceded by the "Umayyad North," used to describe the administrative unit
comprised by the Umayyad provinces of al-Jazīrah, Armīniyah, Arrān, and
Adharbayjān.[2] In the early 1930s, Richard Vasmer made an excellent attempt
through literary and numismatic evidence to develop a general sequence of the
'Abbāsid governors who governed the region for about a century from the reign of
al-Ṣaffāḥ (AD 750–754) to that of al-Maʾmūn (AD 813–833).[3] Vasmer's observations
were of the highest importance at the time and even today, some 85 years later,
his work can be used as a general guide, though it is somewhat obsolete due to
new coin discoveries. A much more updated treatment of the topic was offered in
the doctoral thesis of Norman Douglas Nicol who some 50 years after Vasmer's
publication discussed the main features of the caliphal governorship in Armīniyah
and Arrān.[4] Armed with both historical narratives and recently revealed coins,
Nicol produced a revised list of provincial governors with historical commentary
and offered a brief discussion of the general structure of the governorship in the
region. Despite the importance of this work, Nicol, like Vasmer, primarily used
the evidence of precious metal coinage and failed to give adequate attention to
that of the copper coins. Meanwhile, the contribution of copper coinage to local
history is obvious while it demonstrates a wide range of names that belonged to
minor officials. The catalogue placed at the end of this paper offers an up-to-date
list of copper coins struck in the region in the discussed period. Their discussion
in the general historical context might be useful for a better understanding of the
model of administrative relationship that existed in different 'Abbāsid provinces,
and those forming the Transcaucasia and Caucasia in particular.

The emission of copper coins in the northern provinces of the caliphate
began in the Umayyad period, but was interrupted by the bloody revolution that
culminated in the overthrow of the Umayyad dynasty and the ultimate victory of
the 'Abbāsid clan. Copper coins were again struck in the province by governors
approved by the new authorities starting in the late 130s AH (750s AD). Yazīd ibn
Usayd ibn Zafir al-Sulamī was one of the first governors appointed in the 'Abbāsid
North. His rule in the region can be divided in three main periods. The first began
in the early 750s when he served as deputy for the major governor, the 'Abbāsid
heir al-Manṣūr (AD 754–775). It cannot yet be ascertained when Yazīd abandoned
his post, nor have we information when the next major governor, the prince
al-Mahdī assigned him to Armīniyah. His second period of rule took place over

1 See Michael Bates's remarks regarding this geographical unit in Bates 1989: 89–90.
2 Spellberg 1988: 119.
3 Vasmer 1931.
4 Nicol 1979: 83–112.

much of the 140s AH (760s AD) and is confirmed by a series of copper *fulūs* initiated in Barda'ah in AH 142–143 (AD 759–761).[5] The third period of his governorship began in AH 159 (AD 775/6) and continued into the early 160s AH (780s AD).[6] Between his second and third periods Bakkār ibn Muslim al-'Uqaylī and al-Ḥasan ibn Qaḥṭabah al-Ṭā'ī controlled the provinces on behalf of al-Mahdī. They struck coins not only in Armīniyah and Arrān, but also in Bāb al-Abwāb, the chief city of the Daghastān province. However, a largely uninterrupted issue of copper coins is attested in the region only for the early 180s AH (800s AD). During this period, the local economy was supplied with copper coins struck by the Shaybānid governors of Armenia, particularly Yazīd ibn Mazyad and his sons Asad and Muḥammad. Late in the rule of Hārūn al-Rashīd (AD 786–809) copper coin production in Armīniyah greatly increased as can be seen from the varieties of coin types we have from the mint of Dabīl dated to this period.

The large number of coins struck in Dabīl in AH 185 (AD 801/2), 187 (AD 802/3) and 189 (AD 804/5) and citing Mahdī, 'Abbād, al-Qāsim, and Hishām sheds further light on local governorship and suggests the administrative structure.[7] Even if contemporary chroniclers considered their activities not important enough to be mentioned in their narratives, there is little doubt that all the officials named on the coins in this period were connected to the city's administration. Thus, Mahdī, whose name appears on coins dated AH 185, should have ruled in Dvin for the caliphal governor Asad ibn Yazīd, mentioned on some Armīniyah *dirhams* dated AH 186 (AD 802).[8] The same task was evidently given to 'Abbād who is named on *fulūs* of AH 187 and who served as Asad's successor and administered Dvin on behalf of Muḥammad ibn Yazīd in AH 186–187 (AD 802–803).[9]

In AH 187, the governor in the northern provinces was Khuzaymah ibn Khāzim al-Tamīmī. Silver *dirhams* struck between AH 187 and 192 (AD 803–808) indicate that Bishr ibn Khuzaymah, Isma'īl ibn Ibrāhīm, Nu'aym ibn Bishār, and Salāmah were his probable deputies in Armīniyah and Arrān.[10] In AH 189, Khuzaymah's representative in Dvin was al-Qāsim as evidenced by copper coins alone. Before the end of AH 189 Khuzaymah had appointed Bishr ibn Khuzaymah from the al-Asadī clan as governor of Armīniyah and Arrān. He subsequently dismissed the local administration and appointed to Dvin Hishām ibn 'Amr al-Taghlabī, a Mesopotamian general who together with the aforementioned Bishr had been a

---

5 Vasmer 1931: 9–10.

6 The copper coins dated AH 164 (AD 780/1) currently provide the terminal date for Yazīd's rule in the province (Paghava 2008: 4–6).

7 Besides it, some copper coins citing Yazīd ibn Usayd and dated AH 164 (AD 780/1), have an illegible name within the inscription على يدي engraved in the upper segment of the obverse. Unfortunately, all known to me specimens of this type have the name of that official too worn to be deciphered.

8 Vardanyan 2011: 57.

9 Vardanyan 2011: 58–60.

10 Vardanyan 2011: 61–70, 136–144.

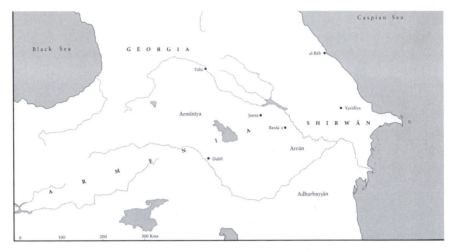

Figure 1. Map of the 'Abbāsid North.

governor of Mawṣil under Umayyads.[11] Finally, some Armīniyah silver *dirhams* dated AH 189–190 (AD 804–806) mention a certain al-Haytham whose name is found between the annulets of the obverse,[12] and who is apparently identical with Saʿīd ibn al-Haytham, from the same al-Tamīmī clan, and included by al-Yaʿqūbī among Khuzaymah's deputies in the region.[13] As I have argued elsewhere, in the early ʿAbbāsid period all silver *dirhams* marked with the mint name Armīniyah were minted in Dabīl.[14] Accordingly, this official could have been attached to Dvin's municipal administration or that of the local mint.

B. Sub-governors in provincial administration

As in the Umayyad period, the inscriptions on ʿAbbāsid copper coins were strictly limited to the use of the profession of faith and inscriptions referring to the provincial ruling elite. The governor of the province was normally introduced on coins through the inscription مما امر به الامير ("from what was ordered by the *amir*"), placed in either the marginal section or the central field. In some cases, the governor's name could be split into two parts engraved above and below the phrase naming the Prophet Muḥammad on the reverse. However, even with a relatively clear concept of the caliphal administration in particular provinces, we still have a very limited knowledge of the persons introduced on coins by the formula على يدي ("by the hands"). In the early ʿAbbāsid period, the governorship in the northern provinces included a major governor, his deputies in the provinces and their

11 Crone 1980: 167f.
12 Vardanyan 2011: 66–67.
13 al-Yaʿqūbī 2002: 300.
14 Vardanyan 2014: 10.

officials in the cities and other settlements. This hierarchy was also reflected in contemporary coinage. Thus, the major governor was normally mentioned on both silver *dirhams* and copper coins. The names of his deputies in the provinces were often engraved under the names of their patrons on the reverse. Finally, the names of minor officials who ruled in particular provinces or cities were indicated by the inscription على يدي. The names of these minor officials were usually inscribed on the copper coins and less frequently on precious metal coins. When they appear on silver *dirhams* the names are given in their entirety or abbreviated on the obverse. The considerably lower status of such persons can be confirmed by the fact that their names (*ism*), in most cases, lack a patronymic (*nasab*). Available coins and the evidence of the literary sources provide us with the names of many individuals who served as sub-governors in the region. Such officials, as a rule, represented local Arab tribal aristocracy or military elite. They represented governor's power on the huge territories with many cities and smaller settlements, having as their duties military, financial and judicial aspects of administration.

a. 'Abdallāh ibn Muḥammad. According to the literary sources, Muḥammad ibn Zuhayr ibn Musayyib al-Ḍabbī, a former governor of Egypt in the 790s AD,[15] was the last governor appointed to Armīniyah by Hārūn al-Rashīd.[16] His rule was short as a new governor was appointed to replace him in the same year. Silver *dirhams* prove that in AH 194–195 (AD 809–811) the province was controlled by Asad ibn Yazīd, who had been appointed governor of Armīniyah ten years before. The administrative authority of Asad was not limited to Armīniyah alone but also included the neighboring province of Arrān, where his deputy may have been a certain Mazyad cited on some rare *dirhams*.[17] Similarly, a *fals* of Dabīl struck in the name of a previously unknown 'Abdallāh ibn Muḥammad in AH 194 (AD 809–810) raises the question of whose authority, if not his own, this represented. Taking into account that 'Abdallāh's name appears on coins within the inscription مما امر به الامير, one can assume that he served as governor in Armīniyah. However, with the only help of available copper coins it is impossible to determine precisely the length of 'Abdallāh's governorship. New coins with his name may shed more light on the duration of his rule in the region.

15 al-Kindī 1912: 135.

16 al-Ya'qūbī 2002: 301.

17 Qatar I: 1581 (2.92 g) = Vardanyan 2011: 131 (with wrong date); Morton & Eden 59 (13–14 Nov. 2012), lot 333 (2.97 g). Another possibility is that *Mazyad* refers here not to a particular person, but to the name of the clan to which Asad belonged.

Table 1. Governors, deputies, and minor officials on copper coins struck in the ʿAbbāsid North

AH	Mint	Governor	Deputy	Minor official
134–135	Armīniyah	Yazīd ibn Usayd [al-Sulamī]		
142	Bardaʿah	Yazīd ibn Usayd		
143	Bardaʿah	Yazīd ibn Usayd		
153	Arrān	Bakkār [ibn Muslim al-ʿUqaylī]		
153	al-Bāb	Bakkār		
154	al-Bāb	al-Ḥasan		
155	al-Bāb	[al-Ḥasan ibn Qaḥṭabah al-Ṭāʾī]	Qaḥṭabah [ibn al-Ḥasan]	
158	Bardaʿah	al-Ḥasan [ibn Qaḥṭabah al-Ṭāʾī]		
158	al-Bāb	al-Ḥasan [ibn Qaḥṭabah al-Ṭāʾī]		
159	al-Bāb	Khālid ibn Yazīd [ibn Usayd]		
159	Dabīl	Yazīd ibn Usayd		
159	Bardaʿah	Yazīd ibn Usayd		
163	Bardaʿah	Yazīd ibn Usayd		
164	No mint name	Yazīd ibn Usayd		?
169	al-Harūniyah	Khuzaymah ibn Khāzim [al-Tamīmī]		
170–171	al-Harūniyah	Yazīd ibn Mazyad	Sharāḥīl [ibn Maʿn ibn Zāʾyda]	
170–173	No mint name	ʿUbaydallāh ibn al-Mahdī	سـ [Sulaymān ibn Yazīd]	
177	Arrān	Khālid ibn Yazīd [ibn Usayd]		
178	Arrān	Mūsā ibn ʿĪsā [al-Hāshimī]		
178	al-Bāb	Yaḥyā [al-Ḥarashī]		

AH	Mint	Governor	Deputy	Minor official
182	Dabīl	Saʿīd [ibn Salm al-Bāhilī]	ʿAbdallāh ibn Salm	
184	Arrān	Aḥmad ibn Mazyad		
184	Arrān	Asad ibn Yazīd [ibn Mazyad]		
185	Arrān	Asad ibn Yazīd		
185	Dabīl	Asad ibn Yazīd		Mahdī
186	Arrān	Muḥammad ibn Yazīd [ibn Mazyad]		
187	Dabīl	Muḥammad ibn Yazīd		ʿAbbād
187	Bardaʿah	Muḥammad [ibn Yazīd]		?
189	Dabīl	Khuzaymah ibn Khāzim	Bishr ibn Khuzaymah al-Asadī	al-Qāsim/Hishām
193	Arrān	al-ʿAbbās ibn Zufar [al-Hilālī]	Muṭrif	
194	Dabīl	ʿAbdallāh ibn Muḥammad		
197	Arrān	al-ʿAbbās ibn Zufar	Isḥāq ibn Sulaymān	
204	Armīniyah?	Aḥmad ibn Yaḥyā	al-Baʿyth [ibn Ḥalbas]	Jabbār ?
208	No mint name	ʿĪsā al-Maʾmūnī	Muḥammad ibn Sālim	
214	Mad. Arrān	Khālid ibn Yazīd [ibn Mazyad]	Ibrāhīm ibn ʿAttāb	

b. ʿAbdallāh ibn Salm. At the very end of the eighth century AD the caliphal
governor in Armīniyah and Arrān was Saʿīd ibn Salm al-Bāhilī. ʿAbdallāh's
probable linkage to Saʿīd as brother might explain his assignment to a
provincial governorship. Taking into account that his name appears on
copper coins of Dabīl dated AH 182 (AD 798/9), one can assume that his
authority extended over not only Dvin, but also the whole province of
Armīniyah. Unfortunately, this hypothesis cannot be confirmed by other
sources since the official in question is only known from the coins.

c. al-Baʿyth. This official was a member of the Arab al-Rabīʿah tribe. His father
was Ḥalbas, a ruler of Marand, Khūy, and Urmiyah in western Adharbayjān
in the late Umayyad period. The position of al-Baʿyth's father might have
helped him to enter the service of al-Rawwād ibn al-Muthannā al-Azdī, one
the early Rawwādids who controlled Adharbayjān from the eighth century AD
onwards. Both silver *dirhams* and copper *fulūs* struck in AH 204 (AD 819/20)
prove that al-Baʿyth briefly controlled some parts of Armīniyah and accepted
Aḥmad ibn Yaḥyā as caliphal governor in the province. The crude style of the
inscriptions allow us ascribe these copper coins to the mint of Armīniyah
only conventionally. It may be that an official named Jabbār (?) who appears
on the obverse might have been involved with the municipal administration
of Dvin where the coins were obviously produced.

d. Ibrāhīm ibn ʿAttāb. The name of this official appears on copper coins struck
in Madīnat Arrān (Bardaʿah) in AH 214 (AD 829/30) along with Khālid ibn
Yazīd ibn Mazyad (AH 211–217 [AD 826–833]) who was appointed to the
ʿAbbāsid North by al-Maʾmūn in reward for his brilliant military service. It is
very likely that Khālid was occupied with other military tasks from Baghdād
and therefore entrusted the provincial administration to Ibrāhīm. At least,
his name appears on *dirhams* struck on behalf of Khālid ibn Yazīd in both
Armīniyah and Madīnat Arrān in AH 215–217 (AD 830–833). The dates on
the copper coins extend Ibrāhīm's rule in the province for at least one more
year. None of the contemporary literary sources mention Ibrāhīm in any
connection with Armenia and adjacent areas. It is however possible that he
was the brother of Muḥammad ibn ʿAttāb who rebelled in Georgia about
that time and whose submission was obtained by Khālid ibn Yazīd.[18]

e. Isḥāq ibn Sulaymān. The career of Isḥāq ibn Sulaymān al-Hāshimī in the
capacity of governor began under Hārūn al-Rashīd. Al-Kindī remembers
him among the governors appointed to Egypt in AH 177 (AD 793/4). During
this period his chief of police (*al-shurᴿah*) was Muslim ibn Bakkār al-
ʿUqaylī, the son of the governor of Armīniyah in the days of al-Manṣūr.[19]

18 Ter-Ghewondyan 1976: 28.
19 al-Kindī 1912: 136.

Ishāq was granted a governorship in the 'Abbāsid North by AH 196 (AD 811/2) judging from a silver coin of Arrān (State Hermitage, inv. no. OH-B-M-1719). However, his rule in the region was short. In AH 197 (AD 812/3) Ishāq's authority in Arrān was lost to a certain Sulaymān known only from coins (State Hermitage, inv. no. OH-B-M-1724). Copper coins also show that his rule in Armīniyah was also brief. He was replaced by al-'Abbās ibn Zufar al-Hilālī,[20] who had been appointed to Armīniyah first in AH 193 (AD 808/9), but because of his unsuccessful struggle with the al-Sanāriyah rebels, was soon removed from his post.[21] A *fals* indicates that Ishāq ibn Sulaymān was subordinate to al-'Abbās ibn Zufar.

f. Muhammad ibn Sālim. Copper *fulūs* struck in the name of 'Īsā al-Ma'mūnī and his official Muhammad ibn Sālim in AH 208 (AD 823/4) are of some interest. Although the coins do not explicitly identify the place of their issue, judging from both inscriptions and findspots they probably have a Caucasian origin. 'Īsā al-Ma'mūnī, otherwise known as 'Īsā ibn Muhammad ibn Abī Khālid al-Ma'mūnī, was a caliphal freedman whose governorship in Armīniyah and Arrān spanned the short period of AH 206–208 (AD 821–824).[22] Muhammad ibn Sālim appears to have belonged to the provincial administration.

g. Mutrif. *Dirhams* struck in the name of al-'Abbās confirm his rule over Arrān only in AH 193 (AD 808/9). His copper coins indicate that this governor had an assistant called Mutrif. Vasmer, quoting Tiesenhausen, reported the existence of an Armīniyah *dirham* of AH 193 struck on behalf of Yahyā ibn Zufar.[23] It has not been possible to locate such a coin, and therefore I would suggest that the coin in question actually carries a blundered legend naming al-'Abbās ibn Zufar.

h. Qahtabah. See the section on the administration of Bāb al-Abwāb for this official.

i. Sharāhīl. Sharāhīl ibn Ma'n ibn Zā'yda was a member of the Banū Shaybān, a powerful Arab tribe which, along with the Banū Sulaym, governed Armīniyah and Arrān on behalf of the Umayyad caliphs. Sharāhīl was the paternal uncle of Yazīd ibn Mazyad and his father Ma'n had served both the Umayyads and 'Abbāsids. Sharāhīl made his career at the court of Hārūn al-Rashīd. Sharāhīl participated in the caliph's campaign against the Byzantines

---

20 *SICA* 2, 1400.

21 al-Ya'qūbī 2002: 301.

22 Vasmer (1931: 76) suggested the period AH 205–208 (AD 820–824) for the rule of this official, although available coins cannot yet confirm 'Īsā's assignment to his post as early as in AH 205 (AD 820/1).

23 Vasmer 1931: 44.

in AH 190 (AD 805/6),[24] but some 20 years earlier he had been a deputy of Yazīd ibn Mazyad in parts of Armenia, including the mint of al-Hārūniyah. Silver *dirhams* citing Yazīd ibn Mazyad were struck at al-Hārūniyah in AH 170–171 (AD 786–788), hence the coppers inscribed with the names of Yazīd ibn Mazyad and Sharāḥīl should be placed within the same period of time.

It has been suggested that the al-Hārūniyah of the coins could have been the name of a mint producing coins from silver mined in the Apahunikʿ (Bājunays, also spelled Bāḥunays or Bāḥunis) district of Armenia and therefore should not be connected with a particular city, but rather a fortified administrative center in the vicinity of mines in the Turuberan region of Armenia.[25] However, it is worth noting that the beginning of coinage at Hārūnābād and al-Hārūniyah coincided chronologically with the cessation of the mint activities in Armīniyah and Arrān respectively. This coincidence leads to the tentative conclusion that both Hārūnābād and al-Hārūniyah might have been new names or epithets for the provincial mints that operated before. These new mints, or more probably, the old mints with new names, had previously struck coins for Hārūn al-Rashīd as provincial governor in AH 168 and 169 and he clearly wished to continue issuing coins from these mints bearing his name during his rule as caliph. The local authorities continued to strike coins with the mint name of Hārūnābād in the subsequent years as evidenced by rare coins dated AH 173 (AD 789/90).[26] However, for some reason, perhaps due to the subsequent separation of the northern provinces from Baghdād, the use of the mint names Hārūnābād and al-Hārūniyah was stopped.

j.   Sulaymān ibn Yazīd ibn al-Aṣam al-ʿĀmirī. In the early 790s AD, ʿUbaydallāh ibn al-Mahdī disputed power with his brother Hārūn al-Rashīd. This conflict led to a civil war resulting in the division of the empire. ʿUbaydallāh received Armīniyah, Adharbayjān, and Arrān, while Hārūn retained the other parts of the empire. In his lands ʿUbaydallāh implemented administrative changes and replaced previous officials with new ones. Among these was Sulaymān ibn Yazīd ibn al-Aṣam al-ʿĀmirī, an old, naïve, and weak-willed man, whose task was to control Armenia as ʿUbaydallāh's deputy.[27] Sulaymān left his initial mark on the contemporary coinage too. On silver coins struck in Armīniyah in AH 172 and 174 (AD 788–791) there is letter س engraved below the reverse area. It is notable that the same letter also appears on ʿUbaydallāh's *fulūs* that do not indicate their place and date of issue.[28]

24 Crone 1980: 169.
25 Bates 2012: 14.
26 Vardanyan 2012: 187a.
27 al-Yaʿqūbī 2002: 301; It is interesting that Armenian sources describe this person as a crucial man (Łewond 1982: 131).
28 Vardanyan 2012a.

k.   Unidentified official. Some rare *fulūs* of Bardaʿah dated AH 187 (AD 802/3)
bear the name of a certain Muḥammad inscribed above the central legends of
the reverse and another uncertain name split into two parts on the obverse.
Muḥammad could be identified theoretically with the contemporary
governor of Armīniyah and Arrān, Muḥammad ibn Yazīd. The name divided
between the upper and lower segments of the obverse apparently belong
to an official who was attached to either the provincial administration or a
mint established in Bardaʿah.

Some Remarks on the Administration in Shirwān and Daghastān

Bāb al-Abwāb (Darband)

As an extension to the history of Daghastān, it seems worthwhile to offer a short
discussion of a few copper coins minted at Bāb al-Abwāb in the early 'Abbāsid
period as well. Only six types of coins struck at al-Bāb in AH 153–155 (AD 770–
772), 158 (AD 774/5), 159 (AD 775/6) and 178 (AD 794/5) can be attested so far.
The coins dated AH 153, 154, and 158 name Bakkār and al-Ḥasan al-ʿUqaylī who
governed Armīniyah and Arrān in AH 152–153 (AD 769–770). Bakkār changed
the style of silver *dirhams* to include an inscription pointing out the princely status
of the future caliph al-Mahdī. His copper coins dated AH 153 (770) use the same
style. It is remarkable that copper coins struck in Arrān have the name of Bakkār
inscribed in the margins of the obverse, while it is in the upper segment of the
reverse on coins minted at al-Bāb.

Al-Ḥasan ibn Qaḥṭabah al-Ṭāʾī, who had already been assigned to Armīniyah
in the early 'Abbāsid period,[29] held his post again in AH 154–158 (AD 770–775),
until the Armenian nobility rebelled against the local Arab authorities and expelled
him from the country. It took a few years until 'Abbāsid control was restored
in Armenia.[30] As a result, no coins were minted in Armīniyah until AH 161
(AD 777/8), while the mint of Arrān produced no coins before AH 166 (AD 782/3).
This stagnation may have coincided with a period described by Armenian sources.
The historian Łewond recorded that there was a time when 'Abdallāh (here, the
caliph al-Manṣūr) closed the treasuries and increased the taxes. Only in the days of
Muḥammad al-Mahdī (AD 775–786) were new silver mines discovered in Armenia
and the mints reopened.[31] This was definitely the time when the population
enjoyed a reduction in taxes in the early 160s AH (late 770s AD). According to the
literary sources, al-Ḥasan resided in Bardaʿah, but managed to control his huge
territories with the help of his sons. Thus, he sent Muḥammad as his deputy to
rule over the Armenian territories stretching westwards from Akhlāṭ. His other

29 Vasmer 1931: 8.
30 al-Balādhurī 1966: 329.
31 Łewond 1982: 123.

son Ibrāhīm was entrusted with the Juzjān (Georgia) and Tiflīs, while Qaḥṭabah received Bāb al-Abwāb.[32] The literary evidence for Qaḥṭabah's assignment to Darband is confirmed by *fulūs* of al-Bāb dated AH 155 (AD 771/2).

The literary sources do not indicate who succeeded Qaḥṭabah ibn al-Ḥasan in his post. Yet, the copper coins minted at al-Bāb in AH 159 (AD 775/6) bear the name of Khālid ibn Yazīd, another representative of the Banū Sulaym. Disappointed by developments in his northern provinces, the new caliph al-Mahdī entrusted rule in the region to the Sulamid Yazīd ibn Usayd, who then held the position of governor for the third time. Undoubtedly, a return of Yazīd to power in AH 159 facilitated an appointment of his son Khālid to Daghastān. New coins could shed a light on the third period of Yazīd's rule, since we have no information on the administration of al-Bāb over the next two decades.

Our next numismatic evidence for the city derives from the *fulūs* of al-Bāb dated AH 178 (AD 794/5) with the name of a caliphal *mawlā* Yaḥyā. As a son of Saʿīd al-Ḥarashī, a renowned Umayyad military commander, Yaḥyā made a bright career at the court of Hārūn al-Rashīd. Yaḥyā was briefly put in charge of the northern provinces in reward for his military service, especially in the suppression of revolts by Abū Muslim and al-Sakīn ibn Mūsā in Baylaqān. He replaced Mūsā ibn ʿĪsā al-Hāshimī whose name appears on both Armīniyah *dirhams* of AH 178–179 (AD 794–796) and copper *fulūs* minted in Arrān in AH 178. Silver *dirhams* naming Yaḥyā minted in Armīniyah in AH 179 prove that the transition of power in the province took place during that year.[33] However, Hārūn al-Rashīd was soon disappointed with the local administration and dismissed all governors in Adharbayjān and Arrān. Anonymous *dirhams* struck in AH 180 and 181 (AD 796–798) support indirectly the evidence of the literary sources in this respect.[34] Some time passed before the caliph assigned Saʿīd ibn Salm al-Bāhilī, one of the former governors of al-Jazīrah, to Armīniyah and Arrān. He assumed control of al-Bāb and appointed his official Naṣr ibn ʿAnān over the city, thereby replacing another *nāʾib* named Najm ibn Hāshim.[35] Saʿīd ibn Salm ended the anonymous coinage produced in the province as a result of Hārūn al-Rashīd's previous administrative changes and initiated a coin emission in his own name.

32 al-Kūfī 1975: 255.
33 Vardanyan 2011: 45.
34 Vardanyan 2011: 47–48.
35 al-Kūfī 1975: 255–256.

Al-Yazīdyah

A rather extensive emission of anonymous copper coins dated AH 149–150 (AD 766–768) is known for a mint called al-Yazīdiyah in the 'Abbāsid period. The exact location of this site is unclear, but it is very likely that it was located close to Shamākhā. this city may have been named after al-Shamākh ibn Shujāʿ, a king of Shirwān whose reign coincided with the rule of the Arab governor Saʿīd ibn Salm al-Bāhilī in Armenia. The tenure of Saʿīd ibn Salm as governor was short, lasting only for the period of AD 798–799.[36]

Minorsky suggested that al-Yazīdiyah might correspond to Lashkar-gāh, which lay only one *farsakh* away from Shamākhā.[37] It is very likely that in AH 306 (AD 918/19) Shirwānshāh Mazyadid Abū Ṭāhir Yazīd ibn Muḥammad rebuilt al-Yazīdiyah and made it his capital.[38] This may offer indirect proof that al-Yazīdiyah and Shamākhā had been located at some distance from each other initially. However, after centuries of urban expansion the distance between the two settlements may have been reduced to the point that they merged with each other. Such a merging of settlements might explain why Yāqūt al-Ḥamawī, writing in the thirteenth century AD, considered al-Yazīdiyah to be another name for Shamākhā.[39]

Another question is why the settlement was called al-Yazīdiyah and who administered the city when the anonymous coins were struck. In the second century AH (AD 719–816), there were three officials named Yazīd who were appointed to the northern provinces as governors: Yazīd ibn Ḥātim al-Muhallabī, Yazīd ibn Mazyad al-Shaybānī, and Yazīd ibn Usayd al-Sulamī.

Yazīd ibn Ḥātim served as governor of Adharbayjān in the 750s AD and settled a large group of Yamānī Arabs throughout his province over the course of the decade. However, there is no literary evidence to indicate that his authority extended as far as Shirwān.

Another Yazīd, the son of Mazyad, was a powerful commander from the Shaybānid clan. He played an important role in the political life of the northern provinces in the period AH 170–183 (AD 786–800). However, he began his career only in the 780s AD and therefore could not have been involved in the foundation of a city that was already producing coins with the mint name al-Yazīdiyah in AD 766–768.

Finally, Yazīd ibn Usayd was put in charge of the northern provinces three times. Thanks to his military skills, the caliph al-Manṣūr entrusted Yazīd with the running of affairs with the neighboring Khazar Khaganate. This appointment coincided with Yazīd's second assignment to Armīniyah in c. AH 141–148

---

36 al-Balādhurī 1966: 329.
37 Ḥudūd al-ʿĀlam 1937: 404, n.2.
38 Minorsky 1958: 1058b.
39 Yāqūt V: 436.

(AD 758–766).[40] It was probably Yazīd al-Sulamī who ordered the foundation of a new settlement in the chain of fortifications against the Khazars and which received his name, al-Yazīdiyah. However, diplomatic failures with the Khazars, particularly Yazīd's unsuccessful marriage to a Khazar princess, resulted in the loss of his post. The anonymous copper coins minted at al-Yazīdiyah in AH 149–150 (AD 766–768) would fall into the transitional period between Yazīd's dismissal from the province and his replacement by Bakkār in AH 152 (AD 769/70). Such coins were probably struck by the local administration representing Yazīd ibn Usayd's faction in the province.

CATALOGUE

1. Armīniyah, No date (early 130s AH), Yazīd ibn Usayd.

Obverse: (sic!) وحد \ لا الله الا \ ا اله ا لا

Marginal inscription: بسم الله ضرب هذا الفلس بارمينية

Reverse: الله \ رسول \ محمد

Marginal inscription: مما امر به الامير يزيد بن اسيد الله نصره

Reference: Tübingen, inv. no. 91-16-9 = Ilisch coll. (2.40 g) = Vardanyan 2011: 232; Peus 408 (7–9 Nov. 2012), lot 1399 (2.65 g); *Foundation Coll.*, nos. 1674–1675 (2.66 g; 2.11 g) ascribed mistakenly to the mint of Arrān (ill.).

2. Armīniyah (?), AH 204, Aḥmad ibn Yaḥyā with al-Baʿyth and Jabbār (?).

Obverse: له شريك لا \ وحده الله \ الا اله لا. Below (?) جبار.

Annulet pattern: ○-○-○-○-○

Reverse: البعيث \ يحيى بن \ احمد الامير \ امر مما \ لله

Marginal inscription: بسم الله ضرب هذا الفلس بارمينية سنة اربع و مائتين

Reference: Lowick 386. Akopyan coll. (2.16 g) (ill.) = Vardanyan 2011: 233; Tübingen, inv. no. AL3C3 = Shamma 1998: 228, no. 20; Sahakyan coll. (2.50 g).

3. Arrān, AH 153, Bakkār.

Obverse: له شريك لا \ وحده الله \ الا اله لا

Marginal inscription: بسم الله ضرب هذا الفلس باران سنة ثلث و خمسين و مئة. In the top segment of the margin بكار.

Annulet pattern: ○○-○○-○○-○○

Reverse: المؤمنين امير بن \ محمد المهدي \ به امر مما

Marginal inscription: Qurʾān IX, 33.

Reference: Pakhomov 1959: 69; Lowick 369–371; Shamma 1998: 224, no. 2; Tübingen, inv. no. AL3B5 (2.92 g); Tiesenhausen 1873: 824; Nützel

---

40 Vasmer 1931: 9.

1898: 2075a; GIM (2.63 g; 2.74 g; 3.75 g); HMAz, inv. no. 9118 (2.60 g); SMG, inv. nos. 41, 42, 44, 135, 5418 (2.38 g; 1.49 g; 2.45 g; 1.86 g; 3.46 g); Musheghian 1962: 65, no. 26 and 110, no. 537; Hermitage, inv. nos. 41/123 (2.77 g) and 41/123a (2.81 g); ANS 1959.165.39, 1959.165.40 (2.72 g); *Jena* 1253 (2.52 g); Peus 408 (7–9 Nov. 2012), lot 1397 (2.27 g); Zeno, no. 64987 (23 mm) = Vardanyan 2011: 234 (ill.); Zeno, no. 73432 (2.61 g); Alexanyan coll. (2.20 g; 2.80 g); Akopyan coll (1.92 g; 1.70 g; 1.63 g; 2.21 g); *Foundation Coll.*, nos. 1671–1672 (1.91 g; 2.27 g).

4. Arrān, AH 177, Khālid ibn Yazīd.

Obverse: In double square: مما امر به \ الامير خلد \ بن يزيد. Above عز. Left الله. Below نصره. Right باران.

Reverse: محمد \ رسول \ الله. Above ☼. A crescent below.
Marginal inscription: بسم الله ضرب هذا الفلس سنة سبع و سبعين و مئة

Reference: Pakhomov 1963: 89; Lowick 375; Shamma 1998: 225, no. 8 and 228, no. 22? Lemberg coll. (2.72 g) (ill.); Nützel 1898: 2210; Hermitage, inv. no. 405c; HMAz, inv. no. 11535 (2.31 g); Tübingen, inv. no. 91-23-8 (1.98 g) and AL3C3 (1.98 g) = Vardanyan 2011: 235; *Jena* 1263 (2.60 g); Musheghian 1962: 69, no. 42 (1.92 g); Zeno, nos. 71903 (0.99 g), 82451 (2.33 g), 87379 (2.80 g); Akopyan coll. (2.35 g); Private coll. (2.29 g; 2.45 g; 2.64 g; 3.05 g); *Foundation Coll.*, no. 1673 (2.60 g).

5. Arrān, AH 178, Mūsā ibn 'Īsā.

Obverse: لا اله الا \ الله وحده \ لا شريك له
Marginal inscription: بسم الله ضرب هذا الفلس باران سنة ثمان و سبعين و مئة
Annulet pattern: o-o-o-o

Reverse: محمد \ رسول \ الله \ عدل
Marginal inscription: مما امر به الامير موسى بن عيسى اعز الله نصره

Reference: Lowick 376–378; Tübingen, inv. no. AL3B6 (2.72 g) (ill.) = Vardanyan 2011: 236; Bartholomaei 1862: 30, no. 11 = Tiesenhausen 1873: 1255 = Pakhomov 1963: 89 = Shamma 1998: 226, no. 9; Musheghian 1962: 70, no. 44 (2.60 g); Zeno, no. 68236 (2.12 g); Akopyan coll. (2.25 g); more specimens from Dvin excavations.

6. Arrān, AH 184, Aḥmad ibn Mazyad.

Obverse: لا اله الا \ الله وحده \ لا شريك له. A star below.
Annulet pattern: o-o-o-o-o

Reverse: احمد \ محمد \ رسول \ الله \ بن مزيد
Marginal inscription: بسم الله ضرب هذا الفلس باران سنة اربع و ثمنين و مئة

Reference: Pakhomov ---; Lowick 380; Alexanyan coll. (2.14 g).

7. Arrān, AH 184, Asad ibn Yazīd.

Obverse: بخ \ لا اله الا \ الله وحده \ لا شريك له. An ornament below. Decorated margin.
Annulet pattern: ○○-○○-○○-○○-○○

Reverse: اسد \ محمد \ رسول \ الله \ بن يزيد
Marginal inscription: بسم الله ضرب هذا الفلس باران سنة اربع و ثمنين و مئة

Reference: Pakhomov 1963: 95; Lowick 379; Shamma 1998: 226, nos. 11–13;
    HMA, inv. no. 17461 (2.00 g) (ill.); Bartholomaei 1861: 2; Tiesenhausen
    1873: 1370; Nützel 1898: 2203 (with wrong attribution); HMAz, inv.
    no. 9121 (3.10 g); RIC 364 (with wrong attribution) (3.20 g) = ANS
    1973.261.49; *Jena* 1264 (2.93 g) = Vardanyan 2011: 237; Zeno, no. 87378
    (3.00 g), 92442 (2.50 g); Akopyan coll. (2.43 g); Private coll. (2.23 g; 3.30 g;
    4.03 g).

8. Arrān, AH 185, Asad ibn Yazīd.

Obverse: لا اله الا \ الله وحده \ لا شريك له. An ornament below.

Reverse: اسد \ محمد \ رسول \ الله \ بن يزيد
Marginal inscription: بسم الله ضرب هذا الفلس باران سنة خمس و ثمنين و مئة

Reference: Pakhomov 1963: 96; Lowick 381 (with wrong attribution); Shamma
    1998: 227, nos. 14–15; Tübingen, inv. no. AL3C1 (3.78 g) (ill.) = Vardanyan
    2011: 238; Tiesenhausen 1873: 1390 (3 examples); HMAz, inv. no. 9121;
    SMG, inv. no. 5424 (3.71 g); Lemberg coll. (3.15 g); Alexanyan coll. (3.32
    g); Private coll. (2.41 g; 3.50 g; 4.44 g).

9. Arrān, AH 186, Muḥammad ibn Yazīd.

Obverse: In square: لا اله الا \ الله وحده \ لا شريك له. Above: مما امر به. Left: الامير محمد.
    Below: بن يزيد. Right: اعز الله نصره.
Marginal inscription: بسم الله ضرب هذا الفلس باران سنة سبع و تسعين و مئة

Reverse: In square: محمد \ رسول \ الله. Above بسم الله ضرب. From left هذا الفلس.
Below باران سنة ست From right و ثمنين و مئة.

Reference: Pakhomov 1963: 98; Lowick 382; Shamma 1998: 224–225, no. 3 (with
    wrong date) and 227, no. 16; Akopyan coll. (2.73 g) and (2.18 g) (ill.)
    = Vardanyan 2011: 239; Nützel 1898: 2171–2172; GIM (2.75 g); Zeno,
    nos. 68611 (2.67 g) and 87381 (4.00 g); Private coll. (2.92 g; 2.55 g).

10. Arrān, AH 193, al-ʿAbbās ibn Zufar.

Obverse: لا اله الا \ الله وحده \ لا شريك له \ عدل
Annulet pattern: ○-○-○-○-○

Reverse: العباس \ محمد \ رسول \ الله \ بن زفر

Marginal inscription: بسم الله ضرب هذا الفلس باران سنة ثلث و تسعين و مئة

Reference: Lowick 383; Shamma 1998: 227, no. 17; HMA, inv. no. 14682 (2.82 g)
(ill.) = Musheghian 1962: 74, no. 65; RIC 365 (2.89 g); Tübingen, inv. no.
AL3C2 (2.46 g).

11. Arrān, AH 193, al-'Abbās ibn Zufar with Muṭrif.

Obverse: لا اله الا \ الله وحده \ لا شريك له \ مطرف
Annulet pattern: o-o-o-o-o

Reverse: العباس \ محمد \ رسول \ الله \ بن زفر
Marginal inscription: بسم الله ضرب هذا الفلس باران سنة ثلث و تسعين و مئة

Reference: Pakhomov 1963: 107 (partially correct); Lowick 384; Shamma 1998:
225, nos. 4–5 (with wrong date) and no. 18 (with wrong attribution);
SICA 2: 1399 (2.95 g) (ill.) = Vardanyan 2011: 240; Zambaur 1904: 64
(with wrong attribution); HMAz, inv. no. 3047 (2.33 g); GIM (3.09 g);
Private coll. (2.33 g).

12. Arrān, AH 197, al-'Abbās ibn Zufar with Isḥāq ibn Sulaymān.

Obverse: لا اله الا \ الله وحده \ لا شريك له
Marginal inscription: بسم الله ضرب هذا الفلس باران سنة سبع و تسعين و مئة

Reverse: مما امر به الامير العباس بن زفر علا يدي اسحاق ابن سليمان
Marginal inscription: مما امر به الامير \ العباس بن زفر على \ يدي اسحاق ابن سليمان

Reference: Lowick 385?; *SICA* 2: 1400 (2.95 g) (ill.) = Vardanyan 2011: 241.

13. Madīnat Arrān, AH 214, Khālid ibn Yazīd with Ibrāhīm ibn 'Attāb.

Obverse: لا اله الا \ الله وحده \ لا شريك له
Annulet pattern: o-oo-o-oo-o-oo

Reverse: خلد بن يزيد \ محمد \ رسول \ الله \ برهيم بن عتاب
Marginal inscription: بسم الله ضرب هذا الفلس بمدينة اران سنة اربع عشرة و مائتين

Reference: HMA, inv. no. 17674/11 (3.25 g) (ill.); Akopyan coll. (1.30 g; 2.90 g).

14. Madīnat Arrān, AH 214, Khālid ibn Yazīd with Ibrāhīm ibn 'Attāb.

Obverse: لا. لا اله الا \ الله وحده \ لا شريك له. A flower below.
Annulet pattern: o-?

Reverse: خلد بن يزيد \ محمد \ رسول \ الله \ برهيم بن عتاب
Marginal inscription: بسم الله ضرب هذا الفلس بمدينة اران سنة اربع عشرة و مائتين

Reference: Pakhomov 1963: 124; Lowick 387; Shamma 1998: 228, no. 21; Zeno,
no. 11558 (ill.) = Akopyan coll. = Vardanyan 2011: 242; Barda'ah hoard
(1955) (1.51 g; 1.82 g; 2.29 g; 2.36 g).

15. al-Bāb, AH 153, Bakkār.

Obverse: لا اله الا \ الله وحده \ لا شريك له

Marginal inscription: بسم الله ضرب هذا الفلس بالباب سنة ثلث و خمسين و مئة

Annulet pattern: o-?

Reverse: بكار \ مما امر به \ المهدي محمد \ بن امير المؤمنين

Marginal inscription: Qur'ān IX, 33.

Reference: Lowick 388; Zeno, no. 75268 (1.70 g) (ill.); Pakhomov 1959: 70 (2.00 g);
     Tübingen, inv. no. 92-11-58 = Shamma 1998: 238, no. 1.

16. al-Bāb, AH 154, al-Ḥasan.

Obverse: لا اله الا \ الله وحده \ لا شريك له

Marginal inscription: بسم الله ضرب هذا الفلس بالباب سنة اربع و خمسين و مئة

Annulet pattern: o-o-o-o-o

Reverse: الحسن \ المهدي محمد \ بن امير المؤمنين \ مما امر به. Above a six-pointed star and
     three pellets from right.

Marginal inscription: Qur'ān IX, 33.

Reference: Pakhomov 1959: 71; Lowick 389; Tiesenhausen 1873: 839; *Foundation
     Coll.*, no. 1676 (2.10 g) (ill.).

17. al-Bāb, AH 155, Qaḥṭabah.

Obverse: In square of dots: لا اله الا \ الله وحده \ لا شريك له

Marginal inscription: بسم الله ضرب هذا الفلس بالباب سنة خمس و خمسين و مئة

Reverse: قحطبة \ المهدي محمد \ بن امير المؤمنين \ مما امر به. A six-pointed star above.

Marginal inscription: Qur'ān IX, 33.

Reference: Lowick 390; Sibilev coll. (2.22 g) = Vardanyan 2012: 234a; Tübingen,
     inv. no. AK3D5 = Shamma 1998: 238, no. 3 (with wrong mint reading);
     Zeno, no. 110530 (2.56 g) and 110531 (2.03 g); *Foundation Coll.*, no. 1677
     (4.14 g) (ill.).

18. al-Bāb, AH 158, al-Ḥasan.

Obverse: الحسن \ لا اله الا \ الله وحده \ لا شريك له.

Annulet pattern: - - with a star inside each circle.

Reverse: الله \ محمد \ رسول. An ornament below.

Marginal inscription: بسم الله ضرب هذا الفلس بالباب سنة ثمان و خمسين و مئة

Reference: Unknown provenance (ill.). Unpublished!

19. al-Bāb, AH 159, Khālid ibn Yazīd.

Obverse: لا اله الا \ الله \ وحده و لا شريك له. A star above and below.
Annulet pattern: ○-○-○-○

Reverse: محمد \ رسول \ الله. A star above it. A circle with pellet inside and pentagram
     beneath below.
Marginal inscription: بسم الله مما امر به خلد بن يزيد بالباب سنة تسع و خمسين و مئة

Reference: Pakhomov 1959: 73; Lowick 391; Rasmir (3.29 g) (ill.); BNF =
     Shamma 1998: 238, no. 4; HMAz, inv. nos. 1027 (2.83 g), 4270 (2.77 g);
     Private coll. (2.69 g; 2.28 g; 2.18 g); Excavations at Darband (2.13 g).

20. al-Bāb, AH 178, Yaḥyā.

Obverse: A tamgha in the centre? Around لا اله الا الله وحده لا شريك له.
Marginal inscription: بسم الله ضرب هذا الفلس بالباب سنة ثمان و سبعين و مئة

Reverse: محمد رسول \ الله صلى الله \ عليه و سلم
Marginal inscription: مما امر به يحيى مولا امير المؤمنين اعز الله نصره

Reference: Pakhomov 1963: 90; Lowick 392; Zeno, no. 99145 (3.18 g [ill.], 3.10 g;
     2.72 g); Tiesenhausen 1873: 1254 = Markov 1896: 28, no. 408; Nützel
     1898: 2177; HMAz, inv. no. 3049 (2.13 g); Hermitage, inv. no. 86/408
     (2.69 g); Private coll. (2.42 g).

21. Barda'ah, AH 142, Yazīd ibn Usayd.

Obverse: In square of dots: لا اله ا \ لا الله
Marginal inscription: بسم الله—مما امر به—يزيد بن—اسيد

Reverse: In square of dots: محمد \ رسول \ الله
Marginal inscription: ضرب—ببردعة سنة—اثنين و اربعين—و مئة

Reference: Akopyan coll. (1.11 g) (ill.) = Vardanyan 2011: 246.

22. Barda'ah, AH 142, Yazīd ibn Usayd.

Obverse: لا اله \ الا الله. Below •●•.
Marginal inscription: بسم الله مما امر به يزيد بن اسيد
Reverse: محمد \ رسول \ الله
Marginal inscription: ضرب ببردعة سنة اثنين و اربعين و مئة

Reference: Pakhomov 1959: 60–61; Lowick 393, 395; Shamma 1998: 229, no. 1;
     Foundation Coll., no. 1678 (2.62 g) (ill.); Zeno, no. 145147 (1.67 g).

23. Barda'ah, AH 142, Yazīd ibn Usayd.

Obverse: لا اله الا الله \ لا اله \ الله. Above ●. Below ●●●.
Marginal inscription: بسم الله مما امر به يزيد بن اسيد
Reverse: الله \ رسول \ محمد
Marginal inscription: ضرب ببردعة سنة اثنتين و اربعين و مائة

Reference: Pakhomov 1959: 60–61; Lowick 393–395; Shamma 1998: 229, no. 1,
   but without specifying the word hundred written as مائة. Musheghian
   1962: 138; HMAz, inv. no. 14169 (2.57 g); SMG, inv. no. 5394 (2.78 g);
   BNF; Tübingen, inv. no. 2004-2-2 (1.60 g) and AL4B5 (2.78 g); ANS
   1959.165.31 (1.60 g); MM AG 75 (4 Dec. 1989), lot 375 (2.06 g); Zeno,
   nos. 23438 (1.78 g), 47455 (2.30 g), and 86763 (1.75 g); Akopyan coll.
   (2.33 g) = Zeno, no. 95966 = Vardanyan 2011: 244 (ill.); Zeno, no. 124675
   (2.46 g); Private coll. (2.64; 3.19 g); *Foundation Coll.*, no. 1680 (2.21 g).

24. Barda'ah, AH 143, Yazīd ibn Usayd.

Obverse: لا اله الا الله \ لا اله. Below ●●●.
Marginal inscription: بسم الله مما امر به يزيد بن اسيد

Reverse: الله \ رسول \ محمد
Marginal inscription: ضرب ببردعة سنة ثلث و اربعين و مئة

Reference: Pakhomov 1959: 62; Lowick 396; HMA, inv. no. 6293 (2.48 g) and
   16268/12 (2.33 g) = Vardanyan 2011: 245 (ill.); Musheghian 1962: 64, no.
   23; Hermitage (2.48 g) and inv. no. 48/50 (3.07 g) = Shamma 1998: 229,
   no. 2; Akopyan coll. (2.76 g); Alexanyan coll. (2.08 g); *Foundation Coll.*,
   no. 1681 (2.10 g).

25. Barda'ah, AH 143, Yazīd ibn Usayd.

Obverse: لا اله الا الله \ لا اله. Below ●●●.
Marginal inscription: بسم الله مما امر به يزيد بن اسيد

Reverse: الله \ رسول \ محمد
Marginal inscription: ضرب الفلس ببردعة سنة ثلث و اربعين و مئة

Reference: Pakhomov ---; Lowick ---; Jafar coll. (2.33 g) (ill.). Unpublished!

26. Barda'ah, AH 158, al-Ḥasan.

Obverse: لا اله الا \ الله وحده لا \ شريك له \ الحسن.
Annulet pattern: ○ ● ○ ● ○ ● ○

Reverse: الله \ رسول \ محمد.
Annulet pattern: ○-○-○-○-○
Marginal inscription: بسم الله ضرب هذا الفلس ببردعة سنة ثمان و خمسين و مئة

Reference: Pakhomov 1959: 72; Lowick 397-398; Shamma 1998: 230, no. 5; HMA,
   inv. no. 14304 (3.76 g) (ill.); Tiesenhausen 1873: 850, 2766; Markov 1896:
   19, nos. 164–165; Nützel 1898: 2133; GIM (4.00 g); SMG, inv. nos. 114
   (3.77 g), 128 (4.37 g); *Jena* 1254 (3.75 g), 1255 (3.74 g) = Vardanyan 2011:
   247; Hermitage, inv. no. 71/164 (3.80 g), 72/165 (4.08 g); Tübingen; ANS
   1959.165.32; BNF; Morton & Eden 46 (11 Nov. 2010), lot 119 (3.72 g);
   Akopyan coll. (4.31 g); Alexanyan coll.; Private coll. (Yerevan) (4.50 g).

27. Bardaʿah, AH 159, Yazīd ibn Usayd.

Obverse: لا اله الا \ الله وحده لا \ شريك له. Below ☼.
Marginal inscription: مما امر به الامير يزيد بن اسيد اعز الله نصره

Reverse: محمد \ رسول \ الله. Below ☼.
Marginal inscription: بسم الله ضرب هذا الفلس ببردعة سنة تسع و خمسين و مئة

Reference: Pakhomov 1959: 73–74; Lowick 399–400; Shamma 1998: 230, no. 6;
   Jena 1256 (4.04 g) (ill.) and five more ex. 1257–1261 (3.63 g; 3.68 g; 3.94
   g; 3.03 g; 3.16 g); Tiesenausen 1873: 887, 1465; Lavoix 1887, 1557 (3.53
   g); Markov 1896: 20, nos. 169–170; Nützel 1898: 2134–2135; HMAz, inv.
   no. 14297 (3.92 g); GIM (4.15 g); Khar'kov, inv. no. 5926; Hermitage (4
   ex.); ANS 1959.165.33–35, 1991.3.350 (3.63 g); Tübingen, inv. no. 91-16-
   11 (3.73 g) = Vardanyan 2011: 248; Musheghian 1962: 67, no. 34; Spink
   22 (17 March 1987), no. 315 (4.14 g); Morton & Eden 37 (9 June 2009),
   lot 633; Lemberg coll. = Peus 408 (7–9 Nov. 2012), lot 1401 (3.69 g); Rare
   Coins 17 (19–21 Sept. 2013), lot 198 (3.99 g); Zeno, nos. 86796 (3.70 g),
   95967 (3.80 g) and 119564 (3.69 g); Ilisch coll.; Limbada coll.; Akopyan
   coll. (3.78 g); Alexanyan coll. (3.37 g); Rasmir (3.79 g); *Foundation Coll.*,
   nos. 1682–1683 (3.72 g; 3.99 g).

28. Bardaʿah, AH 163, Yazīd ibn Usayd.

Obverse: لا اله الا \ الله وحده \ لا شريك له
Marginal inscription: بسم الله ضرب هذا الفلس ببردعة سنة ثلث و ستين و مئة
Annulet pattern: o-o-o-o-o-?

Reverse: محمد \ رسول \ الله. Below a crescent.
Marginal inscription: مما امر به الامير يزيد بن اسيد اعز الله نصره

Reference: Pakhomov 1959: 76; Lowick 401; Shamma 1998: 230, no. 7; HMA, inv.
   no. 17596/37 (3.00 g) (ill.) = Musheghian 1962: 67, no. 35; Tiesenhausen
   1873: 726, 2769; Tübingen, inv. no. AL5C4 (3.14 g) (ill.) = Shamma 1998:
   234, no. 3 = Vardanyan 2011: 253; SMG, inv. no. 8549 (2.52 g); *Jena*
   1262 (2.53 g); ANS 1917.215.395 = RIC 367 (2.84 g); ANS 1959.165.41,
   1965.123.1; Tübingen, inv. no. 91-16-12 (2.67 g) = Vardanyan 2011: 249;
   Zeno, no. 95949 (2.80 g); Sahakyan coll. (2.40 g).

29. Barda'ah, AH 187, Muḥammad.

Obverse: لا شريك له \ وحده \ الله الا \ لا اله الا. Above and below unclear Arabic letters.
Annulet pattern: o-o-o-o-o-o-o

Reverse: عدل \ الله \ رسول \ محمد \ محمد
Marginal inscription: بسم الله ضرب هذا الفلس ببردعة سنة سبع و ثمنين و مئة

Reference: Tübingen, inv. no. AL4C1 (2.49 g) (ill.) = Shamma 1998: 231, no. 11 =
   Vardanyan 2011: 250.

30. Dabīl, AH 159, Yazīd ibn Usayd.

Obverse: لا شريك له \ وحده \ الله الا \ لا اله الا. Below ☼.
Marginal inscription: بسم الله ضرب هذا الفلس بدبيل سنة تسع و خمسين و مئة

Reverse: الله \ رسول \ محمد. A decorated crown (?) below.
Marginal inscription: مما امر به الامير يزيد بن اسيد اعز الله نصره
Annulet pattern: o-o-o-o-o-?

Reference: Lowick 406–407; Shamma 1998: 234, no. 2; Rare Coins 12 (13–14 Jan.
   2012), lot 191 (3.57 g) = *Foundation Coll.*, nos. 1684 (ill.), 1685–1686
   (3,88 g; 4.51); *SICA* 2: 1441 (4.43 g) = Vardanyan 2011: 252; Tiesenhausen
   1873: 837 (with wrong date), 1465 (with wrong attribution); Markov
   1896: 18, no. 132; Zambaur 1904: 48; Musheghian 1962: 66, no. 30;
   ANS 1917.100.3; Tübingen, inv. no. AL5C3 (3.96 g); *Jena* 1207 (3.35 g);
   Limbada coll.; Akopyan coll (3.60 g; 3.44 g; 2.76 g; 3.09 g; 2.70 g);
   Alexanyan coll. (3.98 g); Zeno, no. 68610 (3.53 g).

31. Dabīl, AH 182, Sa'īd with 'Abdallāh ibn Salm.

Obverse: لا شريك له \ وحده \ الله الا \ لا اله الا. Three points below.
Annulet pattern: o-o-o-o-o

Reverse: سعيد \ مما امر به \ الامير عبدالله \ بن سلم
Marginal inscription: محمد رسول الله ضرب هذا الفلس بدبيل سنة اثنين و ثمنين و مئة

Reference: Lowick 408; HMA, inv. no. 17816/1 (2.66 g) (ill.); Musheghian 1962:
   70, no. 45 (2.35 g).

32. Dabīl, AH 185, Asad ibn Yazīd with Mahdī.

Obverse: لا شريك له \ وحده \ الله الا \ لا اله الا. Three points below.
Annulet pattern: o-o-o-o-o

Reverse: لمى يدي \ مما امر به \ الامير اسد \ بن يزيد \ مهدي
Marginal inscription: بسم الله ضرب بدبيل سنة خمس و ثمنين و مئة

Reference: Lowick 409; Lemberg coll. (2.63 g) = Peus 408 (7.-9. Nov. 2012), lot
   1411 (ill.); Tiesenhausen 1873: 2549; Nützel 1898: 2204; HMA, inv.

no. 6370 = Musheghian 1962: 71, no. 46 (3.12 g); ANS 1972.100.3 = Vardanyan 2011: 254.

33. Dabīl, AH 187, Muḥammad ibn Yazīd.

Obverse: لا اله الا \ الله وحده \ لا شريك له. An ornament below.
Annulet pattern: o-oo?

Reverse: محمد بن \ محمد \ رسول \ الله \ يزيد
Marginal inscription: بسم الله ضرب هذا الفلس بدبيل سنة سبع و ثمنين و مئة

Reference: Tabataba'i 1373: 201 (2.40) (ill.) = Shamma 1998: 235, no. 5 = Vardanyan 2011: 255.

34. Dabīl, AH 187, Muḥammad ibn Yazīd with ʿAbbād.

Obverse: لا اله الا \ الله وحده \ لا شريك له. A crescent above and ☼ below.
Annulet pattern: o-o-o-o-o

Reverse: على يدى \ مما امر به \ الامير محمد \ بن يزيد \ عباد
Marginal inscription: بسم الله ضرب هذا الفلس بدبيل سنة سبع و ثمنين و مئة

Reference: Lowick 410; HMA, inv. no. 19357/3 (2.50 g) (ill.) = Vardanyan 2012: 255a; Musheghian 1962: 72, no. 52 (1.85 g); *Foundation Coll.*, no. 1687 (2.57 g).

35. Dabīl, AH 189, Khuzaymah ibn Khāzim with al-Qāsim.

Obverse: بخ \ لا اله الا \ الله وحده \ لا شريك له \ بخ
Annulet pattern: oo-oo-oo-oo-oo

Reverse: علا يدي \ مما امر به \ الامير خزيمة \ بن خازم \ القسم
Marginal inscription: بسم الله ضرب هذا الفلس بدبيل سنة تسع و ثمنين و مئة

Reference: Lowick 411–413; HMA, inv. no. 6321 (2.67) (ill.) = Vardanyan 2011: 257; Musheghian 1962: 72, no. 53 (2.93 g), 73, no. 54 (2.20 g) and 73, no. 57 (2.15 g); Alexanyan coll. (2.42 g; 2,24 g).

36. Dabīl, AH 189, Bishr ibn Khuzaymah with Hishām, a mule?

Obverse: لا اله الا \ الله وحده \ لا شريك له. An ornament below.
Annulet pattern: o-o-o-o-o

Reverse: على يدي مما امر به الامير بشر بن خزيمة هشام
Marginal inscription: بسم الله ضرب هذا الفلس بدبيل سنة تسع و ثمنين و مئة

Reference: Lowick 414–416; HMA, inv. no. 17600/33 (1.70 g) (ill.); Berlin, inv. no. 129/1903; Tübingen, inv. no. AN1A1 (2.67 g), 2004-2-6 (2.35 g) = Vardanyan 2011: 256; Musheghian 1962: 73, no. 58 (2.75 g); *Jena* 1213 (2.94 g); Zeno, no. 48014 (1.90 g); Sahakyan coll. (2.60 g); Akopyan coll. (2.35 g; 2.80 g; 2.78 g; 1.61 g).

37. Dabīl, AH 194, ʿAbdallāh ibn Muḥammad.

Obverse: لا اله الا \ الله \ وحده \ لا شريك له. Below an Arabic letter *mīm* or *fā*.
Annulet pattern: ○-○-○-○

Reverse: مما امر به \ الامير عبد الله \ بن محمد \ عدل. A sign above.
Marginal inscription: بسم الله ضرب هذا الفلس بدبيل سنة اربع و تسعين و مئة

Reference: Lowick 417; Reva coll. (1.84 g) (ill.); HMA, inv. no. 17563/12 (2.50 g) =
Vardanyan 2011: 251 (with wrong date) = Vardanyan 2012: 251;
Musheghian 1962: 75, no. 69 (2.30 g); Private coll.

38. al-Hārūniyah, AH 169, Khuzaymah ibn Khāzim in the name of the caliph
al-Hādī.

Obverse: لا اله الا \ الله \ وحده \ لا شريك له
Marginal inscription: بسم الله ضرب هذا الفلس بهارونية سنة تسع و ستين و مئة
Annulet pattern: - - - - .

Reverse: الخليفة \ محمد \ رسول \ الله \ الهادى
Marginal inscription: مما امر به الامير خزيمة بن خازم عز الله نصره

Reference: Bonner 1989: 5; Lowick 419; HMA, inv. no. 6314 (2.62 g) = Vardanyan
2011: 259; Bartholomaei 1861: 7, no. 1 = Bartholomaei 1862: 30, no. 10 =
Tiesenhausen 1873: 1093; ANS 1959.165.36–37; *Jena* 1234 (2.59 g), 1235
(2.53 g); Tübingen (2 ex.); Private coll. (3.00 g) (ill.).

39. al-Hārūniyah, No date (c. AH 170–171), Sharāḥīl in the name of Yazīd ibn
Mazyad.

Obverse: لا اله الا \ الله \ وحده \ لا شريك له
Marginal inscription: بسم الله ضرب هذا الفلس بالهارونية

Reverse: محمد \ رسول \ الله \ شراحيل
Marginal inscription: مما امر به الامير يزيد بن مزيد اعز الله نصره

Reference: Lowick 420; Gorny&Mosch 209 (17–19 Oct. 2012), lot 4751 (ill.); Ilisch
coll. (3.95 g) = Vardanyan 2011: 260; Arslan coll. (4.20 g).

40. al-Yazīdiyah, AH 149, anonymous.

Obverse: لا اله الا \ الله \ وحده \ لا شريك له. Above and below ☼.
Annulet pattern: ○-○-○-○-○

Reverse: محمد \ رسول \ الله. Above and below ☼.
Marginal inscription: بسم الله ضرب هذا الفلس باليزيدية سنة تسع و اربعين و مئة
Annulet pattern: ○-○-○-○-○

Reference: Pakhomov 1959: 65–66; Lowick 421; Sahakyan coll. (2.60 g) (ill.);
Markov 1896: 17, no. 104; GIM; SMG (2.73 g); ANS 1965.123.2;

Foundation Coll., no. 1669 (2.83 g); al-Saadi coll. (2.55 g); Private coll. (3.05 g); Zeno, no. 77221 (2.75 g).

41. al-Yazīdiyah, AH 150, anonymous.

Obverse: لا اله الا \ الله وحده لا \ شريك له. Above and below ☼.
Annulet pattern: o–o–o–o–o

Reverse: محمد \ رسول \ الله. Above and below ☼.
Marginal inscription: بسم الله ضرب هذا الفلس باليزيدية سنة خمسين و مئة
Annulet pattern: o–o–o–o–o

Reference: Pakhomov 1959: 66–67; Lowick 422; Shamma 1998: 239, no. 5; Zeno, no. 117048 (ill.); HMAz, inv. nos. 11534 (2.74 g), 11549 (2.80 g); GIM (3.04 g; 3.22 g); SMG, inv. nos. 5406 (2.73 g), 6220 (2.71 g); ANS 1917.216.219, 1940.125.3, 1965.159.123.2; BM, inv. no. 1973.4.22.1 (3.15 g); Hermitage, inv. no. 68/104 (3.06 g); Iraq Museum, inv. no. 19516; Lavoix 1887: 1641 (2.45 g); Siouffi 1891: 10; *SICA* 2: 1628 (2.94 g); Limbada coll.; Private coll. (2.73 g, 3.06 g, 3.02 g).

42. No mint name, AH 164, Yazīd ibn Usayd.

Obverse: لا اله الا \ الله وحده \ لا شريك له. A crescent above. Below a ring surrounded by dots.
Annulet pattern: o–o–o–o–o–o. Between the upper annulets: على يدي ....؟

Reverse: محمد \ رسول \ الله. Above and below ornaments.
Marginal inscription: مما امر به الامير يزيد بن اسيد اعز الله نصره سنة اربع و ستين و مئة
Annulet pattern: o–o–o–o–o

Reference: Paghava 2008 (ill.) and a few more specimens; Sahakyan coll. (1.30 g), (1.90 g) = Vardanyan 2011: 243 (with wrong attribution).

43. No mint name, AH 208, ʿĪsā al-Maʾmūnī and Muḥammad ibn Sālim.

Obverse: لا اله الا \ الله وحده \ لا شريك له \ ع. Above a six-pointed star.
Annulet pattern: - - - - -?

Reverse: محمد \ محمد \ رسول \ الله \ بن سالم
Marginal inscription: بسم الله مما امر به الامير عيسى المأموني سنة ثمان و مائتين
Annulet pattern: o–o–o–o–o–?

Reference: Pakhomov 1963: 117; Lowick 854; Akopyan coll. (3.65 g; 2.89 [ill.]) = Vardanyan 2011: 262; Bardaʿah hoard (1955) (3.37 g; 3.47 g; 3.95 g; 4.35 g; 4.48 g); Zeno, no. 74924 (2.70 g).

44. No mint name, AH 208, al-Ma'mūn.

Obverse: لا اله الا \ الله وحده \ لا شريك له \ ع. Above a six-pointed star.
Annulet pattern: o-o-o-o-o-o

Reverse: د or ك \ المأمون \ الله \ رسول \ محمد \ الخليفة
Marginal inscription: بسم الله ضرب هذا الفلس سنة ثمان و مائتين

Reference: HMA, inv. no. 17600/18 (2.80 g) (ill.); Sahakyan coll. (2.80 g); Alexanyan coll. (1.92 g; 3.40 g).

45. No mint name, No date, 'Ubaydallāh ibn amīr al-mu'minīn.

Obverse: لا اله الا \ الله وحده \ لا شريك له
Annulet pattern: o • o • o • o •.

Reverse: بخ \ محمد \ رسول \ الله \ س
Marginal inscription: مما امر به الامير عبيد الله بن امير المؤمنين

Reference: Ilisch coll. (2.77) (ill.) = Vardanyan 2011: 261; Tübingen, inv. no. 90-6-2 (2.53 g); Pakhomov 1963: 87 (2.41 g); Akopyan coll. (2.47 g).

CONCLUSION

One must admit that *dirhams* are of little help in reconstructing the structure of local administration, since minor officials were rarely mentioned on this imperial coinage. Furthermore, the frequent interruptions in mint operation that resulted in lacunas in the regional numismatic history makes our perception of local historical realities more complicated. For instance, silver *dirhams* cannot help much in clarifying the sequence of governors appointed to 'Abbāsid Armīniyah and Arrān from the early 770s AD to AD 783. Likewise, the lack of locally produced silver coinage in Arrān between AH 170 and 181 (AD 786–798) causes certain difficulties for understanding the structure of local provincial administration during the first decade of Hārūn al-Rashīd's caliphate. Thus the evidence of copper coins plays an extremely important role. The copper coinage is a significant historical source that allows us to enrich our current knowledge concerning provincial and municipal administration, local mint organization, etc.

The coins catalogued in this article confirm the evidence of both silver *dirhams* and available literary sources on the joint nature of the 'Abbāsid rule in the provinces bordering the Khazar state. As in the Umayyad period, the 'Abbāsid governor controlled the vast territories lying between the Alanian Gates in the North and the faraway provinces bordered by the Taurus Mountains in the South. This area included the provinces of Armīniyah, Arrān, Shirwān, and Daghastān, which together represented a single administrative unit. This organizational policy aimed to pool the frontier provinces in the face of a permanent Khazarian danger.

Within this northern administrative unit, Bāb al-Abwāb was a significant stronghold defending the northernmost frontier. Together with other fortresses and settlements built in the area, it represented part of much larger defensive system. Among these fortified settlements was al-Yazīdiyah, which was established by Yazīd ibn Usayd during his second period as governor of Armīniyah and Arrān in the 140s AH (760s AD).

The administrative system in the 'Abbāsid North, which had no longer included the province of al-Jazīrah and Mawṣil, repeated the main features of the system that had existed in the Umayyad period. The major governor of the entire province was from the 'Abbāsid family, normally, a caliphal heir. He used to stay in either the capital Dabīl, or Barda'ah, the second most important city of the region at that time,[41] but managed to control his lands through provincial governors (deputies) representing either the local tribal aristocracy or military elite. In turn, a large number of minor officials drawn from the indigenous Muslim and Christian populations helped the provincial governor to effectively manage finances, courts, palace, and a huge bureaucratic apparatus. Thus, some copper *fulūs* minted in Dabīl provide us with names of several officials mentioned without patronym and cited within the formulae على يدي. It is to suggest that they were attached to local administration and controlled Dvin on behalf of the provincial governor. These persons were responsible for tax collecting, *kharāj*, and military affairs.

It is worth noting that copper coin emissions with the mint name Armīniyah appear to have ceased at the beginning of 'Abbāsid rule in the region. Apart from a few early issues naming Yazīd ibn Usayd, dated in the early 130s AH (750s AD), and copying the style of Umayyad coppers, no other coins from this mint are known so far. Some crudely struck pieces citing Aḥmad ibn Yaḥyā and his officials dated AH 204 (AD 819/20) can be ascribed to the mint of Armīniyah only by conventions. It seems as if the mint located in Dabīl was responsible for producing copper coins in quantities that would fulfil the need for small coins in parts of inner Armenia. Likewise, along with a massive emission of Armīniyah *dirhams* produced at Dvin, only a few occasional types of *dirhams* inscribed with the mint name Dabīl are attested so far.

---

41 Kałankatvac'i 1969: 254.

References

Primary Sources

al-Balādhurī, Aḥmad ibn Jābir. 1966. *Kitāb futūḥ al-buldān*, translated by P. Hitti. Beirut: Khayats.

Ḥudūd al-ʿĀlam. 1982. *The Regions of the World. A Persian Geography 372 A.H.— 982 A.D.*, edited by V. Minorsky and C. Bosworth. London: E. J. W. Gibb Memorial, new series, vol. XI.

Kałankatvacʿi, Movses. 1969. *Patmutʾyun Ałuanicʾ ašxari*, translated by V. Arakelyan. Yerevan: Hayastan Publishing House.

al-Kindī, Muḥammad ibn Yūsuf. 1912. *Kitāb el-ʾumarāʾ (el-wulāh) wa kitāb el-quḍāh of el-Kindī*, edited by R. Guest. London: E. J. Brill & Luzac & Co.

al-Kūfī, Aḥmad ibn Aʿtham. 1975. *Kitāb al-futūḥ*, vol. VIII, edited by ʿAbd al-Wahḥāb al-Bukhārī. Haydarabad: Dāʾirat al-Maʿārif al-ʿUthmāniayh.

Łewond. 1982. *Patmutʾyun*, edited by A. Ter-Ghewondyan. Yerevan: Sovetakan Grogh Publishing House.

al-Yaʿqūbī, Aḥmad ibn Isḥāq. 2002. *Tārīkh al-Yaʿqūbī*, edited by Khalīl al-Manṣūr. Beirut: Dār al-Kutub al-ʿĀlamiyah.

Yāqūt ibn ʿAbdallāh al-Ḥamawī. 1977. *Kitāb muʿjam al-buldān*, vol. V. Beirut: Dār Ṣadr.

Numismatic and Historical Works

Bartholomaei de, J. 1861. "Seconde lettre de M. le Général J. de Bartholomaei a M. F. Soret, sur des monnaies koufiques inédites." *RNB* 5: 21–72.

Bartholomaei de, J. 1862. "Troisième lettre de M. le Général J. de Bartholomaei a M. F. Soret, sur des monnaies koufiques inédites." *RNB* 6: 23–102.

Bates, M. 1989. "The dirham mint of the northern provinces of the Umayyad caliphate." *Armenian Numismatic Journal* 15: 89–111.

———. 2011. "A second Muḥammadiyya, and the four mints of the Bājunays mine." *JONS* 209: 14–17.

Bonner, M. 1989. "The mint of Hārūnābād and al-Hārūniyah." *AJN* 1: 171–193.

Crone, P. 1980. *Slaves on Horses. The Evolution of the Islamic Polity*. Cambridge: Cambridge University Press.

Foundation Coll. = Darley-Doran, R. and E. 2015. *The Foundation Collection of the early copper coinage of the Muslim community*. London: Piers & Dominic.

Jena = Mayer, T. 2005. *Sylloge der Münzen des Kaukasus und Osteuropas, Orientalisches Münzkabinett Jena. Mit Beiträgen von Stefan Heidemann und Gert Rispling*. Wiesbaden: Harrassowitz Verlag.

Lavoix, H. 1887. *Catalogue des monnaies musulmanes de la Bibliothèque Nationale.* Tom I. *Khalifes Orientaux*. Paris: Arnaldo Forni Editore.

Lowick, N. 1996. *Early ʿAbbāsid coinage. A type corpus 132–218 H / AD 750–833*, edited by E. Savage. London: No publisher.

Markov, A. 1896. *Inventarniy katalog musul'manskikh monet imperatricheskago Ermitazha.* vols. 1-2. St. Petersburg: Tipografiya Gos. Ermitazha.

Minorsky, V. 1958. *A History of Sharvan and Darband in the 10th and 11th Centuries.* Cambridge: Cambridge University Press.

Musheghian, Kh. 1962. *Denezhnoe obraschenie Dvina po numizmaticheskim dannym.* Yerevan: Izdatel'stvo Akademii Nauk.

Nicol, D. N. 1979. *Early 'Abbāsid administration in the central and eastern provinces, 132-218 A.H./750-833 A.D.* PhD thesis, Ann Arbor, Michigan.

Nützel, H. 1898. *Katalog der orientalischen Münzen. Königliche Museen zu Berlin.* Bd. I. Berlin: W. Spemann.

Paghava, I. 2008. "The prolongation of Yazīd b. Usayd's reign in the north-west of the caliphate." *JONS* 198: 4–6.

Pakhomov, Ye. 1959. *Monety Azerbaidzhana.* vyp. I. Baku: Izdatel'stvo Akademii Nauk.

———. 1963. *Monety Azerbaidzhana.* vyp. II. Baku: Izdatel'stvo Akademii Nauk.

Qatar = Abū-l-Faraj Muḥammad al-'Ush. 1984. *Arabic Islamic coins preserved in the National Museum of Qatar.* Vol. I. Doha: Ministry of Science of Qatar.

RIC = Miles, G. 1950. *Rare Islamic coins.* New York: American Numismatic Society.

SICA 2 = Nicol, D. 2012. *Sylloge of Islamic coins in the Ashmolean,* vol. 2, *Early Post-Reform coinage.* Oxford: Ashmolean Museum.

Shamma, S. 1998. *A catalogue of 'Abbasid copper coins.* London: Al-Rafid.

Shams Eshragh, A. 2010. *Silver coinage of the caliphs.* London: Spink & Son Ltd.

Siouffi, N. 1891. *Catalogue de Monnaies Arabes et Supplément N1.* Mossoul: No Publisher.

Spellberg, D. 1988. "The Umayyad North: Numismatic evidence for frontier administration." *ANS MN* 33: 119–127.

Tabataba'i, S. T. 1373. *Sikkeha-ye Islāmiyye Īrān Tabrīz.* Tehran: Antashadat.

Ter-Ghewondyan, A. 1976. *The Arab emirates in Bagratid Armenia.* Lisbon: Livraria–Bertrand.

Tiesenhausen, V. 1873. *Monety vostochnago khalifata.* St. Petersburg: Tipografiya Imperatorskoy Akademii Nauk.

———. 1891. "Numizmaticheskie novinki." *Zapiski vostochnago otdeleniya rossiyskogo arkheologicheskogo obschestva* VI: 229–264.

Vardanyan, A. 2011. *Islamic coins struck in historic Armenia. Early 'Abbāsid period (142–277 AH / 759–891 AD).* Yerevan: Tigran Mets Publishing House.

———. 2012. "Some rare coins of the Armenian mints: Addendum to the *Islamic coins struck in historic Armenia,* vol. I." *JONS* 212: 10–16.

———. 2012a. "The accession of Hārūn ar-Rashīd to the throne and some aspects of 'Abbāsid administration in Armīniyah as reflected in sources," 24–29 September 2012, State Hermitage, St. Petersburg.

———. 2014. "Where was the mint of 'Armīniya' located? A case for provincial mint organization." *JONS* 221: 9–14.

Vasmer, R. 1931. *Chronologie der arabischen Staatshalter von Armenien unter den Abbasiden, von as-Saffach bis zur Krönung Aschots I., 750–887.* Wien: Mechitharisten–Buchdruckerei.

Zambaur von, E. 1904. "Contributions à la numismatique Orientale." *NZ* 36: 43–122.

Auction Catalogues, Collections and Other Resources

Gorny & Mosch Gießener Münzhandlung (München)

Münzen und Medaillen AG (Basel)

Morton & Eden Ltd. (London)

Dr. Busso Peus Nachfolger (Frankfurt a. M.)

Stephen Album Rare Coin Auction Catalogues (Santa Rosa)

Spink Coins of the Islamic World (Zürich)

ANS—The American Numismatic Society (New York)

ArmNS—Armenian Numismatic Society (Los Angeles)

Berlin—Staatliche Museen zu Berlin (Berlin)

BM—The British Museum (London)

BNF—Bibliothèque National de France (Paris)

GIM—Gosudarstvenniy Istoricheskiy Muzey (Moscow)

Hermitage—The collection of Islamic coins in the State Hermitage Museum (St. Petersburg)

HMA—History Museum of Armenia (Yerevan)

HMAz—History Museum of Azerbaidzhan (Baku)

Iraq Museum—The collection of Islamic coins in the National Museum of Iraq (Baghdad)

Khar'kov—Collection of Islamic coins in the Khar'kov University (Kharkov)

SMG—State Museum of Georgia (Tbilisi)

Tübingen—Forschungsstelle für Islamische Numismatik, Universität Tübingen

Rasmir—Rasmir online coin database (St. Petersburg)

Zeno—Zeno online coin database (Moscow)

Akopyan coll.—Alexander Akopyan collection (Moscow)

Alexanyan coll.—David Alexanyan collection (Moscow)

Arslan coll.—Ali Arslan collection (Amsterdam)

Christianian coll.—Jirair Christianian collection (USA)

Ilisch coll.—Lutz Ilisch deposits in the Tübingen University's collection (Tübingen)

Jafar coll.—Yahya Jafar collection (Dubai/London)

Lemberg coll.—Yevgen Lemberg collection (Odessa)

Limbada coll.—Mohammad Limbada collection (London)

Mosanef coll.—Farbod Mosanef collection (Tehran)

Reva coll.—Roman Reva collection (Novosibirsk)

Al-Saadi coll.—Fahad al-Saadi collection (Saudi Arabia)

Sahakyan coll.—Bagrat Sahakyan collection (Yerevan)

Sibilev coll.—Ruslan Sibilev collection (Bryansk)

AJN Second Series 28 (2016) pp. 231–257
© 2016 The American Numismatic Society

Ancient Roman Colonial Coins in Renaissance Europe

PLATES 51–60   DAMIANO ACCIARINO*

Thanks to the gradual advancements of antiquarian erudition that brought together different academic disciplines, scholars from all over Europe were able to comprehend the ancient Roman colony and the specific coin type associated with this institution. The study of the Roman colony was a cultural process that had a strong impact on sixteenth-century intellectual life leaving its mark on epistolary exchanges and influencing both numismatic scholarship and contemporary artworks. The Renaissance interest in Roman colonial coinage fully embraced the spirit of humanistic antiquarianism, showing how numismatists interacted with the multiform cultural experiences of the time.

INTRODUCTION

Ancient Roman colonial coins[1] emerged as one of the most interesting antiquarian topics debated by scholars during the Renaissance. The understanding of this numismatic type developed only after years of confrontation, meditation, and sedimentation of thought. It evolved from a complex cultural system and the conjunction of several different areas of study, which ultimately generated a chain of repercussions for sixteenth-century intellectual life.

* Ca' Foscari University, Venice, Italy (damiano.acciarino@unive.it).

1 During the Renaissance, ancient coins were classified according to their territory of origin and of circulation, which permitted sixteenth-century humanists to comprehend the

Initially, scholars only took up a renewed interest in the Roman colony as an institution, but, soon after, evidence was found that pointed to the existence of local public treasuries ordering specific monetary policies. This important discovery established a first connection with the numismatic findings circulating among collectors and scholars. But the real tie between colonial institutions and money gradually came about throughout the years, growing hand in hand with the advancements of antiquarian studies that opened new doors to the comprehension of ancient history. Thanks to this collaboration, a new awareness slowly developed over decades, and, within the extensive, confused, and incomplete numismatic corpora of the time a new numismatic type was identified: the colonial coin.

Many scholars from Italy, Spain, Germany, France, and the Netherlands contributed to the general cultural progress from which numismatics often benefited, influencing the advancement of the debate on colonial coinage, assembling multidisciplinary data and information and cross-referencing sources from various fields—i.e. archaeology, philology, history, geography, juridical studies, zoology, iconography, and mythology.

In this context that embraced more than one century, the theoretical formulation of antiquarian erudition emerged, placing empirical evidence at the center of research. The antiquarian method tried to associate every single statement to a corresponding source as a witness of time and real proof of past life. Its application was different for each humanist according to his personal vision; but, from this multiform picture, it is possible to grasp a common spirit of investigation, the sum of all experiences through which Renaissance culture as a whole flourished in sixteenth-century Europe.

THE FIRST STUDIES OF ROMAN COLONIES

The first Renaissance humanist to deal with Roman colonies was Flavio Biondo (1392–1464), whose *Roma Triumphans* reconstructed the administrative apparatus of ancient Rome.[2] Here, he dedicated a few pages to the *coloniae*, particularly to the *origo deducendarum coloniarum* and to the *colonorum praemia iugerum*, where general aspects tied to the structure and functioning of this institution were described.

Biondo indicated the strategic role of colonies in the foreign policy of Republican Rome, illustrating how colonies founded by Roman citizens acted as a defensive instrument (*contra suspicione periculi*) for the mother-city and, at the same time, served as an outpost for territorial expansion (*propugnacula*).[3]

function of their local economic and coinage policy and to identify new iconographic types representing the institutions themselves; see Caro 1957–1961: II 374, 109–111; see also Davis 2012. Today, colonial coins are known as provincial coins: see Woytek 2012: 329–330; Ripollès 2012: 362–366; *RPC* I: 14-17 and 36-37; Wallace-Hadrill 1986.

2 Other authors who have treated institutional antiquarianism without dealing with colonies include Pomponio Leto (1515) and Raffaele Maffei (1559).

3 Biondo 1503: III, 64–65

Biondo seized one of the most important points of the issue, i.e. the rite of allotting land: the ridge-and-furrow that the colonist was able to trace with two yoked oxen and a plow during the course of one day's work corresponded to the boundry of their landholding (*quantum unius diei labore duo boves arare*).[4]

This is the first time that oxen and plow are mentioned in relation to colonies, but only as a rural element. In the following decades, however, the pair "oxen-plow" will represent the crucial knot for the advancement of the entire colonial debate tied to urban founding.

In illustrating how laws (*iura*) and institutions (*instituta*) were set up, the humanist also identified the cultural interdependence between the mother-city and the colonies, which included the transmission of customs and traditions in order to recreate political and social entities in its image (*effigies populi Romani*). Biondo's scholarship influenced subsequent antiquarians who added new information to the topic.

The Neapolitan scholar Alessandro Alessandri (1461–1523), in his *Genialium dierum libri* (1522), tried to distinguish Roman institutions—mainly *colonia* and *municipia*—and identify the various types of colonies (*coloniarum genera*).[5]

The twelve *Commentarii reipublicae Romanae in exteris provinciis* (1551) by the Austrian humanist Wolfgang Laz (1514–1565), dedicated a few pages to the colonies in order to distinguish them from other urban structures of Roman society and to put some order to the differing terminology (*romanae, latinae, Augustales, veteranorum*) used by the ancient sources.[6]

The humanist who brought a substantial change to the debate on the nature of Roman colonies was Alessandro Sardi (1520–1588) from Ferrara. Thanks to his work, *De moribus et ritibus gentium libri III* (1557), Sardi became the first scholar to describe the ritual of Roman colonial foundation involving the demarcation of the sacred boundary (*pomerium*) by a priest plowing with a yoked ox and cow (*tauro dextra, vacca sinistra iunctis*).[7] Sardi's discussion of colonies blends and contaminates various unspecified sources traceable to Macrobius, Servius, Festus, and Varro.[8] It was Varro's *De lingua latina*, however, that played a key role in the development of Sardi's thought, because this was the only text that explicitly connected the foundation ritual to colonies. However, as in the case of his predecessors, Sardi was not yet able to discern the link between colonial rituals and numismatic iconography, even though his antiquarian interests went beyond

---

4 Biondo 1503: III, 64–65

5 Alessandri 1522: IV 10, 202.

6 Laz 1551: XII 2, 891.

7 It should be pointed out that the Latin words *bos* (ox) and *taurus* (bull) were used indiscriminately to indicate the male bovine in the ancient sources for colonial foundation. This ambivalence was received and continued by Renaissance scholars.

8 Sardi 1557: II [1], 75–76. Cf. Macrob. *Saturn.* V.19.13; Serv. ed. Estienne, 389; Thilo and Hagen 1961: V.755.3; Plut. *Vit. Rom.* 10–11; Fest. ed. Lindsay, 270–272; Forcellini 1858–1879: s.v. *Primigenius sulcus*; Varr. *LL*, V. 143-146.

the study of texts. In 1579 he published his *Liber de nummis* (1579), a booklet on the weights and names of ancient coins.[9]

The construction of a complex antiquarian system on colonial rituals—including the use of both archeological and literary evidence—soon after led to a new focus on coins and colonies.[10]

Colonies and Coins

During the second half of the sixteenth century, humanists started to analyze systematically the Roman state in relation to its laws. The first significant monographs written on Roman civilization in this period displayed a substantial growth and a new maturity in erudite scholarship. The work that marked a clear change was the *Reipublicae Romanae commentariorum libri* (1558) by Onofrio Panvinio (1529–1568), an antiquarian monk from Verona. An entire section, entitled *De iure coloniarum*, was dedicated to the juridical mechanisms of the colonies. Among the various aspects examined, a list of judiciary powers and roles were explicitly compared for the first time.[11] Panvinio established that the colonies were structured as city-states reflecting Roman institutions, customs, and judiciary system (*populi Romani imaginem referebant*). There were magistrates who looked after the safety and security of the city, the infrastructure and census, and the public treasury (*aerarij publici curam*). This last aspect represented a major innovation: the institutional layout of the colony included the administration of money. Panvinio did not offer evidence or explain how the treasury was organized, but by assigning this function to the colonial administration, he suggested that the colonies had their own identities and their own monetary systems. As a consequence, a link was made between Roman colonies and coins.

The studies of numismatists and ancient coin collectors, who identified different varieties of coin types and questioned their meaning, confirmed Panvinio's views. In his *Discorso sopra le medaglie degli antichi* (1558), Enea Vico (1523–1567), an engraver and numismatist from Parma, noticed the stylistic variety of coins ("tanta diversità di cogni nelle medaglie"), suggesting the activity of more than one authorized mint ("in più d'una zecca [...] si stampassero").[12] The use of *De asse et partibus eius* (1514) by the French scholar Guillaue Budé (1467–1540)[13] shows that Vico considered metrological aspects in his numismatic studies, allowing him to examine in detail and from a different perspective the iconographic aspects of coins.

9 Sardi 1579.

10 The general interest in colonies during the mid-sixteenth century can be also perceived through the epistulary exchange of the time. See Carbonell (1991: 158–161) and Sigonio (1732–1737: VI, 996–997).

11 Panvinio 1558: III, 683.

12 Vico 1558: 50.

13 Budé, *Ass.*, IV, 311.

Only through this crossing over of spheres was it possible to understand how ancient Roman coin production, metrology, and iconography were all part of a whole. Budé was the first to identify the factors that led to the comprehension of a specific colonial coinage policy, including the decentralization of mints that marked their own coins independently from the central authority. This insight may have generated in careful scholars, such as Vico, an awareness that coin minting (and therefore its iconography) was subject to geographical, cultural, and historical variables.

Geography and Numismatics

Between 1554 and 1560, ancient geographical texts were used extensively in the study of Roman colonies. The most important of these were the *Itinerarium Antonini*,[14] a register that mapped cities located near the Roman imperial road network, and the *Liber Coloniarum,* attributed to Frontinus, that described the subdivision of Italian territory under the Julio-Claudian emperors.[15] Both texts provided a rich source of data for ancient geographical locations and toponyms. The epistolary exchanges of the sixteenth century illustrate the wide interest of these two works.[16]

The Spanish humanist and Catholic bishop Antonio Agustín (1516–1586) used these texts to identify city names that could be connected to the various *elementa linguarum*[17] found on ancient coins (mostly naming places of origin or dedication) and thence decode the coin legends. It was a natural consequence that, among the toponyms present on the coins, the names of colonies were to be discovered. The observation of coins bearing names associated with the ancient geographical texts and linked to data on institutional mechanisms assisted in their identification and decodification.

In a letter to the Spanish scholar and historian Jéronimo Zurita (1512–1580) dated April 1557, Agustín specifically defined the colonial coin type and its iconography, starting from considerations and interpretations tied to the names of locations ("de medallas de las nombres de lugares").[18] Agustín's words are the

---

14 In the first half of the sixteenth century, the *Itinerarium* was printed in three editions. Achille Maffei delegated Gabriel Faerno to produce a new version of the precious manuscript in his possession, as mentioned by Pantagato in a letter to Onofrio Panvinio dated 21 May 1558 (see Soler i Nicolau 2000: 195–197).

15 There were two sixteenth-century editions of the *Liber Coloniarum*: a French one by Adrien Turnèbe (1554) and another anonymous Roman version (1560). See Front. *Col.*[1] and *Col.*[2].

16 See, for example, the letters of Antonio Agustín, Carlo Sigonio, and Vincenzio Borghini: Carbonell 1991: 115–121 and 175–181; Sigonio 1732–1737: VI, 1013; Carrara 2008: 367; Dati 1743: IV 4, 140 and 164.

17 This Latin expression indicating the coin legends is taken from an undated letter of Carl Lange to Fulvio Orsini. See Nolhac 1887: 438–440.

18 Carbonell 1991: 115–121.

first evidence that he recognized the existence of a specific colonial coin type ("en las mas de las Colonias"). He stated that the typical imagery of colonial coins involved a pair of oxen pulling a plow ("dos bueyes unzidos arando con el que lleva el aradro, cino sono toro y vaca"), representing the ritual tracing of the sacred boundary of a new city ("para denotar que eran Colonias, pues se guardava en su primera fundacion la orden que se tuvo en lo de Roma"), as reported by Varro ("come dize Varron"). Agustín anticipated the conclusions that other scholars, like Sigonio, reached later.

THE CIRCULATION OF A CONCEPT

After a long cultural process that lasted decades and reached maturity only at the end of the 1550s, the colonial coin type was also defined by Carlo Sigonio in his work *De antiquo iure Italiae*, printed in Venice in 1560. In this antiquarian juridical treatise he dedicated a large section to colonies (*de coloniis*).[19] He declared that the explicit symbols representing colonies were oxen/cows (*tauro et vacca iunctis urbi condendae locum circumarasse*), the plow (*aratro coloniae deductionem*), and military standards (*signis militaribus*) (Pl. 51, 1–3). To support his statement Sigonio employed numismatic evidence (*in nummis veteribus demonstrari*). It is unclear if this development evolved from exposure to the views of Agustín, or if they were reached in parallel and independently.[20]

The effects of this progress were soon to appear. During the same year, Enea Vico, in his *Ex libris XXIII commentariorum in vetera Imperatorum Romanorum numismata*, openly recalled what Sigonio had brought to light and considered this new perception from a purely numismatic viewpoint.[21] Vico, for his part, gave a central role to ancient coins, as they represented a "monument" (*monumentum*), witnessing concrete historical dynamics, in which the coin was the leading element.[22]

The method pursued by Vico in analyzing sources and his strong antiquarian interests, in this case, were most likely influenced by Sigonio's work. In fact, he declared that he used Sigonio as a model and Vico identified him as the author of the perspective that he adopted (*de quibus omnibus apud Sigonium*).[23]

---

19 Sigonio 1560: II 2, 63–64.

20 It would be interesting to explore the unpublished letters of Carlo Sigonio and Antonio Agustín from 1556 to 1557. In these letters there may be tangible evidence of this circulation of ideas. A certain cultural affinity may have derived from Sigonio's collaboration with Agustín on the Spanish edition of Festus, completed during those years. The synergy between the two scholars is well known. Sigonio and Agustín wrote to the same addressees and belonged to the same circle as they shared similar antiquarian interests. See the letter to Fulvio Orsini, dated 20 August 1573, included in ms. BAM G. 271 inf. ff. 34–35.

21 Vico 1560: 108–110.

22 Vico 1548: 1.–2.: Augustus, tav. 3–4; 3.: Tiberius, tav. 1.

23 Vico 1560: 111–112. Totally different was the experience of another epigone of Sigonio, Giovanni Andrea Gilio, in the appendix of his *Due dialogi* , entitled "Discorso sopra la Città,

A MISSED AWARENESS

In order to gain an overall picture of the entire colonial discussion and to understand the series of factors that contributed to the growth of the antiquarian perspective in Renaissance scholarship, it is useful to consider the works of other scholars who did not or could not take account of the advancements in understanding colonial coinage up to this point.

The *Commentariorum vetustorum numismatum specimen exile* (1558) by Wolfgang Laz described and explained a selection of coins belonging to the imperial collection in Vienna. In interpreting coins of Augustus depicting a single bull (Pl. 51, 4–5),[24] he referred to the sacrificial symbolism of the auspices, including those related to the founding of colonies,[25] but made no concrete connections between the numismatic evidence and ancient colonial institutions.[26] From this it emerges that the awareness of the foundation ritual was still not sufficient to understand the entire cultural mechanism behind the ritual itself because it was not contextualized in its original institutional framework. Likewise, without the support of a wide range of numismatic examples, it was impossible to reconstruct the iconographic type of an ancient institution.[27]

Different and significant is the case of Sebastiano Erizzo (1525–1585), a Venetian humanist and rival of Enea Vico in numismatic theories.[28] In his *Discorsi sopra le medaglie antiche* (1559), he identified the colonial coin type, but was unable to offer a detailed interpretation of it.[29] He gave the iconography only a general rural

---

l'Urbe, Colonia, Municipio etc." (Gilio 1564: 133–135). The *Colonia* section omitted all the numismatic references. This lack of information was brought to light by Carlo Sigonio himself, in a letter of September 1564 addressed to Onofrio Panvinio, in which he seemed willing to amend Gilio's errors in a specific publication (Sigonio 1732–1737: 1020).

24 The iconography of the single bull on colonial coins has a complex sedimentation that can be reconstructed through the Renaissance sources: Alessandri 1522: 218; Valeriano (1556: 27) considered the type of *BMC* 17, pl. XV, 9; Cartari (1556) applied Alessandri's observations to the iconographic field; Vico 1558: 44; and the late metrological treatise by the German scholar Matthäus Host written in 1580 (I. II. 1–2, 58; I. III. 32, 112; III. III. 1, 443–449); see also Ligorio (2010: 124) and the 1557 letter of Agustín published by Carbonell (1991: 116), where it is stated by both authors that the bull alone symbolized the Roman *municipium* in contrast with the colonial oxen. A different opinion was expressed years later by Agustín (1587: 250–257).

25 Laz 1558: 27.

26 For the *Auspitia coloniarum*, see Laz 1558: 27. The coin under discussion is *RIC* 167a, an issue of the Roman Imperial mint at Lugdunum and not a colonial coin.

27 Nevertheless Laz (1588: *praef.*), in composing his greatest numismatic work never published, claims to have studied the entire Palatine collection made up of thousands of specimens. In the introduction to this small treatise, he boasts that he studied a corpus of 700,000 ancient coins.

28 See Palumbo Fossati 1984 and Bodon 1997.

29 Erizzo 1559, 126–127; see also *BMC* 53.

meaning, affirming that the ox symbolized cultivation ("il bove [...] ci dichiara lo studio dell'arare").[30] Considering the methodological framework already provided by Agustín, Sigonio, and Vico, it could be said that Erizzo underestimated the question of interpretation. Nevertheless, he managed to decode the legend COL as an abbreviation of *colonia*, but was incapable of reconstructing an historical and cultural context.

A similar approach can be found in the *Hyeroglyphica* (1556) written by Giovanni Pierio Valeriano (1477–1558). This work represented the broadest ancient iconographic collection accessible to scholars and artists in the mid-sixteenth century. In his inventory, Valeriano included ancient coins with oxen and plow types (Pl. 51, 6–7).[31] He underlined the agricultural symbolism (*nimirum arationis partes procuratas, et rei frumentariae commoda*) noted by various scholars (*coniectores*), but never connected this to colonies or colonial institutions. This limitation reflects the vision of an entire antiquarian season.[32]

Two reverses (Pl. 51, 8–9) mentioned by Valeriano feature all the characteristics that were identified a few years later by those scholars that connected their sources to the function of ancient institutions.[33] He almost certainly had the literary sources available to reach the same conclusions that were reached by a later group of antiquarians. In describing the plow, Valeriano indicated the path toward a contextualized iconographic interpretation. He attributed to this instrument sacred allusions ascribed to rituals of power and religion, capturing a symbolic importance that was not only agricultural but also connected to rituals used to found (*in condendis*) as well as destroy (*delendisque*) cities.[34] This awareness of the function of the plow in founding might have permitted him to discover the missing link between the ongoing colonial discussion and the coins.

---

30 The tie between the plow and agriculture lies in the erudite studies of the sixteenth century. An ideal archetype of this interpretation can be identified in the *De rerum inventoribus* of Polidoro Virgili (1470–1555). See Virgili 1596: III 2.

31 Valeriano 1556: 26–27.

32 The passage appears to be the main source of the interpretation given by Sebastiano Erizzo on the same iconography: the meaningful link becomes clear especially in the lexical calque, "ci dichiara [...] i comodi dei frumenti"/ *et rei frumentariae commoda declarant*.

33 1: *.BMC* 209; 2.: Crawford 378–1c.

34 Valeriano 1556: 354. The interpretation of the plow as an instrument of foundation could be found in the section *Urbibus aratrum circumducere quid sit* of the *Antiquarum lectionum commentarii* of Ludovico Ricchieri (1469–1525) (Ricchieri 1517, XIV, 5) and in *De consulibus Romanorum* of Johann Speißmeister (1473–1529) (Speißmeister 1553: 128 a).

The Impact of Colonial Coins
in the Second Half of the Sixteenth Century

From the 1560s and with the advancements achieved by earlier antiquarian experience, Renaissance scholars openly considered colonial coins as an autonomous numismatic type, easily recognized and originating from defined cultural dynamics interdependent on the functioning of ancient institutions.[35] In these decades, throughout all of Europe, many numismatic works dedicated specific sections to colonial coinage.

The Flemish antiquarian Hubert Goltz (1526–1583) included colonial coins in several treatises, starting with his *C. Iulius Caesar siue Historiae imperatorum Caesarumque Romanorum ex antiquis numismatibus restitutae*, first issued in 1563 and then in 1571, and the *Fastos magistratuum et triumphorum Romanorum ab vrbe condita ad Augusti obitum ex antiquis tam numismatum quam marmorum monumentis restitutos*, published in 1566. Both works illustrated this coinage, but no clear definition was yet formulated. A detailed analysis of the type was carried out in Goltz's subsequent work, *Caesar Augustus siue Historiae imperatorum Caesarumque Romanorum ex antiquis numismatibus restitutae* (1574). Here the description and explanation of typical colonial iconography was explicated through many engravings (Pls. 51–52, 10–13).

Goltz's overview of colonies and coins continued in his subsequent work, *Historia urbium et populorum Graecae ex antiquis numismatibus restitutae* (1576), which included coins from Sicily and Magna Graecia. At the end of this treatise, he made a brief exposition on the function of ancient institutions in relation to the coin types. Under the influence of Sigonio, he repeated that the Roman colony was always founded with oxen and plow under a military banner (*deductis sub vexillo in agros Colonis aratro urbem et agrum tauro et vacca iunctis*). He further added the innovation that colonies were founded with the same rite both under the Roman Republic and the Empire. This assertion was based on his observation

35 Evidence of this phenomenon can be found in a letter of Antonio Agustín to Fulvio Orsini, dated 20 August 1573, to which a list of colonial coins with images and explanatory notes was attached (ms. BAM G. 271 inf. ff. 34–36). In 1567, Agustín described Goltz's numismatic work as a work for beginners in an epistolary exchange with Onofrio Panvinio (Andrés 1804: LIV, 378–379), but he changed his opinion of the Flemish scholar many times. For example, in Book 4 of *Diálogos de medallas* (1587), Agustín criticized him for having only an indirect knowledge of ancient sources and also for falsifying types in illustrations and explanations (Agustín 1587: 132. See also Stenhouse 2009: 49–51 and Napolitano 2012: 177–188). However, in Book 9 he states that the works of Goltz were a great example of antiquarian erudition, very well illustrated (Agustín 1587: 466). The first statement (Book 4) matches what was said in his 1573 letter to Orsini. Retrospectively, Agustín revised his opinion, perhaps even in relation to the development of Goltz's antiquarian studies that had to be recognized by the Spanish scholar. In the end, Antonio Agustín seems to have rehabilitated his colleague.

of the numismatic material (*in veterum numismatibus tam consularibus quam imperatorijs*).[36]

Goltz's work also brought developments in colonial nomenclature. In the *Thesaurus rei antiquariae huberrimus* (1579), he dedicated two entire sections to the naming of colonies in light of numismatic types and inscriptions. The first of these was entitled, *Coloniarum municipiorumque romanorum nomina et epitheta*[37] and the second, *Nomina propria eorum qui in magistratu aliquo fuerunt, quae in numismatibus romanorum et coloniarum spectantur et leguntur.*[38]

It is clear that by the end of the 1570s, Roman colonial coins had become easily recognizable and widely known among Renaissance scholars. In 1577, Fulvio Orsini (1529–1600), a famous scholar living in Rome in the service of Cardinal Alessandro Farnese, published his *Familiae Romanae quae reperiuntur in antiquis numismatibus*. In this antiquarian work that retraced the history of Roman families through coins,[39] he did not offer a special section on colonial coins. Orsini did, however, include three colonial pieces from his own collection and briefly discussed their iconography (Pls. 52–53, 14–16).[40]

In the *Discours sur les medalles* (1579), a treatise by the French humanist Antoine Le Pois (1525–1578), there is an entire section specifically dedicated to colonial coins.[41] The description of the iconography follows the usual pattern: a plow pulled by oxen ("d'une charruë trainee par deux bœufs") and driven by a priest ("au derrier desquels estoit le Sacerdote") who traces the furrow of the new city ("faisant la limitation de la place") under the supervision of the magistrates ("suyvant l'ordonnance des Duumvirs ou Triumvirs").

Le Pois refers to a colonial type of L. Munatius Plancus from Lyons (ancient Lugdunum) which has not yet surfaced in the numismatic corpus available today, but traces of it are found in Hubert Goltz's works (Pl. 54, 17).[42] He chose this colonial coin instead of others, perhaps because Le Pois had an interest in connecting a French city to an ancient Roman foundation. Similar expedients were later utilized in other antiquarian treatises in a more structured way.

---

36 Goltz 1576: 204.

37 Goltz 1579: Chapter 18.

38 Goltz 1579: Chapter 20.

39 Nolhac 1889: XIX, 28–29: (1571) and XX, 29–30 (1574).

40 Orsini 1577: 56. In a letter dated 20 August 1573, Antonio Agustín sent him a list of illustrations of the colonial coin type in Figure 11. The coins illustrated by Orsini may have been taken from this list.

41 Le Pois 1579: 18 v.

42 Le Pois (1579: 2–4) lists among his forerunners Andrea Fulvio, Enea Vico, Sebastiano Erizzo, Costanzo Landi, Jacopo Strada, Gabriel Symeoni, János Zsámboky, Hubert Goltz, Guillaume Du Choull, and Wolfgang Laz. The connection to Goltz (1566: 194) encourages us to suspect that the Lyons coin was one of the falsifications for which the Flemish scholar was famous.

In Adolph Occo's (1524–1606) catalogue, *Impp. Romanorum numismata* (1579), only one coin is mentioned as an example of the *coloniae deductae*.[43] Occo was an important German physician, numismatist, and antiquarian renowned throughout Europe for his trips to Italy and his contacts with scholars and prestigious collectors of antiquities.[44]

Due to the brevity of this work, explanations were reduced and no comparisons of sources and iconographic analyses were made. He just mentioned briefly the typical colonial elements (*Signum cohortis sive vexillum, aquila legionaria, aratrum, decempeda*). The coin described is noteworthy: it is openly indicated as a colonial founding coin but it does not depict the usual iconography of oxen; however, other symbols representing colonies (the banner, the plow, the *pertica*, the eagle) are depicted, perhaps directly inspired by the ones represented in Goltz's works (Pl. 54, 18).

Research concerning colonial coins continued, showing developments and reinterpretations of studies and sources already utilized. This was the case of the *Antiquitatum Romanarum libri* by the German scholar Johann Roszfeld (1550–1626), published for the first time in 1583 and subsequently expanded in 1613 by the Scottish scholar Thomas Dempster (1579–1625). In his *editio princeps*, Roszfeld broadly described the colonial type and reconnected it to the rite of foundation. He described the usual imagery of colonial coins (*vexillum, aquilam, aratrum decempedam, sive perticam agri mensoriam, tertius sacerdotem agentem iugum boum*) and named the works of Goltz as his main sources. He also mentioned those typical objects of colonial founding that Goltz and Occo depicted (Pl. 54, 19–20).[45]

Further details were included in the addenda to Dempster's edition. In contrast with Roszfeld, who mentioned only Goltz, the Scottish scholar looked further back to the work of Sigonio, declaring that it was necessary to offer a more extended description of the function of colonies (*descriptio videretur maximopere esse necessaria*), without which the numismatic aspects would have not been altogether clear.[46]

The *Libri delle Medaglie* by Pirro Ligorio

The *Libri delle Medaglie* of the Neapolitan scholar Pirro Ligorio (1514–1583), part of the 30-volume *Libri dell'Antichità* written between 1550 and 1583, encapsulate the history of colonial coinage during the Renaissance.[47] This numismatic treatise,

---

43 Occo 1579: 10

44 Carbonell: 451. It is very probable that Occo was directly in contact with Fulvio Orsini and that he came into contact with the numismatic collection of the Farnese and of Antonio Agustín. Missere Fontana (2009: 305) describes the work of Occo as the "greatest attempt to write a numismatic corpus that revives the sixteenth century."

45 Roszfeld 1583: 311–312.

46 Dempster 1613: 746 (X 22).

47 Ligorio 2010: Introduction. The *Libri delle Medaglie* remained unpublished, even

compared to other contemporary works, had the greatest number of colonial coin illustrations in terms of iconographic variety. Thus, it would be interesting to know what other contemporary numismatic works Ligorio might have had access to for enriching his knowledge and to what extent his acquaintance with contemporary antiquarians influenced the composition of his work.[48] The fact that the *Libri delle Medaglie* only circulated as a manuscript may have reduced its impact on the numismatic culture of the time. It nevertheless reflects the sedimentation of views developed over the course of a decade and, therefore, is deserving of great attention in the context of Renaissance scholarship.

His first description of colonial coins relates to the iconographic representation of the equipment involved in founding a colony. This is founded directly upon Sigonio's antiquarian scholarship and to Goltz's numismatic texts, in which these coin types are broadly represented (Pl. 54, 21).[49] This is followed by the description of coin series depicting yoked oxen during the foundation ritual. The coins were initially attributed to different colonies without explanation, but later Ligorio discussed the reverse side of the coins following the paradigm of his sources.[50]

Ligorio also used a new method to interpret the colonial coin: beyond the representation of the ox/cow, he proposed the reading of the acronym C·C·A on issues now known to have come from Caesaraugusta as a colonial inscription (*Colonia Cercanita Augusta*). He deduced that the first C stood for *colonia* on the basis of the colonial iconography and the legend naming the *duumviri* (Pl. 54, 22).

Other interesting contributions by Ligorio emerged when he identified additional types employed by colonies.[51] He interpreted, for example, a colonial coin minted by the city of Troas as honoring the Trojan origins of Rome (Pl. 54, 23). The legend COL permitted him first to identify the coin as a colonial issue since this was already recognized by Sebastiano Erizzo as the abbreviation for *colonia*. Ligorio then recognized the reverse type of the wolf and twins as a tribute to the birth of Rome and a celebration of the mythological origin of its people in Troy. The colony thus represented a concrete extension of Rome and the coin clearly presented the relationship between the founding city and colony.

though the manuscript was ready for printing from 1567, but there is evidence that the author was still working on it in 1581. This treatise on colonial coins never reached Rome; see Carbonell 1991: 560 (22 March 1567) and Wickersham Crawford 1913: 583 (12 October 1566); see also BAM G.: 271 inf. ff. 34–36: (20 August 1573).

48 Ligorio 2010: X–XI. In addition to his own collection (also sold to the Farnese family), he consulted the Estense collection in Ferrara and the texts of Enea Vico.

49 Ligorio 2010: 16

50 Ligorio 2010: 134.

51 Ligorio 2010: 227 and 435.

Two other colonial medallions of Troas connected to Rome's Trojan origins show on the reverse side a hexastyle temple (Pl. 55, 24) and an eagle with an ox between its claws. These coins were struck under Marcus Aurelius and Commodus in the second century AD, but before Ligorio, no Renaissance scholar had connected their types to colonies.[52] He furthermore distinguished the hexastyle temple as a specifically colonial element but did not offer evidence to support this view. One may hypothesize that it had to do with those temples that were built in the first circle of the city where sacrifices took place.[53]

The most curious of his colonial examples is represented in a drawing of a coin that is not documented in modern catalogues (Pl. 55, 25). It depicts a female figure riding a bull—a design found on the provincial coinage of Amphipolis in Thrace and representing the local goddess Artemis Tauropolos or Artemis Tauridea (Pl. 55, 26). Perhaps Ligorio came across an example of the Amphipolis series when preparing the drawing.[54] If the Greek legends of the coin were worn, this might have encouraged him to invent a colonial legend (COL·IVL·CORINTHVS) based on the use of the bull/ox as the central iconographic element.[55]

COLONIAL COINS IN FLORENCE:
VINCENZIO BORGHINI AND GIORGIO VASARI

The Florentine scholar Vincenzio Borghini (1515–1580) explored the matter of colonies in the first book of his *Discorsi sopra l'origine di Firenze*, published posthumously in 1584. In order to gain a greater understanding of the origins of Florence, and more precisely of its foundation as a Roman colony, Borghini opened a long discussion in which he carefully explained the political mechanisms behind the colonial institution. This was divided into three parts (4. De' Municipi, e Colonie Romane; 5. Delle Colonie Latine; 6. Delle Colonie Militari) and, for size and completeness, it is the richest treatise on colonies written in the sixteenth century.[56]

The second volume of the *Discorsi sopra l'origine di Firenze* (1585) included a section dedicated to the coinage of Florence ("Della moneta fiorentina") that also dealt with colonial coins. Within this extensive section, Borghini considered monetary organization a central issue, without which important turning points in the history of Florence could not be understood. He questioned the economic function that may have been connected to the colonial institution and addressed one of the original problems concerning colonial coins: whether or not they were tied to the treasury of the colony, which would imply an autonomous monetary policy. Borghini left the question unanswered, even though he considered that the

---

52 Ligorio 2010: 435.
53 Plut. *Vit. Rom.* 10–11.
54 *RPC* I, 1635 (Amphipolis).
55 This was a frequent practice even among the most rigorous antiquarians. See below.
56 Borghini 1584: 367–455.

coins could have been an effective colonial currency with a general circulation ("che potevano servire per ispendere").[57]

Borghini also mentioned a colonial coin apparently minted for the foundation of Florence with the legend COL. FLOR,[58] reinforcing the identification of the city as an original Roman colony. Borghini had not actually seen this coin ("io non ne ho vedute"), but he learned of its existence from his friend Panvinio whom he considered a reliable source ("per l'autorità dell'uomo si debbe credere"). The information was obtained through an epistolary exchange between the two humanists about twenty years before the publication of the *Discorsi*. Today it is possible to read only Borghini's reply of 18 February 1566, in which he requested further information about the coin and noted that it depicted the image of Hercules, a supposed ancient symbol of the city ("il sigillo pubblico della città è Ercole").[59]

The question of authenticity opened a debate between Florence and Rome in which other scholars participated. Borghini probably consulted his erudite friends for additional evidence to support Panvinio's report and to reinforce its credibility. A letter of Fulvio Orsini to the great Florentine philologist Piero Vettori (1489–1585), dated 27 July 1574, expressed skepticism regarding the coin.[60] Orsini further declared in the letter that no such Florentine colonial coin existed ("né credo si trovi tal moneta") and impugned Panvinio's reliability ("soleva ben spesso dire delle bugie").[61]

57 Borghini 1585: 151–152.

58 Borghini 1585: 151–152.

59 Dati 1745: 66–68.

60 Nolhac 1889: XX, 29–30. It was no coincidence that Vettori, among all the scholar friends of Borghini, asked Orsini for an explanation of this coin. Along with his other antiquarian and numismatic interests, Vettori dealt with colonial coinage in his *Variae Lectiones* (XXXV, 23) on Greek cities. The coins discussed are *SNG ANS* 1366 (Veleia) and *SNG Cop.* 729 (Massalia). He explained the colonial origin of these two Greek cities, which both produced coins depicting a lion (*In argenteo nummo Veliensium imago leonis impressa est* [...] *In aversa itidem parte nummorum, quos cudebant Massilienses, leonem sculptum vidi*). He then discussed the literary sources treating the foundation of these Greek colonies. In recognizing analogous iconographic elements and connecting them with the colonial origin of the two cities found in the literary sources (*Velienses et Massilienses e Phocide oriundi erant*), Vettori concluded that similar types corresponded to a similar institutions (*Tuebantur igitur illi patrium institutum, ut mos erat omnium coloniarum*). This methodology was derived from the study of Roman colonial coins, which employed iconography related to specific rituals and institutions generally attributed to the mother-city. For Vettori's methodology see Drusi 2012: 15–38.

61 It can be said that the fame and authority of Panvinio were differently regarded: Ottavio Pantagato's epistolary complains of Panvinio's sloppiness (Soler i Nicolau 2000) while Fulvio Orsini, writing to Antonio Agustín on 12 October 1566, derogatorily refers to Panvinio as a "carrot planter" (Wickersham Crawford 1913: 583–584).

Although Borghini was not able to confirm the existence of the Florentine colonial coin, it is conceivable that a coin of Caesarea Maritima as a Roman colony under the emperor Hadrian (AD 117–113) could have been mistaken by Renaissance scholars as Florentine issues (Pl. 55, 27).[62] The legend refers to the city as COL·FL·AVG (*Colonia Flavia Augusta*), but it is easy to see how a worn specimen could have led to the misreading of the inscription as COL FLO (*Colonia Florentia*). The presence of Hadrian's image could have increased the confusion, because he was portrayed wearing a beard and a laurel wreath to express his identity as a philosopher emperor. These same iconographic features were also commonly associated with images of Hercules. The oxen and plow reverse added the final piece to make the coin perfectly compatible with Borghini's antiquarian needs.

A prototype of a colonial coin with similar characteristics (Pl. 55, 28) can be found in a drawing in another book by Borghini, stored at the Biblioteca Medicea Laurenziana in Florence (ms. Antinori 143).[63] This work included a wide range of colonial specimens, many with faithful illustrations, all drawn by Borghini himself.[64] Thus he may have had reason to put faith in the information given to him by Panvinio, in consideration of his personal experience.

Borghini's meditations became useful in a controversy with Girolamo Mei (1519–1594), a Florentine scholar living in Rome, that took place during the years 1566 and 1567. Mei disputed Borghini's idea that Florence had a Roman colonial origin.[65] In the end Borghini prevailed in the debate despite his mistaken colonial coin.

The whole issue of the founding of Florence probably grew out of the studies for the iconographic program devised by Giorgio Vasari (1511–1574) to decorate the vault of the Palazzo Vecchio in 1563–1565. In both Vasari's preparatory cardboard sketch and in the painting (Pls. 55, 29–30 and 59, 45),[66] the figurative repertoire adopted (oxen with plow that trace the furrow delimiting the *pomerium*) is inextricably connected to the research on colonies. The years in which the debate on colonies reached a turning point (1557–1560) represent a cultural *terminus post quem*, in which the role of numismatic studies emerged as an essential source.

62 The types are as Sofaer, pl. 24, 26; Kadman (Caesarea) 27; Rosenberger 24.

63 See Scorza 1987; Belloni and Drusi 2002.

64 BMLF, ms. Antonori 143, c. 22 r. I am grateful to Rik Scorza for providing the image.

65 On this matter, Eliana Carrara has written extensively already (Carrara 2008: 317–380). However, the foundation of Florence as a Roman colony was established by Onofrio Panvinio in his *Commentariorum reipublicae romanae libri* (1558) on the authority of Frontinus. This was called into question by Girolamo Mei in the dispute with Borghini: Carrara 2008: 358–396; Panvinio 1558: II, 741.

66 The preparatory cardboard draft can be found at the Harvard Art Museum, placement n. 1932.157 B. I am grateful to Isabella Donadio for providing the image.

Vasari himself talked about this iconography in a letter to Cosimo I de'
Medici dated 3 March 1563,[67] and in his later treatise, *Ragionamento*, published
posthumously in 1588, in which he explained the meaning of his work to Duke
Francesco I, son of Cosimo.[68] In both texts, Vasari used the same terminology that
derived from the colonial coinage debate (*segnio—insegna—primo cerchio*). What
emerges is that the painted imagery was the product of a cultural sedimentation
of the colonial discussion that intersected different disciplines and became an
expression of the "rebirth of antiquity" in modern times.

COLONIAL COINS IN THE *DIÁLOGOS DE MEDALLAS* OF ANTONIO AGUSTÍN AND ITS REPERCUSSIONS

As a last step to reconstruct all facets of the colonial coinage discussion, the
Diálogos de medallas of Antonio Agustín must be considered. Published for the
first time in Spain in 1587 after 30 years of numismatic studies,[69] it is perhaps the
most important and detailed work on the subject written in the sixteenth century.[70]

Colonial coins were specifically treated in Book 6, starting with the
interpretation of a piece thought to be from the African city Leptis Magna, but
which is actually an issue of the Iberian city of Lepida-Celsa (Pl. 57, 31). The
Spanish humanist entered in the heart of the debate on this coin type, touching on
both iconographic aspects and those tied to institutional mechanisms.[71]

This coin was recognized as colonial, first through the obverse legend
COL·VIC·IVL·LEP· ("que quieren dezir Colonia Victrix Iulia Leptis") and then
through its design representing a man driving two oxen with a plow ("dos bueyes
y un hombre detras"). From the legend, Agustín was able to resolve the acronym
C·V·I. as an abbreviation of COL·VIC·IVL, just as Ligorio did with C·C·A.

He also tried to interpret the bovine iconography,[72] demonstrating great
originality: for example, when he specified the bovine gender during the
colonial founding ritual ("en la medalla el uno ha de ser buey y el otro vaca"),
he enriched this notion with details, which were based on neither sources nor
archeological evidence. He claimed that the shape of the horns of the ox/cow was
linked to gender: inward for the female and outward for the male ("Los de la vaca
son como los cuernos de la luna, […] los de toros y bueyes salen ma a fuera").[73]

---

67 Frey 1934: I, 722–731. The images are described synthetically: it is possible to find a
polysemic connotation in the word *segnio* that can refer either to the banner (*vexillum*) or to
the boundary (*terminus*), as witnessed also by the *Vocabolario degli Accademici della Crusca*
(1612) and serving as a reliable parameter for the literary use of this word *VAC* 1612, 781.
    68 Vasari 1588: 172–173.
    69 Carbonell 1991: passim.
    70 See Stenhouse 2009: 49–66.
    71 Agustín 1587, 226.
    72 Agustín 1587: 226.
    73 Agustín 1587: 273.

The zoological distinction of ox from cow through horn shape may have derived from the antiquarian culture of the period but also from new scientific publications issued throughout the sixteenth century. On the one hand, Agustín could have been inspired by the Latin grammarian Festus. In his *De verborum significatione,* which Agustín edited himself in 1559, Festus reported that bovines had horns that extend in different directions (*Et patuli boves, quorum cornua in diversum supra † modum patent*).[74] On the other hand, Renaissance zoological treatises also classified bovine gender according to horn shape. Many examples can be adduced, but the most relevant are the *De differentiis animalium* (1551) of the English scholar Edward Wotton (1492–1555), where the question of classification is discussed in detail, and the four-volume *Historia animalium* (1551) written by the Swiss humanist Conrad Gesner (1516–1565). Both works treated the shape of the horns as a trait related to gender,[75] but they do not fully agree with Agustín.

Gesner's treatise is notable for its many illustrations. Curiously enough, in the pictures of the ox and cow (Pl. 57, 32–33), the horns could fit the description given in Agustín's *Diálogos*:[76] the horns of the male curve outward while those of the female curve slightly inward. However, there is no proof that Agustín's statement was derived from this illustration, even though it seems to be the only iconographic model to support his view.

There are no signs of this particular iconography in the numismatic treatises of the time, not even in the *Diálogos,* since the illustrations end at Book 4. However, in the translation made by Dionigi Ottaviano Sada in 1592, this detail of horn shape was faithfully included in the drawing of a coin of Caesaraugusta following the description in the text, even though it is not present on the original coin (Pl. 58, 34–35).[77]

In two other translations of the same work—an anonymous Italian version dated 1592[78] and a Latin one by Agustín's secretary, Andreas Schott (1552–1629), dated 1617—this treatment of the horns was not carried through in the accompanying drawings. The illustrations in Agustín's original work were placed at the end of every section, while those of all three translations were created *ex novo*.[79] In the anonymous Italian and Schott's Latin versions, the illustrations were placed at the beginning or at the end of the treatises, and the relation between image and description was not immediately clear. On the contrary, the images in Sada's translation followed one by one the corresponding text descriptions for ease of reference. Probably, the omission of the iconographic detail of the horns in the

---

74 Fest. (ed. Agustín), 383.

75 Wotton 1551: 72–73; Gesner 1551: 27 and 104.

76 Gesner 1551: 24–25.

77 Agustín 1592a: 208; *RPC* I, 305.

78 The translator is thought to be thought to have been Alfonse Chacon. Missere Fontana 2009: 61–72.

79 Missere Fontana 2009: 61–72.

other two editions was due to the disposition of the images in the text: when it was necessary to create a link between word and image, the collaboration between translator and illustrator was better controlled, as emerges from Plate 57, 36–38.[80]

Not all colonial coins with oxen and plow illustrated in the Italian translation of Sada distinguished two different horn types, reinforcing the hypothesis that the iconography of this work was extremely faithful to Agustín's description in the text, and the adoption of different horns for the colonial coins was not a free choice of the illustrator but the consequence of a specific textual situation (Pls. 58–59, 39–42).[81]

This treatment of horns deriving from the study of colonial coins evolved into a tradition of its own in contemporary figurative art, as indicated by the frescos of the Founding of Rome cycle at Palazzo Magnani in Bologna painted by the Carracci brothers from ca. 1589 to 1592 (Pl. 60, 46). In the scene with the motto *In urbe robur et labor*, where Romulus uses the plow to trace the furrow delimiting the *pomerium*,[82] the two oxen are depicted with two different types of horns— one with an inward-curving shape in the foreground, representing the female, the other in the background with an outward-curving shape, representing the male (Pl. 59, 43). The archetype could have been taken directly from the Spanish *Diálogos* of 1587. However, considering the low circulation of this work (only 60 copies were published in Tarragona),[83] it is possible that the fresco found its model in Sada's version, where the differences in the bovine gender are also indicated by horn shape.

One must also consider that the coins used as examples for this Italian edition belonged to the collection of the Bolognese antiquarian Lelio Pasqualini (1549– 1606), who moved to Rome as canon of Santa Maria Maggiore. He retained close relations with his city of origin and with its artistic environment, including the Carracci brothers, whom he included among his closest friends.[84] Notes in the manuscript of the Vatican Library Barb. Lat. 2113 prove that Pasqualini knew very well the original work of Agustín, as he was also author of the appendix of Sada's translation.[85] In light of this, he may have contributed to the Carracci brothers' conceptions of the iconographic program of the Palazzo Magnani, where the influence of a numismatist appears almost certain to justify the imagery.[86]

---

80 Agustín 1592b: Tables 69–70; Agustín 1617: Table 16.

81 Agustín 1592a: 215 and 238.

82 On the fresco in general see Vitali 2011; Bettin 2009; Emiliani 2000; Stanzani 2000; Rubinstein 1979.

83 Missere Fontana 2009, 61; see also Stenhouse 2009, 50–51.

84 Missere Fontana 2009, 72.

85 Missere Fontana 2009, 72.

86 However, Giovanni Pietro Bellori and Carlo Cesare Malvasia, two art historians of the seventeenth century originating from the area of Bologna, do not mention a possible relation between Pasqualini and the Carracci brothers. Even the most recent studies do not mention consultants called to contribute ideas for the decorations, following the order of

It was confirmed that the main source for the Carracci brothers was the Italian version of the *Vitae Parallelae* of Plutarch translated by Battista Alessandro Jaconello in 1492,[87] in which Romulus traced the furrow of the city of Rome with a plow pulled by two oxen whose horn shapes are not specified.[88] The classical source does not fully explain the imagery, which, at this point, could have derived from the development of the debate between institutions and numismatics, in particular colonial studies.

As already seen in the case of Florence, the theme of this fresco could also find an ideal correspondence in the *Historia Bononiensis*[89] of Sigonio, published for the first time between 1571 and 1574, in which it was stated that Bologna was a Roman colony (*eodemque tempore Bononiam colonia deducta*).[90] Thus the depiction of the founding rite of Rome becomes a concrete reference to the shared identity of colony and mother-city. The fact that Bologna had Roman origins also justified the use of this iconographic theme that, echoing Biondo, made the colony in the image and a likeness of Rome.[91]

The detail regarding the shape of the horns took on a life of its own in a fresco depicting an episode of the *Storia di Coriolano* (sixteenth–seventeenth century) painted by an apprentice of the Carracci brothers, Lucio Massari (1569–1633), in the Palazzo Bonfiglioli Rossi in Bologna. In the scene with the motto *Vincuntur praelio Volsci*, two bovines with horns of different shapes (curving inward on the left and outward on the right) are depicted from behind (Pl. 59, 44).[92] This feature could be identified as the sex-linked trait used to distinguish the ox from the cow. The fact that here it is represented outside a colonial context, may show the free-standing life of this iconographic element.

Lastly, one could see further repercussions of this cultural dynamic in Bolognia, but in a different context. In 1621, when the extensive zoological treatise, *De quadrupedibus bisulcis*, was published by the naturalist and scholar Ulisse Aldrovandi (1522–1605), the horns as a trait for distinguishing gender returned in a very curious way.[93] Aldrovandi, in describing the differences of the

Lorenzo Magnani. Nevertheless, if the detail of the horns does carry a humanist thought, it would be necessary to identify its palingenesis in the discussion of Roman colonies and colonial coins. See Bellori 1672; Malvasia 1678; Rubinstein 1979. Samuel Vitali, who recently completed a detailed analysis of the frescos in Palazzo Magnani, does not recognize a precise model for the painting, connecting it only with an image of Neptune leading a plow in Vincenzo Cartari's iconographic repertoire. He defines it only as a "figurative option" and not as a "programmatic choice" (Vitali 2011: 140–143).

87 Stanzani 2000: 21–25.

88 Jaconello 1537: 27–28.

89 The editorial history of the work, and the controversies with the local inquisition, are narrated by Paolo Prodi (1959).

90 Sigonio 1732–1737; *Hist. Bon.*, III, 18.

91 Stanzani 2000: 21.

92 Negro and Pirondini 1995: I, 236.

93 Aldrovandi 1621: 36–37.

horns between male and female bovines, affirmed that the horns of cows can be recognized by their inward curve, recalling a rising moon (*et uno flexu conspicua, cuiusmodi fere sunt novae lunae cornua*). This expression, as seen before, apparently does not derive from previous zoological publications, but evokes the words Agustín used to distinguish the gender of cows in his numismatic work ("Los de la vaca son como los cuernos de la luna"). This situation shows how this detail continued its history beyond numismatics into other disciplines; and probably it could indicate the vitality of a cultural environment that shared information and readings, constructing the antiquarian narrative through a strong multidisciplinary approach.

Conclusions

In conclusion, it is possible to say that Roman colonial coins during the Renaissance period were identified according to two criteria: their legends and their iconography. The legend had to have the inscription COL or at least the abbreviation C—sometimes an acronym as in the case of C·V·I (*Colonia Victrix Iulia*) or C·C·A (*Colonia Cercanita Augusta*)—and the name of the magistrates; during the Roman Empire, the names of the emperors and the names of their families were also engraved.

With regard to the imagery, the first element that acted as a distinguishing element was the oxen with plow and the priest delimiting the *pomerium*. The second element was the depiction of military banners, the eagle of the legion, the plow and the agrimensorian *pertica*. Further unconventional imagery was also identified by Pirro Ligorio.

Without the reconstruction of the relation between colonies and public treasury established by Onofrio Panvinio, it probably would have been more difficult to connect colonial institutions to coins. However, the revolutionary turning point for the study of colonies that opened the doors to the numismatic world was the critical analysis of the passage on urban founding of Varro's *De lingua latina*. Those who gave impulse to the new interpretation of this work were Antonio Agustín, Carlo Sigonio, and Enea Vico, who, most probably, were in contact with one another. Sigonio offered a more structured contribution in juridical antiquarian studies, consolidating the connection between coinage and institutions; Vico provided a broad representation of coins confident in the views of Sigonio, who saw the colony as an independent entity, but submitted to specific mechanisms; Agustín found confirmation of these phenomena starting from the geographical sphere.

All of this pushed forward research and a renewed understanding of the sources, which also created an intersection of viewpoints, emerging remarkably from the use of geographical texts, like the *Liber coloniarum* attributed to Frontinus and the anonymous *Itinerarium Antonini*.

Once the relation between oxen, plow, and colonies was established the entire iconographic system that had developed previously around these elements had to be reconsidered. The new antiquarian knowledge modified the earlier accepted views of scholars like Valeriano and Erizzo.

In the cases of Vasari and the Carracci brothers it is clear that their projects would have not been possible without decades of sedimentation of scholarly and antiquarian views on the subject. For the decoration of Palazzo Vecchio in Florence, it emerges that the entire figurative arrangement derived from the studies on colonies—especially the detail of the plow delimiting the territory of the first city. In fact, it did not have to do with just an ordinary city, but with a colony regulated by its own mechanisms with its own specific characteristics. All of this is well outlined in the experience of Vincenzio Borghini.

An inverse path is made for the Palazzo Magnani in Bologna, where it was the theme (The Founding of Rome) that evoked a colonial context, in virtue of the fact that the colony wanted to reproduce the layout and image of the mother-city. Thus Bologna, identified as a Roman colony by Sigonio, became a tacit reference point for the entire cycle.

Lastly, that the iconography of colonial coins, particularly the ones with oxen, could have been influenced by zoological reasoning is an appealing assumption. From an anatomical detail (the shape of the horns), unexpected pathways of circulation of culture (theoretical and figurative) could have perhaps been opened, starting from the Spanish work of Antonio Agustín and its Latin and Italian translations (especially that of Sada and Pasqualini), to the frescos in the Palazzo Bonfiglioli in Bologna and the work of Ulisse Aldrovandi.

From this cultural journey of European numismatics during the Renaissance, it emerges that a series of dynamics were activated thanks to the progressive growth of antiquarian studies, modifying throughout the decades the perspectives of humanists on the subject; even underground flows can be denoted, which sometimes contributed, only dimly, to broaden the possibilities of a critical interpretation of the past.

Acknowledgements

My special thanks for having contributed to the successful outcome of this paper go to Tomaso Maria Lucchelli, professor of numismatics at Ca' Foscari University of Venice, Italy.

References

Agustín, A. (ed.). 1559. *M. Verrii Flacci, Quae extant et Sex. Pompei Festi Deverborum significatione lib. XX. [...] Ex bibliotheca Antonij Augustini*. Venezia: Bonello.
Agustín, A. 1587. *Diálogos de medallas, inscripciones y otras antiguedades*. Tarragona: Felipe Mey.
———. 1592a. *Dialoghi di don Antonio Agostini arciuescouo di Tarracona intorno alle medaglie inscrittioni et altre antichita tradotti di lingua spagnuola in*

italiana da Dionigi Ottauiano Sada et dal medesimo accresciuti con diuerse annotationi, et illustrati con disegni di molte medaglie et d'altre figure. Roma: Guglielmo Faciotto.

————. 1592b. *I discorsi del s. don Antonio Agostini sopra le medaglie et altre anticaglie diuisi in XI dialoghi tradotti dalla lingua spagnuola nell'italiana con la giunta d'alcune annotationi e molti ritratti di belle e rare medaglie si e messo di piu nel fine l originale spagnuolo per sodisfattione di molti.* Roma: Donangeli.

————. 1617. *Antiquitatum Romanarum Hispaniarumque in nummis veterum dialogi XI. Latinè redditi ab Andrea Schotto Societ. Iesu, cuius accessit Duodecimus, De prisca religione, diisque gentium. Seorsim editae Nomismatum Icones a Iacobo Biaeo aeri graphicè incisae.* Antwerp: Hendrik Aertssen, 1617.

Aldrovandi, U. 1621. *Quadrupedum omnium bisulcorum historia.* Bologna: Girolamo Tamburini.

Alessandri, A. 1522. *Genialium dierum libri sex.* Rome: I. Mazochi.

Amandry, M. 2012. "The coinage of the Roman provinces through Hadrian." In *The Oxford handbook of Greek and Roman coinage,* edited by W. E. Metcalf, 391–404. Oxford: Oxford University Press.

Andrés, J. (ed.). 1804. *A. Augustini Archiepiscopi Tarraconensis, Epistolae latinae et italicae, aedite a Ioanne Andresio.* Parma: Mussi.

Belloni, G. and R. Drusi. 2002. *Filologia e invenzione nella Firenze di Cosimo.* Firenze: Olschki.

Bellori, G. P. 1672. *Le vite de' pittori, scultori et architetti moderni.* Roma: Mascardi.

Bettin, S. 2009. *Palazzo Magnani in Bologna.* Bologna: Unicredit Banca.

Biondo, F. 1503. *De Roma triumphante libri decem.* Brescia: Angelo Britannico.

Bodon, G. 1997. *Enea Vico. Fra memoria e miraggio della classicità.* Roma: L'erma.

Borghini, V. 1584–1585. *Discorsi di monsignore don Vincenzio Borghini. Al serenissimo Francesco Medici gran duca di Toscana. Parte prima [–seconda]. Recati à luce da' deputati per suo testamento.* Firenze: Filippo and Iacopo Giunti.

Budé, G. 1528. *De asse et partibus eius.* Köln: Johann Soter.

Carbonell i Manils, J. 1991. *Epigrafia i numismàtica a l'epistolario d'Antonio Agustin (1551–1563).* PhD thesis. Universitat Autònoma de Barcelona.

Caro, A. 1957–1961. *Lettere familiari, edizione critica a cura di A. Greco.* 3 vols. Firenze: Le Monnier.

Carradice, I. 2012. "Flavian coinage." In *The Oxford handbook of Greek and Roman coinage,* edited by W. E. Metcalf, 375–390. Oxford: Oxford University Press.

Carrara, E. 2008. "Il ciclo pittorico Vasariano nel Salone dei Cinquecento e il carteggio Mei–Borghini." In *Testi, immagini e filologia nel sixteenth secolo,* edited by E. Carrara and S. Ginzburg, 317–380. Pisa: Edizioni della Normale.

Cartari, V. 1556. *Le Imagini con la spositione de i Dei de gli antichi.* Venezia: Marcolini.

————. 1996. *Le immagini degli dèi di Vincenzo Cartari,* edited by C. Volpi. Roma: De Luca.

Dati, C. R. 1743. *Raccolta di prose fiorentine. Volume terzo, parte quarta, contenente lettere*. Firenze: Tartini-Franchi.

Davis, M. D. 2012. "Il rovescio della medaglia no. 1: Two letters by Annibal Caro: numismatic methods and ancient coin reverses." *FONTES* 72: 4–32.

Dekesel, C. E. 1988. *Hubertus Goltzius, the father of ancient numismatics: An annotated and illustrated bibliography*. Gand: Bibliotheca Numismatica Siliciana.

————. 1997. *Bibliotheca nummaria: Bibliography of the sixteenth century numismatic books*. London: Spink.

Dempster, T. 1613. *Antiquitatum Romanarum corpus absolutissimum in quo praeter ea quae Ioannes Rosinus delineauerat, infinita supplentur, mutantur, adduntur. Ex criticis, et omnibus vtriusque linguae auctoribus collectum, Thoma Dempstero à Muresk, I.C. Scoto, auctore*. Paris: Jean Le Bouc.

Drusi, R. 2012. *Ricercando scrittori e scritture. Studi su Vincenzio Borghini*. Padova: Il Poligrafo.

Eckhel, J. H. 1728–1739. *Doctrina numorum veterum*. 8 vols. Vienna: F. Volke.

Emiliani, A. 2000. "Genus unde latinum." In *Gli affreschi dei Carracci: studi e disegni preparatori, Bologna, Palazzo Magnani, 24 May–2 July 2000*, edited by C. Loisel, 13–14. Bologna: Rolo Banca.

Erizzo, S. 1559. *Discorso sopra le medaglie antiche, con la particolar dichiaratione di molti riuersi*. Venezia: Vincezo Valgrisi.

Fest. ed. Lindsay = Sexti Pompei Festi. *De verborum significatu*, Stuttgard/Leipzig: Teubner, 1997 (ed. stereotypa 1913)

Front. Col.[1] = *De agrorum conditionibus, & constitutionibus limitum, Siculi Flacci lib. I. Iulii Frontini lib. I. Aggeni Vrbici lib. II. Hygeni Gromatici lib. II. Variorum auctorum ordines finitionum. De iugeribus metiundis. Finium regundorum. Lex Mamilia. Coloniarum pop. Romani descriptio. Terminorum inscriptiones & formae. De generibus lineamentorum. De mensuris & ponderibus. Omnia figuris illustrata*, Paris: Turnèbe, 1554.

Front. Col.[2] = *Sex. Iulius Frontini De coloniis libellus*. [Roma], c. 1560.

Forcellini, E. 1858–1879. *Totius latinitatis lexicon, opera et studio Aegidii Forcellini*. 6 vols. Leipzig/London: Kollmanni/Black and Armstrong.

Frey, K. 1934. *Der literarische Nachlass Giorgio Vasaris herausgegeben und mit Kritischen Apparate verschen von Karl Frey*. München: G. Muller.

Gesner, K. 1551. *Historiae animalium liber I. De quadrupedibus viviparis*. Zürich: Christoph Froschauer. 1551.

Gilio, G. A. 1564. *Due dialogi. Nel primo de' quali si ragiona de le parti morali, e ciuili. Nel secondo si ragiona de gli errori de pittori circa l'historie. Con un discorso sopra la parola urbe, città, colonia, municipio*. Camerino: Antonio Gioioso.

Gitler, H. 2012. "Roman coinage of Palestine." In *The Oxford handbook of Greek and Roman coinage*, edited by W. E. Metcalf, 485–498. Oxford: Oxford University Press.

Goltz, H. 1566. *Fastos magistratuumque et triumphorum romanorum ab Urbe condita ad Augusti obitum ex antiquis tam numismatum quam marmorum monumentis restitutos.* Bruges: Hubert Goltz.

―――. 1571. *C. Iulius Caesar siue Historiae imperatorum Caesarumque Romanorum ex antiquis numismatibus restitutae liber primus.* Bruges: Hubert Goltz.

―――. 1574. *Caesar Augustus siue Historiae imperatorum Caesarumque Romanorum ex antiquis numismatibus restitutae liber secundus.* Bruges: Hubert Goltz.

―――. 1576. *Graecia siue Historiae vrbium et populorum Graeciae ex antiquis numismatibus restitutae libri quatuor.* Bruges: Hubert Goltz.

―――. 1579. *Thesaurus rei antiquitatis huberrimus, ex antiquis tam numismatum quam marmorum inscriptionibus pari dilingentia qua fide conquisitus ac descriptus, et in locos communes distributos.* Antwerp: Christophe Plantin.

Host, M. 1580. *Historiae rei nummariae veteris libri quinque, quae continet exquisitam nummorum veterum Romanorum, Graecorum, Hebraicorum et externorum inter se, et cum praecipuis nummis Germanicis collationem, cum indice copiosiore.* Frankfurt an der Oder: Johann Eichorn.

Itinerarium 1512 = *Itinerarivm prouinciarum omnium Antonini Augusti, cum fragmento eiusdem, necnon indice haud quaque aspernando.* Paris: Henry Estienne, 1512.

Itinerarium 1518 = *Pomponius Mela Iulius Solinus Itinerarium Antonini Aug. Vibius Sequester P. Victor De regionibus vrbis Romæ. Dionysius Afer De situ orbis Prisciano interprete.* Venezia: Aldo Manuzio, 1518.

Itinerarium 1550 = *Itinerarium prouinciarum Antonini Augusti. Vibius Sequester de fluminum, et aliarum rerum nominibus in ordinem elementorum digestis. P. Victor de regionibus urbis Romae. Dionysius Afer de situ orbis Prisciano interprete.* Lyon: Vincent Simon, 1550.

Itinerarium 1600 = *Itinerarium Antonini Augusti, et Burdigalense. Quorum hoc nunc primum est editum: illud ad diuersos manusc. codices & impressos comparatum, emendatum, et Hieronymi Suritae Caesaraugustani, doctissimo commentario explicatum.* Köln: Arnold Mylius, 1600.

Jaconello, B. A. 1537. *Le vite di Plutarcho, di greco in latino et di latino in volgare tradotte. Nouamente da molti errori corrette: et con le sue historie ristampate.* Venezia: Bernardino Bindoni.

Laz, W. 1551. *Commentariorum reipub. Romanae illius, in exteris prouincijs, bello acquisitis, constitutae, libri duodecim.* Basel: Johann Oporinus, 1551

―――. 1558. *Commentariorum vetustorum numismatum maximi scilicet operis et quatuor sectionibus multarum rerum publicarum per Asiam, Aphricam et Europam antiquitatis historiam nodosque Gordianis difficiliores comprehendentis Specimen exile.* Vienna: Michael Zimmermann.

Le Pois, A. 1579. *Discours sur les medalles et graueures antiques principalement Romaines. Plus, vne exposition particuliere de quelques planches ou tables estans sur la fin de ce liure, esquelles sont monstrees diuerses medalles et graueures antiques, rares et exquises*. Paris: Mamert Patisson.

Leto, P. 1515. *Opera. Romanae historiae compendium, ab interitu Gordiani iunioris vsque ad Iustinum tertium. Pomponius. De Romanorum magistratibus. De sacerdotiis. De iurisperitis. De legibus ad .M. Pantagathum. Item De antiquitatibus vrbis Romae libellus, qui Pomponio adscribitur. Pomponii Epistolae aliquot familiares. Pomponij vita, per. M. Antonium Sabellicum*. Strasbourg: Mathias Shuerer.

Ligorio, P. 2010. *Libri delle medaglie da Cesare a Marco Aurelio Commodo; a cura di Patrizia Serafin Petrillo*. Roma: De Luca.

Macrob. *Saturn.* = Macrobius, *Saturnalia, recognovit brivique adnotione critica instruxit R. A. Kaster*. Oxford: Oxford University Press, 2011.

Maffei, R. 1559. *Commentariorum vrbanorum, octo et triginta libri, accuratius quàm antehac excusi, praemissis eorundem indicibus secundum tomos ut ab autore conscripti fuerunt: quibus accessit nouus, res ac uoces in philologia explicatas demonstrans, quo superiores editiones carebant hactenus*. Basel: Froben.

Malvasia, C. C. 1678. *Felsina pittrice. Vite de' pittori bolognesi*. Bologna: Domenico Barbieri.

Missere Fontana, G. 1999. *La collezione Missere di monete romane provinciali*. Modena: Aedes Muratoriana.

———. 2009. *Testimoni parlanti: le monete antiche a Roma tra Cinquecento e Seicento*. Roma: Quasar.

Morel, A. 1734. *Thesaurus Morellianus, sive familiarum romanarum numismata omnia, diligentissime undique conquisita, ad ipsorum nummorum fidem accuratissime delineata*. Amsterdam: William Smith.

Napolitano, M. L. 2012. *Hubertus Goltzius e la Magna Grecia. Dalle Fiandre all'Italia del Cinquecento*. Napoli: Luciano.

Negro, E. and M. Pirondini (eds.). 1995. *La Scuola dei Carracci. I seguaci di Annibale e Agostino*. 2 vols. Modena: Artioli Editore.

Nolhac, P. de. 1887. *La Bibliotheque de Fulvio Orsini: contributions a l'histoire des collections d'Italie et a l'étude de la Renaissance*. Paris: Vieweg.

———. 1889. *Piero Vettori et Carlo Sigonio : correspondance avec Fulvio Orsini*. Roma: Vaticana.

Occo, A. 1579. *Imperatorum Romanorum numismata a Pompeio Magno ad Heraclium: quibus insuper additae sunt inscriptiones quaedam veteres, arcus triumphales, et alia ad hanc rem necessaria*. Antwerp: Christophe Plantin.

Orsini, F. 1577. *Familiae Romanae quae reperiuntur in antiquis numismatibus ab Vrbe condita ad tempora diui Augusti ex bibliotheca Fului Vrsini*. Roma: Giuseppe De Angelis.

Palumbo Fossati, I. 1984. *Il collezionista Sebastiano Erizzo e l'inventario dei suoi beni*. Venezia: Ateneo Veneto.

Panvinio, O. 1558. *Reipublicae Romanae commentariorum libri tres*. Venezia: Vincenzo Valgrisi.

Prodi, P. 1959. *Il cardinale Gabriele Paleotti, 1522–1597.* Roma: Edizioni di storia e letteratura.

Ricchieri, L. 1517. *Lectionum antiquarum libri 16th.* Basel: Johann Froben.

Ripollès, P. P. 2012. "The ancient coinages of the Iberian peninsula." In *The Oxford handbook of Greek and Roman coinage,* edited by W. E. Metcalf, 356–374. Oxford: Oxford University Press.

Roszfeld, J. 1583. *Romanarum antiquitatum libri decem ex variis scriptoribus summa fide singularìque diligentia collecti à Ioanne Rosino Bartholomaei F. Isennacensi Thuringo.* Basel: Pietro Perna.

Rubinstein, B. R. 1979. *The Palazzo Magnani: an iconographic study of the decorative program.* PhD thesis, Florida State University.

Sardi, A. 1557. *De moribus et ritibus gentium, libri III.* Venice: Giordano Ziletti.

———. 1579. *Liber de nummis.* Mainz: Caspar Behem.

Schmidt, J. 1555. *Differentiae animalium quadrupedum secundum locos communes, opus ad animalium cognitionem apprimè conducibile.* Zürich: Andreas e Jakob Gessner.

Scorza, R. A. 1987. *Vincenzio Borghini (1515–1580) as iconographical adviser.* PhD Thesis, University of London.

Thilo, G. and H. Hagen (eds.). 1961. *Servii grammatici qui feruntur in Vergilii carmina commentarii.* 3 vols. Hildesheim: Georg Holms.

Serv. ed. Estienne = *P. Virgilii Maronis Opera. Mauri Servii Honorati grammatici in eadem commentarii, ex antiquis exemplaribus suae integritati. Castigationes et varietates Virgilianae lectionis, per Ioannem Pierium Valerianum.* Paris: Robert Estienne, 1532.

Sigonio, C. 1560. *De antiquo Iure Italiae libri tres.* Venezia: Giordano Ziletti.

———. 1732–1737. *Opera Omnia,* edited by L. A. Muratori and F. Argelati. 6 vols. Milano: Palatina.

Soler i Nicolau, A. 2000. *La correspondència d'Ottavio Pantagato (1494–1567).* PhD thesis, Universitat Autònoma de Barcelona.

Speißmeister, J. 1553. *De consolibus romanorum.* Basel: Johann Oporinus.

Stanzani, A. 2000. "Gioco delle apparenze, allusione ed ironia nella cornice del fregio." In *Gli affreschi dei Carracci: studi e disegni preparatori, Bologna, Palazzo Magnani, 24 May–2 July 2000,* edited by C. Loisel, 21–25. Bologna: Rolo Banca.

Stenhouse, W. 2009. "Antonio Agustín and the numismatists." In *The rebirth of antiquity. Numismatics, archaeology, and classical studies in the culture of the Renaissance,* edited by A. M. Stahl, 49–65. Princeton: Princeton University Library.

VAC 1612 = *Vocabolario degli Accademici della Crusca,* Venezia: Giovanni Alberti, 1612.

Valeriano, G. P. 1556. *Hieroglyphica siue de sacris Aegyptiorum literis commentarii.* Basel: Michael Isengrin.

Varr. *LL* = Varro, M. Terentius. *De lingua latina quae supersunt, recenseverumt Georg Goetz et Friedrich Schoell.* Amsterdam: Adolf M. Hakkert, 1964.

Vasari, G. 1588. *Ragionamenti del sig. caualiere Giorgio Vasari pittore et architetto aretino. Sopra le inuentioni da lui dipinte in Firenze nel Palazzo di loro altezze serenissime. Insieme con la inuentione della pittura da lui cominciata nella cupola,* Firenze: Filippo Giunti, 1588

Vettori, P. 1582. *Variarum lectionum libri XXVIII.* Firenze: Giunti.

Vico, E. 1548. *Le imagini con tutti i riuersi trouati et le vite de gli imperatori tratte dalle medaglie et dalle historie de gli antichi.* Parma: Enea Vico.

———. 1558. *Discorsi sopra le medaglie degli antichi.* Venezia: Gabriel Giolito.

———. 1560. *Ex libris 23. commentariorum in vetera Imperatorum Romanorum numismata.* Venezia: Paolo Manuzio.

Virgili P. 1596. *De rerum inventoribus libri octo.* Lyon: Antonio Gryphio.

Vitali, S. 2011. *Romulus in Bologna: Die Fresken der Carracci im Palazzo Magnani.* München: Hirmer.

Wallace-Hadrill, A. 1986. "Image and authority in the coinage of Augustus." *Journal of Roman Studies* 76: 66–87

Wickersham Crawford, J. P. 1913. "Inedited letters of Fulvio Orsini to Antonio Agustín." *Publications of Modern Language Association of America* 28: 577–593.

Wotton, E. 1551. *De differentiis animalium libri decem.* Paris: Michel Vascosan.

Woytek, B. E. 2012. "The denarius coinage of the Roman Republic." In *The Oxford handbook of Greek and Roman coinage,* edited by W. E. Metcalf, 317–334. Oxford: Oxford University Press.

AJN Second Series 28 (2016) pp. 259–271

Review Article

Aux origines de la monnaie fiduciaire: traditions métallurgiques et innovations numismatiques. Actes de l'atelier international des 16 et 17 novembre 2012 à Tours. Edited by Catherine Grandjean and Aliki Moustaka. Bordeaux: Ausonius, 2013. ISBN: 978-2-35613-092-1.

The editors' introduction lays out the stakes of this collective volume. In the past, collectors and numismatic specialists concerned with ancient coins were far more interested in coins made of precious metal than in bronze coins. While it is true that they have never been neglected entirely, bronze coins of the ancient world have long been the poor stepchild of research. But today the situation has changed radically. By the 1960s, the works of Georges Le Rider and those of Martin Price opened the way for new studies of bronze coinage—studies that have multiplied in recent years. The various authors of papers in this volume are among the foremost specialists in the field. The work has a well-defined theme: it addresses the question of the origins of bronze coinage. It was in the fifth century BC that the first issues of bronze coinage began, and it was the Greek states that took the initiative. As a metal, bronze had a value roughly one hundred times less than that of silver, at least at Athens. Minting bronze in place of small denominations of silver meant moving to a fiduciary system, at least for small denominations. Towards the end of the fourth century, the minting of bronze had become, if not universal, at least extremely common in the cities and kingdoms of the Greek world. What were the conditions of the creation of these bronze coinages? And what were the causes that led to the minting and circulation of a bronze coinage? To these questions, this volume does not present a comprehensive answer, strictly speaking; but it does offer a wealth of information and of highly welcome illumination concerning the question.

The volume is divided into two sections. The first part, in five chapters, presents some "new approaches." The second, in seven chapters, presents some "regional assessments." A brief conclusion strives to reassemble the threads of the debate. This division is, however, slightly artificial: thus, for example, the fine paper of Sélènè Psoma concerning the introduction of bronze coinage in mainland Greece, which is in the first part, could just as well have appeared beside that of Christos Gatzolis on northern Greece, which is in the second. The paper of Catherine Grandjean, which is in the second part, takes as its theme the birth of bronze coinage in the colonial worlds, but offers a broad analysis on the origins of bronze coinage and would fit comfortably in the first part. Also, in taking account of the book, it seems preferable to depart from the order of the essays. Therefore, we shall first focus upon the regional assessment (with the modifications that have just been indicated), which provides an overview of the first issues of bronze coinage, and which permits us to fix some important chronological points; then we shall touch upon the more general issues raised by the issuance of bronze coinages.

Where did matters begin? In a rich paper, Louis Brousseau presents a detailed account of the origins of bronze coinage in Magna Graecia and Sicily. The idea that the first bronze coins were struck in the West was already the consensus opinion; but this account provides some new details. On the basis of a recently published specimen, the author puts forward the claim that it was in the city of "Sybaris IV," newly refounded in 446, and in the period (to be extremely precise) between 446 and 444, that the first bronze coins were struck—thus, prior to the arrival of the Athenian and Panhellenic contingent in 444, at the beginning of the new city of Thurii (after a falling-out with the new colonists, the Sybarites went off to found Sybaris V around 440). The literary tradition informs us that an Athenian politician, Dionysios, had advised his fellow citizens (in vain) to adopt a bronze coinage, which earned him the surname Chalkous (from the name of the small bronze piece). According to Louis Brousseau (pp. 82–83), this Dionysios was one of the new colonist-founders of the new Sybaris IV in 446. Dionysios would, then, have had more success in his new city than at Athens (which only struck bronze coins from about the middle of the fourth century onward). Thurii, which succeeded Sybaris on the same site, continued to strike in bronze with the same types, but with a different legend. We must note that, in the same volume, Catherine Grandjean (p. 101) and John H. Kroll (p. 112) also offer their judgments in the case of Dionysios Chalkous, whose arrival in the West they place around 443 (that is to say, with the arrival of the second Athenian contingent, which marked the foundation of Thurii). It is unfortunate that the editors did not clarify this discrepancy, because the reader is left in a state of uncertainty.

Louis Brousseau further notes that Rhegion, Poseidonia, Metapontum, and Hyele swiftly followed the example of Sybaris. In neighboring Sicily, it was apparently in the third quarter of the fifth century (or a little earlier), first at Agrigentum and Selinus and subsequently at Himera, that the first bronze coinages appeared. However, these coinages had a different appearance from those of Italy. In fact, they were of conical or ovoid shape, and they were cast, not struck. The other peculiarity of the four basic denominations, issued on a duodecimal base, viz. the ounce (1/12), the *hexas* (1/6 = 2 ounces), the *tetras* (1/4 = 3 ounces), and the *trias* (1/3 = 4 ounces), was that they were tied to the standard of the *litra* of the indigenous Siculi. The theoretical weight of the bronze *litra* was, at Selinus, 45.72 g for heavy series and 30.48 g for light series (but at Lipara, we even find bronze *litrai* of which certain specimens have a weight greater than 100 g). The cities also issued silver coins on the basis of an equivalent with the indigenous *litra*.

The analyses of Louis Brousseau concerning Sicilian bronze coins invite some additional remarks. These bronze coinages, which copied the standards of the indigenous currency, itself based upon the use of bronze weights, were in one way or another coinages whose value was based upon their metal value, and not fiduciary coinages. On the basis of the weight of the bronze *litra*, which was not identical from one city to another and clearly experienced rapid changes, and also on the basis of what we know of the value ratio between the bronze *litra* and the silver *litra* (concerning which see the evidence given by Louis Brousseau on pp. 90–94), the question must be raised whether the value ratio between bronze and silver did not experience some rapid changes. In any case, in contrast to the bronze coinages that were introduced in the same years in Italy, the Sicilian bronze coinages were thus not intended as fiduciary coinages, at least at the outset. One also notes that the rapid devaluations of the *litra* evoked by Louis Brousseau illustrate the difficulty of maintaining what was, at least at the start, a "bimetallic" silver-bronze system.

John H. Kroll's paper presents a small bronze coinage whose chronology and significance have been discussed; the article sheds decisive light upon the question. We are concerned with a small bronze coinage (diameter 16–19 mm, weight 3–4 g) issued on the island of Salamis (as the legend and the types explicitly show—the nymph Salamis on the obverse, the shield and sheathed sword of Ajax on the reverse). It is a surprising coinage, because Salamis was—and permanently remained—linked to the Athenian state in the Classical period. On the basis of the context and chronology of the examples of these coins that have been discovered— in the cemetery of the Kerameikos (thus in the mainland territory of the city of Athens), in tombs of the 420s—it is clear that these coinages were issued by the *dēmos* of the Salaminians. Additionally, whereas Athens did not adopt a bronze coinage until much later, during the 430s the Salaminians undoubtedly possessed the right to issue a small coin that was uniquely their own, and which, inevitably, circulated in Attica also.

The paper by Sélènè Psoma raises the question of the circumstances of the transition from small silver units to bronze coins. The article is founded upon a vast selection of examples taken from the whole of mainland Greece, and even beyond, and thus has value as a synthesis. It is stressed that a number of Greek states (beginning with Colophon in Asia Minor, but also the kingdom of Macedon and numerous Peloponnesian cities) struck very small silver coins at the end of the Archaic period and in the Classical period. These coinages were very frequently of a weight less than their theoretical weight. Additionally, while the great majority of Greek coins, especially the large denominations of precious metal, did not normally bear an indication of their value, these small units bore an explicit indication of value, in letters or in symbols, such as, according to the case, E, H, HM for the hemiobol, EEE for the trihemiobol, T for the tetartemorion, and TTT for the *tritetartemorion*. The transition to small coinage in bronze (for example, in the kingdom of Macedon, under Archelaos I at the end of the fifth century) generally occurred in northern Greece, central Greece, and the Peloponnese from the end of the fifth century onward and into the fourth century. Small units were frequently struck: the *chalkous* (1/12 of an obol in the Aeginetan system, 1/8 in the Attic system) and its multiples, the *dichalkous* and the *tetartemorion* (3 *chalkoi* in the Aeginetan system). The word *chalkous* signified "(a small coin of) bronze," the smallest unit being designated by this name. Although the *chalkous* seems to have ordinarily had a weight between 1.6 and 2 g (see below for some cases of a *chalkous* of lower weight), one must nevertheless be attentive to the fact that, from one region to another, coins of the same nominal value did not necessarily have the same weight (which is obviously a characteristic trait of the fiduciary character of bronze coinages). Another characteristic of bronze coinages, well-established by the observations that one can make at the sites of Olynthos, Akanthos, Maronea, and Pydna (for the coinages of the kingdom of Macedonia), is their strictly regional circulation. This is a characteristic trait of fiduciary coinages: they had a circulation constrained by the boundaries of the state, and enjoyed practically no or only limited circulation beyond them.

Christos Gazolis introduces the results of his research concerning the bronze coinages of Chalkidike and Macedon. The Chalkidian League, Mende, the kings of Macedon, and perhaps Akanthos issued bronze coins from the end of the fifth century. Mende issued its first bronze coinage (*chalkoi* of a very light weight, on average 0.95 g) at the end of the 420s, or rather at the beginning of the 410s. What is more, it now appears certain that the Athenian colonists of Potidaea (who occupied the city from 430/429 until their expulsion in 404) issued a bronze series bearing a female head on the obverse and a bull in sacrificial position on the reverse. These coins, of which 15 specimens are presently known (the figure of 14 in the table on p. 122 must be supplemented by the mention of a fifteenth one on p. 125), circulated in various cities of Macedon and Chalkidike (Pydna, Methone, Dikaia, Olynthos, Mende, Stageira). One must note that these cities were under the direct or indirect control of Athens in this period, though not necessarily until 404. Moreover, the case of Pydna is particularly interesting. The recent discovery of coins of the cleruchs of Potidaea in a pit at Pydna, sealed by a destruction layer corresponding to the siege and capture of the city by the king of Macedon Archelaos I, implies that this coinage began to be issued prior to 410, and may even reach back to the 420s.

The analysis of Christos Gazolis opens up some stimulating lines of inquiry. Despite the limited numbers of the coinages of the cleruchs of Potidaea, one can indeed ask, based upon their zone of circulation, whether, beyond Potidaea *stricto sensu*, these monies did not circulate in all the cities of the region under Athenian control. In contrast, if we retain the proportions and not the absolute numbers, the bronze coins of Olynthus issued up to 361 BC circulated nearly exclusively in the territory of that city: 179 examples have been found there out of a total of 190 examples—but it is true that we do not possess information for Potidaea comparable to that which the excavations at Olynthus have furnished us. It should also be noted that for the third time in the fifth century—after Dionysios Chalkous at Sybaris-Thurii and the coinages of the Salaminians—we find Athenians taking the initiative in the creation of a bronze coinage. If, then, the city of Athens did not adopt a bronze coinage before roughly the middle of the fourth century, this was clearly not because they lacked inventiveness in monetary matters; as early as the period c. 446–420, and even before the poor bronze coins temporarily issued at the end of the Peloponnesian War in a period when the city no longer had reserves of precious metals at its disposal, not only were bronze coinages struck at the initiative of certain Athenians, but these Athenians were clearly among the very first Greeks to take the initiative in this innovation. The Athenians were, therefore, not "late" in comparison to the other Greeks, a point also made by Raymond Descat in his conclusion (p. 186). In a famous passage, Thucydides (1.70.1–71.3) emphasizes that Athens was the city of innovation *par excellence*. The case of bronze coinage, too, demonstrates that, if not Athens as a city, at least certain Athenians were able to be at the forefront of innovation.

Pierre-Olivier Hochard offers a detailed study of the debut—comparatively late (the second half of the fourth century BC)—of bronze coinage in Lydia. In chronological terms, this essay does not deal with the Classical period, as the other articles in the volume do, but with the Hellenistic period. It was Alexander, in fact, who began the minting of bronze coins at the mint of Sardis. Next, we must draw a clear distinction between two periods: up to the turn of the third and second centuries, only the royal mints at Sardis and additionally at Magnesia ad Sipylum struck in bronze. After that, concomitantly with the Attalids' taking control of the region, a series of cities (often those newly created by the new hegemonic power) began to issue civic series. In terms of quantity, however, it is Sardis that remains by far the most active mint throughout the entire period. This chronology merits attention. For Pierre-Olivier Hochard, Lydia (understood in a restricted sense: the region of Lydia and not the territory of Croesus's Lydia, which covered the lion's share of western Asia Minor) was rich in gold, silver, and iron, but only a very small amount of copper was to be found there. So far as the production of lead, zinc, and above all tin in Lydia is concerned, it is "not at all clear" that it occurred.

The author adds that "the correlation 'minting of bronze'/'proximity of a vein' and its opposite are thus not proven." In other words, in contrast to that which we observe in the case of precious metal, the presence or absence of the principal components of "bronze coinages" in terms of sources of metal, viz. copper, tin, but also lead as well, has no importance in the introduction of a bronze coinage. The remark is correct, although it is undoubtedly necessary to pose the question differently with regard to sources of metal, including in the case of bronze coinages. For Lydia, in a context where as elsewhere in the Aegean basin bronze had been readily used for well over a millennium, the "lateness" of the introduction of bronze coinage could not have been for technical reasons. The true question is to determine why the Great King did not judge it to be useful to strike a bronze coinage. Now, the answer is more complex than it may seem.

In any case, as the paper of Frédérique Duyrat shows, an analogous phenomenon can be observed in Syria. Before the Macedonian conquest, which saw the opening of six royal mints (Myriandros, Ake/Tyre, Arados, Byblos, Sidon, and Poseidion), only two Phoenician cities, Sidon (chiefly) and Arados, struck in bronze, and even then scarcely before the middle of the fourth century. For Frédérique Duyrat, the fact that the cities of the region had previously issued miniscule fractions of silver rendered the minting of bronze useless. It will be observed however that as we have seen, among others for northern Greece, the minting of small units of silver appears to other authors as a preparatory stage in a transition to a small bronze coinage. This leaves the question open of why the same phenomenon did not present itself in Syria. In any case, in Syria too, the Achaemenid king did not mint any bronze coinage. The difference from the Macedonian monarchy is thus striking.

On this point, the data usefully assembled by this book thus invite us to pose a broader question, that of the Achaemenid monarchy's disinterest concerning bronze coinage, which contrasts with the attitude of the Greek cities and monarchies, and also with that of certain Phoenician cities under its control. It is very likely that we should see here the mark of a lack of integration between "the base and the summit," with the far-off power of the Great King not concerning itself with what might occur in the local agoras. In any event, while masses of shekels and darics were being struck at Sardis, it is out of the question that the Achaemenid government could have been ignorant of the developments that were taking place in Asia Minor at the very same time. In concentrating its attention on Lydia without making mention of the other regions of western Asia Minor, the volume could lead the unsuspecting reader to conclude too hastily that Asia Minor only experienced its first issues of bronze coinage with the arrival of Alexander. In reality, on the west coast of Asia Minor and on the neighboring islands, a number of Greek and Carian cities—as well as certain Persian satraps, such as, *inter alios*, Tissaphernes and Pharnabazos—were minting a bronze coinage from the late fifth century or at the beginning of the fourth century.[1] Thus, for example, Kamiros struck a bronze coinage before 408/7 BC, the date of the synoecism of the island of Rhodes.[2] The Carian city of Keramos also struck a coinage probably in the late fifth century.[3] The existence of these coinages makes the choice of the Great King (but not of his satraps) to abstain from minting in bronze all the more significant. We thus find ourselves brought back to a fundamental question, posed by Pseudo-Aristotle in the second book of his *Economics* (1345b): that of the motivations of monetary authorities in minting this or that coinage, in this particular case, bronze.

The thematic portion of the volume is first illustrated by two papers which deal with bronze as a metal. The title of Sophie Descamps-Lequime's contribution, "From wax to copper alloy: techniques of Greek bronzes," demonstrates her concern to link her subject to the theme of the work. However, the "bronzes" with which the paper is concerned are not *coinages* of bronze, but rather *statues* of bronze. The article presents an excellent overview of the techniques used to fabricate bronze statues. In any event, however, the gradual development of the "lost wax" technique for casting bronze statues at the end of the Archaic period does not have any direct link with the minting of the first bronze coins in the fifth century, which is part of a different technological and institutional setting: that of the minting of metal coinage. The transition to minting in bronze does not correspond to any technical innovation that could have served as the trigger—which, even so, does not mean that the mints charged with minting in bronze did not profit from the experiments carried out in the domain of statuary. So far as minting bronze coins is concerned, the contribution thus constitutes a useful background concerning certain points, such as the golden color of alloys rich in tin (15%).

The essay of Maryse Blet-Lemarquand presents, in a synthesizing manner and with vigor, the results of her own studies as well as those of analyses carried out at the laboratory of Orléans over three decades concerning multiple series of Greek bronze coins, covering the period from the fifth to the first century BC. In this regard, one must emphasize the fundamental role of the late Jean-Noël Barrandon in these investigations. The cities or regions concerned range from Marseilles to Ptolemaic Egypt, passing through Sicily, northern Greece, Boeotia, Elis, Messene, and Miletus. The method is that of Fast Neutron Activation Analysis

1 Konuk 2011.
2 Ashton 2006.
3 Konuk 2000.

(FNAA) using a cyclotron. The author mentions that copper melts at 1083° C, but that the addition of tin lowers the melting point, ranging from 1025° C for an alloy containing 10% tin to 760° C for an alloy containing 30% tin. With an alloy containing between c. 13% and 16% tin, bronze attains its maximum toughness. In addition, bronze can be cast more easily than copper. The addition of tin permits the melting temperature to be lowered; the addition of lead, meanwhile, permits one simultaneously to save on the cost of metal (lead being considerably cheaper than copper and, above all, than tin) and to once again lower the melting temperature. But, for reasons of stability, a ternary alloy where lead reaches 20 to 25% requires the proportion of tin to be lowered. On these bases, the analysis of Greek bronze coinages shows that initially an alloy was used that was made from separate ingots of copper and tin. Soon enough, the mints began to make use of recycled bronze, with additions of lead of up to 15–20% (sometimes as high as 30%, for example at Marseille in certain bronzes of series II, and in the bronze coins of Alexandria in the second century BC) We may note that the bronze statuettes of the Classical period were also made of alloys with a lead content of a similar order, which indicates that the mints benefited from the technical knowledge of sculptors' workshops (and vice versa, no doubt).

Several papers return to the question of the circumstances in which a transition occurred to bronze currency. Hélène Nicolet-Pierre discusses the mention in Cretan inscriptions of the Hellenistic period of payments in "cauldrons" and "spits." She believes (rightly) that we should see here the legacy of an ancient period in which these words referred to concrete objects, while in the Hellenistic period, they should only be seen as indications of value (one should only add that these indications of value—staters, "cauldrons" and "spits"—must therefore have formed an integrated system).

Olivier Picard presents a synthetic overview of all the coinages of the Greek cities, which permits him to analyze the relationship between bronze coinages and coinages of precious metals. Since in the majority of cases (and despite the remarkable exceptions noted above) a coin's value was not indicated in an explicit fashion, it was its size that would have allowed the user to determine its value. Even if their actual weight was less than the theoretical standard—whether because they had undergone wear and tear in the course of usage (the notion of "attrition"), or whether because they had been deliberately calibrated to a weight less than the standard by the issuing authority—the coins were counted, and not weighed: this rule was true for coins of precious metal, and thus *a fortiori* for bronze coins. There is a point here, however, to which it will be necessary to return. We may, in any event, agree with Olivier Picard: the well-established nature of the usage of coinages of precious metal, and a certain form of fiduciarity in their circulation, constitute the necessary background for the possibility of a transition to minting in bronze, that is to say, to a coinage that was now entirely fiduciary. One of the original characteristics of bronze coins was that the flans used to strike them had a weight that varied much more widely than in the case of coinages of precious metals. We must certainly see two reasons for this: one in the technical sphere—that flans were fabricated with far less care, and thus at less cost, than in the case of precious metals; and the other in the institutional sphere—that the fiduciary nature of bronze coinage did not require any great precision of weights.

Brigitte Lion's paper deals with the second millennium. It is placed in the volume before that of Pierre-Olivier Hochard, undoubtedly for chronological and geographical reasons. This paper touches upon a fundamental question: that of bronze as metal- or commodity-currency. We know that the tradition of the Near East from the end of the second millennium and into the first millennium favored weighed silver as a monetary instrument. But, as Brigitte Lion stresses, there are two cases that serve as an exception: the archives of the small city of Nuzi (in northern Mesopotamia) in the fourteenth century BC, and two inscriptions of the Assyrian king Sargon at the end of the eighth century BC. It is to the rich evidence from Nuzi that Brigitte Lion devotes her paper. The palace archives record payments in bronze in exchange for barley. Bronze likewise appears in the private archives of Pula-hali as an instrument of loans at interest and as a means of payment (in parallel with head of cattle and barley). Silver is practically absent from transactions, but we should also take note of the evidence for heavy fines of one silver mina and one gold mina. Bronze, which also appears constantly in the archives as a raw material for the making of various objects, is thus quite plainly a metal-currency here (albeit in an exceptional manner), and not a fiduciary currency.

Now, if the use of bronze as metal-currency remained very limited in the states of the Near East, the situation was quite different in the states of the western Mediterranean, as Raymond Descat argues (p. 186). The tradition of bronze coinage (as merchandise-money) among non-Greek populations is emphasized for Italy by Catherine Grandjean (p. 103) and for Sicily by Louis Brousseau (p. 94). It is this tradition that explains the existence in western Sicily of this metal-currency in the Greek cities. In the same fashion, it is the tradition of bronze as a metal-currency (albeit once again cast, not struck) that we find in the Greek cities of the western part of the Black Sea, which were also in contact with the barbarian world. In particular, we find here coins in the shape of arrowheads or dolphins.

The inevitable conclusion, then, is that we must admit the simultaneous co-existence of two different monetary practices. Certain Greek cities (in western Sicily and in the western part of the Black Sea) adopted bronze coinage as a metal-currency taking various shapes. Other Greek cities chose to develop a properly fiduciary currency, and for the shapes of the coins they followed the tradition of the coinage first struck in the seventh century in western Asia Minor. Catherine Grandjean sees the greatest counterexample to the theory of Martin Price (who has maintained that bronze coins were put in circulation to facilitate retail commerce) in the first bronze coins of Sicily and northern Pontus; to her, it rather seems that these coins "were purposely made to be inconvenient: the large dolphin of Olbia in the British Museum and the bigger pieces cast at Olbia and at Lipara weigh more than 100 g." But this reasoning lumps into the same category of "bronze" two very different types of coinage: on the one hand, fiduciary coinages, which Martin Price was thinking of; on the other, coinages in which bronze originally had its value of commodity, or at least mimicked a commodity money. In reality, the two types of coinages must be clearly distinguished, and we should instead keep in mind that, in the face of the difficulty of maintaining a bimetallic system, it was the path of fiduciary bronze coinage within a system of silver monometallism that triumphed. The use of bronze as commodity-currency was rapidly abandoned by the cities of Sicily and the Black Sea.

Still, the question of the reasons for the transition to a fiduciary coinage in bronze deserves to be posed. Several papers, such as those by Sélènè Psoma (p. 57) and Louis Brousseau (p. 82), take as the starting point of their analyses the idea that replacing small silver monetary units was at issue. These coins were inconvenient in that they were tiny (c. 0.18–0.19 g for the Attic *tetartemorion*). Louis Brousseau notes, however, that the idea that bronze coinage was issued "to facilitate daily transactions within the city is biased by our modern conception, although it is not impossible that this was one reason (or rather one consequence) among others." He adds that we should no doubt see instead an "economic" reason (one might rather say a financial reason): "The making of a fiduciary coinage in bronze is necessarily more profitable for the cities than the making of a coinage in small silver units." In fact, "the coinage receives a legal value that is greater than the value of the metal it contains."

These remarks are interesting and deserve to be extended. It is indeed clear that, on a proportional basis, minting small precious metal units was always more costly than minting large denominations: the "big problem of small change," to quote the title of Thomas J. Sargent and François Velde's book (which, oddly, is not cited in the volume).[4] It is thus also clear that it was in the cities' interests to economize above all in the minting of small denominations. Minting in bronze, rather than silver, for small values provided the wished-for remedy. And yet, in terms of Martin Price's thesis, the concept of replacing small units of silver with bronze, as being less expensive and easier to handle, does not serve as an explanation for the minting of small coinages in and of itself. In any case, we are thus merely deflecting the question, which becomes: for what reasons did the movement toward minting in small units of silver occur, and that from the end of the sixth century? In fact, we can scarcely see anything that could replace the thesis of Martin Price, according to which the smallest denominations, in silver and then in bronze, served as a means of making the most modest payments (purchases in

4 Sargent and Velde 2002.

the agora, payment of civic or sacred taxes, payments of civic indemnities, etc.)[5] That the circumstances presiding in this or that issue were varied (according to the case, in a military context or a civil context, but without being able to establish a single rule), we cannot doubt. But we should not confuse the overall usage of currency with the motive for this or that particular issue, as happens too frequently. We should also add a point that, strangely, is not brought up in the volume: that of the lowering of the "monetary floor." While, to use the Attic standard as an example, the smallest silver monetary units were normally the *tetartemoria*, or quarters of an obol, weighing ca. 0.18–0.19 g (units of weight less than 0.1 g were very rare), the ongoing minting of *chalkoi* representing 1/8 of an obol permitted payments at an even more modest level. Henceforth, and all the way to the end of the Roman Imperial period, bronze ruled in the agora where retail commerce was concerned, and it is this that explains why the overwhelming majority of coins found in excavations in Greek agoras are of bronze.

We see the idea appear in certain essays that the transition to bronze may have been linked to a specific context, and in particular to a context of war. Olivier Picard (p. 77) thus argues that we should place the introduction of bronze coinage in relation to the Peloponnesian War and the difficulties that the cities encountered. How, indeed, could we fail to notice the overall synchronism between the first development of bronze coins and the famous Peloponnesian War? However, at the outset one could raise the objection to this theory that war in Greece was a permanent state of affairs. It should also be remarked that the first bronze coinages at Sybaris and then at Thurii were prior to the beginning of the war, as Louis Brousseau's essay shows. Nevertheless, the question remains of why it was in the second half of the fifth century that a form of currency in bronze began to be struck. Perhaps we should direct our search for an answer toward the variations that occurred in the price of silver. It will be noticed that Athens, a producer of silver, did not commence its issuances in bronze until about the middle of the fourth century, while most cities had made the leap long before, as if for that city, for a very long time at any rate, the cost of minting small units in silver had not posed any problem. Among the reasons for the adoption of bronze currency by so many cities in the late fifth and early fourth century (almost all of them deprived of sources of silver), there was certainly the comparative advantage that it represented in terms of cost of minting, source of profit for the state, and ease of usage for the user. These observations, in their turn, invite us to propose two more general remarks.

The first concerns the institutional level. There was clearly no spontaneous, autonomous (in the sense of a purely interpersonal relationship, of a private character, by means of simple "imitation") process of creation of bronze coinage. From the very first, bronze coinage had a civic character. This series of studies concern-

---

5 On small change in the early phase of the development of coinage, see Kim 2002; Kim and Kroll 2008; Kagan 2006; Warren 2009.

ing the first Greek bronze coins shows, if such a demonstration was necessary, that they did not circulate because of confidence that had been spontaneously accorded to them by their users, but rather in accordance with a decision by the civic authorities, who had imposed their usage as a means of payment. The decree of Olbia from the fourth century, which Sélènè Psoma (p. 61) has opportunely reminded us of, equally comes to emphasize to how great a degree the use of silver and bronze coinage in that city was thoroughly defined and regulated.[6] We also know, from a decree of Gortyn dating to around the middle of the third century, that when that city introduced new bronze obols to replace the silver obols that had been circulating until then, it was obliged to impose their use all at once and to forbid any *agio* for a payment in bronze in place of one in silver, with those who violated the decree rendering themselves liable to heavy fines.[7] What we have, then, is not "spontaneous confidence" in the new coinage, but institutional constraint from the very beginning. The new bronze coinage, of a plainly fiduciary character inasmuch as the value of the metal content was inferior to the declared value, could, then, only be imposed at the cost of civic constraint. This was the one important difference from coinages made from precious metals, whose fiduciarity only came into play at the margin, if a denomination was slightly inferior to its theoretical weight. Confidence is certainly essential for ensuring monetary circulation. But what is at issue in confidence is the stability of an institution capable of making sure that each person finds some advantage for himself in making use of a monetary instrument for the conservation and exchange of value.

The second remark, which we can only sketch here, concerns the conceptual leap represented by fiduciarity in bronze coinages. Certainly, as we have seen, a partial form of fiduciarity existed with coinages of precious metal, in particular with small units; but it remained limited to a few fractions of percentage. But the "utility" represented by the use of a coinage that enjoyed legal circulation, in comparison to the custom of weighed silver, certainly made up for the difference in the eyes of the users. In return, when, with coinage in bronze, the Greeks had a coinage whose value was on the order of one-tenth that of its metal content (and even much less, in the case of an alloy with lead), they had now clearly entered the realm of fiduciarity. These are the forms and limits of fiduciarity in ancient Greece that we ought now to explore. As Olivier Picard (p. 71) opportunely emphasizes, all was not set in stone at the start. The Greek world explored diverse paths, and we have insisted here on two paths that were explored concurrently in the fifth century, that of bronze commodity-currency and that of fiduciary bronze, the first having been swiftly abandoned to the advantage of the second, which became a universal system. Even the heaviest bronze coins of the Ptolemies, which were clearly not small change but rather were intended to replace the lower denominations in silver, were not minted at their metal value. The introduction

6 *I. Kalchedon* 16.
7 *IC* IV, 162.

of bronze money thus also constitutes an outstanding example of the process of trial and error, followed by stabilization, in the establishment of a new institution.

This book will thus be indispensable henceforth for anyone who is interested in the question of the origin of bronze coinages. Certain adjustments should have been made to harmonize the points of view of authors working on the same questions. But, by virtue of the new information it provides and the debates to which it will give rise, the work will nevertheless have a place in all good libraries.

Alain Bresson
The University of Chicago

BIBLIOGRAPHY

Ashton, R. H. J. 2006. "The beginning of bronze coinage in Karia and Lykia." *NC* 166: 1–14.

Kagan, J. H. 2006. "Small change and the beginning of coinage at Abdera." In *Agoranomia: Studies in money and exchange presented to John H. Kroll*, edited by P. Van Alfen, 49–60. New York: American Numismatic Society.

Kim, H. 2002 "Small change and the moneyed economy." In *Money, labour and land. Approaches to the economies of ancient Greece*, edited by P. Cartledge, E. E. Cohen, and L. Foxhall, 44–51. London and New York: Routledge.

Kim, H. S., and J. H. Kroll. 2008. "A hoard of archaic coins of Colophon and un-minted Silver (*CH* I.3)." *AJN* 20: 53–103.

Konuk, K. 2000. "Coin evidence for the Carian name of Keramos." *Kadmos* 39: 159–164.

————. 2011. "War tokens for silver? Quantifying the early bronze issues of Ionia." In *Quantifying monetary supplies in Greco-Roman times*, edited by F. de Callataÿ, 151–160. Bari: Edipuglia.

Sargent, T. J., and F. R. Velde. 2002. *The big problem of small change.* Princeton: Princeton University Press.

Warren, J. A. W. 2009. "Sikyon: A case study in the adoption of coinage by a polis in the fifth century BC." *NC* 169: 1–13.

Plates

Plate 1

Seleukos I's Victory Coinage of Susa Revisited

Plate 2

12

13

14

15

20

22

23

Seleukos I's Victory Coinage of Susa Revisited

Plate 3

28   30   31

34   35   40

43

Seleukos I's Victory Coinage of Susa Revisited

Plate 4

44   45   46

48   51   52

53

Seleukos I's Victory Coinage of Susa Revisited

Plate 5

54   57   58

59   63   64

65

Seleukos I's Victory Coinage of Susa Revisited

Plate 6

59

72

73

76

77

78

81

Seleukos I's Victory Coinage of Susa Revisited

Plate 7

82

83

86

88

89

91

94

Seleukos I's Victory Coinage of Susa Revisited

Plate 8

103   104   105

106   107   111

112

Seleukos I's Victory Coinage of Susa Revisited

Plate 9

114 117 121

123 124 126

127

Seleukos I's Victory Coinage of Susa Revisited

Plate 10

128

130

133

134

135

136

137

Seleukos I's Victory Coinage of Susa Revisited

Plate 11

138   139   142

144   145   146

148

Seleukos I's Victory Coinage of Susa Revisited

Plate 12

152   154   155

157   167   173

174

Seleukos I's Victory Coinage of Susa Revisited

Plate 13

175   177   179

180   182   183

188

Seleukos I's Victory Coinage of Susa Revisited

Plate 14

189   190

192   193   196   198   200

201   202   204   205   207

Seleukos I's Victory Coinage of Susa Revisited

Plate 15

209 214 216 217 218

220 223 226 230 236

237 239 240 242 244

Seleukos I's Victory Coinage of Susa Revisited

Plate 16

246

247

248

249

251

252

254

255

257

259

260

261

262

263

Seleukos I's Victory Coinage of Susa Revisited

Plate 17

265   266   267   268

271   272   273   274   276

A1   B1   B2

Seleukos I's Victory Coinage of Susa Revisited

Plate 18

B3

C1

C2

C3

D1

E1

F1

Seleukos I's Victory Coinage of Susa Revisited

Plate 19

F2   G1   G2

H1   I1   J1

K1

Seleukos I's Victory Coinage of Susa Revisited

Plate 20

K2   K3   L1

M1   N1   O1

O2

Seleukos I's Victory Coinage of Susa Revisited

Plate 21

P₁

Q₁

R₁

S₁

T₁

Seleukos I's Victory Coinage of Susa Revisited

Plate 22

Antioch on the Orontes

1

10

14

15

19

20

The Reactions of Mint Workers

Plate 23

22

23

36

37

48

56

The Reactions of Mint Workers

Plate 24

60

71

77

92

95

105

The Reactions of Mint Workers

Plate 25

116   120   122

126   128   129

The Reactions of Mint Workers

Plate 26

135 139 142

149 153 155

The Reactions of Mint Workers

Plate 27

158

160

163

The Reactions of Mint Workers

Plate 28

164

165

166

167

The Reactions of Mint Workers

Plate 29

The Reactions of Mint Workers

Plate 30

Damascus

The Reactions of Mint Workers

Plate 31

16   21   28

30   39   40

The Reactions of Mint Workers

Plate 32

51

55

56

57

60

68

The Reactions of Mint Workers

Plate 33

76   83   88

96   102   112

The Reactions of Mint Workers

Plate 34

114 123 124

129 130 133

The Reactions of Mint Workers

Plate 35

135

136

138

140

The Reactions of Mint Workers

Plate 36

1

2

3

4

5

6

The Koinon of Athena Ilias and its Coinage

Plate 37

The Koinon of Athena Ilias and its Coinage

Plate 38

13 14 15

16 17 18

The Koinon of Athena Ilias and its Coinage

Plate 39

The Koinon of Athena Ilias and its Coinage

Plate 40

25   26   27

28   29   30

The Koinon of Athena Ilias and its Coinage

Plate 41

31   32   33

34   35   36

The Koinon of Athena Ilias and its Coinage

Plate 42

The Koinon of Athena Ilias and its Coinage

Plate 43

43

44

45

46

47

48

The Koinon of Athena Ilias and its Coinage

Plate 44

49

50

51

52

53

54

The Koinon of Athena Ilias and its Coinage

Plate 45

55   56   57

58   59   60   61

The Koinon of Athena Ilias and its Coinage

Plate 46

62

63

64

65

66

The Koinon of Athena Ilias and its Coinage

Plate 47

1 2 3 4

5 6 7 8

9 10 11 12

The Administration of the ʿAbbāsid North

Plate 48

13   14   15   16

17   18   19   20

21   22   23   24

The Administration of the ʿAbbāsid North

Plate 49

25 26 27 28

29 30 31 32

33 34 35 36

The Administration of the 'Abbāsid North

Plate 50

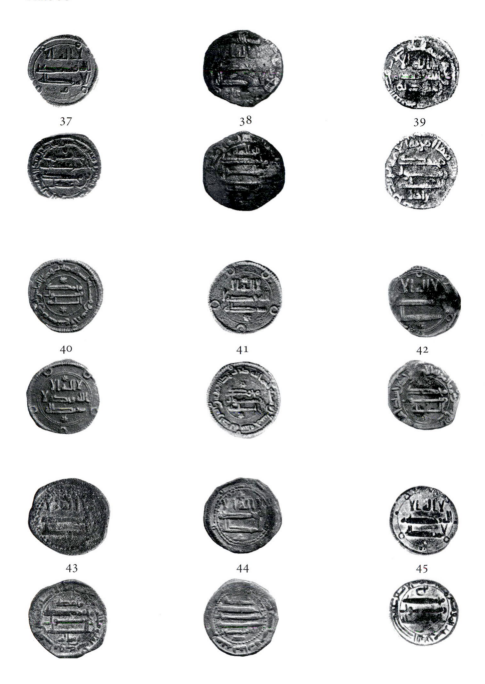

37   38   39

40   41   42

43   44   45

The Administration of the ʿAbbāsid North

Plate 51

1

2

3

4

5

6

7

8

9

Ancient Roman Colonial Coins in Renaissance Europe

Plate 52

10

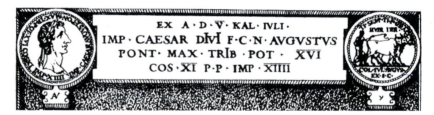

11

12

Ancient Roman Colonial Coins in Renaissance Europe

Plate 53

13

14

15

Ancient Roman Colonial Coins in Renaissance Europe

Plate 54

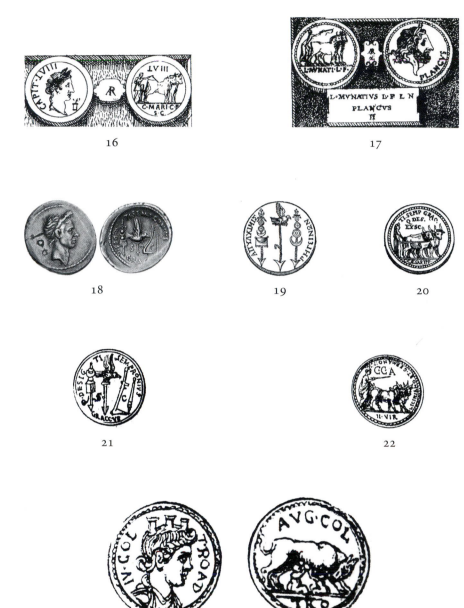

16

17

18

19

20

21

22

23

Ancient Roman Colonial Coins in Renaissance Europe

Plate 55

24

25

26

27

28

Ancient Roman Colonial Coins in Renaissance Europe

Plate 56

29

30

Ancient Roman Colonial Coins in Renaissance Europe

Plate 57

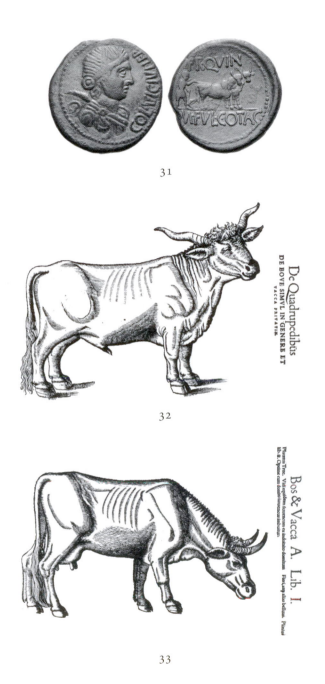

31

32

33

Ancient Roman Colonial Coins in Renaissance Europe

Plate 58

34

35

36

37

38

39

Ancient Roman Colonial Coins in Renaissance Europe

Plate 59

40   41   42

43

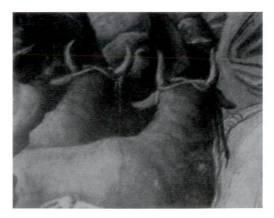

44

Ancient Roman Colonial Coins in Renaissance Europe

Plate 60

45

46

Ancient Roman Colonial Coins in Renaissance Europe